The Dilemma
of the Modern in
Japanese Fiction
◆

◆
A Study of the East Asian Institute

STUDIES OF THE EAST ASIAN INSTITUTE, COLUMBIA UNIVERSITY

The East Asian Institute is Columbia University's center for research, publication, and teaching on modern East Asia. The Studies of the East Asian Institute were inaugurated in 1962 to bring to a wider public the results of significant new research on modern and contemporary East Asia.

The Dilemma of the Modern in Japanese Fiction

◆

Dennis C. Washburn

Yale University Press
New Haven & London

For Ikuko

The publication of this book was made possible through the generous support of the Japan Foundation and the Dartmouth College Burke Award for junior faculty research.

Excerpt from "Burnt Norton" in *Four Quartets,* copyright © 1943 by T. S. Eliot and renewed 1971 by Esme Valerie Eliot, reprinted by permission of Harcourt Brace and Company.

Copyright © 1995 by Yale University. All rights reserved. This book may not be reproduced, in whole or in part, including illustrations, in any form (beyond that copying permitted by Sections 107 and 108 of the U.S. Copyright Law and except by reviewers for the public press), without written permission from the publishers.

Printed in the United States of America

Library of Congress Cataloging-in-Publication Data

Washburn, Dennis C. (Charles), 1954–
The dilemma of the modern in Japanese fiction / Dennis C. Washburn.
    p. cm.—(Studies of the East Asian Institute)
Includes bibliographical references and index.
ISBN 0-300-05997-3
1. Japanese fiction—1868–   —History and criticism. 2. Modernism (Literature)—Japan. I. Title. II. Series.
PL747.57.M577W37   1995
895.6'3409—dc20   94-31373
                                             CIP

A catalogue record for this book is available from the British Library.

The paper in this book meets the guidelines for permanence and durability of the Committee on Production Guidelines for Book Longevity of the Council on Library Resources.

10   9   8   7   6   5   4   3   2   1

contents

◆

Acknowledgments
ix

Note on Names
x

List of Abbreviations
xi

Introduction
1

part one
Mutability and the Floating World:
The Classical Notion of the Modern
17

chapter one
The Makings of a Modern Hero: The "Eawase"
Chapter in *Genji monogatari*
21

Contents

chapter two
The Burden of the Future:
Asserting the Literary Self in *Hōjōki*
37

chapter three
Epiphanies of Modernism and the
Floating World
53

part two
Futabatei Shimei and the
Meiji Sense of the Modern
77

chapter four
Literary Darwinism:
The Crisis of Language and Canon Formation
80

chapter five
The Limits of Realism and the Dilemma
of Futabatei
94

chapter six
The Skeptic as Artist: *Sono omokage*
109

chapter seven
Like the Slobber of a Cow:
A Mediocre Literary Life
126

Contents

part three
Inner Horizons:
The Modern Narrative Voice
139

chapter eight
The Dilemma of the Modern and
the Autobiographical Confession
142

chapter nine
The Sense of an Ending:
The Apocalyptic Individualism of Natsume Sōseki
164

chapter ten
The Individual in History:
The Narrative Voice of Mori Ōgai
180

chapter eleven
Nostalgic Narratives:
The Primitivistic Voice of Nagai Kafū
195

part four
Narrative Relativism and Cultural Amnesia
211

chapter twelve
The Apotheosis of the Artist:
The Transcendent Perspective of Shiga Naoya
214

chapter thirteen
The Narrative Subversions of Akutagawa
and Kajii Motojirō
226

Contents

chapter fourteen
A Dizzying Descent into Self:
Kawabata and the Problem of Cultural Amnesia
246

Epilogue
265

Notes
269

Bibliography
289

Index
307

acknowledgments

◆

Many individuals helped in the preparation of this book. Edward Kamens, Angela Yiu, J. Thomas Rimer, and Paul Anderer all read the manuscript at an early stage and made many valuable comments and suggestions. I want to express my sincere thanks to Ken Ito and to my colleague at Dartmouth, Alan Tansman, for providing detailed readings and constructive criticism. Their advice on matters of form and content helped improve the manuscript in ways I could not have managed on my own.

I also want to thank Carol Gluck and Madge Huntington of the East Asian Institute at Columbia University for their support and encouragement in bringing my manuscript to publication.

The assistance and encouragement of my wife, Ikuko Watanabe, was invaluable, and I have dedicated this book to her. I want to acknowledge as well the support of her family, especially her sisters, Miwako and Kazuko, and her brothers, Mitsuaki and Hiroshi. They provided financial help that made my research possible, and I am very grateful to them all.

I began this book as a dissertation at Yale University. My deepest gratitude goes to my adviser, Edwin McClellan.

note on names

◆

Japanese words are generally romanized according to the system used in the standard *Kenkyūsha's New Japanese-English Dictionary*. Macrons are not used for well-known Japanese place names. Names of Japanese persons are given in the traditional order, surnames first. When using one-name references to authors in the text I follow customary usage: for example, Shiga for Shiga Naoya, but Ōgai for Mori Ōgai.

abbreviations

◆

The following abbreviations are used for citations in the text:

FSZ-I	*Futabatei Shimei zenshū* (Iwanami shoten)
FSZ-C	*Futabatei Shimei zenshū* (Chikuma shobō)
HZ	*[Iwano] Hōmei zenshū*
KZ	*[Nagai] Kafū zenshū*
KMZ	*Kajii Motojirō zenshū*
KYZ	*Kawabata Yasunari zenshū*
NKBT	*Nihon koten bungaku taikei*
STZ	*Shimazaki Tōson zenshū*
TSS	*Tsubouchi Shōyō shū*

introduction

◆

> Words move, music moves
> Only in time; but that which is only living
> Can only die. Words, after speech, reach
> Into the silence.
> —*T. S. Eliot, "Burnt Norton"*

Being a high modernist was probably not much fun, even under the best of circumstances. In these lines from *Four Quartets,* Eliot struggles with the fundamental dilemma inherent in the modern. To be modern is to possess a heightened sense of the significance of one's present moment: a significance expressed through forms or patterns that seek a still point transcending the human experience of time. But the sense of one's modernity is also something that can be made manifest only through the flow of words in time; that is to say, the very effort to express the significance of the present moment, to enclose the infinite notion of timelessness in a finite pattern of language, creates a temporal sequence of words highlighting the fact that no human experience is transcendent.

The central problem in a modernist narrative, then, is time. Narratives create sequences that cannot be sustained indefinitely; and just as death, in human time, ends the sequence of our consciousness, so the running-out of words makes narrative closure inevitable. The present moment is always being closed off to become an irretrievable past. Though we may be able to imagine, with Eliot, epiphanies or still points where the impossible exists, where we can locate an eternal present, such imaginings require, finally, a leap of faith or of sentimentality. We can express the modern only through time, and so modernists are driven toward an end that makes them ever more aware of the futility of the effort to freeze the sense of presentness into a permanent state.

The intractability of this dilemma is why so much depends upon the meaning of *modern*; and it is why so few critical tasks are as significant and as daunting as defining the term. The word's fundamental meanings—"the present," "just now," or "up-to-date"—convey a sense of contemporaneity, of shifting temporal perspectives that are relative and thus problematic. However, the word is also used to denote a set of shared essential characteristics that provide a sense of cultural identity. The contradictory tendency in modernist narratives is always replicated in specific historical understandings of the meaning of *modern*. The creation of the inner narrative that constitutes the sense of selfhood involves a constant resituating and reforming of our past selves in both particular and universal contexts. Selfhood, which is the constantly emerging narrative of identity, is created out of the struggle to assert one's presentness against the past. Personal and cultural identity are forms of narrative in which an understanding of the modern is the central constitutive element.

The meaning of the term *modern* is thus a synthesis shaped by a historically grounded notion of particular, parochial values and by a universally shared process of narrative that locates the sense of presentness in the past. For literature, the term encompasses any narrative in which a sense of self, both public and private, emerges from an awareness of cultural discontinuity. Through that awareness, the word *modern* creates a concept of tradition and thereby establishes a descriptive polarity that specifies the range within which a common cultural identity may be located. We are compelled, therefore, to try to come to grips with a critical understanding of the term when we examine historical moments where the project of constructing a common narrative of the modern is seen as a prerequisite for defining, or re-creating, a sense of cultural identity. One of the most compelling examples of how the dynamics of change has evolved to a large extent from a general preoccupation with what it means to be modern is provided by the experience of Japan during the Meiji period (1868–

1912). How that experience manifests itself in experiments with narrative voice and perspective in selected works of Japanese prose fiction is the subject of this study.

The two Japanese words most commonly used to denote *modern* are *kindai* and *gendai*, and they possess an ambiguity similar to that of their Western counterpart. *Kindai*, which appeared in Japanese literary usage as early as the eighth century (in the *Shoku Nihongi* [Chronicles of Japan, continued]) and thus has an etymology almost as old as the late Latin word *modernus* (sixth century), is for the most part interchangeable with *gendai* when denoting the meanings "the present," "just now," or "up-to-date." However, *gendai* more clearly suggests contemporaneity, while *kindai* has the sense of "near-contemporary" or "of recent times." This difference came about as a result of the historicist tendency to use *kindai* and *gendai* to describe different periods in Japan's cultural development from the mid-nineteenth century on. *Kindai* is generally, though not exclusively, used to indicate the period between the Meiji Restoration in 1868 and the end of World War II in 1945, and it points to the breakup of the feudalistic Tokugawa regime and subsequent Westernization of Japan. *Gendai* is used to indicate the so-called contemporary period of Japanese culture since the war.[1]

Kindai and *gendai* each suggest both a universal process of temporal discrimination and a particular set of cultural values. This ambiguous usage does not stem simply from the relative nature of the perspective that determines what is contemporaneous. The usage of *kindai* and *gendai* to indicate historical periods and to point to specific moments of extreme dislocation and discontinuity clearly indicates that *modern* is understood to be an intrinsic characteristic of Japanese cultural identity as it diverged from what came to be identified during Meiji as the traditional culture of the Tokugawa period. At the same time, both Japanese words indicate that the modern is defined by the process of Westernization, which involved the adoption of a set of social or ethical values extrinsic to the native culture. This process was not significantly different from the modernization of Europe and America, insofar as Japan shared experiences such as industrialization, urbanization, and the rise of nationalism, as well as the problems of alienation and the loss of traditional values.

These similarities with Western experience have created a misleading picture of the nature of Japan's modernization. There has long been a tendency within Japan to view modernization from a Western perspective, which has led to wild swings between seeing Japan as essentially

Western, in the sense that its progress is part of a universal evolutionary process of cultural development, and seeing the country as peculiar and unique. Moreover, while many Japanese recognized the predicament of their self-identity—that they could never be wholly modern in the Western sense nor wholly Japanese in the traditional sense—the process of Westernization marginalized Japanese culture and created the extreme self-consciousness and sense of belatedness reflected in the historicist usage of *kindai* and *gendai*. Understanding of the modern from the Meiji period on is thus ambiguous not only because of the contradiction implied by the descriptive term *modern Japanese* but also because of the willingness in Japan to adopt a relativist outlook that decenters all cultural values as a way to cope with marginalization and belatedness when adopting the political, ethical, or aesthetic standards believed to constitute modernity.

There are several reasons why the need for a common understanding of the meaning of *modern* seemed so urgent in Meiji Japan. The threat posed by Western imperialism and the danger of extreme economic and cultural marginalization forced a reevaluation of social norms. This led to the belief that the only way to protect Japan from the West was to sweep aside the traditions of the immediate past and forge a new cultural identity in order to compete with the Western powers. It comes as no surprise that this movement for reform was coupled with the political legitimation of the Meiji oligarchy, so that modernity came to serve as the ideological justification for rule by an authoritarian regime. The extreme nature of the perceived threat and the equally extreme reactions to meet the threat and to secure domestic political power are reflected in the scope of cultural change that has taken place over the past century and a half. An early Western observer, Basil Hall Chamberlain, noted that "to have lived through the transition stage of modern Japan makes a man feel preternaturally old; for here he is in modern times . . . and yet he can distinctly remember the Middle Ages. . . . Old things pass away between a night and a morning." Although Chamberlain looked at Japan through the confident and at times condescending eyes of a nineteenth-century European, his remarks express the predicament that confronted the Japanese in their pursuit of modernity: the creation of a modern cultural identity inevitably meant the loss of received identity. As Chamberlain put it, the "educated Japanese have done with their past. They want to be somebody else and something else than what they have been and still partly are."[2]

Although Japan's modernization appears to have been dramatically successful when judged from the narrow criterion of the speed with which the country adapted Western technology and bureaucratic organizations and thus joined the club of the Great Powers, in fact the project of creating a modern identity was always on the verge of collapsing under the contradiction inherent in Japanese modernity. The Meiji oligarchy needed support for change, but it also needed a means to assert its authority. There was simply no way to determine the limits of change, and so the government was susceptible to wild swings between radical reform and strict retrenchment. As the founding ideological statements of the Charter Oath (1868) make clear, the authorities were in the awkward, contradictory position of justifying modernization at the expense of tradition in order to become equal with Western nations and thereby protect the native cultural identity against outside encroachment. Later, the same ruling clique tacitly acknowledged—through the structure of the Meiji Constitution (promulgated in 1889), for example—that it would not tolerate change that threatened to extinguish what its leaders identified as the native identity, which by then was routinely expressed by the notion of *kokutai* (national essence) and symbolized by the figure of the emperor, both new constructs of the ideology of modernity.

Meiji culture was defined by a heightened awareness of its historical predicament; and it is that awareness, or self-consciousness, that ultimately defines the modern in Japan. The official sanctioning of modernization on the part of the Meiji oligarchy represented a deliberate acceptance of cultural discontinuity, an acceptance that brought with it a simultaneous sense of liberation and loss. The sanctioning of the modern, even when there was no universally accepted understanding of its meaning, threatened a break in cultural memory that could be compensated for only by reconstituting a cultural self through an act of mythic confabulation that narrated a new understanding of the Japanese tradition into being. Accordingly, the problem of the language required to construct a notion of modern Japanese identity was at the heart of Meiji discourse on modernization, and that problem reflects the underlying ambiguities of the meaning of *modern*. It was thought that language must be rooted in reality and descriptive in a positivist sense to provide the means for redefining the self. At the same time, language was felt to be transcendent and essential, unconnected with transient reality, and a means for establishing continuity and supporting authority. The expression of the modern was both innovative (or adversarial), in that it strove to connect with changing reality to create a new cultural identity, and conservative, in that it moved toward stasis, authority, and canon formation.

Although the dilemma of modernization was never resolved in Meiji Japan, internal economic pressures and growing tensions with the West forced the achievement of a precarious balance. Modernization was accepted as a tool to be used against the West and was at the same time viewed, within limits, as legitimizing Japan's unique role in the world. Even before the Second World War destroyed that balance, however, many observers in Japan were fully aware of the implications of this dilemma. For example, in an essay titled "Kindai e no giwaku" (Doubts about the modern), the critic Nakamura Mitsuo directly confronts this issue. Nakamura's essay was published in 1942 in the journal *Bungakkai*, but it had been first presented as a paper at a wartime conference dealing with the subject "Kindai no chōkoku" (Overcoming the modern). In his essay Nakamura notes the ambiguity of the subject under discussion and expresses strong doubts about the possibility of achieving the aim proposed by the conference title. According to Nakamura, if the subject of the conference is understood as pointing to the decline of the West and encouraging self-awareness in Japan, then the meaning of *modern (kindaiteki)*, which is taken to be "Westernized," is clear. "However," he continues, "if the intention is to arrive at such a simplistic idea, it is unnecessary to put forward this kind of new slogan. The very fact that we borrow Western ideas in order to negate the West is already an implicit dilemma. The fact that we express the subject of modern culture [*gendai bunka*] with the slogan 'Overcoming the modern' [*kindai no chōkoku*] is because we are nothing more than a part of Western intelligentsia."[3]

In spite of his wartime sympathies, Nakamura is cognizant of the fact that he has been co-opted intellectually by the process of Westernization and that the more he tries to break free of that process, the more he binds himself to it. He reiterates this point several times in the course of the essay and observes that at the very moment of composition he is using tools (an electric lamp, a fountain pen) that serve as constant reminders of the influence of the West. He even goes so far as to argue that the strongest proof of the inescapable presence of a Western-based understanding of modernity is that the Japanese have grown so accustomed to extrinsic objects and ideas that they mistakenly assume them to be intrinsic to the culture. One reason he gives for this confusion is the speed with which Japan achieved modernization, an accomplishment that was often viewed as a miracle. For his part, Nakamura is deeply disturbed by the sacrifice involved in achieving that so-called miracle, and here his doubts about the conference give way to an undercurrent of sympathy for its aims.

Introduction

Nonetheless, behind the accomplishment of that miracle, how great was the sacrifice paid for its achievement? How have the sudden changes in our lifestyles forced by the necessities of this miracle led our identities [*seishin*, more literally, "spirit"] down the path of confusion; in other words, how have the requirements of this sort of ruthless age, in which we live by adapting to those necessities without opposition, distorted our identities? Is this not perhaps the most pressing problem that our nation's "modernity" *kindai* presents to us?[4]

Nakamura argued that the ambiguity of the meaning of *modern* arose from the uncritical tendency to simply equate modernity with the West and to see Europe only in terms of its modernity without taking into account its traditions. For him, the price of this ambiguity was a severe identity crisis that led to demoralization. He was, however, writing early in the war during the successes of the Japanese military; and despite his doubts, there is still a degree of detachment in his view of the problem. Four years later the novelist Shiga Naoya (1883-1971) would make a more striking connection between the dilemma of the modern and the problem of cultural identity in a famous short essay titled "Kokugo mondai" (The national language problem). Surveying the destruction of the war and despairing over the magnitude of the difficulties facing his country— among them, hunger, disease, crime, unemployment, and inflation— Shiga nevertheless cites the national language as the greatest. He acknowledges that solving this problem is not an immediate need but argues that it must be addressed if the future of Japan is to be secured.

> We have been made to grow accustomed to the present language since childhood, and to that extent we do not sense [its deffciencies]. However, I think there is nothing as imperfect and as inconvenient as the Japanese language. As a result, when we consider how the development of culture has been hindered by it, this is a serious problem that must be solved at all costs now. If we lose this opportunity, it is no exaggeration to say there is no hope of Japan ever becoming a truly cultured nation in the future. (7:339)

Shiga does not clearly explain why he ascribes such an impact to the Japanese language, and he admits he cannot really give concrete illustrations of its imperfection and inconvenience, since his observations are based solely on his impressions as a novelist. Nonetheless, his proposal strongly implies that Japan's predicament was the result of its incomplete modernization. He states that during the war he recalled from time to time the proposal made sixty years earlier by Mori Arinori for Japan to adopt English as the national language and states, "Had that proposal become a reality, I considered at the time what the consequences might have been. I imagined that Japanese culture would probably be far more advanced than it is now. I even thought that perhaps the war might not have occurred" (*SNZ* 7:340). Shiga asserts a profound connection here between language and modern cultural identity, and for that reason he is very pessimistic about the prospects for reform of the national language. He claims wholesale change, for which he proposes the adoption of French as the official language of Japan, is the only solution.

There is a tone of uncertainty in Shiga's essay about the feasibility of his project—a project that seems to grow out of a sense of desperation over Japan's situation in 1946. Nonetheless, as ridiculous as his proposal seems by virtue of its extremism and by the way in which it would permit absolute co-option of Japanese culture by the West, Shiga's argument has an uncanny logic to it that reveals the trap of Japan's search for the modern. Like Nakamura, Shiga realizes that in one sense the very idea of a modern Japanese identity is an impossibility. One can either be Japanese, and thus not modern as defined by the Western model, or modern, in which case it is perhaps best to be done with the traditional altogether by getting rid of the most basic element of the Japanese identity—its language. Although both men wanted somehow to break free of the trap of modernity, their essays point to a recurring element in the expression of the modern as an obsessive and ambivalent preoccupation with the present as a significant moment; that is, as a break that creates cultural renewal and the loss of received meaning and identity. Moreover, this narrative of the modern was deeply intertwined with developments in literature because it presupposed a link between identity and cultural memory and because it focused heavily on issues of language.

Analyzing Japanese modernity along these lines—that is, viewing the modern as encompassing narratives that define notions of cultural and personal selfhood—allows us to reconcile the usage of the term *modern* to denote a universal process of change with its usage to indicate particular values arising at historical moments of discontinuity. This permits us to balance the misperception that Japanese modernity is essentially Western. The key is not to seek to identify how Japan either conforms to a model of modernization or provides a unique case but to examine how Japan's interaction with the West resulted in new expressions of self-identity. To that end a brief overview of similarities between Japanese and Western understandings of the self is in order, keeping in mind that these similarities are the product not of Western influence but of elements common to the process of cultural transformation.

A strategy typically employed to constitute modern identity and to differentiate it from traditional notions of the self is to ignore the modernity of the past. The modern self views the past not merely as past but as unified, monolithic, and static. This view is implicit in the following characterization by Charles Taylor of premodern and modern notions of self-understanding.

> For the modern I am a natural being, I am characterized by a set of inner drives, or goals, or desires and aspirations. Knowing what I am really about is getting clear about these. If I enquire after my identity, ask seriously who I am, it is here that I have to look for an answer. The horizon of identity is an inner horizon.
>
> For the pre-modern, I want to argue, I am an element in a larger order. On my own, as a punctual existence outside of it, I should be only a shadow, an empty husk. The order in which I am placed is an external horizon which is essential to answering the question, who am I? I could not conceivably answer the question with this horizon shut off.[5]

Taylor's general distinction points to a number of aspects that constitute the modern self. Identity is reflective and inward-looking as subjective experience becomes the cornerstone of reality. The emphasis on subjective experience as the arbiter of reality means that not only is identity more strongly individuated but the individual is defined, or set off, in terms of a plurality of social worlds. It is for that reason that the modern self tends to view the past as unified and coherent, while the present is always seen as open-ended, unfinished, and discontinuous. Identity is also open-ended and possesses the potential for change, growth, and development; and the narrative forms most expressive of the modern sense of self are the confession and the *bildungsroman*, since both attempt to impose order on the chaos of subjective experience and growth while at the same time implying a lack of formal closure that simulates the discontinuity of modern experience.

A sense of discontinuity is therefore an essential element in all modern literary projects. T. E. Hulme, in the opening essay of *Speculations*, drew a sharp distinction between the mode of thought of the nineteenth century and that of the twentieth. He wrote that the achievement of the nineteenth century "was the elaboration and universal application of the principle of *continuity*. The destruction of that principle is, on the contrary, the urgent necessity of the present." This assertion of the value of discontinuity reflects sentiments that underlie many of the common elements of Japanese and European literary productions of the first quarter of the twentieth century. The use of technical, urban settings to convey a sense of alienation or isolation, the cosmopolitan, internationalist aspirations of the avant-garde, a heightened sense of relativism and individualism, and a preoccupation with the traditional and with narrative form and language all suggest an extreme self-consciousness on the part of artists—an awareness of both their dislocation and their freedom. This awareness is at once creative and destructive. It is both an emancipation from orthodoxy and convention and a cultural disinheritance, a loss of tradition and meaning. The key characteristic of the modern is that these contradictory elements act together in a symbiosis. As Roland Barthes has observed, "There is therefore in every present mode of writing a double postulation: there is the impetus of a break and the impetus of a coming to power, there is the very shape of every revolutionary situation, the fundamental ambiguity of which is that Revolution must of necessity borrow, from what it wants to destroy, the very image of what it wants to possess."[6]

The ambiguity created by actively seeking out discontinuity has a number of potential effects on narrative form. Because the modern implies a high degree of historical consciousness, narratives in turn become the product of a more highly developed critical outlook that adopts the strategy of misreading the past in order to make it represent continuity. A modern outlook tends to ignore the contradictions and ambiguities of the past, reducing them instead to unchanging ideal forms. The expression of the modern finds its voice in increasingly formal considerations in which art and performance gain prominence over ethical injunctions or shared cultural values transmitted through the vehicle of communal myth. There is consequently greater self-awareness by the author of his literary role and greater possibility for parody and irony.

Even if seeking out discontinuity makes a renewal of narrative form, and thus a modern narrative, possible, narrative never wholly loses its function as a means to bridge discontinuity and confer order on the political and social culture. In a sense, all narratives, which are orderings of experience, are analogous to human memory; and when one's present moment is thought to be especially significant, then the function of narrative is, like the function of memory, to establish cultural and personal identity and to give meaning to the individual and to the present. The notion that narrating is a response to extreme discontinuity is suggested by the clinical observations of patients suffering from Korsakov's syndrome (amnesia). In the case of a man who has totally lost his memory, the primary symptom is not a silence induced by mental incoherence—that is, by the inability to remember anything long enough to give it order—but by a desperate attempt to narrate his life into existence. Such patients are in a situation where they are

> continually creating a world and self, to replace what was continually being forgotten and lost. Such a frenzy may call forth quite brilliant powers of invention and fancy—a veritable confabulatory genius—for such a patient *must literally make himself (and his world) up every moment.* We have, each of us, a life-story, an inner narrative—whose continuity, whose sense, *is* our lives. It might be said that each of us constructs and lives a "narrative," and that this narrative *is* us, our identities.[7]

The difficulty for patients with amnesia is that the attempt to narrate the self into being lacks any absolute point of reference and is thus so relative that the act of narration itself becomes a stumbling block in the attempt to give an integral form to identity.[8]

My citation of the predicament of a Korsakov's patient is in no way intended to endorse a psychoneurological approach to Japanese culture and literature. Nonetheless, that predicament provides what I believe to be a good analogy to the cultural paradox that many writers in Meiji confronted. A sense of discontinuity gives rise to a tendency to redefine the concept of tradition by placing the individual at the center of the culture through increasingly personal forms of narrative. The need to create identity through narrative is, paradoxically, evidence of how cut off the individual is from the universal values implied by the notion of tradition. The creation of literature is necessary to resolve the sense of discontinuity and yet symptomatic of it. The act of storytelling, like remembrance and nostalgia, attempts to validate the present either by idealizing, or universalizing, its particular values or, conversely, by extending the mythic orders of the cultural tradition into the present, appropriating and familiarizing those ideals. The ambiguities of the modern arise from the conscious attempt to present both the ideal and the particular together in the narrative process.[9]

To seek out discontinuity is to assume the pretense of maintaining particular values as ideals; but, like any other cultural narrative, such a pretense can never be sustained indefinitely. A sense of discontinuity provides the literary artist with the opportunity to stress the unique and particular experiences of the present moment. However, because a sense of discontinuity also cuts the artist off from commonly shared cultural narratives, it brings with it problems of isolation and intelligibility. For that reason, modern literature tends to emphasize the formal conventions of narrative, elements such as perspective and voice, stylistic or linguistic play, and allusion, as means to reinterpret the cultural tradition and resolve discontinuity. Yet the emphasis on formal qualities has its own cost, because all narrative, even as an expression of the avant-garde, becomes conventional and ideal to some degree, and thus the particular expressions of the modern can never be completely reduced to or encompassed by a literary form. Jean-François Lyotard has observed that

> modern aesthetics is an aesthetics of the sublime, though a nostalgic one. It allows the unpresentable to be put forward only as the missing contents; but the form, because of its recognizable consistency, continues to offer to the reader or viewer matter for solace and pleasure. Yet these sentiments do not constitute the real sublime sentiment, which is in an intrinsic combination of pleasure and pain: the pleasure that reason should exceed all presentation, the pain that imagination or sensibility should not be equal to the concept.[10]

By compelling a breaking and then remaking of traditional standards and practices, the modern suggests a process that is a source of literary renewal and of integration of the present into the cultural tradition. It represents a drive toward freedom from convention and is a necessary condition for the possibility of original literature.[11] At the same time, the expression of the modern requires a sense of discontinuity it cannot sustain, for in reinterpreting the concept of tradition, the present is reduced to a conventional form that destroys novelty and reasserts a sense of cultural continuity. This dilemma is, as I will show, expressed in Japanese narratives by a recurring pattern of irreconcilable polarities: descriptive pairs such as deep and shallow, constancy and mutability, intuitive and scientific, idealistic and realistic, orthodox and heterodox. The modern, however, is never defined by one or the other but lies instead in the ambiguous space whose boundaries are marked by these complementary extremes of language.

If discontinuity is so important in the creation of narrative, it may also be argued that in this narrow sense all literature is modern. Yet what distinguishes the works and authors studied in this book is the intensity with which discontinuity is felt and the degree of formal innovation that results from that intensity. For that reason, the primary focus of this book is on works written from mid-Meiji to the decade following the Second

Introduction

World War. As noted above, during this time Japan went through a series of rapid cultural changes and dislocations unparalleled in its history, and the catalyst for these changes was the increased contact with the West forced on Japan. Since the Western world was at that time also undergoing profound economic and social revolutions, the problems associated with Westernization were relatively more important issues for Japanese authors. Nevertheless, Meiji writers could not achieve an absolute discontinuity that totally obliterated all memory of the past. They looked to pre-Meiji narratives for the forms and critical vocabulary that would allow them to renew their culture without wholly losing the traditional elements that defined their identities in the face of Western norms. Therefore, I shall briefly examine three pre-Meiji works in the opening chapters to provide a control for my study. Identifying how the dilemma of the modern is expressed in pre-Meiji works will help to indicate how Meiji writers reinterpreted their tradition and also moved to salvage it under the pressure of Western influences.

In part 1, I shall examine how narrative strategies reveal the dilemma of the modern in three works: Murasaki's *Genji monogatari* (The tale of Genji, early eleventh century); Chōmei's *Hōjōki* (The record of a ten-foot-square hut, 1212); and Saikaku's *Kōshoku ichidai onna* (The life of a woman of passion, 1686). These works provide examples of the kind of narrative resources that may be called both native and modern, in the sense that Meiji readers felt them to possess the relevance or contemporaneity that permitted the appropriation of these works for a new literary language. In the case of *Genji monogatari*, the fusion of political and aesthetic values that marked Heian court society finds narrative expression in the problematic hero, Prince Genji, and in the employment of an ironic narrating voice that is frequently skeptical about the actions of the hero. There is a strong dissonance in the text created by the disparity between the pretense of Genji as the ideal romantic hero and the narrator's awareness that his behavior is less than ideal. The importance of this aspect of the characterization of the hero is highlighted by the aesthetic ideology that shapes him. Genji strives to exert absolute political and aesthetic control over his age but is ultimately defeated by the fact that central to his ability to exert control is the ability to exemplify the dominant aesthetic value of his moment, which is an awareness of the transience of experience.

A similar sort of dissonance is created in *Hōjōki* through the narrator's high degree of self-consciousness. The text, ostensibly a religious meditation, is so self-referential and self-aware that it highlights the limits imposed by the motives of the narrator and thus points to the ultimate impossibility of achieving the aims of his narrative. In the case of *Kōshoku ichidai onna* the parodistic, episodic, and aleatory nature of narrated experience illustrates a strong degree of self-consciousness in the narrative voice and an awareness of how immediate experience constantly reshapes the contours of self-identity by forcing a reinterpretation of the remembered past. The anecdotal structure of the work is used to support a satirical view of human experience in the floating world, but it also suggests that even in mundane matters epiphanic moments force a self-conscious awareness of the significance of the present.

The narrative strategies of these three works share several elements: the concept of ephemerality or mutability, which is elevated into an ideology of discontinuity; the conflict between the narrating self and the authority of tradition; self-consciousness about the act of narrating; and the conflict between dominant and subordinate cultural voices (for example, between high and low culture, between province and capital, between Chinese and native, between masculine and feminine). These common features reflect the ambivalence of the modern, with culturally subordinated voices embracing discontinuity to empower the new against the authority of the past and with dominant voices often assuming the guise of subordinated voices to reaffirm orthodox values.

In part 2 my discussion shifts to the Meiji period, and the primary subject will be the works of Futabatei Shimei (1864–1909). Although he wrote only three novels, his fiction is highly representative of the period, marking out many of the key literary issues of his day. The most important of these issues include the crisis of language—that is, the need to make literary language relevant to the new configurations of Meiji society through the creation of a realistic idiom—and the parallel problem of canon reformation. Futabatei strove to renew the literary tradition and saw modern literature as different from the past in terms of its seriousness and sincerity. At the same time he understood that by emulating the formal qualities of the Western novel he had to accept a sense of the modern alien to his culture that cut him off from his own tradition and denied the validity of his understanding of the modern as a Japanese. The result was that he came to view all literary convention and practice in a skeptical light and the modern literary project as an impossibility.

Part 3 expands on Futabatei's response to the dilemma of the modern by examining the tendency of some of his important contemporaries to

Introduction

link explicitly the creation of a new self-identity with the modernization of literary practice, especially through experiments in narrative voice and perspective. This tendency, seen in its extreme form in the naturalist movement, did not result from the influence of Western notions of individualism, nor is it simply a return to traditional notions of the isolated self seen in the confessional narratives of certain pre-Meiji works. The self-awareness that arises with cultural discontinuity is heightened in late Meiji literature to the point that narrative perspective becomes increasingly interior and relative. This interiority brought with it a sense that the heroic was no longer available to modern artists. The attempt by the naturalist writers Shimazaki Tōson (1872-1943) and Iwano Hōmei (1873-1920) to resolve the dilemma of the modern by merging art and life in the autobiographical confession, Natsume Sōseki's (1867-1916) apocalyptic vision of the isolated individual as the source of modern art, the efforts by Mori Ōgai (1862-1922) to integrate individual consciousness into the ideal form of historical narrative, and Nagai Kafū's (1879-1959) embrace of primitivism as a means to make the marginal individual central to the text are all experiments that extend Futabatei's understanding of the dilemma of the modern.

Part 4 examines how the Meiji concern with narrative voice and perspective led to increased experimentation with perspectivism and narrative relativism in subsequent generations of writers. The growing tendency among Meiji writers to focus the perspective through a central protagonist or narrator was a strategy intended to create original and sincere narratives, but that strategy also made it difficult to integrate narrative experience into the literary tradition or to claim universal validity for it. In reaction to this predicament, literary experiments moved between two extremes during the Taishō period (1912-1926) and the early years of Shōwa (1926-1989). One extreme is represented by the limited perspective of Shiga Naoya, who sought to insert a transcendent notion of the artist—a kind of modern heroism—into his narratives. The other extreme is represented by the work of Akutagawa Ryūnosuke (1892-1927), who frequently explored the possibilities offered by narrative relativism. Between these extremes lies the writing of Kajii Motojirō (1901-1932), who, although he adopts a limited perspective in the manner of Shiga, nonetheless remains skeptical about a self-centered point of view. The perspectivism and relativism of these authors set the stage for the narrative experiments of the immediate postwar period, when cultural discontinuity was at a new height. The works of Kawabata Yasunari (1899-1972), which are concerned with the problems of narrative solipsism and the loss of cultural memory, illustrate the impact of the discontinuity created by the war.

My aim is not to seek a grammar or poetics of Japanese literature. First of all, my survey is not extensive enough to achieve that aim, and in any case to try to force a rich and diverse tradition into the confines of a single critical construct would be a dreary and ultimately futile exercise. Moreover, it is not my intention to try to incorporate the Japanese tradition into an international literary culture. Imputing to Japanese literature a narrative of the modern as central to the storytelling process runs the risk of perpetuating the biases inherent in applying Western critical approaches to the study of a non-Western tradition.[12] My use of the term *modern* not merely as a definition of particular cultural values but as a shaping element of narrative voice and perspective is obviously a reading strategy to present a personal and perhaps idiosyncratic literary history. Having pointed out that limitation, however, I would add that a critical point of view—more bluntly, a cultural bias—does not automatically invalidate observations made on that basis. Given the constraints inherent in any critical project, my aim is to be descriptive and not programmatic: to focus on the awareness of discontinuity and of the ambiguities of the modern exhibited by particular authors and on the ways in which that awareness leads them to reinterpret their tradition and express a more general understanding of what it means to be modern.

part one

◆

Mutability and the Floating World: The Classical Notion of the Modern

Inherent in the definition of *modern* is an irresolvable dilemma involving two fundamentally opposed impulses. One is an adversarial effort to gain priority for the present by creating discontinuity and thus the possibility for cultural renewal. The other is a conservative effort to preserve or re-center traditional values and forms by integrating the present into canonical or orthodox ideals. This dilemma recurs over a long period in the Japanese tradition as a major concern in a number of important prose narratives. The classical notion of the modern is perhaps best expressed by the oxymoronic concept of *eterne in mutabilitie,* a concept that struggles to elevate the ephemeral, evanescent nature of the material world to a permanent ideal by seeing in the process of change a constant of human experience. It is a concept structurally identical to the notion of beauty set forth by Baudelaire in his essay "The Painter of Modern Life." "Beauty," he writes, "is composed of an element that is eternal, invariable, and exceedingly difficult to measure, and of another element that is relative and circumstantial, such as period, fashion, morality, emotion, taken either one by one or all together." This duality of art, he concludes, is the inevitable result of the duality of mankind.[1]

Mutability and the Floating World

The notion of mutability as a law of nature became the basis for a self-renewing aesthetic ideology that sought to encompass both aspects of the modern. It affirmed the aesthetic value of individual experience and self-cultivation in the ephemeral world—that is, in the changeable reality of the here and now. However, pre-Meiji affirmations of self-cultivation, which in general were aimed at defining the self in relation to tradition by striving to master inherited practices and standards, in no way approached the highly reflective, plural, and open-ended qualities that we in the West now associate with aspects of modern identity. The notion of mutability clearly balanced the appeal of the up-to-date with a traditionalism that validated the modern in terms of its resemblance to ideal standards. Accordingly, the sense of self in Japan before the Meiji period was never defined outside of a rigidly conceived social or cultural context. It would be wrong to assume that even in the strictly hierarchical status society of the Tokugawa period (1600-1868) there was no degree of personal autonomy, but for the artist, self-cultivation involved both a constraining sense of moral discipline and a measure of freedom to define one's own identity.[2] Mutability was an aesthetic notion that conveyed both these elements of self-cultivation. It was not only an explanation, and by extension a justification, for discontinuity and renewal but also a universal concept that served as a point of comparison, and thus a link, between the past and the present.

In terms of narrative voice, there were two ways in which a strong sense of individual identity was asserted in the classical tradition. There was a detached sense of self, a private identity, conveyed through the convention of the narrator as hermit or recluse. This convention achieved the pretense of detachment by removing the narrating voice from the social contexts, or external boundaries, that defined the individual and thereby provided a high degree of autonomy and interiority by limiting narrated experience to subjective observation or remembrance. A similar kind of detachment was achieved through private forms of writing such as the diary (*nikki*) or the miscellany (*zuihitsu*), in which authors were able to create complex narrative voices that posited the existence of a reader while maintaining the pretense of writing only for themselves. Such private narrative conventions were especially important to women authors, whose social identities were rigidly defined and whose access to public utterance was severely restricted.

The alternative to the detached sense of self was a notion of the self as defined within some larger institutional or social framework on the basis of common values. For example, the elitist ideal of the literati (*bunjin*)—artists, connoisseurs, educated men of taste—provided a model in which the cultivation of the self was directed toward a mastery of tradition. The artist bound himself to tradition in order to express himself through it. The problem was that this socially defined identity always threatened to overwhelm the individual and deny freedom and autonomy. Such a problem was the reverse of the difficulty encountered with the use of a detached, private voice. The detachment of the hermit, if fully realized, amounts to an extinction of the self—a figurative death that removes the individual from collective memory.

The three works examined in this section utilize narrative strategies to deal with the dilemma of the modern in ways that resemble literary developments in Meiji Japan. In the "Eawase" (A picture contest) chapter of *Genji monogatari,* by Murasaki Shikibu, the narrative attempts to transform the aesthetic sensibility of a particular cultural epoch into a permanent set of values through the idealization of its hero, Prince Genji. At the heart of that sensibility is an appreciation of ephemeral beauty, a sensitivity to immediate sensation, and an awareness that beauty exists because of change. *Hōjōki,* by Kamo no Chōmei (1155-1216), gives greater emphasis to the religious notion of mutability, the Buddhist concept of *mujō* (a term that I shall broadly equate with mutability for the purpose of this discussion), in an effort to arrest the flux of the present by placing it within the framework of established religious and cultural ideologies. Chōmei is not as concerned with making the aesthetic of the modern permanent as he is with making the aesthetic ideals of the past comprehensible in the present. *Kōshoku ichidai onna,* by Ihara Saikaku (1642-1693), seeks to confirm the underlying truth of the idea of mutability while asserting the priority of the present through a parody of traditional ideologies and literary forms. Saikaku's preoccupation with the ephemera of human experience is an expression of the aesthetic values of an emerging social group, the townsman class, that dominated the literary scene before the Meiji period.

The classical sense of the modern is defined in these works, then, by the recurring concept of mutability as both an expression of particular values and a constant element in human experience binding the present to the past. It is represented as a narrative element by the struggle to give priority to individual experience and by the awareness of the impossibility of achieving that aim. In examining aspects of *Genji monogatari, Hōjōki,* and some of the *ukiyo-zōshi* (fiction/accounts of the floating world) of

Saikaku, my purpose is to indicate how the sense of a significant present and the preoccupation with literary novelty, as expressed through the idea of mutability, determine narrative voice and create a sense of cultural identity. It is not my intent to claim that these works are modern because they foreshadow later developments (although Meiji writers often misread them as containing the seeds of modernity), for such an argument would be anachronistic. However, it is not anachronistic to discuss the modernity of pre-Meiji works within the context of how narrative conventions are used to construct a sense of modern identity or modern aesthetics. As Kermode puts it, there is in theory "nothing very new about the New."[3] Moreover, since the problem in defining the modern in the Meiji period was compounded by the danger of being co-opted by the West, it is important to look at how the modern is defined in pre-Meiji texts in order to provide a control that balances Western-biased readings of the tradition. As powerful as the influence of the West has been, an understanding of the sense of the modern lies more in the narrative process by which Meiji authors confronted the new by rereading their tradition.

◆

chapter one
The Makings of a Modern
Hero: The "Eawase" Chapter
in *Genji monogatari*

Arthur Waley, in discussing some of the literary techniques in *Genji monogatari* that appeared modern to him, once compared the use of foreshadowing in Murasaki Shikibu's novel with that in the fiction of Proust. He later seemed to have regretted the comparison, insisting that because of the great cultural divide between Murasaki's epoch and our own, any such general resemblances were the result of accident.[1] In fact, though he argued that an awareness of the present pervaded Heian aesthetics, Waley was careful to stress the difference between that awareness and the understanding of modernity he associated with his own times. Describing Japan in the tenth century, he writes that it was

> a purely aesthetic and, above all, a literary civilization. Never, among people of exquisite cultivation and lively intelligence, have purely intellectual pursuits played so small a part. What strikes us most is that the past was almost a blank.... It is indeed our intense curiosity about the past that most sharply distinguishes us from the ancient Japanese.... Their absorption in the present, the fact that with them "modern" was invariably a term of praise, differentiates them from us in a way that is immediately obvious.[2]

Waley points to the word *imamekashi* as the aesthetic term closest in meaning to *modern*. Interestingly, he interprets the modern in Heian literature as being remarkably free-floating because of a total absence of historical consciousness. It may be that for Waley's literary generation— a generation so acutely preoccupied with its own historical uniqueness that it was possible to conceive, in the manner of Virginia Woolf, that "on or about December, 1910 human character changed"—it was natural to look on Heian aesthetics as lacking historical grounding.[3] Waley's historically bound use of the term *modern* to distinguish his own age from Heian court society placed limits on his view of the aesthetics of the period. These limits are apparent when we consider the aesthetic terminology presented in the "Eawase" chapter of *Genji monogatari*.

At the level of subject matter, "Eawase" gives evidence of a strong historical consciousness by revealing an awareness of both literary tradition and genre. This historical awareness appeared negligible to Waley because of its seemingly narrow literary scope. Yet it is precisely because the chapter is so self-conscious about critical matters and preoccupied with formal qualities that it is helpful in determining the sense of the modern in the work as a whole. Moreover, the "Eawase" chapter is not, in fact, limited to purely literary concerns. It details an extremely crucial period in Genji's life after his return from exile in Suma and Akashi during which he is engaged in reestablishing and solidifying his political position at the court. The picture contest becomes an important test of Genji's political power, with the measure of that power being the quality of his aesthetic judgment.

The picture contest is a direct outcome of the political rivalry between the two factions at the court of the young emperor, Reizei. Reizei is the son of Genji and Fujitsubo, though Genji's paternity, and his quasi-incestuous adultery with Fujitsubo, are the well-guarded secrets throughout the work that form an ironic counterpoint to the depiction of Genji as the ideal courtly figure. Fujitsubo is worried that her young son lacks the presence of an older, more experienced woman to look after him, and so she turns to Akikonomu to fill that role. Genji, partly because of his stormy relationship with Akikonomu's mother, Lady Rokujō, and partly to further his own position, quietly sponsors the move to make Akikonomu an imperial consort.

Akikonomu's entrance upon the scene immediately creates tension with the consort of the Kokiden, who is the young daughter of Genji's friendly rival, Tō no Chūjō. When Akikonomu first arrives, Reizei is put off by her age, afraid that her maturity will make him appear childish. The consort of the Kokiden, who is younger, thus has an initial advantage. However, Reizei is very fond of painting, and when he learns of Akikonomu's skill in this art, he is increasingly drawn to her. This situation prompts the competitive Tō no Chūjō to collect interesting and unusual illustrations, and to have new pictures made by the best artists for his daughter's salon. Genji responds by selecting, with the help of Murasaki, those drawings he deems appropriate for Akikonomu. Most importantly, he includes some of his own work painted during his days in exile.

The first of two picture contests takes place, a preliminary contest among the court ladies held in the presence of Fujitsubo. It is decided that the Umetsubo, or Akikonomu faction, will represent the Left and the Kokiden faction the Right. The first round of the contest pits an illustration of the old man from *Taketori monogatari* (Tale of the bamboo cutter), which is presented by the Left, against an illustration of Toshikage from *Utsuho monogatari* (Tale of the hollow tree), which is presented by the Right.

> The Left stated, "This has grown old over the generations like graceful bamboo piling joint on joint; and though there is nothing particularly elegant about it anymore, Kaguyahime's destiny, which was to ascend to the far heavens without being defiled by the corruption of the world, was lofty. Because it is a tale from the age of the gods, it is no doubt beyond the understanding of superficial women."
>
> The Right responded, "Since the heavens to which Kaguyahime ascended are in truth beyond human conception, no one can know of it. As for her ties to this world, because she was born inside a stalk of bamboo, it would appear that she was a person of humble lineage. Though her radiance shone throughout a single house, it could never compare with the gracious light of the emperor. Abe no Ōshi threw away a thousand pieces of gold thinking he would buy the robe made of the fire-rat's skin. That it disappeared in an instant was a waste. Kuramochi no Miko, while knowing the deep truth about Hōrai, made a forgery. That he damaged the reputation of the jeweled branch is a flaw of the story."
>
> The *Taketori* picture was by Kose no Ōmi, and the caption was by Ki no Tsurayuki. It was mounted on broidered silk on Kan'ya paper with a magenta binding and a sandalwood spindle. It was an ordinary presentation.
>
> The Right stated, "Although Toshikage was buffeted by heavy waves and wind and borne to an unknown country, still he was able to reach his planned destination. Subsequently, in China and Japan, he spread his wonderful talents, and left his fame behind him. The picture combines Chinese and Japanese elements. It has many beautiful points and is without equal."

It had white paper, blue binding, and a yellow jade spindle. Because the illustration was by Tsunenori and the caption by Michikaze, it was up-to-date, with a lovely air about it, and it seemed to shine before the eyes. The Left had no response. (15:179-180)

The judgments expressed here are most notable for the style of argumentation, a kind of rhetorical one-upmanship. The participants also take into account considerations not always directly related to the quality of the picture under discussion. Literary criteria occupy a central place in the discussion, the question of literary merit having been introduced initially by the narrator's remark that *Taketori monogatari* is the parent or ancestor of the *monogatari* form.[4] This remark indicates in a rudimentary way a critical sense of tradition that acknowledges the historical position of *Taketori* in relation to the development of fictional narrative at the Heian court.

The strong historical sense of tradition is further revealed by certain features of the contest. First, the two sides are divided in a manner that pits the earlier works of the tradition against works presented as decidedly contemporary. The Left, the side representing the interests of Fujitsubo and Genji, is tied to works that have acquired a reputation as classics, while the Right represents the new and fashionable works of the present. It is on the basis of that critical divide that the opening round is decided. The Left loses decisively, even though they cite the depth of *Taketori* and its unchallenged position in the canon and argue that works of current fashion, lacking the weight of tradition, are as superficial as the understanding of their female readers. In spite of this defense of tradition, the participants for the Left are swept away by the up-to-date beauty of the Right's presentation. The critical standards applied in the opening judgment are thus clearly based on a temporal sense of the development of the tradition.

Also indicating a strong historical sense is the understanding of genre revealed by the form of the debate. Mitani Kuniaki sees the pairing of *Taketori* with *Utsuho monogatari* as a reflection of prevailing notions about narrative types; and the standards by which they are judged are appropriate to their genre. Mitani argues that both works belong to a subgenre involving recognizable settings and foreign or unearthly elements and thus are judged according to a form he terms "romances of a visit to a foreign land."[5] *Taketori* loses in part because it does not adequately meet the criteria of its genre, which requires a mix of foreign and familiar elements. *Utsuho,* in contrast, gives an adequate depiction of exotic settings, which

Taketori does not, and Toshikage is an adventurous hero who overcomes the trials of his journey, whereas the courtiers in *Taketori* refuse to act in an appropriately heroic manner.

An even more telling argument against *Taketori* is the problem of Kaguyahime's lineage. She is not a creature of this world, and when at the end of the story she leaves behind the old man and woman who had reared her, putting on once more her heavenly robe of feathers, she also leaves behind her humanity. She belongs to a supernatural world "beyond human conception," and yet this apparent source of her timeless and otherworldly beauty is also responsible for her greatest flaw. She lacks the human awareness of the evanescence of life and thus cannot appreciate the aesthetic values of the court. She may be an ideal woman in that she is immortal and unchanging, but she could never embody the values implied by the term *imamekashi,* which refers to the beauty inherent in the ephemeral present. For that reason her radiance "could never compare with the gracious light of the emperor."

Further evidence of a critical sense of genre is provided by the method of argumentation in the second round of the contest, where the pictures depict scenes from a different subgenre, *uta monogatari* (poem-tales) that deal with matters of love.[6]

> Next, pictures from *Ise monogatari* and *Jōsammi* were brought together. Again it was difficult to decide. In this case as well the picture of the Right, which engagingly and brightly depicted the appearance of the palace and of the contemporary world, was exceedingly beautiful. For the Left, Heinaishi argued,
>
> With no regard for the deep spirit
> of the sea of Ise,
> must the waves wash away,
> indiscriminately,
> the ancient remains?
>
> "Put down by a common love story, however well told, must the reputation of Narihira be sullied?" She was, however, unable to argue with any spirit. Daini countered for the Right.
>
> To a heart that has risen
> above the clouds of Heaven,
> the thousand-fold depths
> of that sea appear
> quite shallow indeed.

Fujitsubo remarked, "Though the noble heart of Hyōei no Ōkimi is truly difficult to set aside, Narihira's fame cannot be sullied."

At a glance these bays
may perhaps have grown tiresome,
but does that submerge the fame
of the fishermen of Ise
passed down through the years?

Arguing back and forth in feminine disputation, they exhausted their words on this one scroll, unable to come to a judgment. (15:180-81)

The *Jōsammi* has been lost, so any classification of it according to narrative type is speculative. However, the same critical standards that operated in the first round appear to remain valid for the second: the modern stands in contrast to the classical, with the modern described as either interesting or shallow, and the classical described as either tiresome or deep. In addition, the form of disputation, in which the arguments are presented in verse, fits the subgenre under discussion. This indicates that the awareness of tradition was based as much on a sophisticated recognition of a variety of types of prose literature as on the simple polarity of modern versus tradition. Such recognition greatly expands the sense of the modern as it is presented in the contest. The modern is linked to representations of the contemporary world of the court. The Right uses the appeal of the immediacy of their works to assert the superiority of the present-day court, turning their critical position to political advantage. The importance of this connection between aesthetics and politics is not lost on Fujitsubo, who is forced to intervene on behalf of Narihira's reputation, which has come to represent that of her own faction.

The sense of the modern is expanded by the use of the terms *shallow* and *deep*. They appeared in the first round as well but seem to gain some specificity and weight in the second. They are of course used throughout in a conventional manner that takes advantage of the possibilities for wordplay, but they gain critical significance as descriptions of the degree of interest the novels and pictures hold for the audience. This interest is defined according to the general positions of the two sides. For the Right, a successful evocation of the present is more deeply moving and elegant, and they state a preference for the immediate—for what might be termed, with some qualifications, a realistic presentation. The Left is forced to defend, reluctantly it seems, the classical mode and must fall back on that mode's timeless quality, the depth of its ideal representation, in contradistinction to the ephemeral and shallow present. The arguments presented in the preliminary contest suggest historical awareness in their critical distinction between past and present. The results of the two rounds further suggest that although the values of the past are appreciated, political considerations force the sympathies of the courtiers to lean toward contemporaneity as their primary aesthetic value.

The critical judgments of the court ladies remain at the level of content in the story, and so the understanding of the modern implied by their arguments cannot be separated from its context. The political motivations behind the judgments render them suspect as a guide to the aesthetic sensibility that guided the creation of *Genji monogatari*. Moreover, the arguments have a real-life historical model. Both the preliminary contest and especially the formal contest, which is held later in the presence of the young Reizei, are based on descriptions of the important imperial *uta awase* (poetry contest) of 960.[7] Murasaki's use of historical precedent indicates that her primary concern is to present a credible fictional account, and that calculation on her part requires that we be very cautious in assuming that the critical views it presents are relevant to her own storytelling techniques. On the contrary, she appears to have subordinated those received critical standards to the needs of her own fiction. We must therefore look at how Murasaki's awareness of contemporary critical values guided her in the development of her narrative and its problematic hero.

The arguments of the preliminary rounds assume the coexistence of two competing modes of representation in both fiction and painting. The first mode, represented by the value of the modern and up-to-date, may be described as realism and appears to be defined by the creation of a familiar narrative context and by a sense of plausibility. The pictures from *Utsuho monogatari* and *Jōsammi* are judged superior, or at least equal, to works of the past, and their appeal evidently lies in their ability to evoke a sense of recognition or presentness in the reader/observer. The aesthetic language of these works is apparently felt to be more firmly rooted in the realities of courtly experience. Lacking this realistic quality, *Taketori monogatari* and *Ise monogatari* are judged to be less immediate and compensate for that failing only by virtue of the ideals they represent. Their mode, then, may be described as idealistic.[8]

The recognition in critical terms of two competing modes of representation points to an important development in Heian narrative techniques. In her study of *Izumi Shikibu nikki* (The diary of Izumi Shikibu; also known as *Izumi Shikibu monogatari*),⁹ Janet Walker notes that two modes of presentation coexist in the text. There is a realistic mode in which individual experience is the focus. In this mode "change is possible and growth can occur in a direction expressing individual desire and energy. Feelings are not set patterns of experience, as in the poetic anthology, but dynamic responses of the individual to his or her environment."¹⁰ In *Izumi Shikibu nikki*, the function of the realistic mode is to present the factual aspects of the real-life love affair. The function of the idealistic mode is "primarily to celebrate the Heian courtly rituals and ideals of poetry and love."¹¹ The coexistence of these modes indicates that Izumi Shikibu sought to remake the standards of courtly behavior by asserting as an aesthetic value the immediacy, interest, and truthfulness of her own affair with Prince Atsumichi. To give the account of her love formal priority she appropriated the idealistic mode found in earlier works like the love poems of the *Kokinshū* or *Ise monogatari*. Her work is subjective and interior by virtue of being based on her experience, and because the story is in essence about her growth and development as a romantic heroine, the text is open-ended. However, by narrating her particular story in a literary form that stresses universal, unchanging patterns of human experience, the author also attempts to idealize and conventionalize her story. The historical distinction implied by an awareness of the modern as an aesthetic value is revealed not as a matter of content, as in the arguments in "Eawase," but in the formal structure of the narrative and its presentation of the characters. A similar formal effect is seen in *Genji monogatari*.

Although Murasaki Shikibu's narrative is more complex than *Izumi Shikibu nikki*, it, too, is a hybrid of both idealistic and realistic modes. The presence of the idealistic mode is felt in the heavy emphasis on ritual, in the use of allusion, and in the appropriation of earlier narrative elements. At the same time, there is throughout the text a pronounced critical awareness of the literary tradition, a self-consciousness about the debt to the past and its forms. The burden of that debt increases the need to assert the validity of present experience and observation against the authority of the past, thereby contributing to the emergence of a realistic mode. The attempt to bring together idealistic and realistic modes is perhaps the distinctive formal characteristic of the *monogatari* in general, a feature that developed from an earlier tendency in Japanese narratives to fuse ritual and historical elements. For example, a good deal of liturgical and legendary material found its way into the *Rikkokushi*, the six national histories modeled after the authoritative Chinese histories.¹² Waley may have been mistaken to assert there was no rigid historical sense in Heian fiction, but his mistake is understandable given that the line between fiction and history was blurred. A realistic mode appears to have evolved in part because fictional language was felt to require a factual, descriptive dimension.

As I noted earlier, *Izumi Shikibu nikki* is also known as *Izumi Shikibu monogatari* in certain textual variants, which further suggests that notions of narrative form were very fluid. If the line between historical writing and fiction was indistinct, then it is likely that fiction was not recognized in a formal, critical sense as denoting a specific category of narrative.[13] The ambiguous meaning of *monogatari* did not preclude the development of the idea of subgenres; it only prevented a clear demarcation between historical and fictional narratives. Iwahashi Koyata argues that the so-called *monogatari ron*, the discussion of *monogatari* that takes place in the "Hotaru" chapter of *Genji monogatari*, provides an example of this particular usage of the term and represents Murasaki Shikibu's view of history and fiction as essentially the same in a formal sense:

> Murasaki Shikibu had read [the six national histories] and had perhaps thought them not very interesting. When [in the *monogatari ron*] she wrote that the histories were one-sided [*katasoba*] . . . she probably meant that they did not tell the main thread of the story. Murasaki thought that you could not understand the true nature of the world if you recorded only what happened in such-and-such a year or month. In contrast she seems to have felt that truthfulness was to be found in the *monogatari*. Naturally you can discover the essential characteristics of human nature or trace the development of culture if you do detailed research and compile the fragmented pieces of historical fact, though it occurs to me that Murasaki Shikibu would have thought about the matter in this way only because she was looking at history from the standpoint of literature.[14]

The context of Prince Genji's remarks about the *monogatari*, which he uses as a means to try to seduce his adopted daughter, Tamakazura, makes it unlikely that they represent Murasaki Shikibu's opinions, as Iwahashi suggests. It does seem, however, that at the time Murasaki Shikibu wrote the appearance of factuality was felt to be an essential part of the *monogatari*, and the stress on factuality put a premium on the present, on the moment of observation, in the narrative process.

A number of technical developments furthered the rise of a realistic mode during the Heian period. The emergence of the kana syllabaries in the ninth and tenth centuries facilitated the writing of vernacular literature, and this widened the reading audience at court, especially among women. The extent to which literacy increased should not be overestimated as an influence, but the realistic mode of narrative, which strives to explain or establish the narrative context more fully in order to bring all the audience into the narrative world, both requires and creates an expansion of the readership. Certainly, the use of kana made it easier to record stories, broadening the scope of literary activity and making possible wider circulation.

The development of the diary form (*nikki*) also facilitated the emergence of a realistic mode through the use of a private, and therefore more subjective, narrative voice. The importance of ceremony at court, with advancement often depending on knowledge of and adherence to set codes of behavior, made it imperative that proper conduct be observed. Many early diaries were nothing more than records of minute observations of ritual and custom, with the factual accuracy of the observations serving a prescriptive function. Powerful social forces worked constantly to reintegrate individual experience back into ideal forms.[15] Over time, the diary became a means by which to set forth and establish aesthetic standards. *Tosa nikki* and *Makura no sōshi*, by Ki no Tsurayuki and Sei Shōnagon, respectively, are examples of the transformation of the form. However, the growing sophistication of the diary, which was focused through the perspective of the narrator, did not change its fundamental nature. The need for knowledge of the literary tradition and of social custom remained strong, demanding attention to factuality and to authentic detail even in literary matters where proper poetic diction and practice were often the subjects under observation.

Standards established in the present are constantly challenged by the authority of tradition and by idealized models of writing. To resist that challenge, authors assert the validity and originality of immediate experience and observation. Georges Gusdorf has observed that "the man who takes the trouble to tell of himself knows that the present differs from the past and that it will not be repeated in the future; he has become more aware of differences than of similarities; given the constant change, given the uncertainty of events and of men, he believes it a useful and valuable thing to fix his own image so that he can be certain it will not disappear like all things in the world."[16] The effort to idealize subjective experience leads authors to transmute their own remembrances, or inner narratives, into permanent literary narratives. The coexistence of realistic and idealistic modes is the product of a literary culture trapped in the modernist dilemma: confident in the aesthetic standards of the present yet forced by historical awareness to confront the impermanence of those standards. The struggle to resolve this dilemma is apparent in various *monogatari* in their attempts to represent the concrete reality of the ephemeral world as an ideal.

This struggle is the dominant element shaping both the overall structure of *Genji monogatari* and the portrait of its shining hero, and it is presented explicitly in the latter part of "Eawase," where the aesthetic values of the present are affirmed in the formal picture contest that is held with full pageantry before Reizei. The splendor of the occasion and the magnificent clothing and preparations are described in careful detail. Genji now and then offers his own opinions, and his taste tends to sweep all before him; but because perfection is ineffable and thus beyond representation, there are none of the specific arguments that appeared in the preliminary contest, and we are told simply that the contest continued through the day into the evening. The outcome appears to be in doubt until the very end, when both sides bring out their final and most magnificent works. The picture scroll offered by the Kokiden side is truly remarkable, but it is forced to compete with a scroll depicting life at Suma—the scroll painted by Genji during his exile. Genji's work evokes a powerful and tearful reaction in all those in attendance.

> To an even greater degree than at the time of his exile, they looked upon the pictures and thought about how sad and painful it had all been. The appearance of the world in those days, and the thoughts they had kept in their hearts at the time, came back to them as if they had just occurred. In drawing the scenery of that place, its strange bays and strands, Genji had kept nothing from view. Here and there kana were mixed in with the cursive characters. It was not a conventional, formal diary, and the manner in which the moving poetry had been incorporated into the work was breathtaking. Everyone was captivated by it. Points of interest and beauty found separately here and there in the other pictures were all contained together in this one scroll. Its beauty was deeply felt. Everything gave way before it and the Left was victorious. (15:184-85)

Throughout "Eawase," the self-conscious artificiality of Tō no Chūjō's efforts to win the contest is contrasted with Genji's more relaxed approach. Genji takes great care in the selection of works he has on hand, but his efforts need not be quite as elaborate because he has a natural gift, an innate aesthetic sense that is the source of his heroism. His scroll of Suma carries the day because of its immediate emotional impact, and the response of the audience takes the place of critical discourse here. There are no specific critical comments about the scroll (apart from the vague description provided by the narrator) or efforts to categorize the work; critical commentary could hardly be expected to explain Genji's success, for an absolute ideal is beyond representation.

It may be said that writing about a picture contest instead of a poetry contest was an inevitable choice for Murasaki Shikibu, since she could abstractly discuss a perfect painting but could never produce a perfect poem for her text. Her narrative strategy is to assume Genji's artistic genius, as well as his claim to political power, without actually having to demonstrate that genius directly. Such a strategy signals the difficulty of portraying a hero who is meant to represent the ideal and once again alerts us to the fact that the author subordinated statements of artistic standards to the needs of her narrative—a practice that points to the deeper values of the text. Genji's scroll brings to life memories and pain that many of the participants, at another time and place, had actually experienced. Indeed, the scroll seems to elicit a response more powerful than the original emotions. The sense of affective reality behind Genji's art gives his work an unparalleled poignancy and beauty; it re-creates the past for the courtiers and makes the foreign shores of Suma seem familiar. The artistic language at work achieves an almost perfect correspondence with reality, but that is a correspondence beyond any author's descriptive ability. The indirect presentation of this aesthetic ideal through the scroll represents an example where an imagined work of art achieves what is essentially the aim of the entire novel as depicted through the actions of its hero: namely, the realization of the ephemeral present as an absolute, timeless value.

The aim of idealizing the standards and values of the modern, of giving the ephemeral a kind of permanence, is expressed by Genji following his triumph in the picture contest. As the banquet wine flows freely and the dawn approaches, Genji, now relaxed, confident, and expansive, begins a drunken reminiscence about his scholarly and artistic training as a young man and recalls his early aptitude for painting. In his moment of triumph, he can afford to be excessively magnanimous, and he asks his brother, Prince Hotaru, who acted as judge, if perhaps he had been conceited to include his own work in the contest. Hotaru assures him that he was not and points out that for painting, as for the game of Go, natural ability is finally what counts most. Musical instruments are brought out, and the chapter ends with the inner thoughts of the two rivals, Tō no Chūjō and Genji. Tō no Chūjō consoles himself on his defeat, thinking that his daughter has not yet lost favor with Reizei. Genji's thoughts are of a different order: "Genji thought that for matters like proper ceremonials he wanted to establish precedents people of coming ages would speak of as having originated in his time. The present reign was an exceptionally high point, and even for trivial private entertainments remarkable ingenuity was shown. However, he also knew that this world was evanescent; and when he was certain that Reizei had matured a little more, he thought then he would surely retire from the world" (15:188).

There is throughout *Genji monogatari* a sense of the present as a significant time. Prince Genji himself reveals a strong historical sense in his preoccupation with cultural beginnings and endings. He is especially concerned with gaining cultural or aesthetic priority for himself, and this aspect of his characterization is one of the most important developments in the *monogatari* form—a development that sets apart Murasaki's work from earlier narratives. The gradual sophistication of the hero is achieved by giving to Genji a heightened self-awareness about those traditional courtly qualities that make him heroic. This self-consciousness, like the disparity between the ideal and its representation, creates tension in the narrative as Genji strives to assert the authority of his own experience in the present, making his experience ideal and heroic and remaking aesthetic standards in his own image. Genji defines himself according to inner expectations; he sees his life, and thus his identity, as a process of growth and potential development; he sees his life as open-ended and thus cannot close off his narrative by taking vows and withdrawing from the world. The "Eawase" chapter reveals a crucial move away from the narrative representation of Genji as a courtly paragon of sexual and aesthetic manners to a representation in which Genji defines the terms of his own heroism.

From the point of the picture contest on, the novel is increasingly an account of a fictionalizing, narrating mind at work as Genji becomes more and more involved with gathering his women around him and building the ideal court. The self-consciousness of his creative project contributes to a growing irony as the contradiction between his attempt to make himself the ideal and the recognition not only of his flaws but also of the impossibility of making his ephemeral vision permanent becomes harder to reconcile. This contradiction runs like a leitmotif through the narrative. It is particularly noticeable in the comments of the narrator, who from time to time remarks on the portrait of her hero, noting either that his behavior is bad or that he is almost too ideal to be believable. Yet the irony in *Genji monogatari* does not stem merely from the pretense that Genji is the ideal hero in spite of his faults and shocking actions nor from the narrator's occasional criticisms. It is also the result of the gap between Genji's awareness of himself as a hero—a heroism that leads him to try to establish the ephemeral present, which he controls politically, as the ideal—and his awareness that his heroism is built on an ephemerality that is lost once it becomes standard and conventional. The predicament Genji confronts arises from his inability to overcome the dilemma of the modern.

Genji is in no way a stand-in for the author, but his attempts to remake his world and to gain permanent power by setting the ideal standards of courtly behavior reveal the critical knowingness that shapes the narrative as a whole. Perhaps it is this knowingness that Motoori Norinaga had in mind when he argued that the underlying sensibility of the work is best described by the phrase *mono no aware* (knowing what it is to be moved).

> What sorts of thoughts and deeds, then, are considered good and evil in the novel? Generally speaking, those who know what it means to be moved by things [*mono no aware wo shiri*], who have compassion [*nasake arite*], and who are alive to the feelings of others [*yo no hito no kokoro ni kanaeru*] are regarded as good; whereas those who do not know what it means to be moved by things and are compassionless and insensitive to the feelings of others are regarded as bad. . . .
>
> The main object of *Genji monogatari*, then, is the understanding of what it means to be moved by things; and hence it stands in opposition to the teachings of Confucianism and Buddhism.[17]

Norinaga argued against a didactic or rationalistic reading of Murasaki Shikibu's work and asserted that the book must be described in aesthetic or intuitive terms. For Norinaga, the intention of the work is the elevation of the awareness of ephemerality to a guiding aesthetic principle, and his identification of *mono no aware* as the guiding ideal highlights the modernist sensibility of the narrative and the dilemma that sensibility reveals through the portrait of its problematic hero.

Genji is driven to define himself by his ability constantly to remake or renarrate his heroism, and on a number of occasions he describes his motivations as the need or desire to make an interesting story. His failed attempt to begin a relationship with Akikonomu, who serves a term as high priestess at Ise, evokes the story in *Ise monogatari* of Ariwara no Narihira and the priestess of Ise. In light of Genji's passionate affair with Akikonomu's mother, the Rokujō Lady, the idea of such a relationship seems outrageous and in fact never comes off. All the same, the attraction to the idea of such an unconventional love story is crucial to the development of Genji's character, for it seems that he needs to elaborate on not only his own earlier affairs but also other literary models, such as Narihira. As was noted above, in his attempt to seduce his adopted daughter, Tamakazura, in the "Hotaru" chapter, he uses a defense of fiction, the *monogatari ron,* as a means to draw close to her. His proposition is that their affair, like the books she has been reading, would make a great story because it would be unconventional and novel (15:433). At the center of Genji's character is an impulse to be original, to embrace discontinuity as a means of achieving political and cultural empowerment, and that impulse embodies the subversive tendency of the narrative to undo cultural norms.

The problem for such a hero is that the re-creative process must be continuous, for when it ceases the hero becomes conventional and passes into tradition. Barthes places this dilemma at the heart of the narrative process, writing, "Thus we find, in the Novel too, this machinery directed towards both destruction and resurrection, and typical of the whole of modern art. What must be destroyed is duration, that is, the ineffable binding force running through existence. . . . But what reconquers the writer is again duration, . . . an order which must be destroyed anew."[18] The repetitive structure of *Genji monogatari* is the result of this process. If Genji is driven by an urge for originality, for establishing a continuous now, he is also bothered by the loss implied in his preoccupation with the present. His sense of disinheritance is exemplified by what Norma Field has described in detail as his longing and search for the ideal woman to substitute for his dead mother.[19] That the novel's structure is determined by this search provides formal evidence of the impact of the sense of the modern. Genji's attempt to establish his ideal parallels the attempt by the novel as a whole to re-create the literary past by constantly elaborating on the paradigm of Yang Kuei-fei, the heroine cited at the beginning of the novel as the model for Genji's mother.

The desire to embrace discontinuity and assert the significance of the present is central to *Genji monogatari,* apparent not simply in the sense of the modern elaborated in "Eawase" or in Genji's attempts to make the modern start with himself. The awareness of change and loss, which is the fundamental aesthetic value in the text, is the primary motivation of the hero, who refuses ultimately to withdraw from the evanescent world, for repeatedly seeking to reaffirm the present and his own heroic qualities.

The emphasis on the modern in his characterization helps explain why Genji's death is not dealt with explicitly and why there is no formal closure to the narrative of his life. Obviously, the work may be open-ended because the author died before she could finish or because parts of the text are lost. Even so, the novel continues long after Genji's story is finished, and it is possible that Murasaki Shikibu may have consciously chosen not to write of Genji's death. The only reason to write such a character out of the story would be if his increasing repetitiveness and conventionality threatened the narrative process. Moreover, the lack of formal closure simulates the discontinuity and open-ended quality of the hero's life. The abrupt handling of the death of Genji suggests that the very nature of his heroism, which is predicated on the creation of discontinuities, makes his death an event that must remain outside the text.

◆

chapter two
The Burden of the Future:
Asserting the Literary Self
in *Hōjōki*

Genji monogatari was the product of an elite class confident of its values and yet cognizant of their transience. This tension shows through the heroism of Prince Genji, and though there is no doubt that the novel's sympathy is with him, as the portrait of Genji turns more toward the fictionalizing aspects of his character, the work becomes increasingly interior, the figure of Genji more and more tired, and the sense of ephemerality darker, more somber. The exit of the Shining Prince, announced at the beginning of chapter 42, leaves an emptiness in the fictional world of the novel, as if now that the paragon of courtly ideals is gone, the tale has the freedom to explore more fully the tangled contradictions of human relationships: an exploration that earlier was constantly, if with some difficulty, deflected by the pretense of Genji as the ideal hero.

The final section of the story, the so-called Ukifune chapters, has often been acclaimed as Murasaki Shikibu's greatest achievement, though the radical difference in tone between this part and the earlier chapters has fueled speculation that someone else, perhaps even Murasaki's daughter, Echigonoben, authored it. There is no credible evidence to support such speculation, however, and because the Ukifune chapters expand on the tendencies already present in the earlier parts of the narrative, it seems likely that the work is the conception of a single author. The qualities that make Genji a problematic hero are still present but split between his supposed son, Kaoru, actually the son of Kashiwagi, and his grandson, Niou, so that their contradictions are more apparent. The result is that the new heroes seem inadequate. A sense of exhaustion, passivity, and resignation pervades the story of their love affairs with Ukifune, who, in despair over her situation, attempts suicide and then, renouncing the world, takes monastic vows. The impossibility of giving permanence to aesthetic values is more pronounced as the story focuses on characters who have little claim to representing the ideal. The desire to turn one's back on the world, stated over and over by Genji, becomes an even more powerful impulse as the work reaches its close. There is at once a despair at being so deeply immersed in the ephemeral and a sense of resignation over the conflicting desires of human experience. With that despair and resignation the overtly religious elements of the novel grow even more prominent.

In turning her back on the world, Ukifune does what Genji cannot. Although the ending of the work is not conclusive, it seems that she rejects Kaoru and Niou, thereby committing a purely literary suicide: that is, she voluntarily, though not without a great deal of anguish, chooses to end her own story. In this she is assisted by the bishop of Yokawa—a figure based on the priest Genshin, the author of the influential tenth-century religious tract *Ōjōyōshū* (The fundamentals of salvation)—and by his sister. The story of Ukifune is an elaboration on the story of Kaguyahime in *Taketori monogatari*. Like Kaguyahime, once Ukifune renounces the ephemeral world, she in effect loses her human capacity for feeling and thereby moves beyond the realm of experience that can be narrated. Whereas for Genji the strong awareness of the present and the need to assert his priority led him to seek after discontinuity and constantly to recreate his own story, that same awareness becomes an intolerable burden for Ukifune. She must choose between either the stable, conventional Kaoru or the fickle, sexually exciting Niou. The values represented by these men have equal attraction for her, but they are as irreconcilable as the complementary aesthetic values of deep and shallow or of the ideal and the particular.

The exhaustion and despair that overtake the last section of *Genji monogatari* presage the cultural crisis that marks the late Heian and early Kamakura periods, and that section provides a literary model for later works that chronicled the social upheavals fueled by the collapse of the power of the court and the spread of the apocalyptic Buddhist doctrine of *mappō*. The work that most directly deals with (and is influenced by) these two underlying causes of the discontinuities of the age is *Hōjōki*, by Kamo no Chōmei. This acutely self-conscious memoir draws a parallel between the social and personal crises experienced by the narrator, who laments the loss of tradition in an uncertain present, and its literary structure shows signs of an awareness of the present as a significant time. *Hōjōki* is the literary testament, couched in the form of a religious confession, of a man seeking to overcome the inevitability of change in human life. The text begins as follows:

> The current of a flowing river never ceases; its water is ever changing. The foam that floats up in stagnant places now disappears, now bubbles up again, but it never lingers. The people and dwellings of the world are like this.
>
> It might be imagined that houses, great and small, which vie roof against proud roof in the capital, remain unchanged from one generation to the next. But when we examine whether this is true, we find that old houses are scarce. Those that burned down last year are this year built anew. Great houses fall apart and become small houses; and it is the same with the people who lived there. Even where places remain unchanged and there are as many people as ever, out of twenty or thirty people there are but one or two known to me. It is taught that it is the way of the world for people to die in the morning and to be born in the evening, just like bubbles of water. It is not known from where people who are born and die come, nor to where they go. Neither is it known for whose sake people go to such trouble over temporary dwellings, or why those dwellings should bring such joy. Which will be the first to pass away, the owner or the house? It is no different from the dew on the morning glory. The dew falls, and the flower lingers for a moment. It lingers, yet soon withers in the morning sun. The flower withers, but the dew has still not disappeared. And though it has not yet disappeared, it will not wait for the evening. (23–24)

These opening lines restate the Buddhist concept of *mujō*, the idea that human existence is relative and contingent, but the narrator's concerns are primarily literary, not religious. The apparent forms of the world are illusory, and the only response is to reject or transcend them. Chōmei looks to the past, to the religious and literary ideal of the hermit/saint, to find a way to overcome the impermanence of the present.[1]

Chōmei's statement of the fundamental nature of human experience is based on a paradox. The narrator of *Hōjōki* sees both his literary project and his building project as means to create an ideal form into which he

Mutability and the Floating World

can retreat. In defining himself through withdrawal from the world, however, he comes to realize that even as a hermit he cannot arrest the flux of experience. This realization creates self-doubt, and the difficulty Chōmei encounters in resolving his predicament is strikingly similar to the problem Freud claimed people face in trying to avoid "unpleasure." One way to avoid "unpleasure" is to regard

> reality as the sole enemy and as the source of all suffering, with which it is impossible to live, so that one must break off all relations with it if one is to be in any way happy. The hermit turns his back on the world and will have no truck with it. But one can do more than that; one can try to re-create the world, to build up in its stead another world in which its most unbearable features are eliminated and replaced by others that are in conformity with one's own wishes. But whoever in desperate defiance sets out upon this path to happiness will as a rule attain nothing. Reality is too strong for him.[2]

Although his remarks address the impossible pursuit of happiness, Freud has described the dilemma expressed by the narrator of *Hōjōki*, who seeks to resolve the problem of impermanence by seeing in mutability the underlying essence of reality. In reducing his expression of this truth to a narrative form, however, the narrator perpetuates the problem and is forced to confront the impossibility of escaping the ceaseless flux of the present moment. The sense of discontinuity he feels is similar to that in *Genji monogatari*, though there is an important difference. Genji, who seeks to assert his own standards, values their immediacy or presentness. For him, the dilemma is that once created they immediately lose their presentness, and he is forced to re-create them. For Chōmei's narrator, on the other hand, the awareness of the flux of the present leads him to seek values in the religious past and what he interprets as the selfless model of nature, yet the burden of a future that will bring only further chaos and Chōmei's knowledge of the inadequacy of his own efforts, which are primarily literary, not religious, make success impossible.

Because *Hōjōki* is a memoir conceived within the language of the Heian courtly tradition, it is necessary to look at the personal, religious, and social contexts that shaped its composition. Kamo no Chōmei was born in 1155, a year before the Hōgen Disturbance set in motion the conflict between the Taira and Minamoto that would last for the next thirty years, culminating in the Genpei War. The triumph of the Minamoto and the founding of the military regime in Kamakura ended all pretense of de facto rule by the aristocracy in Kyoto. Chōmei's formative years coincided with the decline of the court, and the decline of his own personal fortunes, which he recounts in *Hōjōki,* mirrored the greater social unrest around him.

Chōmei was the second son in a family that had held the hereditary position of *negi,* a midlevel position at the Kamo no Mioya Jinja (also known as the Shimogamo Jinja).[3] In accordance with his family's position, he received at the age of seven a peerage and a stipend as *taifu,* a position of the fifth rank. His father, Nagatsugu, retired in 1170 and evidently died sometime during the following decade, probably in 1172 or 1173. Before his death, Nagatsugu had been succeeded by a cousin, Kamo no Sukesue, and this was the key factor in the loss of the family's position. Chōmei was forced to turn to a life in the arts in order to support himself. His social displacement almost certainly heightened his awareness of the mutability of the world, and it is perhaps worth noting here that his circumstances resemble the personal upheavals and displacement experienced by many writers during the Meiji period. He was proficient in both poetry and music, and through those channels he maintained access to court society.[4]

Through these connections Chōmei nearly succeeded in reviving his family's position. From 1191 on he received increasing recognition for his talents as a poet, and he participated as a judge at a number of poetry contests held at the court. In 1200 the retired emperor Go-Toba requested one-hundred-poem sequences from Chōmei, and from that point on it appears he enjoyed imperial patronage. It was perhaps this improvement in his situation that led him to petition Go-Toba for a position at Tadasu no Yashiro in the Kamo Shrine. His petition was opposed by the head of the shrine, Sukekane, the son of Sukesue, who wanted the position for his own son. The fact that Chōmei was turned down and offered another post is evidence of his lack of political influence. His disappointment must have been keen, for shortly after, in 1204, he announced his *shukke,* his renunciation of the world, and became a novitiate, taking the name Shami Ren'in.

Renunciation was not an unusual practice among courtiers, and it was common to take only the vows of the novitiate without becoming a full-fledged monk or residing in a temple. However, it must be noted that Chōmei was far more strict in his religious practice and much humbler in his lifestyle than was often the case among aristocrats. Poverty was probably a major determining factor in his adherence to principle, although in fairness to Chōmei it should be noted that others admired his sincerity. An entry from *Minamoto no Ienaga nikki* describes his character:

> The retired emperor Go-Toba ordered Chōmei to visit and bring the *biwa* called Tenarai with him and had his message conveyed to Ōhara. Chōmei told the messenger that he would attend, and he sent poems written on a plectrum.
>
> While in seclusion
> not even the roar
> of the storms of the peak
> could finally dislodge me,
> but I shall leave here at your command.
>
> The dew has fallen
> even on these hermit robes of moss
> that ought to be pure.
> Such is the way that our attachments
> to this foul world accumulate so.
>
> On reading these poems the retired emperor replied.
>
> Because the dew falls
> even more heavily on the sleeves
> of him who reads these poems,
> how much more so have the attachments
> to this foul world piled up.
>
> Having donned the appearance
> of one who has gone off
> deep into the mountains,
> do you look upon the half-moon
> as a memento of the palace?
>
> Later, when we suddenly met, he was so thin and wasted that we hardly recognized him. Chōmei said, "If only I had no regrets for this world, the darkness of my state of woe would have cleared. Truly I have received his majesty's grace," and his moss robes wilted with tears. "I cannot leave behind the world of woe, and though it is but a small impediment to salvation I have kept this," he continued, taking out from his sutra pouch the *biwa* plectrum on which the retired emperor had sent his reply poems. "If kept in the same place beneath the moss [that is, if I keep it], then it will rot in obscurity," he concluded. It is of course difficult to forget things that have found their way into your heart, and it is touching that he appeared to think such a trifling object could be a hindrance to his salvation.[5]

Chōmei recounts briefly in *Hōjōki* that he spent the first five years of his retirement in a small house in Ōhara, in an area north of present-day Kyoto (36). The area around Ōhara and nearby Kurodani had for a long time been a center for Pure Land Buddhism in conjunction with the Enryakuji temple on Mount Hiei.[6] The area was especially attractive to a kind of hermit/holy man known as *bessho hijiri* who, though not denouncing the major temples outright, sought to break free from what they saw as the secularization and corruption of the temples by the presence of the aristocracy. Perhaps because Ōhara was the site of a great deal of religious activity, it did not provide Chōmei with the degree of seclusion he was seeking, and he made a more complete break by moving to the area around Hino no Yama (or Hino no Toyama). There he became a true hermit, building the tiny hut that provided the title for his most famous literary work. *Hōjōki* was written in 1212, and Chōmei died four years later.

In spite of his religious devotion, he was unable to end his lifelong association with the court and its traditions, and the fusion of his religious and courtly lives enabled him to create an original portrait of himself as a literary artist. In both his life at the court and in his retreat from the world, his sense of the present as a falling off was a conspicuous factor. By the time he wrote *Hōjōki*, the power and prestige of the court had witnessed nearly two centuries of erosion. The decline in the military and economic power of the aristocracy coincided with the acceleration of the general movement within Buddhism away from its position as an elite religion to a religion for the masses.[7] Insofar as this movement eventually gave rise to the Pure Land sects, Chōmei's decision to become a novice at Ōhara reflects part of a larger religious trend. At the same time, his position as a poet at the court placed him within an aesthetic tradition that cultivated an awareness of the passage of time and the evanescence of human life. Having witnessed such vast upheavals in his lifetime and desiring somehow to arrest the decline in his own fortune, the attempt to maintain the ephemeral as a purely literary value must have struck him as a hindrance to his own literary project of renunciation. Yet the language of the courtly tradition was the only resource Chōmei possessed to make a coherent vision.

Hōjōki is heavily indebted to a tenth-century work written in Chinese by Yoshishige no Yasutane (d. 997), the *Chiteiki* (Record of the Pond Pavilion). The first half of *Chiteiki* is a meditation on the mutability of the world, while the second half deals with the withdrawal of the narrator to a small dwelling of his own construction. *Chiteiki* also provides a statement of the fundamental dilemma that Chōmei later confronts. Having succeeded in withdrawing from society into a life that satisfies only the most basic of his needs, the narrator of *Chiteiki* realizes that even his modest lifestyle is an illusion: "Now that I am well along in years, I've finally managed to construct a little house, but when I consider it in the light of my actual needs, even *it* seems somewhat too extravagant and grand. Above, I fear the anger of Heaven; below, I am ashamed in the eyes of men. I'm like a traveler who has found an inn along the road, an old silkworm who has made himself a solitary cocoon. How long will I be able to live here?"[8]

In addition to the structural debt owed to a work like *Chiteiki*, which deals with the theme of renunciation, there are numerous passages in *Hōjōki* that make extensive use of well-worn imagery to connect Chōmei's personal experiences to the literary ideal of the hermit.

> Sometimes, in the still of the evening, at the sight of the moon in my window, I long for people of old, or I weep at the sound of monkeys wailing. The fireflies in the grasses mingle with the fishing lights on Maki Island; the predawn rains sound like a storm blowing through the leaves. Hearing the calls of the mountain birds, I wonder, is it my father or mother? Thinking about how the deer of the peak have grown used to me and come near, I realize how far I am from the world of men. And sometimes, stirring up buried embers of charcoal, I make them companions to the sleeplessness of old age. (39–40)

There are a series of allusions in this passage. The image of the moon in the window is a reference to "Tiao wang shih" (Poems on his dead wife), written by P'an Yueh (247–30), which appears in the twelfth book of *Wen-hsüan* (The anthology of literature, compiled 526–31). The conceit of hearing the voice of his parents in the crying of a mountain bird is a reference to a poem by the priest Gyōgi (668–748), which later appears in the nineteenth book of the *Gyokuyō wakashū* (Collection of jeweled leaves of Japanese poetry, compiled 1312–13). Like the final voice in Eliot's "The Waste Land," Chōmei seems to have shored these poetic fragments against his ruins. His sense of discontinuity and his attempt to reclaim the literary past in some form echo the aesthetic concept of "old words, new heart" formulated by Fujiwara Shunzei (1114–1204)—a formulation that reflects a shared cultural conservatism.

This impulse to reclaim the court tradition for the purpose of a religious testament was to some extent made necessary by the doctrine of *mappō*.

The Burden of the Future

Briefly stated, the doctrine maintains that the dharma, the teachings of the Buddha, would pass through three periods of gradual decline: the period of the True Dharma, when the teaching of doctrines, the practice of disciplines, and the achievement of enlightenment were all possible; the period of the Imitated Dharma, when only teaching and practice were possible; and *mappō*, the period of the final stages of the law when only the teaching remains. The lengths of these periods were subject to various interpretations, but the time frame generally accepted in Japan was that the periods of the true and the imitated law would each last a thousand years, and the age of *mappō* would last for ten thousand years, after which Buddhism would completely disappear.[9]

Notions of the eventual demise of Buddhism are found relatively early in a number of Indian texts.[10] Several reasons were cited for the predicted decline, including the entrance of women into the *sangha* (priesthood), the religious and moral laxity of disciples, the lack of cultivation of the four states of mindfulness, the lack of care in transmitting, understanding, and applying the True Dharma, and external threats such as persecutions or social and political conditions unfavorable to the dharma. Of these causes, it was the last that came to be viewed in later Mahāyāna texts and among Chinese Buddhists as bearing primary responsibility. For the people of Japan, the increasing frequency of civil disorders, the loss of power and economic status by the ruling class, and the corruption of the Buddhist hierarchy typified by the armed struggles between competing factions of *sōhei*, the warrior monks attached to the great monasteries, were signs of a breakdown of society in fulfillment of the doctrine.

Using the time frame mentioned above, the Japanese reckoned the beginning of *mappō* to be the year 1052,[11] and the full implications of the theory were understood in Japan by around the middle of the tenth century. The doctrine's apocalyptic nature was responsible in large part for the pessimistic cast of mind that dominated many Heian and Kamakura works of literature. It is worth noting that an apocalyptic mode of thought was also important in the growth of modernist literature at the turn of the last century and is characteristic of the concern with discontinuity and change. Frank Kermode writes that "it seems to be a condition attaching to the exercise of thinking about the future that one should assume one's own time to stand in an extraordinary relation to it. The time is not free, it is the slave of a mythical end." He goes on to observe that crisis is a way of thinking about one's moment, and not inherent in the moment itself. Transition, like the other apocalyptic phases, is, to repeat Focillon's phrase, an "intemporal agony"; it is merely that aspect of successiveness to which our attention is given. The fiction of transition is our way of registering the conviction that the end is immanent rather than imminent; it reflects our lack of confidence in ends, our mistrust of the apportioning of history to epochs of this and that. Our own epoch is the epoch of nothing positive, only of transition. Since we move from transition to transition, we may suppose that we exist in no intelligible relation to the past, and no predictable relation to the future.[12]

This description is applicable to the doctrine of *mappō* insofar as that doctrine emphasizes the present as discontinuous, transitional, and ultimately degenerative. The collapse of values was believed to be inevitable during *mappō*, and this notion led to a sense of urgency about the present.

The doctrine's impact reached a peak in the religious developments of the late Heian and early Kamakura periods, spurring a movement to reform Buddhism to make its teachings and practices not merely relevant to the age but possible. The reasoning was that, however correct previous practices and institutions were in their historical contexts, they were now neither appropriate nor adequate for the period of decline. The relativistic view of the historical viability of Buddhist doctrine that came to dominate made the present a significant, if deeply troubled time; the need was to find a way to achieve practice and eventual enlightenment in the present. Judging by its rapid growth as a popular religion, the teaching of Pure Land Buddhism was evidently taken to be a possible solution.[13]

The focus of Pure Land belief is the Buddha Amida, and three texts form the core of the sect: the *Muryōjukyō*, the main sutra; the *Amidakyō*, commonly used for liturgical purposes; and the *Kanmuryōjukyō* (the sutra of contemplation). The *Muryōjukyō* tells the story of Dharmākara bodhisattva (the name of Amida/Amitābha before he accepted buddhahood), who, desiring to create a perfect Buddhaland, makes forty-eight vows and swears that his own acceptance of buddhahood will depend on the realization of them. Of these vows, the eighteenth, known as the *hongan*, or primary vow, states that all sentient beings who call ten times upon the name of Amida with a sincere mind, with true faith, and with a desire to be reborn into the Pure Land will be reborn there.[14] Consequently the practice of *nenbutsu*, of calling the name with the formula *namu Amida butsu*, became central to Pure Land practice. More importantly, Pure Land teachings addressed the doctrine of *mappō*. The *Amidakyō* claims that Śākyamuni achieved the highest enlightenment even though he lived in a period of the Five Corruptions: a corruption of the times, when war, natural disasters, famines, and pestilence occur; a corruption of outlook, when confused ideas are widespread; a corruption by inner defilements such as ignorance, greed, and hatred; a corruption of living beings, with the mind and body wracked with infirmities; and a corruption of longevity, with a decrease in the human life span.[15] The concept of the period of the Five Corruptions was known to the Chinese monk Hui-ssu, who systematized *mappō* in the form that gained acceptance in Japan in the sixth century.

The appeal of Pure Land teaching is obvious. It gave hope to all, even in a corrupt age, and its practice was simple enough that it could, and did, become widespread. Though it was initially practiced mainly by the upper classes and the clergy, it became a mass religion in the Kamakura period. In spite of this growth, however, Pure Land Buddhism was not an independent sect until the start of the twelfth century, when Hōnen (1133–1212) espoused the doctrine of *senju nenbutsu,* the exclusive practice of calling the name of Amida, and rejected the preoccupation of other Pure Land sects with good works or ascetic practices.[16] It was this rejection of other practices that moved Pure Land Buddhism toward independent status and started a trend toward reform along sectarian lines.

Although they were contemporaries, it is not clear whether Chōmei was directly involved with or aware of Hōnen's activities. The influences of the general outlook of the times and of specific religious teachings were nonetheless important in the composition of *Hōjōki,* not only in posing the essential dilemma confronting the author but also in shaping the structure of the work. As was the case with *Chiteiki, Hōjōki* breaks into two main sections. The first states the main thesis of the vanity of human life, focusing specifically on the problem of flux and mutability, and offers an overview of the state of the world as evidence to support that view. The second section gives the personal response of one individual to the present crisis.

Most of the first half of the work consists of a description of a series of disasters witnessed by the author during his lifetime. Each disaster is linked to the others, and each section is marked off by the repetitive use of the word *mata* (and again), giving the catalog of events the resigned air of inevitability. The narrator tells of the great fire in the capital in 1177, of the whirlwind that struck in 1180, of the political disorder following the attempt by Taira no Kiyomori to move the capital to Fukuhara, of the famine of 1181, and of the great earthquake of 1185. Each of these events is used to support the general philosophical statement about the impermanence of life put forth in the opening lines, cited above. The significance of these events lies to a great extent in the literary form Chōmei imposes upon them. The five disasters do not correspond directly to the Five Corruptions, but Chōmei's description of his age very closely fits the description of the corruption of the times in the *Amidakyō,* and, as with his use of the language of the court tradition, it is clear that he has employed a literary conceit to confer order on the present. He concludes the first half of the work with an affirmation of his primary thesis about the mutability of the world and the uncertainty of the human condition: "Wherever we may reside, whatever work we may do, we inhabit our bodies but for a short time, and we can rest our spirits for but a moment" (35).

The narrative switches at this point to an autobiographical account of the author's life, especially his later years when he has taken up the life of a hermit. It is in this personal account that we glimpse aspects of a modern identity, for not only is the voice here more subjective and interior but there is an emphasis on the ongoing growth and development of the narrative self. After briefly telling of his early life and loss of position, he describes his house in Ōhara and uses it as an image of the uncertainty of his life to that point. He renounces the world utterly and retreats further to Hino no Yama, where he builds the ten-foot-square hut that becomes the image of his new life. The connection between the physical hut constructed as a means to live out his ideal and the literary hut, an edifice built out of words, is made explicit in the descriptions of the ways in which Chōmei embellishes the original, simple structure of the hut.

> Since retiring to the interior of Hinoyama [*sic*], I have extended the eaves of my hut by more than three feet to the east and made a convenient place to break up and burn firewood. To the south I have spread a veranda of bamboo, and to the west of that I have built a shelf to hold offerings of water and flowers to the Buddha. To the north, inside on the other side of a screen, I installed a painting of Amida and beside it have hung a picture of Fugen. In front of it I have placed the *Lotus Sutra*. At the eastern edge of the hut I spread out strands of straw and make that my mattress for the night. To the southwest I constructed a hanging shelf out of bamboo, and I put three baskets of black hide there. In the baskets I place excerpts from things like poetry, music and the *Ōjōyōshū*. (37)

Chōmei's home improvement project stresses simplicity and devotional functionality, fusing his religious concerns with his aesthetic interests and courtly tastes. He creates an entirely new type of physical and literary edifice that spreads out beyond the bounds of the ten square feet defined by his model, the hut of Vimalakīrti. Moreover, the narrator sees in his physical surroundings the ideal of his renunciation, and he tries not merely to identify with and pattern his life after natural objects but to make physical nature an extension of his edifice. Once more he turns to the language of his poetic tradition to state the connection between nature and his ideal.

> There is an opening in the west, and I am not without a means to contemplate on the Pure Land. In the spring there are waves of wisteria. Like the purple cloud on which Amida arrives, the wisteria shines with a fragrant splendor in the west. In summer I listen to the cuckoo. Each time he speaks he promises to act as a guide in the world after this one. In the autumn the voice of the cicada fills my ears. It sounds like it mourns for the people of this world. In the winter I think fondly of the snow, for its appearance, piling up, then disappearing, may be likened to our sins, which stand between us and salvation. (37–38)

Thomas Hare argues that the double negative in the phrase "not without a means to contemplate" casts serious doubt on the commitment and sincerity with which Chōmei practiced Pure Land teachings.[17] He reads Chōmei as a "deluded ascetic" who is skeptical about the efficacy of his project and his devotions. However, this reading suggests that Chōmei never intended sincerely to follow Pure Land doctrine, and that is by no means certain. There is no question that Chōmei is wracked with doubts about the ultimate value of his literary project, but that skepticism is as much a literary pose as it is a statement of religious belief. The conscious use of the language of the court aesthetic to present the narrator's religious testament sets up competing and equally compelling claims on our reading of the life of the narrator. Doubts about the efficacy of his devotions illustrate the tension inherent in the literary project but do not necessarily constitute a rejection of Pure Land teaching.

More importantly, Chōmei's skepticism reflects a significant doctrinal controversy central to the development of the Pure Land sects in his day. The debate centered on whether good works, or devotions such as the *nenbutsu*, are really effective or even necessary for rebirth in the Pure Land of Amida. The problem with such actions is that they stem from self-power, *jiriki*, which may be a source of self-delusion and thus a hindrance to salvation. This is a particularly acute dilemma for the faithful in the age of *mappō*, for it implies that the only means of salvation is other-power, *tariki*, the compassion of Amida and the transference of his merit.[18] It seems more appropriate, then, to view Chōmei's statements of devotion, casual though they may be, as a narrative strategy to heighten the recognition at the very end of the work that all such devotions are useless anyway. Such a stance does not prove that Chōmei was a devoted follower of the sect, but equally the narrator's expressions of skepticism and his casual attitude to his devotions do not, as Hare claims, prove that Chōmei was in some way a failed Pure Land ascetic. What may be said with more certainty is that the structure of *Hōjōki* owes a debt to the controversy over faith versus good works in Pure Land ideology. The concluding lines of *Hōjōki,* examined below, suggest that Chōmei's skepticism was directed mainly at the possibility of salvation through self-power in a world that is constantly in flux and that cannot be contained within the construct, real or literary, of a hermitage.

Chōmei's strategy for extending the boundaries of his literary edifice, and thus his identity, is based on an attempt to absorb the qualities he observes in his surroundings. There is in nature an absence of a sense of the present, and thus an absence of attachment to the things of this world. Chōmei seeks that lack of self-consciousness and tries to achieve the intuited sense of belonging to the physical environment that he sees in the behavior of birds and fish. His self-reliance makes him consider his hands his servants and his feet his only vehicle. For nourishment he takes only whatever nuts and berries he finds; for clothing and bedding he uses only whatever simple cloth or fiber he comes across (42–43). He compares his body to a drifting cloud and is careful not to recommend his way of life to others lest that signal a purposefulness that he must avoid. The desire to avoid self-consciousness extends to his religious practice as well.

> Should the *nenbutsu* be troublesome, or when I am not inclined to read the scriptures, I rest and neglect my duties. There is no one to interfere with me, nor anyone in front of whom I must feel shame. Though I do not intentionally practice vows of silence, because I am alone I must follow the practice of speaking no evil. Though I do not necessarily keep the precepts, since this is not an environment where you can break the prohibitions, then of course they will not be broken. (38)

Nature is subject to change and flux, but the forms of nature live only for the moment, free of a sense of discontinuity. The wholeness and timelessness in nature provide the narrator with his model for transcendence, which he copies in the construction of his hut, in his religious discipline, and in the structure of his literary work—all of which constitute his identity. The effort to achieve transcendence, however, presents its own paradox, and a clash between his religious and literary aspirations marks the end of the narrative.

> The substance of the teaching of the Buddha is to have no attachments to anything. The fact that I now love my grass hut is a sin. That I am attached to my solitude is a hindrance to my salvation. Why do I write about these useless pleasures and waste precious time?
> One quiet morning before dawn, while carefully considering this problem, I questioned my own heart, saying to myself, "The fact that you fled the world and lived among the mountains was for the sake of disciplining your mind and following the path of the Buddha. Although in outer appearance you are like a holy man, your heart is stained with corruption. Though you claim to follow the path of Jōmyō Koji (Vimalakīrti), who also lived in a hut, in truth your keeping of the practices barely reaches what Shuri Handoku (Suddhipanthaka) achieved. Is it possible that the repayment of the sins of a previous life, which has taken the form of poverty, causes you to trouble yourself? Or is your extremely corrupt heart throwing your intentions out of order?" At that time my heart held no answers. All I could do was use my tongue to chant two or three sections of the *nenbutsu* to Amida, of whom I am unworthy. (39)

The desire for transcendence and enlightenment is a necessary first step on the path to salvation, but that desire may become an obstacle if it leads to a preoccupation with the self. The effort to achieve enlightenment is a project aimed at remaking the self. In the case of the hermit, the project requires the separation of the individual from society, and in literary terms that separation is equivalent to re-creating the self through autobiographical narrative. The search for transcendence is reduced to a temporal act of narration, which defeats salvation and the ultimate unity hinted at by the oxymoronic concept of eternity in mutability. Many commentators, in order to explicate this problematic ending, have focused their attention on the word *fushō*, which I have rendered as "of whom I am unworthy" on the basis of two possible readings. The first, "unwillingly" or "grudgingly," comes from a vernacular usage current at the time Chōmei wrote. The second originates in a Buddhist usage indicating that Amida Buddha will bring salvation "without being asked."[19] These two meanings appear to produce very different interpretations of the narrator's statement. Either he is a skeptic who "grudgingly" goes through the motions of saying the *nenbutsu,* or he is a true believer who knows that Amida will come to him even if he does not ask. These two meanings are not, I believe, mutually exclusive; rather, they are meant to be taken together to indicate ambivalence. The lukewarm attitude toward devotions and the doubts about their efficacy do not, as I noted above, provide evidence one way or the other about Chōmei's adherence to Pure Land belief, and the word *fushō* maintains that ambivalent narrative pose. In my reading, *fushō* refers back to the corrupt condition of the narrator's heart and to the propriety of his ascetic practices, implying that the reason for his unwillingness to say the *nenbutsu* is his realization that he is unworthy of salvation. Conversely, he may be unwilling to say the *nenbutsu* because of his faith in Amida and his knowledge that he will be saved even though he is not worthy of receiving Amida's grace.

William Lafleur reads these final lines as a tongue-in-cheek statement, arguing that the knowingness of the narrator indicates that he has no problem "understanding the meaning and the implications of the Mahayanist principle of nonduality."[20] The narrator's wisdom regarding nonduality in effect resolves the paradox of seeking enlightenment through rejection of the world. This reading is not entirely satisfactory, however, since the narrative structure of the work makes it clear that describing the state of nonduality—like describing the ideal heroism of Prince Genji—lies outside the bounds of the text. To read the final sentiments of *Hōjōki* as the clever posturing of a knowing narrator is to undervalue the tensions inherent in the self-conscious act of narrating a personal religious testament. Chōmei is neither an enlightened sage, nor a failed visionary, nor a manipulative cynic. In his fusion of Buddhist ideology with the aesthetic language of the Heian courtly tradition he created a narrative form whose quicksilver nature is well suited to express the predicaments of his life and age. Chōmei's work shares the sense of urgency found in all modern art. His historical predicament is revealed by his attempt to use narrative to overcome the discontinuities of his experience and to create a new identity for himself and by his eventual understanding that the ability to narrate a new self demands discontinuity. *Hōjōki* states this dilemma through the terms of Buddhist teaching and the recovery of traditional literary images and motifs, revealing in its deeper structure and formal qualities the impact of the dilemma of the modern.

◆

chapter three
Epiphanies of Modernism and the Floating World

Charles Taylor argues that at the center of modern culture in the West since the romantic period is a conception of art "as a creation which reveals, or as a revelation which at the same time defines and completes what it makes manifest." He terms this conception "epiphanic" and explains that what he wants to "capture with this term is just this notion of a work of art as the locus of a manifestation which brings us into the presence of something which is otherwise inaccessible, and which is of the highest moral and spiritual significance; a manifestation, moreover, which also defines or completes something, even as it reveals." This view of art as something higher and significant, as a means to recover wholeness—to join the fleeting ephemeral with the eternal—has resulted in opposing tendencies to give priority to the inward, subjective experience of the artist, on the one hand, and, on the other, to see art as a realm apart, placing the center of interest, not on self-expression, but on language and form.[1] This notion of epiphanic art not only recapitulates the conflicts inherent in Western modernism but also provides a useful point of comparison for examining developments in pre-Meiji literature.

In the Tokugawa period the modern found expression in the changed meaning of the term *ukiyo,* the floating world. *Ukiyo* originally referred to the religious notion of the contingent and illusory nature of the evanescent world, the world of woe and impermanence, and was written with the graph meaning "melancholy" or "pitiable." By the end of the seventeenth century, however, *ukiyo* had become associated with the demimonde of the great cities of Japan, the red-light districts of Shimabara, Yoshiwara, and Shinmachi, and by extension took on the meaning of "fashionable" or "up-to-date." The word had also come to be written with the graph for "floating" or "drifting." At times it seems as difficult to define *modern* as a critical term as it is to find a legal definition for pornography. The Tokugawa usage of *ukiyo,* however, seems to have very nearly encompassed both, for its reference to the fashionable, the ephemera of the up-to-date, took on pornographic connotations. But even though the word carried the meaning that the present-day world is not merely illusory and unsatisfying but also vulgar, for the most part it was associated in the Tokugawa period with notions of gaiety and liveliness, with a sense of joie de vivre, and assumed a subversive tone that became a source for literary renewal throughout the period.

The association of the fashionable with the floating world contrasts sharply with the sadness and the uncertain reality of human life expressed in the earlier meaning of *ukiyo*. The contradictory aspects of the expanded meaning reflect two larger cultural phenomena that also helped shape the general development of Tokugawa literature. The first was the emergence of an entrenched, assertive, and self-renewing tradition, neo-Confucian orthodoxy. Herman Ooms, among others, has urged caution when discussing neo-Confucianism as a monolithic state ideology, arguing that the view of neo-Confucianism as a tradition that dominated continuously from the inception of the Tokugawa regime is in fact a relatively late ideological construct. Nevertheless, he notes that neo-Confucianism provided important "conceptual and mythological material to construct the Tokugawa discourse on society."[2] The crucial function of that discourse was to justify and preserve the power of the ruling elite, and neo-Confucianism was often used in the service of the elite by a literati class on the margins of social power who saw the appropriation of orthodox views as a means of empowerment.

> The broader ideological constructs that marshaled discursive argument for the correctness of the new political system were by and large, however, not commissioned by the bakufu [shogunal government]. The misrecognition of

the new system of domination as a regime of virtue was created primarily through the activity of a new class of schoolmen. Not only does power generate private interests (which it tries to hide by generalizing them); private interests also seek power. Thus a class of learned men that included doctors, monks, ex-monks, déclassé warriors, and teachers, who were left outside the new power structure but who, unlike the peasants and other commoners, had a rich body of knowledge (Buddhist, Shinto, and Neo-Confucian) at their disposal, used this knowledge to draw themselves closer to the center.[3]

The second phenomenon that affected literary developments was the emergence of a vibrant merchant class and the beginnings of a mass literary culture with its own canons of taste, which were by nature opposed to any entrenched orthodoxy. The social stability and general prosperity created by the Tokugawa regime ameliorated to some degree the problems posed by the political discontent and social aspirations of this class, at least until the regime began to show signs of crisis in the late eighteenth and early nineteenth centuries.[4] The attempts by the dominant orthodoxy to suppress or manipulate what it viewed as antitraditional and subversive clashed with the efforts of disenfranchised elements in the society (for example, writers who focused on the demimonde, the merchant class, or those who held forth heterodox ideologies such as *kokugaku* [national learning—a school of linguistic research into the origins of the Japanese language]) to overturn the linguistic and ideological categories embraced by the champions of orthodoxy. These tensions were expressed as a clash between high culture (orthodoxy) and low culture (heterodoxy) and deflected from the social or political spheres to a subversion of the literary tradition, as seen, for example, in the comic impulse of much Tokugawa literature, especially later *gesaku* fiction ("playful works," frequently banned by the authorities for obscenity). Even in tragic works of the period, such as the love-suicide plays of Chikamatsu, there is a temporary sense of affirmation, a kind of ritual catharsis, that comes with giving priority to individual desire over the dictates of social convention. Yet the expression of individual desire is realized only through an act of self-extinction, and these plays ultimately reaffirm orthodox values and the existing social order.

The formal innovations that developed out of the effort to resolve the contradictory aspects of the modern are best represented in the *ukiyo-zōshi* (tales of the floating world) of Ihara Saikaku. Saikaku's use of certain narrative resources—his adoption of a realistic mode, his choice of an anecdotal structure, his use of parody, and his fusion of classical and vulgar narrative elements—are especially noteworthy because they act as markers of a struggle between literary novelty and traditionalism while at the same time indicating how the potential for socially subversive work is turned inward to a narrower type of subversion acceptable to the established regime. Before looking at specific narrative innovations in *Kōshoku ichidai onna* (The life of a woman of passion, 1686), it is worth noting certain general tendencies in Saikaku's work.

Numerous critics and scholars have pointed to the realistic mode employed by Saikaku as the distinctive innovative feature of his fiction.[5] Generally speaking, the argument is that Saikaku's attention to detail, the factuality with which he describes elements of the floating world, constitutes formal realism. The purpose of detail is, in narrative terms, to help familiarize the reader with the fictionalized context. The size and diversity of the intended reading audience will thus determine to an extent the amount and quality of descriptive detail included. As noted earlier, the use of detailed literary settings in works of the Heian period in part grew from the need to establish the context within which court life took place. A similar need for clarification of the narrative context arose when the reading audience grew larger and a preoccupation with fashion became an important part of the culture of the Tokugawa merchants. This preoccupation was already an influential factor in the *kana-zōshi*, the early seventeenth-century forerunner of the *ukiyo-zōshi*. Written, as the name indicates, in the simpler kana phonetic script and in a style that was relatively accessible to a mass audience, these popular booklets contained everything from romances and traditional stories to travelogues, personal anecdotes, and catalogs of the leading actors and courtesans in the licensed quarters. Above all, their key function was to provide a source of information on topics of style and fashion of interest to a particular class, the bourgeois townsman.[6]

Saikaku's use of a realistic mode and his focus on the life and concerns of the merchant class have led a number of critics to compare him with European writers of the same time, most notably Defoe. Such a sweeping comparison of course runs the risk of ignoring vital parochial differences; nonetheless, the term *realism*, when used narrowly to refer to certain formal qualities in the manner of narrative presentation, does serve a comparative purpose. As Ian Watt has suggested, realism, which is usually associated with the narrative form of the novel, implicitly embodies the premise that the narrative is "a full and authentic report of human experience" that satisfies the reader with certain details of the story "through a more largely referential use of language than is common in other literary forms." Beyond the greater use of circumstantial detail, however, is an outlook that relates the formal quality of realism with the modern. Watt argues that realism begins with the assumption that truth can be discovered by the individual through observation. The outlook associated with realism is critical, antitraditional, and innovating. "Literary traditionalism was first and most fully challenged by the novel, whose primary criterion was truth to individual experience—individual experience which is always unique and therefore new. The novel is thus the logical literary vehicle of a culture which . . . has set an unprecedented value on originality, on the *novel.*"[7]

There are of course indisputable differences between the English novel of the early eighteenth century and the *ukiyo-zōshi,* and it must be noted as well that realism, as defined by Watt, is not the only narrative mode operating in Saikaku's fiction. Equally important is the manner in which Saikaku transforms individual experience into ideal forms. He frequently casts the subjects of his works as specific examples to establish a norm of human behavior or to prove the validity of a general observation. He gives his characters ideal features, which he then proceeds to differentiate and vary by detail. This tendency reached its full potential after Saikaku in the *katagimono,* or character sketches, of Ejima Kiseki (1666–1735).

Since realism is a formal convention, the pretense of factuality and accuracy is also a pretense of universal validity for subjective experience. Realism is a narrative pose that attempts to idealize or generalize while pretending to do no such thing. The failure to explore that aspect of Saikaku's realism fully has led some critics, especially in the West, to devalue his work on the spurious grounds that it does not conform to the models of narrative developed at the same time in Europe.[8] Keeping this qualification about the nature of Saikaku's realism in mind, it may be said that the important effect of realism in his work is much the same as that found in the early European novel: that is, the experience of an individual character becomes the focus of the narrative, and the detailed presentation of an individual, subjective point of view creates an implicit challenge to established convention.[9] For Saikaku and his contemporaries, the attempt to maintain ideal forms while giving space to individual details led to narratives based on a dialectic between passions and social norms. Insofar as the literary process demands a challenge of the orthodox, realism plays a vital subversive role in the *ukiyo-zōshi.*

To speak of realism as a subversive element in Saikaku's fiction does not mean that Saikaku was necessarily subversive in a political or ideological way. Ivan Morris has pointed out that the focus on the individual in Saikaku's *ukiyo-zōshi* does not necessarily carry with it political notions of autonomy; indeed, he argues instead that Saikaku's work is essentially apolitical and, to a certain extent, amoral in its outlook.[10] This analysis leads to an unwarranted dismissal of Saikaku's humanism, however, for Saikaku's work confronts the same dilemma found in *Genji monogatari* and *Hōjōki* in its awareness of the contingency and impermanence of human existence, and it presents that dilemma in a similarly dialectic form that pits individual experience and passion against tradition and conventional behavior.

Saikaku's failure to provide an overtly political or ethical response to this dilemma is no indication that he lacks humanism. For Saikaku, political or social ideologies are part of the contingency of life; they participate in the flux of nature. Since there can be no absolutes in the floating world, all one can do is accept contingency, and Saikaku's characters, especially his merchants, often succeed or fail for reasons of accident or chance. A typical example of this view of life is provided by the story of the fan maker, "Nidaime ni yaburu ōgi no kaze" (The breeze of a fan broken in the second generation) in *Nippon eitaigura* (The eternal storehouse of Japan, 1688)—a title suggesting that the stories that follow are lessons in human behavior presented in the manner of parables. A young fan maker becomes a man of wealth when his father dies and spends the next year working industriously and avariciously to maintain his fortune. His life is changed one day by the accident of finding in the street a letter addressed to a courtesan named Hanakawa. The letter is a passionate avowal of love and contains a gold coin intended to pay off debts. Moved, the young man goes to the pleasure quarter of Shimabara to return the coin. Unable to find the rightful owner, he spends the money on himself and soon becomes addicted to the pleasures of the floating world,

> to the extent that other fashionable gentlemen of pleasure began to imitate him. Indeed, he gained the nickname Koikaze the Fan Maker because of the way he blew his money on sex. People are really hard to figure. After four or five years of carrying on in this way, not an ash or ember remained of his inheritance of two thousand *kanme,* and he no longer had the strength to blow on and rekindle the fire of his fortune. All that was left was an old fan to remind him of his family heritage. Living a day-to-day existence as a beggar, he sang the words of a popular ditty, "Once I was a rich man, but

now it's done." Seeing him and hearing his song, the puritanical Mr. So-and-So of the Kamadaya told his children, "What a disgrace to blow your money like that—and in this day and age when it's so hard to come by."[11]

This story is in certain respects indistinguishable from many others Saikaku wrote. The narrator inserts the traditional ethical conclusions appropriate to the observations of the young fan maker's life and character, but, as elsewhere in Saikaku's work, these conclusions are unconvincing, either appended after the fact or related by characters who seem excessively, even humorously upright and didactic. Whatever their validity as principles for behavior, it is clear that ethical ideas are of little use in explaining or controlling human conduct in the floating world. Saikaku's presentation of the fundamental human predicament, his preoccupation with the conflict between individual desire and the longing for the order and predictability represented by ideal ethical precepts and tradition, is the source of his humanism.

Of course an awareness of this dilemma is not a resolution of it, any more than Chōmei's awareness of the nature of his literary project exempts him from the attachments incurred by his undertaking. Accordingly, Saikaku's work often assumes a peculiar narrative pose that seeks a synthesis of both rational and irrational views of life. His observational method of exposition, which often overtly supports the dominant neo-Confucian orthodoxy that emotions are to be distrusted and controlled, contributes to his pose as a rationalist. At the same time, this outlook is counterbalanced by the conclusion that, for better or worse, human life is essentially unpredictable and irrational. His apparent sympathy with the passionate side of his characters and with the accidental nature of human experience is in part a necessity of the search for originality. The characters he created, some of whom were based on historical figures, are often forced by circumstances to assert their self-interest against social norms, and the uniqueness of their passions is the particular, original feature of the narrative that claims the reader's interest. However, although the process of narrative renewal constitutes a subversive element in Saikaku's writing, he limits the effects of that subversion by never seriously challenging the normative values of neo-Confucianism. The contradictions and failures of credibility sometimes created by the uneasy coexistence of rational and irrational outlooks in the narrative are evidence that the gap between ideological orthodoxy and the up-to-date is too great to bridge. Saikaku denies a role for conventional morality in determining literary values while purporting to give a full account of the validity of that morality through a detailed representation of the conflicts inherent in the floating world.

Reading Saikaku as a realist in the narrow sense of Western literary models ignores his effort to synthesize the rational and irrational aspects of human behavior. Such a reading also invites unwarranted comparisons with his European contemporaries, implying that his work lacks completeness. The structure of many of his stories, which admittedly show signs of hasty composition and carelessness, evident in mistakes in grammar or inconsistencies in factual detail, nonetheless reveal an order determined by his attempt to justify the rationalism implicit in orthodox morality and reconcile that view of human nature with the irrational impulses of the floating world. Saikaku was forced to turn back to and parody traditional literary techniques in order to universalize, or idealize, his particular observations of the present-day world.

The structural technique Saikaku most frequently employed in the attempt to achieve his synthesis is the anecdotal narrative. This mode developed from a number of possible sources—medieval collections of short tales, or *setsuwa;* miscellaneous writings such as Yoshida Kenkō's *Tsurezuregusa; kana-zōshi;* Chinese vernacular fiction of the Ming and early Ch'ing Periods; and the convention of serial publication in short formats—and it dominated fictional narrative throughout the Tokugawa Period.[12] As with the old *setsuwa* and some *kana-zōshi,* Saikaku's stories are connected by a general thematic organization. *Saikaku oridome* (Saikaku's weavings, 1694), for example, is divided into two sections, with the stories in the first part dealing mainly with questions of fortune and how to succeed in business and those in part two dealing with questions of human passions and their effects. This type of structural organization is also apparent in the earlier *Nippon eitaigura* and occurs to a greater or lesser degree in nearly all of his work.

Saikaku's anecdotal narrative achieves an especially high level of structural symmetry in *Kōshoku gonin onna* (Five women of passion, 1686). Most of the stories are based on real events that happened within a few years of the composition of the work, and beyond the simple unity of theme the five stories share, they are cast in familiar literary conceits and forms. To begin with, the tales are geographically inclusive. The settings are Himeji, Osaka, Kyoto, Edo, and Satsuma, a selection intended to show that incidents arising from human passion are common throughout Japan. The stories also seek universal appeal by invoking the literary tradition through allusion to, or imitation of, well-known narrative formats. For example, the comparison of women that opens the third story, "Chūdan ni miru koyomiya monogatari" (The tale of the almanac maker in the middle section), echoes the "rainy-night discussion" of types of women in the second chapter of *Genji monogatari*. An even more intriguing example of how Saikaku invokes the literary tradition is provided in the final story, "Koi no yama Gengobei monogatari" (The tale of Gengobei, the mountain of love). The hero, Gengobei, is a paragon of homosexual love, but he at last marries a young woman, Oman, after she has won his attentions by disguising herself as a young man. They are happily married, but circumstances reduce them for a time to a life of poverty as traveling entertainers. Conflating the hero of his story, the up-to-date Gengobei, with Gengobei's literary prototype, the subject of ballads popular at the time, Saikaku has one of Gengobei's specialties be to sing ballads about himself. This is typical of Saikaku's general technique of constantly reintegrating the particular details of his stories into received literary forms.

Another technique that gives structural symmetry to *Kōshoku gonin onna* is the device of the accident or coincidence that sets the plot and the feelings of passion in motion. A forgotten mailbag and some misplaced money lead to the apprehension and unjust execution of Seijūrō in the opening tale. In the second story, "Nasake wo ireshi taruya monogatari" (The tale of the cooper devoted to love), Osen, the cooper's wife, goes to the house of Chōzaemon, the yeast maker, to help him prepare for his father's memorial service. While working in the kitchen, Chōzaemon knocks a bowl off a shelf, striking Osen on the head and undoing her hair. His jealous wife interprets Osen's disheveled appearance as evidence of adultery with her husband and spreads unwarranted rumors. To gain revenge, Osen rashly begins a brief affair with the husband that ends in her suicide. In the fourth tale, "Koikusa karageshi yaoya monogatari" (The tale of the greengrocer who bundled leaves of love), a fire brings the young lovers Oshichi and Kichisaburō together and eventually leads Oshichi to commit the fatal crime of arson. The random, accidental elements of these stories both illustrate the unique aspects of individual behavior and, taken together, impose an archetypal pattern on the narratives of passion.

The use of anecdotal narrative, though certainly not establishing a design in which all the narrative elements or individual stories point to a single, well-defined closure, furnishes Saikaku's work with more than merely a loose thematic organization. Through the realistic technique of closely described vignettes, this type of narrative presents an image of both the individual and society as mutable and evanescent and seeks to establish that quality as a constant in human experience. Human life is a kind of ground against which moments of interest—that is, anecdotal moments— stand out. The juxtapositions of incident, image, and observation in the *ukiyo-zōshi,* though they do not in any formal way resemble linked verse, nonetheless perform the same functions in the narrative: namely, focusing attention on the ephemeral nature of experience and thereby inducing contemplation of the fundamental truth of mutability.[13] Like linked verse, Saikaku's anecdotal narrative is an epiphanic art form, though clearly a parodic one, that reveals a deeper aesthetic significance through its accounts of the ephemera of the floating world.

Saikaku's connection to the world of linked verse and *haikai* (which are nonstandard poetics), in particular to the Danrin school, is well documented. He began his study of *haikai* in 1656, when he was fourteen, and by 1662 he had become a poetry judge. He pursued a prolific career before turning to *ukiyo-zōshi* and abandoning his practice of poetry in 1682. This was a major decision in his life, but Yamaguchi Takeshi argues that the move from *haikai* poetry to *ukiyo-zōshi* was not a major transition for Saikaku, writing that it would have been a great change only if

> Saikaku's *haikai* had been a thoroughly meditative type held for a long time during the final years of his life, or had it resembled the *haikai* advocated by Bashō's school; but his *haikai* and the character of Danrin *haikai,* to which he belonged, were naturally different from the meditativeness of the Bashō school. His interest was not drawn toward the realm of solitude of the mountains and fields but to the songs of the licensed quarters. His interest was exactly in those things of the world of the *ukiyo-zōshi.* When that *haikai* was changed slightly in its form of expression, it was as the *ukiyo-zōshi* and the *kōshokubon* [books dealing with stories of love and passion, a genre of *ukiyo-zōshi*].[14]

In noting Saikaku's connection to *haikai,* Yamaguchi makes a valid distinction between the different subject matter that attracted members of the Danrin and Bashō schools. However, the importance of that difference is overstated. Though it may be true that Saikaku was attracted to the world of the merchants and the licensed quarters, Bashō and his disciples also made great use of vulgar elements. Moreover, the approach to *haikai* taken by both schools shared some crucial similarities.

One commonly held notion in *haikai* aesthetics is that beauty is created by conferring literary form on the change and flux of human experience.

For the *haikai* writer, literary fashions that "resist the mutability of history ... preserve a kind of peaceful constancy within the height of fashion. The beauty of *haikai* ... naturally reaches the point where it promotes an appearance of immutability—an unchanging, undying appearance."[15] A fuller statement of *haikai* aesthetics is provided by Hattori Dohō (or Tohō, 1657–1730), a disciple of Bashō who wrote a three-part account of the master's teachings titled *Sanzōshi:*

> The *haikai* of the master possesses both the immutability of epochs and the changes of the moment. His *haikai* comes down to these two ideals, but there is a single source for them. That source is the sincerity of *haikai*. If you do not understand the immutable, then truly you cannot understand *haikai*. Immutability does not draw on the old and new, nor is it subject to change and fashion. Rather, it is a form that is thoroughly grounded in sincerity.
>
> When you observe the works of poets through the ages, you see the changes from generation to generation. Yet in spite of the presence of the old and the new, there is no difference in outlook between the past and the present, and there are many poems from all ages that move us. This poetic constancy should be understood as immutability.
>
> It is the law of nature that all things undergo change. If there were no change, then *haikai* would not be renewed. If there is no change toward new *haikai,* then to the extent that words are appropriate only for a momentary fashion, the sincerity of *haikai* cannot be achieved. Those who cannot recognize that or do not apply themselves to it will never understand the renewal of *haikai*. They will merely follow after others. For those who do recognize the changes, it is difficult to stay in the same place, and they will advance a step toward nature.[16]

One of the fundamental principles of *haikai* is presented by the oxymoronic formula *fueki ryūkō,* constancy (immutability) and fashion.[17] Fashion stresses the nonstandard, as measured against the traditional, and is an assertion of the significance of the present. The values embodied by a fashion lack permanence, and the impulse is to try to elevate it to the level of an orthodox aesthetic in order to achieve permanence. This phrase recalls the critical distinction between deep and shallow in the "Eawase" chapter of *Genji monogatari* and between mutability and transcendence in *Hōjōki*. Saikaku's concept of the floating world and his narrative depictions of it reveal a notion of the modern similar to that of both Murasaki Shikibu and Kamo no Chōmei.

Forcing the reader to consider the fundamental contradiction of modern experience, in terms of both human behavior and narrative technique, confers a strong sense of cohesion on individual stories and on the larger collections as a whole. The fact that the stories' moral statements may or may not be consistent with or relevant to the stories of human experience is not a narrative lapse but a sign of the uncertainty and contingency of life and thus part of the image of mutability. The anecdotal narrative works somewhat in the manner of the medieval European exempla or like the *setsuwa* in the Japanese tradition. The primary purpose is essentially literary: to convey a story that is intrinsically interesting and new. The didactic purpose of the story is served not so much by the statement of the moral, which itself is a conventional narrative element, as it is by the cataloging of particular incidents that by repetition impose a structure on random experience. The anecdotal form allows the combination of rational and irrational elements, and it encompasses the fundamental dialectic created by opposing what is of interest—the new, realistic elements of the story—against an ideal form that imposes order on the disparate and unique elements of human life.

Saikaku introduces the nonstandard and the strange into his work through anecdotal narrative, which may explain why there is such a variety of stories in his collections. The importance of the nonstandard is also evident in certain stylistic elements that he employs. One particular feature of his style is the way in which he tries to establish a connection between his observations of the ephemeral present and the literary tradition by a mixture of classical and contemporary elements. The awareness of the impossibility of achieving a complete fusion of these elements creates an ironic mood, and Saikaku's humor and literary subversion depend heavily on the parodic or mock-heroic effects created by the jarring juxtapositions between the elegant, *ga,* and the vulgar, *zoku.*[18] Like anecdotal narrative, the mixture of classical and vulgar elements allowed Saikaku to put forth his own reflections on the world within a traditional literary framework that alters and transforms the tradition according to the vision of the individual artist.

It has been frequently noted that parody is a recurring element in the narratives of the Tokugawa Period.[19] The fact that Saikaku used parody primarily for literary effect rather than political statement is an extension of basic *haikai* attitudes, and many of his works, especially the *kōshokubon,* are best described as *haikai* versions of the classics.[20] *Kōshoku ichidai otoko* (The life of a man of passion), for example, owes its structure to the fifty-four-chapter pattern of *Genji monogatari,* though it disguises that debt by the conceit of presenting the biography of a man of the world, Yonosuke (literally "man of the world"), which recounts the hero's sexual exploits.

Yonosuke is an up-to-date (from a Genroku perspective) Prince Genji, and many of his adventures parallel those of his Heian forebear. Such obvious borrowing indicates the degree to which Saikaku consciously elaborated on the tradition of love heroes, and the self-made comparison of his work to the great classic of Japanese literature is an extended joke that points up the contradiction between his subject matter and the idealized way in which he is presenting it.

The work of Saikaku that most completely incorporates the general features of his *ukiyo-zōshi* is *Kōshoku ichidai onna*. Several qualities of this work make it more of a formal breakthrough than the earlier *kōshokubon*. *Kōshoku ichidai otoko*, for example, for all its emphasis on the details of life and love in the world of the merchants, presents a utopian vision of passion that concludes with the hero's departure for the legendary island of women and the complete fulfillment of his sexual fantasies. Such an ending is a narrative expedient that avoids the problem of representing the attainment of Yonosuke's ideals. The problem of death, which would end all passion, is also sidestepped by the figurative passing of the hero, who removes himself from the reader's world to arrive at a place beyond the experience of mortals and achieve the paradoxical life of eternal passion. Yonosuke's achievement of his ideals is equivalent to his death in narrative terms, and, like the depiction of Prince Genji's perfection and death, it must remain an event outside the purview of the narrative.

Kōshoku gonin onna takes a step closer to a narrative form that more fully exploits the dissonance between particular passions and a realization of the ideal of *kōshoku* (passion) by conflating historical incidents and fictional elements. However, even this work, in which the limits of passion are clearly revealed by the deaths of the protagonists, has its utopian aspects. First, each of the heroines achieves in death a kind of immortality as an ideal representative of passion. Second, the narrative structure resembles that of *Kōshoku ichidai otoko* in that the story of Gengobei closes the text on an optimistic note. In spite of all his travails, Gengobei, like Yonosuke, ends by achieving a life in which all of his desires are completely fulfilled. Saikaku attempts to suggest a continuation of passion through idealization that overcomes the deaths of his heroes and the closure of the text.

Kōshoku ichidai onna moves the formal innovations of the *ukiyo-zōshi* a step further. Saikaku takes a woman as his hero and makes her the narrator of her own life story. He thereby creates, through his parody, a strong variation on the work of Kamo no Chōmei. By making the heroine the main narrative voice, Saikaku places a socially marginal character at the center of the text and at the same time creates a higher degree of narrative self-consciousness that results in expanded possibilities for parody, irony, and dissonance. Moriyama Shigeo has noted the modern aspect of the subjective voice of the woman, pointing out that in her narrative, unlike the earlier *kōshokubon,* "passion is no longer a passive, unconscious thing. Rather, like individual consciousness, it depends on and cannot be separated from the self."[21] The self-consciousness with which passion is discussed is most readily evident in the fact that the narrative is cast in the form of a religious confession. The connection between the confessional mode and the self-consciousness of the narrator is important in understanding how the dilemma of the modern, the underlying tension between mutable desires and ideal forms, affects Saikaku's narrative. Karatani Kōjin has written,

> It can be said that "modern literature" in Japan began together with the form of the confession (*kokuhaku*). The form of the modern confession is fundamentally different in quality from the simple confession, for in contrast it creates an interior that must be confessed. Accordingly, however much the confession in a narrow sense is denied or conquered, the form itself remains unscathed. In other words, there is a dichotomy between the thing that must be expressed (the interior) and the thing that has been expressed. . . .
>   The form of the confession, or the system of the confession, gives birth to an interior that must be confessed, that is, the "true self." The problem is not how to confess but the system of the confession itself. If there is something you must hide, it is not something you confess. The responsibility of confessing is to create something that must be hidden, or an "interior."[22]

I have taken Karatani's remarks out of context, because he views the formal qualities of the type of confession that is a codevelopment of modern literature as a critical construct of the Meiji period. I shall return to this matter in later chapters, but at this point it bears noting that Karatani, in describing the formal qualities of the "modern" confession, arbitrarily assigns a chronological origin to that critical category even though he purportedly is not really writing a literary history. Karatani's project is beyond the scope of this study, but my purpose in appropriating his description of the "modern" confession (and reading him like any other literary historian) is that he has observed an important feature of the confessional mode, which is the fundamental dichotomy between the rhetorical devices of the confession and the "true self" those devices supposedly reveal. Since that dichotomy is at work in the other classical texts examined in this section, and since it is structurally akin to the dilemma of the modern, Karatani's formal description may be usefully applied to an analysis of *Kōshoku ichidai onna.*

In *Kōshoku ichidai onna,* the dichotomy is created by the fact that the text is not a "true confession" but a parody of a confession, again playing off the model provided by *Hōjōki.* In fact, Saikaku played off numerous sources to create this parody, the subgenre of *kana-zōshi* known as *bikunimono* being one of the most important. *Bikuni* originally referred to Buddhist nuns who renounced the world and took special vows or precepts (*gusokukai*) that would naturally endow them with virtue. In the Kamakura and Muromachi periods the term came to be used for traveling female singers and *etoki,* storytellers who used pictures during their recitations. By the Tokugawa period the word referred to a type of prostitute, a streetwalker, who dressed up as a nun. *Bikunimono,* works like *Ninin bikuni,* a *kana-zōshi* by Suzuki Shōzan, were for the most part didactic tales in which a woman unexpectedly loses the man she loves or depends on and then seeks religious solace from a nun. This nun then tells of her own past and attachments, leading the woman to understand the true nature of the evanescence of the world and to take vows. This type of story remained popular for a long time and appeared in the Meiji period in works such as Ozaki Kōyō's *Ninin bikuni: iro zange* (Confessions of love).

Although the *bikunimono* were probably the works that Saikaku had foremost in mind when he wrote, other sources also played an important role. One was the *Yu hsien k'u* (The dwelling of playful goddesses; in Japanese, *Yū sen kutsu*), an early T'ang period novella by Chang Tsu (657–730) that was imported during the Heian period and survived because of its popularity in Japan. The story, a mildly erotic fantasy of a traveling official who comes across two beautiful sisters living in an isolated pleasure palace, is so similar in structure to the *bikunimono* that it facilitates the conflation of the two types of stories, the religious confession and the erotic adventure, into a parodic version of both—a conflation realized in *Kōshoku ichidai onna* by the narrative setting, the "hermitage of passion" (*kōshokuan*).[23]

Another source is the *Chiu hsiang shih* (in Japanese, *Kyūsōshi*) by the Sung poet Su Tung-p'o (1063–1101). The title of Tung-p'o's poem refers to the Buddhist idea of the nine stages of decay of the human body following death. Though there is no precise correlation, the organization of the poem provides a narrative model for the gradual degradation of Saikaku's heroine.[24] The influence of the work is especially apparent at those points where the *Chiu hsiang shih* is cited directly to point up the heroine's awareness of her own physical and moral decay (NKBT 424, 454).

Yet another source is *Mumyōzōshi* (ca. 1196–1202), which is part fiction and part criticism. Two of its structural features are relevant to *Kōshoku ichidai onna*. First, like the *bikunimono*, it has an elderly nun assume the role of the main narrator. Second, the work shows an essentially critical sensibility. The story opens with the narrator posing to the younger women at court a serious question, "What has the greatest value in the world?" The correct answer turns out to be *monogatari*, and an evaluation of *monogatari* written by women authors follows. *Kōshoku ichidai onna* follows this structure, with the narrative dealing instead with discussions of love and passion in their various manifestations. *Mumyōzōshi* is particularly important to Saikaku's parody in that it gives him a model on which to base the critical self-awareness of his narrator.

Taniwaki Masachika has noted about *Kōshoku ichidai onna* that the stories told by the woman "in order to enlighten the foolish young men about the limits of love are not confessions but are closer to parables."[25] There is accordingly a sharper critical awareness in the text that establishes a form of confession different from the *bikunimono*. This is apparent from the outset of the work, which begins with a reference to traditional wisdom: "The ancients have said that a beautiful woman is an axe that cuts down life. Who can avoid the fact that the flowers of the heart scatter, and the withered branch becomes the evening's firewood? Even so, how foolish are those who, addicted to the way of passion, die young like flowers blown away on the morrow by an unseasonable storm! There is no end to instances of such folly" (NKBT 328). The opening lines, which may be traced to the *Wen-hsüan*, echo the opening of *Hōjōki*, substituting the images of flowers and firewood for that of foam on the water as the metaphor for the shortness and precariousness of human life. This opening provides a rather conventional moral frame for the story, and it may be said that the text that follows does attempt to confirm the wisdom of the ages. However, in the catalog of human folly that makes up the bulk of the narrative, the emphasis shifts away from the goal of supporting a moral teaching to the interest inherent in such a catalog.

The task is begun by the narrator of the framing story, who sets out on an errand from Kyoto to Saga and encounters two young men greatly troubled by the dilemma of passion. Both long for an ideal they cannot achieve. One wants to give himself over completely to passion and make unceasing the momentary pleasures of sexual intercourse. His companion wants instead to live in a country without any women whatsoever. The text notes that "although these two had completely different ideas, because the term of human life is fixed they were pursuing dreams that had never before been realized" (NKBT 328). The opening moral frame has already been subtly undercut by the two extreme views of life of the young men, whose quests shift the narrative away from proving the supposed danger posed by a beautiful woman to the problem of how to fulfill the desire for ideal passion or ideal abstinence.

Seeking an answer to their paradox, the young men visit the "hermitage of passion" and ask the old woman there to teach them about the ways of love. Their request also serves as a statement of the formal intent of the narrative, for they ask her "to tell of your experience of yore in a modern fashion" (NKBT 328). At this point, the narrator of the frame story becomes an eavesdropper, the reader's narrative ears, and is heard from no more. By narrating this short opening frame, however, he has played a crucial role in directing our reading of the woman's confession. The word I have translated as "modern fashion" here is *imayō*, which stresses the quality of contemporaneity. Although the truth of mutability is confirmed, it becomes secondary to the concern for the originality and up-to-dateness of the narrative as a whole. The opening frame also signals a knowingness or self-awareness about her narrative on the part of the woman of passion, since we know that she is speaking ostensibly with the purpose of educating her audience of two young men. The pretense of narrating with a moral purpose in mind, however, is quickly left behind. There is an understanding that although individual experience can never be transformed into a permanent ideal, it can challenge ideas that are presented as the unchanging truth of the ages. The confessional mode is parodied and subverted in *Kōshoku ichidai onna* by making the most important concern not whether the narrative confirms a universal truth but whether it continually renews itself.

Even though Saikaku creates a parodic ideology of passion, his parody necessarily reflects the problem of reconciling the ideal with the particular, and this is conveyed by the anecdotal mode of the narrative. Every chapter tends to digress, but the general movement is a narrowing down from general to specific cases, from ideal types to practical examples. The chapter "Inpu no bikei" (The beautiful forms of a wanton woman) provides a typical example of the pattern of the whole work. It begins with a foreshadowing of the woman's fate by presenting the sad figure of a great courtesan, the second Katsuragi, who has been reduced to penury. The old woman then shifts the focus back to her own story and tells us that she was sold into a brothel when she was fifteen. Here again she abruptly shifts to an exposition of the special characteristics of the floating trade: the types of dress, the ways of walking, the rules for letter writing, and the tricks used to handle or manipulate customers (NKBT 342–343).

After a detailed discussion of the rules of appearance and conduct of the courtesan, the old woman moves on to discuss the customers. She lists all the characteristics of the ideal, up-to-date man who knows how to conduct himself with women. She then lists several examples of especially desirable customers. The chapter ends, however, on a cautionary note. The woman assures her listeners of the reliability of her observations by informing them that she herself did not follow these rules, came to be regarded as a cold and haughty courtesan, and gradually fell out of favor. The chapter comes full circle, with the opening premonition fulfilled in a way that idealizes her experience, concluding with the maxim "There is nothing in the world as sad as treading the path of the courtesan" (NKBT 348).

Though the narrative is anecdotal and digressive, it constantly strives toward the universalization of particular experience. The woman becomes an everyman figure who can observe all types of human behavior and whose perspective can bring some order to the randomness of life. Her own experience lends an overarching structure to the narrative, which chronicles her gradual but inexorable decline both in social status and in body. She moves from a position in her youth at the very center of traditional (and by Saikaku's day moribund) Japanese culture, the imperial court, to the degraded life of a common streetwalker in her old age. Her retreat to the "hermitage of love" marks the end of the cycle and at the same time reveals the pattern of her life story.

While the anecdotal narrative contains elements that hold the work together, the emphasis on cataloging and vignette also provides ample opportunity for variation and parody. The old woman constantly asserts the truthfulness of her observations about human foibles, but the mock-heroic quality of the stories she uses as her examples continuously undermines the attempt to achieve universality. The old woman's opening story provides a striking example of this ambivalence in the narrative. We learn that she was not born into a noble family, but because of her father's connections she went into the service of a lady at the imperial court. When she was twelve she had her first affair, but when the affair was discovered she was banished to a place near Uji Bridge, and her lover was put to death. She suffered for several days, during which she was visited by a terrifying vision of her dead lover. Moreover, her love affair resembles numerous other ill-fated literary relationships, especially the story of Ukifune, who was forced to resolve her passionate dilemma by attempting suicide.[26] Saikaku's narrative, however, breaks radically with the expectations created by these allusions, and the woman tells us that although she considered suicide, "as the days passed, at last I forgot all about my former lover. When you consider this action of mine, you realize that there is nothing whose heart is as shallow and changeable as a woman's" (NKBT 331).

The abrupt change of heart turns the traditional love story on its head, and it even reverses the treatment of passion that predominates in Saikaku's *Kōshoku gonin onna*, where all the women lose themselves completely to passion, even though they know the consequence may be death. In *Kōshoku ichidai onna*, the heroine is too savvy to fall for the old story. Rather than let her passion destroy her, she controls the direction in which her passion goes, always deciding that it is best to live to love another day. Perhaps the greatest reversal of the narrative is that a woman has usurped the masculine role of narrator. Her efforts to make passion a permanent state are just as doomed, however, and that limitation is illustrated on those occasions where we see that the old woman (and other women) are not really capable of controlling their own lives or their own narratives. In the chapter "Chōnin koshimoto" (A townsman's maid), the old woman tells of the time when she worked as a maid, seduced her master, and tried to have him get rid of his wife. She even put curses on the wife, but to no avail: the curses came back to afflict her, causing her to go mad for a time (NKBT 378–379).

A similar example of the impotence of women appears in the next chapter, "Wazawai no kankatsu onna" (A fine lady of evil curses), during which the old woman tells of her service to the wife of a feudal lord. One day, while playing what is described as the male sport of *kemari*, the wife grows sullen and that evening holds a "jealousy bee" (*rinkikō*) with the women in her service (NKBT 379). They take out a female doll and use it as a scapegoat on which to vent their frustrations over their unfaithful husbands. On this evening the ceremony backfires when the old woman, acting as a proxy for the wife, expresses the cause of the wife's jealousy, which is the presence of a beautiful concubine in her lord's retinue. With this utterance the doll comes to life and frightens the entire party. The wife falls ill until the doll is burned, and when the lord hears of the incident he sends the concubine away and severs relations with his wife. Despite the old woman's sex, her anecdote supports the age-old patriarchal "wisdom" about the dangers of feminine jealousy. Having the woman narrate her own life of love provides opportunities for such narrative reversals and parody, but the limits of that parody are clearly marked throughout, and, like the cathartic effect of a double-suicide play, the narrative acts to reaffirm conventional, patriarchal ethical standards.

The reversals in the narrative are not limited to types of stories; they also extend to include questions concerning narrative modes. In the chapter "Shorei onna yūhitsu" (Etiquette: A female writing instructor),[31] the old woman describes how she once set up shop as a writing teacher and vowed to give up her lustful ways. Recalling an occasion when a young man asked her to write love letters for him, she goes off on a digression about the power of the written word, asserting that

> there is no more expedient means to reveal your true feelings than a letter. Even to distant provinces and villages you can relate your thoughts with a brush. No matter how well-written a letter it may be, when there are many falsehoods contained therein, the letter will of its own accord cease to be of interest and will be discarded with no regrets. A letter that shows traces of sincerity will naturally strike a chord in the heart of the reader, so that he will feel that he has definitely met the person who wrote it. (NKBT 368)

At first glance, this is a defense of affective realism, but this view is quickly undercut by the woman herself, and we are left with a parodic version of the *monogatari ron*. The writing instructor comes to desire the young man for herself and urges him to give up the cold-hearted woman he is pursuing, pointing out that his letters are of little use (NKBT 369). The young man finally agrees to be her lover, but he sets out some rather harsh conditions in a preaffair contract. The woman is put off by his behavior and gains revenge by forcing him to have sex with her constantly, gradually destroying his health and position. The parody of criticism cuts two ways. It is the act of writing that brings the two lovers together, confirming the argument for the affective realism of letters. Yet the fictionality of all writing is exposed by the overriding reality of passion. Once the narrative pretense that passion is the universal condition of human experience is reestablished, the sexual joke of the insatiable woman, which is of course a male fantasy, can be retold in a new fashion.

The parody of the efficacy of letters to convey reality is carried into the next chapter, "Chōnin koshimoto," to include the world of *haikai* poetry. The parodic elements again are introduced by means of a digression. The woman witnesses the funeral procession of a shopkeeper whose wife is renowned for her beauty. This leads to a discussion of whether or not having a beautiful wife is good thing, and the woman cites the go-between Gion Jinta, who says that "while a wife is something you have to look at your whole life, a woman who is too beautiful is not good" (NKBT 374). The woman generally concurs, stating

> In my own experience, it is the same with beautiful women and beautiful scenery: if you look at them all the time you soon grow tired of them. One year I went to Matsushima, and since it was my first time I was enthralled with the place. I thought, "If only I could show this to a singer or a poet!" Yet after gazing out on the view from morning to night the myriad islands began to reek of the seashore, the waves at the beach of Sue no Matsuyama roared in my ears. The cherry blossoms at Shiogama scattered without my viewing them; I overslept and missed the dawn over the snows of Mount Kinka; and I did not give a second thought to the moon over Oshima. Instead I gathered black and white pebbles at an inlet and was soon lost in a game of *mutsumusashi* [a simplified form of *go*] with some children. (NKBT 375)

Saikaku is poking fun at the literary pose that some things are so beautiful they simply cannot be expressed in human language.[28] Here the sights of Matsushima are indeed so beautiful that the woman longs for someone who could give voice to her impressions of the place. However, as she begins to understand the reality beneath the poetic ideal, the sights become conventional and of no interest to one who is the embodiment of the ephemeral and up-to-date. Once again the parody points up its own limits by exposing the artifice of all literary expression.

The parody is constantly delimited by the narrative's contradictory features: its attempts to give the anecdotes of passion universal validity and its affirmation of the conventional notion that everything in the floating world is doomed to pass away because of its particularity. When the physical decline of the woman makes it impossible for her to continue her narrative of passion, the work finds a formal ending by returning to Buddhist ethics. The woman is made aware that the end of her narrative is approaching by a vision of the ghosts of all the children she aborted during her lifetime. This does not prevent her from trying to make a living as the lowest form of streetwalker, but she is so old that even in heavy disguise she cannot attract a man. Shortly after, she visits the Daiunji, which is called a Pure Land paradise in this world, and there she has an epiphanic moment when she recognizes that each of the faces on the five hundred *rakan,* or images of the Buddha, resembles one of her former lovers. The woman is reminded of the wantonness of her life, and she takes the step of renouncing the world. However, the narrative is not a simple reassertion of Buddhist ethics. The lovers are manifestations of the Buddha, and so the parody of religion that is at the heart of the woman's confession comes full circle.

The woman's religion of passion is fused with Buddhist assumptions to form a new narrative, through which she achieves salvation. She closes her account by telling the young men,

> By this confession, the clouds of my body have been cleared, the moon of my heart is pure and bright, and I have provided you with comfort and diversion on a spring evening. Because I am a single woman with no offspring, I can gain no profit by hiding anything from you; and I have told you all the circumstances of my life, from the opening of the lotus in my breast, to the withering of its flower. Though I have bathed in the current of wantonness, does that mean that my heart must be muddied? (NKBT 454)

The woman takes leave of the young men in her role as teacher and of the reader in her role as narrator. She has entered the path of sainthood and reaffirmed religious and ethical ideals, but she has done so through the trick of appropriating the narrative form of the confession to create a religion of passion.

The ending of *Kōshoku ichidai onna* is not especially didactic within the context of its recurring tendency to draw a moral even when one is not warranted. On the other hand, it must be said that it does not really subvert the old order. The narrative ends poised between an affirmation of conventional morality and a satire of that morality. The language of the literary tradition is subverted by applying it in inappropriate ways, but that subversion is purely formal and particular. The withdrawal of the woman makes the confession possible, but it also points up the impossibility of a complete subversion of the tradition.

The developments in Saikaku's narratives—his emphasis on individual experience, on the primacy of emotion and intuition in literary creation, on the mixture of elegant and vulgar elements, and on subordinating ethical conventions to the necessities of narrative—were refined in the work of later Tokugawa writers. As this narrative tradition was forced to seek renewal, the constant extension of the anecdotal, humorous style, with its satiric description of human foibles and the contingency of experience, led to the kind of aleatory narrative that predominates in *gesaku* fiction. Anecdotes seem to be increasingly random and are given order by overarching images of communal life: the constants of human experience summed up by the brothel or the bathhouse, by sweeping metaphors for the condition of human life such as travel, or by ideological constructs such as *giri* (duty) and *ninjō* (human emotion). The transitions from Saikaku to Ueda Akinari, Ōta Nanpo, Shikitei Sanba, and Ryūtei Tanehiko are surprisingly continuous, for the tremendous literary self-awareness that marks much of Tokugawa fiction is a product of a shared sense of the dilemma of the modern. By the age of *gesaku*, that self-awareness brought with it a heightened playfulness that used the emptiness of narrative form as an expression of the reality of contingent experience.

The pose of frivolousness struck by *gesaku* authors made their work the object of critical scorn in the Meiji period, but that judgment was based on the need of Meiji authors to distance themselves from the traditions of the past in order to define their own modern identity, and it does not take into account the historical and ideological contexts of late Tokugawa fiction. As I suggested at the outset of this chapter, the frivolousness of the pose struck by *gesaku* authors ran counter to the assertions of officially sanctioned orthodoxy; and like the more overtly ideological work of *kogaku* (ancient learning) and *kokugaku* scholars, who challenged neo-Confucian learning at its core by researching the history of language and the very origins of discourse, the so-called popular (that is, unserious) writers of the period willfully and gleefully misread the tradition in order to assert the validity and priority of their own modern standards against the authority of the past. In the chapters that follow, I shall explore how the expressions of the modern in the classical tradition, as exemplified by the three works discussed above, were interpreted, or misread, by writers in the Meiji period, and how that misreading is an indicator of both the need for a break with the past and the desire to reestablish a sense of cultural continuity.

part two

◆

Futabatei Shimei
and the Meiji Sense of
the Modern

As the pre-Meiji works discussed in the previous section suggest, the preoccupation with the modern was apparent in the appropriation of the ephemeral for religious, aesthetic, or even political purposes. Prince Genji, for example, seeks to empower himself politically and culturally by trying to establish his own emotional awareness of the ephemeral as a kind of permanent, ideal value or cultural standard. For the narrator of *Hōjōki*, who understands that such an effort can lead only to failure and exhaustion, the ephemeral is instead something to be rejected or transcended—an aim equally impossible to achieve in the present. The tension created by trying to make the present permanent or by trying to transcend it altogether is revealed in the formal qualities of these works.

In the Tokugawa period the preoccupation with the modern acted subversively against the ruling orthodoxy that dominated the political, ethical, and aesthetic landscape. The vibrant merchant culture sought its own forms of expression, and the autonomy that such forms implied threatened the prevailing standards of the ruling elite. The outward forms of social subversion, most apparent in the form of the licensed quarters of the urban centers, were to a degree legitimized by intellectual movements that were also subversive. *Kogaku* and *kokugaku* both sought to re-create neo-Confucian orthodoxy by attacking the reliability of its readings, that is, by challenging it in linguistic terms. Trying to go back to the origins of language, both Chinese and Japanese, these movements sought to regain a mythical state of ethical and aesthetic wholeness and thus to assert the validity of the present against an erroneous past. The tendencies of the literature of the period—anecdotal narrative, the divide between classical and vulgar languages that was consciously manipulated for comic effect, the use of didactic material and fantastic stories—were all means by which to state the condition of the present and to allow it to engage the past on some level. The emphasis on the fleeting present, on the ephemera of human life, permitted the best writers of the period to go beyond mere didacticism. Championing the modern and ephemeral did not so much deny ethical conventions as fuse them with aesthetic values to achieve innovation in narrative form.

These and other classical examples of formal innovation provided precedents for radically rereading the literary tradition in the Meiji period. The literature of the time, in general correspondence with literary trends in Europe and America, is marked by an extremely strong sense of discontinuity and a near-obsession with the modern. The similarity of Japan's literary development at this time to the experience of the West is certainly due to Japanese authors' search for forms appropriate to express their sense of dislocation. However, the intensity of the cultural dislocations that such borrowing implied was more or less unique to the Japanese experience at that time, and it is vital to note that the sense of discontinuity was not a cultural import. This may seem obvious, but it is a crucial distinction in that much historical and critical writing about Japan uses the terms *modernity* and *Westernization* almost interchangeably. Since the ongoing process of defining the modern is so closely tied to innovation in narrative voice and perspective, it is important not to limit the usage of the term to a parochial set of values—that is, to European and American social and literary forms. This is to deny neither the influence of foreign literatures in Japan nor the tendency of Japanese writers to reread their native tradition according to Western aesthetic criteria. It is rather to emphasize the process of temporal discrimination that defines the understanding of what it means to be modern in Japan.

A sense of discontinuity is reflected in three primary concerns that Meiji writers almost universally shared. First and foremost was a concern with the establishment, or more precisely the restatement, of what constituted the tradition; that is, as the sense of discontinuity increased over the period, canon formation and reformation became necessary in order more clearly to define or locate the modern. The mid-Meiji work of Tsubouchi Shōyō is a particularly important expression of this impulse. The second concern was the reformation of the Japanese language. This was to a certain extent a holdover from Tokugawa preoccupations, but whereas the efforts of earlier writers were aimed at recovering the origins of the language for the present, the efforts of Meiji writers, which were the basis of the *genbun'itchi* (the fusion of spoken/vernacular and literary styles) movement, were directed toward the creation of a new literary language. The third major concern, which grew out of the movement for language reform, was the search for a new type of realism, for a literature that would not simply reflect but embody objective fact. The attempt to create a literature in which art and life, form and reality, were wholly synthesized became one of the overriding preoccupations of the period, and it is here that the modern is most evident. The works of Futabatei Shimei provide examples of the primacy of these concerns and are central to understanding the Meiji sense of the modern.

◆

chapter four
Literary Darwinism:
The Crisis of Language and
Canon Formation

The sense of linguistic crisis in Meiji Japan, the sense that the received forms of literary expression were inadequate to signify the realities of the modern age, was widespread. This is evident in the number of solutions offered to create a new literary language, among them, a refinement of the compromise between the elegant (classical) and vulgar styles that had emerged in certain Tokugawa works, most notably in the genre of narrative known as the *yomihon* (literally, "a reading book"; that is, a book without pictures); the adoption of a style based on translations from Western literature; a balance of Sinitic, Japanese, and Western elements; and the advocacy of a wholly new style based mainly on colloquial speech. There were also suggestions for orthographic reform, which included such extreme proposals as the abolition of Chinese characters and the exclusive use of kana or of a romanized script.

In the early years of Meiji there was no widely organized movement for language reform. Changes and experiments in style were ad hoc and piecemeal, undertaken as needs arose. As the political reforms of the period began to take shape, however, there was a growing awareness of a need for a colloquial literary style to support the ideology of modernization. The importation of technology from the West, coupled with the growing number of translations of Western works, highlighted the pace with which the Japanese language was undergoing change. By 1877 newspapers like the *Yomiuri shinbun*, which geared its publications toward the less literate, were, in effect, modernizing their style of writing by including more colloquial vocabulary, standardizing the use of auxiliary verbal forms like -*masu* and *gozaimasu* and the copula *da, desu,* and *nan da* and liberally applying *furigana* (kana written beside Chinese characters to indicate how they are to be read) to Chinese characters.[1] The shifts in language usage were thus closely connected to the sweeping social and political changes promoted by the Meiji oligarchy, and it was the awareness of the magnitude of change that made the linguistic crisis seem so acute.

It is beyond the scope of this study, and in fact not relevant to my aims, to go into a detailed account of the changes that culminated in the fusion of colloquial and literary styles. It is relevant to note that *genbun'itchi* developed gradually as a movement and lasted over the whole of the Meiji period. It is also important to keep in mind that although *genbun'itchi* is now associated with the emergence of a literary style based on colloquial patterns, and thereby associated with reform, the movement itself was a search for a synthesis of literary and colloquial styles, not just the transcription of the vernacular language. There is a strong element of conservatism in the so-called reform of the language. A brief outline will indicate the general trends, as well as language reform's relation to the broader problem of the modern.

Yamamoto Masahide has proposed that the *genbun'itchi* movement may be divided into four periods: the period of mixed styles between 1866 and 1885; the period of the search for a new literary style, which lasted from 1886 to 1899; the period of the establishment of *genbun'itchi* between 1900 and 1909; and the period of full realization of a vernacular style, which took place between 1910 and 1922. This periodization of stylistic developments is a useful way to suggest the ongoing nature of the language crisis and its central place in the creation of Meiji literature.

The literary language of early Meiji was marked by a mixture of styles. Some authors continued in the vein of *gesaku* writers of the *bakumatsu* (late Tokugawa) period, while translators often chose to emulate the rhythmic styles found in *jōruri* or the *yomihon* of the late Edo writer Kyokutei Bakin (1767–1848).[2] Some newspapers, as noted above, adopted colloquial forms, but the prevalent trend in popular publications early on was toward a simplified Sinitic style. Many early experiments focused on orthographic conventions, and the desirability of a literary style generally based on the colloquial language was by no means universally accepted. It was not until the mid-1880s that literary experiments with the colloquial language began on a wide scale, and it is from that point that the specific notion of achieving a style that reflected the spoken language (especially the speech of Tokyo) became the focus of debate.

Two of the central figures in the debate at this time were Yamada Bimyō and Futabatei Shimei. In a short, wry account titled "Yo ga genbun'itchi no yurai" (The origins of my *genbun'itchi,* 1906), Futabatei looked back on his reasons for pursuing this style. "Because I haven't yet researched the matter very thoroughly, I'm afraid that I shall have to make a single confession do in place of my thoughts about *genbun'itchi.* It's really terrible, but the truth is that I first began writing in the *genbun'itchi* style because otherwise I couldn't write at all" (*FSZ*-I 5:170). He implies that he was driven to seek a new literary style in order to express his sense of the age as significant and to avoid being silenced by the lack of a language. Futabatei locates the origins of his own *genbun'itchi* style in his natural inclination to use the vulgar language of everyday speech, even in such an apparently trivial matter as the choice between the forms *desu* and *da.*

> Shortly after the *genbun'itchi* of Yamada Bimyō appeared. I noticed that whereas he used the polite "*Watakushi wa . . . desu*" form, I was of a different school altogether. In other words, mine was the *da* ideology, while Mr. Yamada's was the *desu.* Later I asked him about it and he told me that originally he too had experimented with the *da* form, but that it hadn't gone too well for him so he settled on *desu.* I had tried *desu* first before finally settling on *da.* So as you can see, our approaches were completely different. (*FSZ*-I, 5:171)

Futabatei then describes how he was put out when both his mentor, Tsubouchi Shōyō, and Tokutomi Sohō, the editor of the influential journal *Kokumin no tomo,* suggested that he refine his style a bit. Not only did this advice go against the grain of his talent, but also, he argues, it is useless to refine one's prose by the addition of literary elements like Sinitic vocabulary. Futabatei then cites several examples of the rather ripe vocabulary frequently found in the style of Shikitei Sanba.[3] For all its vulgarity, Futabatei still admires Sanba's style because it is "poetical" (Futabatei uses the English word, written in katakana; *FSZ*-I 5:172).

Futabatei's personal history of *genbun'itchi* is decidedly tongue-in-cheek, but his identification with *gesaku* style, especially that of Shikitei Sanba, and in particular his avowed dislike of ornamentation and preference for directness of expression were taken quite seriously by his contemporaries. His ideal of a literary style based on, or at least reflecting, the language of everyday speech marked a new direction in the development of *genbun-'itchi*. Tayama Katai noted that although different elements of the vernacular language were incorporated into the various styles adopted by writers in mid-Meiji, it was commonly thought that *genbun'itchi* represented the newest and most advanced.[4] In a similar vein, Shimazaki Tōson argued that the Meiji novel did not arise from the efforts of critics like Shōyō to define the form but rather that "the realization of *genbun'itchi* . . . caused the development of Meiji literature."[5]

It has become part of the mythology of Meiji literature, fostered primarily by the naturalists, that Futabatei's literary style was beyond the comprehension of his contemporaries. This conclusion is not warranted. For one thing, Futabatei was widely praised for the contemporaneity of the style of his early works. Also, given the trend toward literary experimentation, a trend of which Futabatei was a prominent exponent, it is inaccurate to say that he was ignored just because his particular fusion style did not gain immediate widespread acceptance. In fact, Futabatei's style occurs in a number of other important works of the period, mainly in works of translation from European literature and in *sokkibon*, which were transcriptions of oral storytelling performances.[6] The inaccuracy of the assessment that Futabatei's style was ahead of its time was not lost on Futabatei, as the ironic tone of his article on *genbun'itchi* clearly indicates. It is perhaps more accurate to state that if the style Futabatei developed in the mid-1880s did not gain wide acceptance right away, it was partly because its primary exponent withdrew from the literary establishment and partly because other writers who shared similar goals were taking different but equally compelling approaches to developing a new literary style.

There were writers, men like Ozaki Kōyō, who were initially reluctant to support the *genbun'itchi* movement on the grounds that Futabatei's colloquial style was simply too vulgar to serve serious literary purposes. However, the greatest challenge to the solution devised by Futabatei came from writers who shared his goal of a new literary style based on colloquial patterns. An important element in the search for a fusion style was a reevaluation of stylistic resources already available in the native tradition. This was the approach taken by Kōyō and his school, the Ken'yūsha (Friends of the inkstone), and especially by those writers who tried to emulate the native realism they found in the work of certain Tokugawa writers such as Saikaku and Ejima Kiseki.[7] This search was, moreover, conducted in an atmosphere in which the resources of the Japanese language were being judged on the basis of their utility in developing native equivalents for the literary conventions, particularly the realistic mode, then prevalent in Western literature. A number of influential writers attempted to retrieve elements of Tokugawa style for the purpose of modernizing the literary language.[8] Apart from their intrinsic literary merits, the works of Kōda Rohan, Higuchi Ichiyō, and Ozaki Kōyō were admired partly because they seemed to be more directly linked to the native tradition, achieving a modern, fresh style using recognizably Japanese elements. In the case of Ichiyō, it was this aspect of her style that attracted the attention and praise of men like Mori Ōgai, who was himself experimenting with a "triple" style that combined Sinitic, Japanese, and Western elements.[9]

The works of writers like Ichiyō and Kōyō became the center of *genbun'itchi* efforts for a short time, but the literary nationalism that was associated with the revival of native realism soon swung back to favor the type of style that marked Futabatei's work. One impetus for this change was the Sino-Japanese War, which brought to the fore again the need for a standard style. National security, the argument ran, was connected to the general education of the populace, a major concern in a rapidly industrializing society, and to the needs of the military with its universally conscripted army.

In the late 1890s the *genbun'itchi* debate was joined by linguists and educators, and the main developments were no longer achieved by literary experimentation. The general trend among the new groups, typified by the work of Ueda Mannen,[10] was to develop a concise style that strove to describe the facts of reality accurately and objectively. The naturalist movement may be seen in some respects to be a direct outgrowth of this concern to find a language that gives an unmediated expression of reality.

It should be noted that the concern for finding a literary language based on colloquial speech, the speech of the common man, resembles the linguistic concerns of romantics like Wordsworth. And as with the romantics this concern seems to have led in Meiji Japan to a splintering among schools that took different approaches to this fundamental question. Harold Bloom has suggested that this fracturing of the modern tradition is the result of a heightened sense of belatedness that forces writers into an obsession with style and language as a technical means of establishing originality.[11] In the case of the *genbun'itchi* movement, certainly, Bloom's observation seems accurate: *genbun'itchi* grew out of an effort to make literature possible by re-creating the linguistic resources necessary to express concerns about the Japanese sense of belatedness in the face of Western imperialism, while the sheer number of approaches suggests a tendency toward fragmentation.

The developments of the late 1890s were important insofar as the *genbun'itchi* movement gradually became the concern of more than a small coterie of writers. Nevertheless, many of the most important changes in style occurred in the literary experiments of the time. Of particular importance was the work of Masaoka Shiki (1867–1902), among others, with *shaseibun*, literary sketches from life (or nature). Disliking the ornamentation he found, for example, in the work of Kōyō, Shiki wanted to create a more objective descriptive style. Much of his energy was spent in the area of poetry, but he also entered into a number of important publishing ventures that supported his literary philosophy. The magazine *Hototogisu* was one such venture, and it serialized a number of important works, including Natsume Sōseki's *Wagahai wa neko de aru* (I am a cat), written in the *genbun'itchi* style. Shiki's work, together with the emergence of naturalism as a convergence between the linguistic aims of *genbun'itchi* and the romanticism of the 1890s, led by 1910 to a general acceptance of a *genbun'itchi* style as the aim for works of literature and journalism.

From around 1910 on the use of a fusion style in literary works was common, and that usage soon spread to other areas. The movement toward *genbun'itchi* was fully realized with the work of the writers of the Shirakaba-ha (White Birch school), whose confidence in their own intuitive aesthetic judgment led them actively to seek freedom in their style of expression. Later writers acknowledged the debt they owed to this school, and both Uno Kōji and Satō Haruo cited the work of Mushanokōji Saneatsu in particular as representing the achievement of a vernacular literary style.[12]

The awareness of cultural discontinuity in Meiji literature manifested itself most directly in the linguistic debates that were the essence of the *genbun'itchi* movement. However, questions of literary style were only part of the complex of issues that revealed an ongoing and urgently felt sense of crisis. An important part of the *genbun'itchi* movement entailed as a matter of course a reevaluation of the native tradition and a new determination of what constituted the canon of Japanese literature. The work that first seriously addressed this issue within the critical context provided by Western realism was *Shōsetsu shinzui* (The essence of the novel), published in 1885 by Tsubouchi Shōyō. Shōyō's book proved to be one of the most influential of Meiji treatises on the novel, and it must be given a certain amount of credit for the direction that stylistic experiments took soon after it appeared.[13] Shōyō's call for change, however, is made within the context of a conservative document that tries to preserve traditional elements of style, plotting, and characterization. A summary of this well-known work's argument will highlight the critical vocabulary Shōyō employed to redefine the canon and to put forth his own notions of what modern literature should be.

The preface provides a brief historical overview of the current state of the Japanese novel and includes Shōyō's famous observation about the poor quality of writing, which he blames on the bad taste of both authors and readers. He then sets out to determine exactly what the novel is, its origins, characteristics, and purpose. In chapter 1 he begins by first settling on a definition of art. He views art as something that acts on the senses and has certain practical purposes: moral instruction, the ennobling of life through beauty, and the practice of art for its own aesthetic value. He then distinguishes between the plastic arts, those arts with a tangible form, and so-called formless arts like dance, music, and theater and asserts that in all cases the highest art is that which acts most directly on the emotions. Shōyō points to poetry as the form that traditionally has come closest to realizing the highest form of art. But for the modern world, he argues, the novel represents yet a higher stage. He cites Western scholars to prove his point, and there is no challenge of Western assumptions in his analysis of how the novel developed from Homer to Scott and Bulwer-Lytton.

In chapter 2 Shōyō observes the changes in the novel form, beginning with the rise of the romance out of mythology. According to his analysis, mythology served several functions, including that of connecting tribes with their ancestral past through history and religious customs. Mythology gradually developed to fables, then to allegory (he cites Spenser and Bunyan at this point), and finally to religious allegory and social satire. Throughout this development, the didactic, moralizing function of literary art is crucial, and Shōyō argues that both the novel and history owe their origins to the development of romance from mythology, the divergence of the novel and history being simply a matter of fictionalization. Looking at the situation in Japan, he observes that drama also began in myth and religious ceremony and served as moral edification. However, while the drama flourished, the novel declined; the Japanese novel was didactic in a narrow sense, but only because morals were tacked on with no regard to substance (*TSS* 12). Nonetheless, he maintains that the novel is still the superior form because it deals with substance over appearance, because its boundaries are broader than those of drama, and, perhaps most revealing of Shōyō's concept of the rhetoric of realism, because drama is a shallow imitation of things that fails to represent reality.

Having tried to establish the superiority of the novel over other art forms, Shōyō moves in chapter 3 to a discussion of the novel's purpose. He begins with a restatement of the traditional affective theory of the origins and purpose of the novel, but he argues (and this is a major critical shift) that in Japan that purpose has been perverted. The emotions portrayed are usually just desires, and so moral judgment is impaired. He then states his main thesis that the novel should be a real critique of human life. The purpose of the novel is not the mere arousal of emotion, but the credibility and relevance of the portrait of human beings. Above all, the novel should show an understanding of cause and effect, and here he quotes Norinaga's praising of *Genji monogatari* as a lotus out of muddy water for exhibiting just this kind of understanding in a world where cause and effect are hard to discern (*TSS* 19–20). The argument here allows Shōyō to claim a native lineage of realism from the Heian period right through Tokugawa conceptions of fiction.

The types of novels are listed in chapter 4. Shōyō returns to his classification of fiction as two types, the romance and the novel, and further breaks the novel down into two types, the didactic and the descriptive, or artistic.

> The artistic novel is of an altogether different character from the so-called didactic novel. Its sole aim is to reveal the conditions of the world and nothing more. Accordingly, although it may fictionalize characters or contrive a plot, it nonetheless complies with the primary aim mentioned above and possesses the power to draw near the truth simply by creating fictional characters or bringing to life fictional worlds. Just as, for example, the poet composes a song and portrays a real scene or gives vent to real emotions, or the painter depicts nature through his work, or the sculptor carves the shapes of man and beast with his chisel, so the artistic novel is mainly concerned with verisimilitude. (*TSS* 21)

These narrative forms in turn may be either historical or present-day, a distinction that reflects the terminology of Kabuki, in which plays are divided into *jidaimono*, historical plays, and *sewamono*, "domestic" plays that deal with contemporary subjects. The debt to Kabuki terminology is made clearer by Shōyō's further subdivision of the present-day (*sewamono*) novel into works dealing with the lower class (as an example he cites the work of Tamenaga Shunsui), the middle class, and the upper class. Shōyō places all types of novels into this basic classification, which establishes a distinction between high subject matter and low subject matter.

Shōyō concludes the first part of his book with a chapter outlining the benefits of the novel, and here he returns to his initial definitions of the uses of art. The novel can inspire feelings of aesthetic wonder, and thus the novelist should strive for perfect beauty. The novel is capable of ennobling the spirit of men, of giving moral instruction, of supplementing authentic history, and of being in the forefront of modernizing all literary forms. He ends by urging the improvement of the novel in Japan as a means of achieving these benefits.

The second part of *Shōsetsu shinzui* deals with the rules of composition for the novel. Shōyō argues that since natural laws govern all things (terminology that demonstrates a debt to Western assumptions), there have to be rules for the novel as well. He points out, however, that the novel is not merely the record of ordinary affairs but governed by its own rhetorical methods (*TSS* 29). He goes on to discuss those methods in great detail, but I shall touch on only some of the more pertinent observations on style, plotting, and characterization.

For Shōyō, style in general was both decoration and the machinery of thought, but he believed that the question of style was much more important in Japan than in other countries. He makes no attempt to prove this assertion of linguistic uniqueness, which suggests the pressure he felt to reclaim his tradition in the face of what seemed to be the universal validity of Western aesthetics. Instead, he points to the existence of three styles to support his argument about the importance of choice. The first, the classical or elegant style, which he likens to a willow being buffeted in the wind, is not powerful, but it is adequate to convey three of the four aspects of literary style delineated in Chinese critical theory: namely, sublimity, beauty, and pathos. It is not, however, appropriate for the fourth aspect, energy (or ludicrousness). The elegant style is particularly appropriate for the creation of a narrative ground, and Shōyō cites examples of that usage even in *gesaku* writers like Shikitei Sanba.

The second style is the colloquial. Because the expression of this style is direct, simple, and easy to comprehend, it has the vital quality of energy. Because of its vulgarity, however, it is not appropriate for certain types of work, especially the historical novel. It is during his discussion of this style that Shōyō notes the proposal to combine the colloquial and literary languages, and this brings him to the third style, which is a compromise between the first two. This compromise permits complementary aspects of grace and energy, although the proportions of elegant and colloquial elements should vary depending on the type of novel being written; that is, a historical novel should contain a greater proportion of the elegant style, while novels of the present-day world should have more colloquial elements, once more equating a colloquial style with low culture. Shōyō goes on to point out that this compromise is different from the earlier style of the *kusa-zōshi*, popular illustrated fiction in which colloquialisms greatly outnumbered Chinese elements. He also argues that too great a reliance on colloquialisms will actually diminish the style's comprehensibility, its great advantage (this is the basis no doubt of his advice to Futabatei to refine his work). If the novel follows the colloquial patterns of a writer like Ryūtei Tanehiko, then the style becomes a dialect, lacking universal, standard elements, and is thus so parochial that it is difficult to understand. This third style represents Shōyō's conception of *genbun'itchi*. The important things to note about his classification here are, first, that he recognizes a fusion style and gives it priority for the novel before it had actually been achieved as a standard; second, that he attempts to generalize his notion of a fusion style on the basis of a narrow ideal of narrative form, the historical novel; and, third, that his conception of *genbun'itchi* loses out eventually.

Shōyō brings a similarly conservative frame of mind to the rules of plotting, but in this section of the work (chapter 3) he resorts to the traditional rules established by earlier writers, Bakin, in particular. The terminology of the argument, with plot classifications like pairing, foreshadowing, coloring, correspondence, contrast, ellipsis, and reverberation, suggests that Shōyō is not so much interested in creating a radical new poetics for the novel as he is concerned with a conservative reclamation of proper rules that have been forgotten. As if to support this view, he recites a litany of the faults in the contemporary Japanese novel, including the lack of organization and confusion of circumstances, the failure to delineate character fully, and the inclusion of too many incidents and characters with the result that cause and effect become difficult to observe, all of which can be traced to a failure to conform to previously established norms for plotting.

In chapter 4 of the second part Shōyō discusses the historical novel at length, citing it as the form most revered in the West. He does not believe that history and the novel are exclusive but considers that the novel can supplement the history of customs and mores and fill in gaps left by historical writings. The noteworthy aspect of his argument here is that just as historians look for discrepancies in dates and for mistakes in facts and descriptions of customs, so the novelist must be concerned first and foremost with the accuracy of his narrative. Shōyō sides here with the European naturalist/realist approach to the novel by his positivist insistence that the novel performs a scientific, epistemological function for society as a tool of observation, while restating one of the primary guidelines that governed the composition of Heian *monogatari*. Style and plotting, then, are the means to attain a realistic mode of writing.

The argument for realism is carried on in the last two chapters. In chapter 5 Shōyō discusses the ways in which the hero of a novel must be portrayed. He distinguishes between two modes of characterization: the realistic, which he associates with writers like Tamenaga Shunsui and forms like the *ninjōbon* (prose narratives dealing for the most part with stories of love), and the idealistic, which he generally associates with the *yomihon* and writers like Bakin (*TSS* 54–55). He looks for a compromise, stating that the portrait of a hero must strike a balance, that it should be neither too noble nor too base (*TSS* 56). The key is credibility and verisimilitude, and he ends his treatise by discussing descriptive method, echoing the terminology of European writers, especially the practical criticism of Henry James. The novel may describe either in a hidden manner by showing, through the actions or words of the characters, or in an open manner by telling, with the narrator presenting motives and descriptions directly. Once again, the emphasis is on a balance of elements appropriate to the types of novel classified earlier.

The argument of *Shōsetsu shinzui* is not original to the author. The work is a pastiche of ideas from a wide range of Western and Japanese critics (from Aristotle to Fenellosa, from the Heian poet and critic Ki no Tsurayuki [ca. 872–945] to Bakin). Its importance, however, cannot be overstated. It stirred interest in literary experimentation centered on developing a realistic style of narrative for Japanese fiction. It also focused attention on the problem of defining what the novel should be and how it should reflect the new values of a modernizing nation. *Shōsetsu shinzui*, by dealing with questions of technique and critical values, expresses as a central concern the dilemma of the modern and how it should be dealt with in literature, and its influence arose from its view of the literary past and from the way it redefined the canon.

The key element in Shōyō's rereading of his tradition is the tendency to discuss Tokugawa fiction not purely on its own terms but as a foreshadowing of modern literary developments. He observes his own tradition through the lens of a Western developmental schema and consequently attacks the fiction of the late Tokugawa period in particular for being flawed either by its overbearing didacticism or by its lack of seriousness (*TSS* 3–4). He rejected the public function of literature as defined by the moralists because it produced artless works, that is to say, works that were not believable from the standpoint of everyday human experience. For Shōyō, the overwhelming influence of didactic literature, as exemplified by the works of Bakin, reflected too strong a reliance on neo-Confucian ethical principles that judged a work on the basis of how closely it adhered to the principle of *kanzen chōaku*, the promotion of virtue and the chastisement of evil. At the same time, he decried the lack of any public function in a fictional narrative and pointed out that fiction written only for private amusement was often frivolous or pornographic.

Nonetheless, Shōyō's reading of his tradition was not a rejection of it. His approach was a kind of conservative incrementalism that reflected the influence of Social Darwinist theories of the evolution of peoples and cultures. It was an attempt to maintain the sanctity that had been claimed for literary studies during the Tokugawa period by scholars like Norinaga and to reclaim for Japanese literature the seriousness that in the eyes of Shōyō and many of his contemporaries distinguished Western literature and served as an important feature of an enlightened civilization. The goal was to reform native literary practice, not to abandon it altogether, and to this end he sought to appropriate elements from that tradition to act as models for the present and to provide evidence that the progress toward civilization, and thus toward a serious literature, was in spite of parochial differences a universal condition of human society. He believed that a fundamental divide had opened up between literature that was a personal artistic pursuit and literature that claimed a serious social purpose. Accordingly, his proposals for reform included a reinterpretation of critical categories from his own tradition within a framework borrowed from naturalist/realist Western literary theory.

Because of the reformist character of *Shōsetsu shinzui*, it is easy to overlook the role of the native critical tradition in the formulation of Shōyō's critical approach. Yet, as I noted above, Shōyō relied on the work of Bakin and Norinaga, among others, and the basic categories he used to describe the novel—the artistic and the didactic—while serving to support his critique of the imbalance in pre-Meiji fiction, reveal his debt to Tokugawa conceptions of fiction as a vehicle for teaching morals and as a means of self-cultivation worthy of study and practice for its own sake. Thus, while attacking the current state of the Japanese novel according to Western standards, he managed to salvage his own tradition by incorporating many of its assumptions into his theory.

This fusion of Western and native critical ideas grew out of the need to reconcile larger competing cultural values. Kenneth Pyle has observed that

> for many Japanese in this period of intense national consciousness, alienation from their own cultural heritage posed perplexing dilemmas. Building a powerful nation required supplanting much of Japanese tradition with techniques and practices borrowed from the West. Young Japanese were troubled by the implications of this process, for the very modernity they sought had in some sense to be regarded as alien in origin. They were in fact painfully sensitive to the self-effacement that cultural borrowing implied.[14]

Shōsetsu shinzui was an attempt to move the Japanese tradition into the mainstream of world civilization—or at least to show that it partook of the process of civilization—while still preserving the cultural autonomy of the nation. Though he condemned the tradition he had inherited, Shōyō nevertheless saw in it one redeeming quality: namely, that it contained, according to his evolutionary view of the development of civilized culture, the seeds of modernity. In his reading of the tradition, then, he reinterpreted earlier critical notions, especially notions concerning the purposes and forms of literature, and established an approach that placed the values of the past within a modern context, thus giving priority to the progressive critical values of the present.

The legacy of *Shōsetsu shinzui* is apparent in the critical methodology of the Meiji period that read and judged the Tokugawa tradition on the basis of its resemblances to modern conceptions of fiction. Important parts of the canon were established according to that approach. As has already been noted, Saikaku was "discovered" as a protorealist by the mid-Meiji critic and antiquarian Awashima Kangetsu, who recommended his works to a number of writers. Similarly, Shiki "discovered" the great *haikai* poet-painter Yosa Buson, a discovery closely linked to Shiki's efforts to reform Japanese poetics along the lines of his *shaseibun*. Late in the Meiji period, Nagai Kafū, striking the pose of latter-day literatus, began his efforts to preserve the legacy of *gesaku* authors like Tamenaga Shunsui. The status accorded these so-called premodern authors is not based solely on the quality of their writing. As a result in great part of the critical methods of Meiji literature, there continues to be a resistance to reading even the recognized classics of Tokugawa literature within the context of values contemporary to the time of their composition.[15]

It is frequently noted that Shōyō's novel, *Tōsei shosei katagi* (Characters of present-day students), published shortly after his prescription for reform, deals with a contemporary topic, the life of university students, within the traditional anecdotal form of the *katagimono* (character sketch). Yet the work is an almost perfect extension of his critical theory. That it was acknowledged as a failure even by the author stemmed from a sense that it did not achieve what could be called a breakthrough, that it did not create either a new language or a new form for the novel. This judgment was perhaps inevitable, since Shōyō's evolutionary theory of the development of the novel stressed the importance of formal continuity. Unable to embrace discontinuity and thereby radically remake his tradition, Shōyō could develop in his novel neither the language nor the form appropriate to express the sense of cultural crisis that emerged in the mid-1880s. For all that, Shōyō's novel inaugurated a period of experimentation that culminated in the brilliant explosion of literary activity of the late Meiji period.

◆

chapter five
The Limits of Realism
and the Dilemma of
Futabatei

Hasegawa Tatsunosuke, better known by his pen name, Futabatei Shimei, is often credited with writing the first modern novel in Japan: *Ukigumo* (Drifting clouds), which was serialized in the journal *Miyako no hana* from 1887 to 1889. Of course, to call *Ukigumo* the first modern novel is problematic, since that description emphasizes the chronology or historical position of the work over the qualities that make it modern. Perhaps it is best, however, not to challenge such a well-established critical judgment. At the least, it must be acknowledged that this judgment, though not very precise in critical terms, is a fairly accurate assessment of the dominant position the novel was thought by Futabatei's contemporaries to occupy in the history of Meiji literature.

Perhaps even more than his literary efforts, the almost-mythic significance attached by other writers to the life and work of Futabatei is the best measure of his influence on twentieth-century literature in Japan. His importance is not simply the result of his historical position, nor is it to be seen in the direct influence he had on other authors. He is an emblematic figure who gave expression to many of the concerns that came to define modern literature. Other authors may have faced these concerns on their own and in their own way, with no influence from Futabatei, but the literary terrain he first mapped out is roughly the same landscape that later writers had to cross. Much of the significance attached to his career centers on his struggle to define the modern, and thus he is, in spite of his small output of three novels, one of the central figures of my study.

Futabatei's importance is suggested by a number of essays written by various authors that were collected as a memorial tribute to him by his friends Tsubouchi Shōyō and Uchida Roan following his death in 1909. *Ukigumo* is prominent in the minds of many of these men. Mori Ōgai writes,

> I was quite startled by *Ukigumo*. That book marked the first time in Japan that a novel had moved in a psychological direction. One could not help but be surprised that such a work could have been written in those days. It is startling because it was that period. Even though writers were still using hackneyed, conventional pseudonyms—Tsubouchi Shōyō was Harunoya Oboro, Yasaki Chinshirō was Saganoya Omuro, and Hasegawa was Futabatei—a work like *Ukigumo* nonetheless appeared. Of course pseudonyms are used in every nation. They had them in the past, and they have them now. They will probably have them in the future. But those words on the title page, "*Ukigumo* by Futabatei Shimei," will remain forever in literary annals as a curious contradiction, an extraordinary anachronism.

Shimazaki Tōson, a romantic poet of the 1890s who became a leader in the naturalist movement, makes similar observations. Futabatei, he writes, reminded him of a typical Turgenev character, a kind of "realistic-idealist" who was torn between his contradictory impulses toward the practical and toward the arts. The fact that Futabatei had spent much of his life studying and translating Russian literature "was the reason he achieved the psychological analysis such as is found in *Ukigumo,* and it was, I think, the reason that he was attracted to the life of an artist. Nonetheless, it seems that such an inclination was unable to satisfy him for long. At the same time that he was an artist, he also possessed the soul of a reformer. These two qualities left a contradiction he could not resolve for a long time. He was silent. Silent for a long, long time." Finally, there are these remarks by Masamune Hakuchō, a critic and naturalist writer, which seem to echo and expand on the comments above.

> The recognition that Futabatei has done work of the highest importance in the history of Meiji literature has come only in the past two or three years. I have only recently come to think, along with many others, that the plain

writings and translations of men like Futabatei have more significance than the more celebrated activities of the Ken'yūsha and that *Ukigumo* was the first work to try to portray human life sincerely, without a sense of playfulness and without ostentation. In spite of the fact that I have little admiration for writers of that era, men like Kōyō and Rohan, I admire Futabatei in the way I admire Doppo. It may seem that there is little to be learned from their works, but that is because of Doppo's farsightedness and because Futabatei was a forerunner of today's intellectual current. However, while I consider his achievement in the Meiji literary establishment significant, especially with works he wrote in his spare time, I am not able to give his works themselves such a high position. They are works of a transitional age. They reveal a tendency, the result of the influence of Russian literature, that is different from the Ken'yūsha, and yet there still remains the odor of the Tokugawa period with its many elements of playfulness and ostentation.[1]

These remarks constitute a kind of cross-section of opinion from three literary generations. Ōgai emerged as a prominent literary figure at about the same time as Futabatei, Tōson gained his first successes as a poet nearly a decade later, and Hakuchō appeared on the scene just as naturalism was becoming a dominant movement. All three men make roughly the same judgment about Futabatei's early career, albeit from very different perspectives. They see *Ukigumo* as the first significant novel of the Meiji period; they cite as strengths its plain language and psychological verisimilitude; and, most importantly, they see it as full of contradictions, as if it emerged at the very beginning of the modern moment and was on the boundary between what they understood as modern and what they sensed to be traditional. More than any other quality of the work, its language or its method of characterization, those contradictions indicate the influence of a strong sense of discontinuity on Futabatei's writing.

Although the preoccupation with language, such as that exhibited in the *genbun'itchi* movement, and with technical innovations like the development of psychological realism suggest a heightened awareness of discontinuity, that sense alone does not constitute the modernity of *Ukigumo*. The book's modernity is also the product of the outlook on literature, especially his ideas about realism, that led Futabatei to experiment with those techniques in the first place. It follows that clarifying the elements that truly made his work original requires examination of those experiments. This is especially important in discussing the narrative voice Futabatei developed, because, as I already noted, certain conventions of pre-Meiji narrative literature survive in his work, and Futabatei himself acknowledged his debt to the Tokugawa tradition.

The Limits of Realism

In an essay on *shaseibun* he wrote in 1907, Futabatei points to the influences shaping his style. He writes that he objects to the current practice of *shaseibun* because it is used mainly to depict nature, not humanity. His own notion of *shaseibun* is rather different: "Glancing at real scenes, incidents, and people and capturing their essential points, a painter will create a picture with broad brush strokes. *Shaseibun* may be thought of in exactly the same way—though my wording may seem a little strange—as a kind of broad-brush-stroke writing" (*FSZ*-I 5:204). Futabatei does not care for minute, detailed description as such, since that approach limits the range of voice and perspective. He prefers the technique of suggesting detail by capturing essential points and thus implies a distinction between the art of writing narrative, which requires a controlling hand, and the simple cataloging of experience. He cites Russian literature generally and Shikitei Sanba's *Ukiyoburo* (Bathhouse of the floating world, 1809–1813) specifically as the models for the type of descriptive writing he prefers. With respect to the latter, Robert Leutner has noted that "the most outstanding formal characteristic" of the classic *sharebon* (literally, "stylish/clever books," popular fiction mainly dealing with redlight districts) and of the later *kokkeibon* (literally, "books of humor"—humorous or witty popular fiction) is the "heavy reliance on dialogue," and he goes on to point out the connection between that style and the oral storytelling traditions of *rakugo, niwaka, kōshaku,* and other forms.[2] The heavy use of dialogue bearing a marked resemblance to the kind of dialogue found in the works of Sanba and other *gesaku* writers is one of the major stylistic features of *Ukigumo*.

The debt to writers like Sanba is made clearer by a comparison of sample passages of their writing. Because of the difficult nature of the wordplay in Sanba's *Ukiyoburo*, the translation that follows is an extremely rough approximation of the original that substitutes English puns when no other means of literally rendering the text is available. Because the lines of each speaker are clearly marked in the original, my translation renders the text as though it were dialogue in a play. The scene is an exchange between the bathhouse operator, Bantō, and a drunken man, Namayoi (designated as B and N below).

N: What's that? Medicine ads?
B: Yes, that's right.
N: Say, you're a greedy one. Sell anything, won't you?
B: Well . . .

N: Can't make a living just on the bath?
B: You know how it is. I get requests from all over to put them up, so I can't avoid using them. He-he-he-he-he he-he-he-he-he.
N: Hmm. "Chapped skin cured without a helping hand." Bantō?
B: Yes?
N: Can you cure chaps without a helping hand?
B: Sure, he-he-he-he-he.
N: Now just a second. When you get chaps on your legs and can't walk, it's good to have a helping hand. But when you get chaps on your hands, whoever heard of getting a helping leg? I mean, I've heard of cases where the chaps hurt, and you can't lift a leg, but that doesn't mean you can't get somebody to lift a hand. Am I right or what, Bantō? How can you cure chaps without a helping hand?
B: It just means you're cured before you know it.
N: God, you're dumb. How can you be cured without knowing it? Now then, what about this ad? "Tasteful Eight-Part . . ." How do you read that character . . . pill? Eight-Part-Potion? Eight-Part-Powder?
B: That's read "Eight-Part-Performer."
N: Performer? Never heard of that one before. Oh well, it says it tastes good, so I guess you take it for a cold.
B: No, no, I said "Eight-Part-Performer." One person does eight people.
N: Boy, you sure sell some queer people. How much do they go for?
B: They're not something you sell, or even look at. They perform.
N: Well, as long as they're effective, that's all that counts.
B: They cost about sixty-four mon.
N: Wow, that's cheap. Only eight mon per person. That's less than the bath. You take the treatment, and when you get the Eight-Part-Performer, that's eight mon per person, so . . . eight times eight . . . you get sixty-four mon. But when you enter the bathhouse you pay ten mon for one person. When you subtract that you're left with fifty-four mon profit. Now wait just one second here, Bantō. You may not sell something like this, but couldn't you at least give me a half-portion?
B: Dammit, you don't get anything. I said, "Eight-Part-Performer!" It's a person!

The Limits of Realism

N: I know it's a person.

B: In any case, they don't do it here, they perform elsewhere.

N: That's why I'll take one. What use is a treatment that doesn't perform?

B: For God's sake, it's a blind person who performs.

N: Say what? This Bantō doesn't make any sense. Aw shit, (drunken belch) what a pain you are. (Squints face and looks around unsteadily.) Now what's that? It's written so I can't read it. And if I can't read it nobody can. Hey, Bantō! What's that say?

B: You read it "Playful Anecdotes."

N: Hmm. "Playful Antidotes?"

B: No, no. It's storytelling.

N: Man, you sell everything. You don't let anything get by, do you? No wonder it's such an expensive place. Ha-hah, that over there, the medicine on number one. By all means (belch), Battō (belch), aw shit, am I drunk. That medicine called "Night-Wooer?" No matter what, I have to have it. This time, even if you say you don't sell it, I'm going to buy some.

B: Which one?

N: That one right there. The one called "Night-Wooer."

B: Huh? That one? Ha-ha-ha-ha-ha-ha-ha-ha-ha-ha. That's "Night-Wetter."

N: "Night-Wetter?"

B: It's a treatment for bed wetting. Oooh-ha-ha-ha-ha-ha-ha-ha-ha-ha. (83–84)

Although the passage I have chosen from *Ukiyoburo* is an extreme example of the verbal play present in much of Sanba's narrative (and thus perhaps not as realistic as some other vignettes), several features make it representative of his work. First, dialogue is made to carry most of the narrative, and the few authorial interjections present are usually more like stage directions than commentary on the meaning of the action. This does not mean that no authorial presence is felt, for the visual presentation of the narrative, especially the marking of the speakers, calls attention to the recorder, the implied narrator of the verbal action taking place.

A second feature of the narrative, one that also reveals an authorial presence, is the way in which the language of oral performance arts such as *rakugo* has been adapted to a literary format. This vaudevillian shtick is based on mistakes in language comprehension that in turn suggest a strong consciousness of the difference between the high, literate culture represented (at least in this scene) by the Bantō and the low, semiliterate culture represented by the Namayoi. As was noted earlier in reference to the language of Saikaku, this copresence of high and low elements is a sign of the essentially literary nature of Sanba's project. This is especially apparent in the puns that depend not merely on a confusion of sounds, an element taken from oral narrative techniques, but also on the play of those sounds with the characters used to represent them on the page.[3] One is *fūryū*, "elegant" or "tasteful," a word with a long history of use as an aesthetic term that would have been immediately recognized by Sanba's readership. The semiliterate Namayoi, however, mistakenly reads the characters for *fūryū* according to their *kun*, or native Japanese, pronunciation (making the word come out as *kazenagashi*) and thus confuses the aesthetic term with an advertisement for a cold (*kaze*) remedy. A second pun strikes even closer to home for Sanba in the misreading of *gedokudan* (talks on playful readings) as *gedokugan* (antidotes for poison). Sanba is highly self-conscious about the literary nature of his project even at those points where his narrative deals with vulgar subjects or humor of the lowest possible kind.

These stylistic features were not overlooked by Futabatei, who as a young man was an avid reader of *gesaku,* and they appear throughout *Ukigumo*. The book is an account of the struggle of its protagonist, Bunzō, to find a place for himself in a modern society that is undergoing rapid change. Bunzō is something of a stick-in-the-mud who has very strong, old-fashioned notions about proper behavior. His inability to adapt to the shallow, materialistic outlook of his age causes him to lose his job and, as a result, to lose the attention of the woman he loves, Osei. Bunzō is hardly a heroic protector of traditional values, however, since his indecisiveness and penchant for introverted behavior and self-pity prevent him from tackling the problems caused by his personal dislocations. The story of Bunzō is therefore by nature less anecdotal than *gesaku* fiction, since it reproduces the larger, more continuous structure of Western novels that present the inner psychological development of a character. This overall shift to a Western mode of narrative is precisely why the presence of certain *gesaku* elements of style is so relevant to understanding the nature of the experiments undertaken by Futabatei. The following passage is taken from a crucial point in the novel, after Bunzō falls out with Osei and before he breaks off his relationship with Noboru, his crass and thoroughly up-to-date (that is, superficial and amoral) acquaintance. Bunzō has just returned home.

> When he peeked into the inner room, Noboru was standing, with round pieces of white paper stuck to his back, loitering in the midst of things scattered around as if there had been a drunken revel. Osei and Onabe [the maid] were nearby holding their sides and convulsed with laughter, though he couldn't see all of Osei. Even though their eyes met his, no one welcomed him home, or asked him about his aunt, or answered him. When Bunzō moved past the door in a funk, suddenly from behind him he heard a ruckus of loud voices.
>
> NOBORU: All right now, who's the wise guy?
> OSEI: It's not me. It's Onabe. Ho-ho-ho-ho.
> ONABE: What are you saying? It's the young mistress. O-ho-ho-ho-ho.
> NOBORU: It's neither one, it's both of you. Let's start with this little piggy.
> ONABE: Hey, it's not me! O-ho-ho-ho-ho. Stop that . . . Hey, Miss Osei!
>
> Bunzō also heard the sound of feet scurrying, *dotapata dotapata,* and another voice laughing, "O-ho-ho-ho." He also heard Osei shouting over and over, "Scratch him, scratch him!" (*FSZ*-I 1:89–90)

This passage shows both a visual debt in the clear marking out of the dialogue and the speakers and a linguistic debt in the colloquial speech Futabatei imitated. However, the most important aspect of this *gesaku*-like scene is the use Futabatei makes of it within the context of the narrative. After nearly running into Osei in the hallway and being scolded by her, Bunzō retires to his room upstairs and tries to read a work written in English on British political parties. Apart from the tedious subject matter and the incomprehensibility of the foreign language, which is reproduced on the page to make a stark visual contrast between the alien English and the native Japanese, the noise of the young people downstairs having fun distracts him so that he cannot continue. Soon Noboru comes up to visit with him, and the contrast between the serious, boring Bunzō and the shallow, witty Noboru is starkly drawn, especially in the repetition of the latter's ingratiating, scornful laugh, which throughout the book is always visually spelled out on the page.

Noboru's visit leads to an argument and the breaking off of their friendship, but when Noboru insists that Bunzō explain why he is being cut off, Bunzō cannot answer. He is caught between the language of Noboru, the nonserious language of *gesaku,* and the foreign language he is studying. When Noboru presses him for an explanation, Bunzō counters that everything Noboru says is an "evasion." Asked to explain what he means, Bunzō is reduced to asserting, in English, that it is a "Self-evident truth" (*FSZ*-I 1:99). True to his character, Bunzō is always outside the action as a passive observer. Futabatei has extended the literary nature of his *gesaku* model in part by showing the psychological basis for the misunderstanding of language among the characters and more importantly by making the basis of misunderstanding not a mistake in interpretation, but the very lack of language. Bunzō has no words to express himself. He is trapped, in a way like Futabatei himself, between two alternatives, neither of which is acceptable to him.

In the discussion of the development of his own *genbun'itchi* style, Futabatei readily admits his preference for vulgar language and connects his own work with the techniques of *rakugo*. He ties his realistic style quite closely to narrative modes established in Tokugawa fiction. Hakuchō seems to have been justified in detecting a strong Tokugawa aroma, and, as he suggests, the modernness of Futabatei's style may have been a critical construct of later writers based on accidental similarities between Futabatei's literary aims and their own. It is not, then, merely the technique of colloquial style that makes *Ukigumo* modern. The style adopted by Futabatei is a rather conservative element forcing the work into, rather than freeing it from, the context of the tradition. Instead, the modern element of the work's style is the self-conscious use made of Tokugawa narrative techniques. The frivolous language of *gesaku* was recycled for the purpose of creating a realistic narrative. Futabatei's aims were essentially the same as Shōyō's in the sense that he was concerned with giving Japanese literature a new seriousness, and like Shōyō he was interested in reform that did not altogether abandon native literary practice. It is this dual nature of the aims of his reforms that Ōgai, Tōson, and Hakuchō looked on as the defining, albeit contradictory element of his achievement.

The seriousness of his aims is revealed in a brief, somewhat dense essay titled "Shōsetsu sōron" (An overview of the novel), written in 1886. The argument, which borrows heavily from the work of Vissarion Belinsky (1811–1848), is constructed around three main ideas: (1) that all phenomena, objects, and events are the manifestation (or expression) of an idea; (2) that because all phenomena and objects possess unique forms and qualities, their particularity acts to impede or obscure the complete expression of the idea they should by nature express; and (3) that art, especially the novel, recognizes, through an intuitive comprehension of the real nature of all things, that ideas are blocked from their complete manifestation and thus borrows from phenomena and objects in order to express those intuited ideas. "Because the novel gives directly a sense of the state of nature (ideas) within the various phenomena (forms) that appear in the floating world, it should convey that sense directly to people. In order to achieve directness the novel must copy [*mosha*]. That being the case, it is clear that copying is the seriousness [or honesty, *majime*] of the novel" (*FSZ*-I 5:10). As used here, *mosha* suggests mimesis, not reproduction, and is an early statement of the idea that Futabatei later developed into his personal definition of *shaseibun*, which is a style of writing that captures the essence of a scene or character. Futabatei continues his argument by attacking the didactic novel for being too limited in its aims and asserts that copying the world is the sole serious purpose of the novel. Such a theoretical conclusion seems to be very much in line with Futabatei's fondness for the techniques and forms of Tokugawa narrative.

Futabatei seems to start his essay with a rather extreme notion of narrative realism that virtually equates art with the life it represents. This functional approach reflects a strong European influence, and it is perhaps what prompted Tōson to label him a "realistic-idealist" in his memorial essay. The presence of certain traditional critical values should not, however, be overlooked. There is a subtle balance between the positivist approach assumed by his realism, in which knowledge of the world is thought to be possible through observation and analysis, and the idealism that views the novel as a means for giving more complete expression to the ideas that underlie all phenomena. The balance he tries to strike, though expressed through a different critical vocabulary, recalls Tokugawa critical theory.

In spite of his admiration for elements of *gesaku* style and his debt to native critical theory, Futabatei can hardly be described as a late *gesaku* author. As noted above, what makes him different, what creates the discontinuity that so profoundly affects *Ukigumo*, is his self-conscious awareness that he is different from the past and his desire to re-create and reform his tradition. He was brought up in an atmosphere where the values of *chōnin* (townsman, or bourgeois) culture were still very strong—values reflected in the admiration he held for *gesaku*, even though he felt that it was essentially a frivolous literature. Given his upbringing, it is not surprising that he sensed he was losing his cultural bearings in the effort to make literature new and serious. The dilemma inherent in his embrace of discontinuity, a dilemma faced by all writers strongly aware of the present, became a central personal concern that also shaped the structure and narrative logic of his first novel. Harold Rosenberg has defined the dilemma faced by the literary realist.

> To honor fact, art must honor itself. After noting that, given the vision, actual life may reveal greater depths than Shakespeare, Dostoevsky backs away: "But the whole question," he exclaims, "is *whose* vision? Indeed, not only to create and write artistic works, but also to discern a fact something of an artist is required." That modern literature has decided to pursue reality is only half the story; the other half is its discovery that the subversion of literary form cannot be accomplished except by literary means, that is, *through an effort that is essentially formal*.[4]

"The subversion of literary form" in this context refers to the effort of realists to make literature the vehicle for representing fact, a purpose for which fiction is by nature unsuited. In trying to depict the world as it is, there is a fundamental clash between the forms of what is observed and the necessities of artistic form. The notion of the novel as an artistic means of copying reality expounded by Futabatei in 1886 is vulnerable to this dilemma, for absolute mimesis makes the novel form impossible. Although the anecdotal narrative that dominated Tokugawa fiction provided a model for realistic writing in that it could be used to represent the ephemerality and fragmentation of human experience, for Futabatei and others of his generation, the outlook on human experience suggested by that model was no longer valid, and the anecdotal narrative was formally inferior to the Western novel. In the effort to adapt a Western narrative model, Futabatei understood that the transitory formlessness of reality, which is suggested by the title of the work, *Ukigumo*, forces any so-called realistic depiction to be similarly formless and open-ended, with no hope of resolution in an artistic sense. The impossibility of absolutely reducing reality to (or encompassing it by) narrative form is illustrated most brilliantly in the eighteenth-century English novel, *Tristram Shandy*. I do not know if Futabatei ever read Sterne's work, but he was certainly aware of the humorous possibilities of the paradox of realism. In his last novel, *Heibon* (Mediocrity), he satirizes the narrative convention of detailed, lifelike description as a means of conveying reality. The narrator spends a great deal of time on his earliest recollections and then in chapter

7 writes, "But wait a minute now. I said I was going to write like the naturalists, but if I keep writing sluggishly in this way it will take me thirty-nine years just to write about my thirty-nine-year half-life" (*FSZ-I* 4:110).

The modernity of *Ukigumo,* then, is revealed not only by the theme of discontinuity portrayed in the characterization of Bunzō but also by the narrative's open-ended, inconclusive structure. Indeed, the main achievement of the work is the way in which the structure of the narrative meshes so well with the consciousness of the central character. Bunzō is a man out of his time. His problems stem from his inability to reconcile his ideals, which are presented as belonging to the past, with the economic realities and practical needs of the new Japan. Here, as Tōson suggests, the influence of Russian literature seems evident in the seriousness with which Futabatei tried to achieve a psychological realism. Bunzō's inability to redefine himself leads to both his inner turmoil and the central crisis of the novel, which is the problem he begins to have with Osei after he loses his job. He is by nature inclined to inactivity and thus is more of an antihero, a figure whose inability to control or create his fictional world creates the modernist predicament at the core of the book. The sense of discontinuity is so strong within Bunzō that he is rendered incapable of resolving his dilemma. Marleigh Ryan's formulation of Bunzō as a superfluous hero certainly suggests the central problem of the narrative—the protagonist's marginality in his fictional world—but her phrasing is a little misleading, for it stresses that the portrait of Bunzō emerges from Russian literary prototypes rather than from the impulse to reread the native tradition stimulated by the encounter with those prototypes.[5] Futabatei discovered in the course of writing his work that, in an extreme case of dissociation, heroism is not possible, and without a hero a modern narrative becomes difficult to sustain.

Ukigumo, for all its technical borrowings from Tokugawa fiction, altered fictional narrative in Japan by employing shifting perspectives that complicated the determination of what is true in the text, and that introduced a greater self-awareness or self-consciousness on the part of the characters. The narrator often intervenes to explain or judge the actions of the characters or to interject humorous digressions, but that voice is not the sole source of information, and the characters, especially Bunzō and Osei, frequently assume the narrative function of commenting on or judging their own actions or those of the other figures. The characters provide perspectives that call into question the absolute reliability of the text and raise the crucial issue of how a realistic mode reconciles its attempt to present fact/truth with the formal demands of fictional narrative. This represents a significant shift from the practices of *gesaku* fiction, for although the contrived moral pronouncements and humorous asides of the narrator's voice in Tokugawa fiction draw attention by their intrusiveness to the rhetorical nature of the text, it is less common for characters to step out of their narrative roles. *Ukigumo* is often praised for the psychological realism of its characterizations, but the source of that realism, and of the novel's technical innovation, is its more sophisticated handling of voice and perspective.

The irony of Futabatei's breakthrough is that, instead of opening up possibilities for creating a new literature, it caused him to adopt a skeptical stance concerning those possibilities, as though he recognized that he could never be true to the ideals that initially inspired his narrative experiments. Shimizu Shigeru has observed that

> in a sense, the composition of *Ukigumo* was, for Futabatei, an internal struggle with the *gesakusha* [writers of *gesaku*], and especially with Sanba. The fact that *Ukigumo* had to be abandoned in the end means that he was finally unable to overcome the *gesakusha*, the Sanba, within himself. . . .
>
> What was it about the *gesakusha* and Sanba that Futabatei was fighting in *Ukigumo?* First, he was opposed to a fictitious consciousness that had no ideology and that was decadently playful. Second, he was opposed to the petty, self-serving utilitarian outlook and morality of the urban masses.[6]

Futabatei tried to salvage his tradition through realism, but he also wanted to create a literature that was new by virtue of being a serious expression of ideas. He found instead that fictional narrative must by its nature betray the seriousness he sought.

Looking back on the composition of *Ukigumo* in an essay he wrote in 1908, he discusses the dilemma he faced. Since the essay, "Yo ga hansei no zange" (Confessions of my half-life), is a retrospective interpretation of his life and career, his comments are by no means the authoritative view of the problems his first novel caused him. Nonetheless, it is interesting that he describes his own difficulties in terms similar to those he used to create his character, Bunzō: namely, an irreconcilable split between idealism and practicality. He recalls that he wrote the novel in order to make money but that at the same time he was driven by a desire to live a lifestyle that was guided by the ideal of honesty (*shōjiki*). Futabatei tells us that this ideal was evidently the product of several influences, primarily Russian literature, Confucianism, and socialism. He wonders whether ideology really has any bearing on the composition of literature and then proceeds to outline the troubles caused by his attempts to write within the dictates of his ideal of honesty. Although he was guided by humility, honesty, and a reverence for art, the demands placed on him by family and society led him to desire money. Thus his efforts to write became an affront to his ideals. He tells us that he used Shōyō's name to get published, putting his own petty interests first and deceiving the readers as well. He writes,

> This was an extreme dilemma. It was a clash between the practical and the ideal. I could not resolve it, but because the necessities of life were pressing in more and more, writing *Ukigumo* to make money became unavoidable. Looking at it from the vantage of my ideals, I had become an outrageous person. The more money I took, the more self-conscious I became about how unclean I was. Then, at the extreme of my anguish a voice cried out *kutabatte shimae*—drop dead! (Futabatei Shimei).[7]
>
> There have been many explanations offered about the origins of my pseudonym, but the truth is just as I have told it now. At the time that command was made I thought there was a possibility of carrying it out. —If the dilemma were to be solved, it would be because my life was brought to a settlement first. Even now, *kutabatte shimae* rings with meaning for me. . . .
>
> During that period I grew very worried about the problems of humanity. This was because my honesty began to crumble. My honesty first lapsed when I wrote the novel, and then various things began falling apart. In short, my life began crumbling around me. (*FSZ-I* 1:89–90)

Futabatei's account of his early years seems somewhat exaggerated, but when we consider that at the center of his career is a nearly twenty-year period in which he did not write another novel, it is hard to question the extent to which the dilemma posed by his attempts to create a new literature affected him. As the composition of *Ukigumo* continued, he grew increasingly skeptical about his own aims for literature, and he felt no other recourse but to withdraw from literary activity. His silence was perhaps the strongest statement he could make to express his skepticism. Shortly after the third part of *Ukigumo* appeared, he became a civil servant. Although he continued with his work as a translator, his long silence contributed to the impression that he was ahead of his time, both a pioneer and an anomaly.

The interruption of Futabatei's career should not be construed as evidence that he was, in Masao Miyoshi's phrase, an "accomplice of silence."

The notion that there is a "typical Japanese dislike of the verbal" is a questionable generalization that implies, intentionally or not, an endorsement of the argument for Japanese linguistic and cultural uniqueness.[8] The impulse typical of a modernist sensibility is toward not silence but confabulation and the assertion of narrative form. Futabatei provides an instance of a writer acutely aware of the need for a narrative form and language to establish or empower himself over the tradition. The problem he faced was that the language and forms he observed to be new were Western. He understood that in reinterpreting his tradition according to the normative values of the West, he was subscribing to universal ideals that would always place him at the margins of modern culture. To renew the tradition on those terms meant extreme dissociation and cultural alienation. The fact that it was possible to identify traditional narrative techniques within the Western realistic novel may have helped assert priority for native practices, but that merely underscored the Western novel as the norm by which such practices were judged. Futabatei's silence, then, was the result not of a distrust of realistic narrative but of a perceived inability to write a realistic narrative. He felt that, perhaps like his character Bunzō, he did not possess a voice that would enable him to constitute his literary self against either the West or his native tradition.

Eventually the skepticism that led Futabatei to abandon fiction brought him back to writing and determined his development as a literary artist. His novels *Sono omokage* (A shadow of himself) and *Heibon* were not simply afterthoughts in a difficult literary career. *Sono omokage* is Futabatei's most completely realized work in a formal sense and one of the most finely crafted examples of realistic writing in Meiji literature. *Heibon* is also an extremely important novel that more fully explores the problems of narrative form and the question of the possibility of a modern literary life. By looking more closely at the circumstances surrounding his decision to stop writing, we can better understand how his skepticism brought him to try to create a new literature in the novels he wrote late in his life.

◆

chapter six
The Skeptic as Artist:
Sono omokage

Aside from literary considerations, the most compelling reason for Futabatei to give up writing was his family's financial situation. In 1886 his school was split off from Tokyo University and merged with what is now Hitotsubashi University. Futabatei opposed this administrative change and resigned a fairly secure position as an instructor of Russian language as a matter of principle. Shortly after he quit, *Ukigumo* began to appear in print, but the proceeds from its publication were not enough to provide an adequate living. He had been promised ninety yen for the first part, which was then not an inconsiderable sum. He actually received eighty yen, of which he gave thirty-five to Shōyō, who had lent his name to the publication. Shōyō tried to refuse the money, but Futabatei, in a display of the stubborn and at times self-defeating honesty characteristic of him, virtually forced his mentor to accept it. Over the three years that the book was being serialized, the author's share averaged less than ten yen a month.[1] This was not a living wage, and he had to supplement it by teaching literature at Sakurai Women's School. When his father's health began to fail, this arrangement also proved inadequate, and in August 1889 he found a position in the Government Printing Office of the Treasury. He held this job for about eight years.

His family circumstances, aside from being a major consideration in his decision to change careers, were a source of the feelings of personal failure, mediocrity, and frustration Futabatei suffered for the rest of his life. However, as I indicated above, his abandonment of fiction is not explained by financial or family pressures alone. Shortly after he stopped writing *Ukigumo,* he was approached by Yoshioka Tetsutarō, a publisher who was planning a series of novels by new writers.[2] Futabatei was evidently tempted to accept the offer, and he writes in his diary that it had made him feel very happy to be asked. At the same time, he felt a sense of regret and notes that had he been more than merely an average writer, he would have easily achieved success (*FSZ-C* 5:94). He was truly torn between his desire to continue writing and his need for a more secure livelihood. He was also perversely humble about his work, despite the praise and support he had received, and believed he did not have the talent to write. This lack of confidence certainly contributed to his choosing a government career.

Given his strong idealism and his inflexible temperament, it was probably inevitable that he would suffer a loss of confidence. As a young man, he was by nature more of a critic than an artist. He was also a perfectionist. Like Shōyō, his goal in the mid-1880s had been nothing less than the reform of literary practice in Japan. He was a harsh critic of contemporary Japanese society and literature, but his extreme honesty led him to criticize his own work just as severely. Thus when he failed to make a living at writing and when he failed to complete *Ukigumo* to his satisfaction, he took both as indications of his lack of talent.

This personal disillusionment coincided with, and was reinforced by, the general conservative reaction to the excesses of modernization that began in the late 1880s and continued for almost a decade. Although Futabatei's efforts to create a realistic fiction were supported and encouraged, the conservative trend forced the literary experiments of the time in a different direction, exemplified by the writers of the Ken'yūsha, many of whom, as I noted earlier, looked to models from the native tradition, such as Saikaku, to make a new literature. The impact of their work on Futabatei was unfortunately very great, for he not only viewed his work as an artistic failure but also came to believe that he was out of the mainstream of literary developments.[3]

There is no simple explanation for Futabatei's decision to stop writing. His sense of personal failure, his disillusionment, and his intellectual temperament were all important factors, and taken together they led to the skepticism with which Futabatei came to view literary activity. It is important to recall that he had been developing a systematic skepticism almost from the beginning of his career, when he took up the study of Russian language and literature, and his ideology was not merely an emotional reaction to the circumstances in which he found himself in 1889. No doubt his personal failures deepened his skepticism, but the philosophical framework by which he could justify his decision not to write anymore was in place well before he had finished *Ukigumo*. The following entry from his notebook of 1889 provides an indication of his attitude.

> According to [religious believers] the truth cannot be understood by the intellect alone. Instead you must be inspired by the entire soul. (*The truth of God can't be comprehended unless by the whole man*.) Do these believers maintain that as a certainty? If so, I am not surprised by their audacity. . . . [These believers point out that] the shortest line between two points is the straightest, and so it follows that we must comprehend [the truth] by what is called "*the wholeman*" and not by intellect alone. However, can we really claim that truth is a certainty—can we believe *absolutely*? It has been said in the past that "*One can never be sure of what he knows*." I think, "*One can never be sure of what he knows and feels, that is, comprehended by the whole man*."⁴ (FSZ-C 5: 64)

This excerpt reveals a subtle shift in the position Futabatei had held three years before in "Shōsetsu sōron." Whereas earlier he had explored the possibilities offered by the novel form to present an intuitive knowledge of the world through mimesis, here he is saying that no knowledge, either rational or intuited, is absolute or certain. This skepticism, a sense that there were no absolutes, that no assertion of the truth could be taken at face value, and that particular circumstances and universal ideals would always be in conflict, forms the core of his personal convictions and his artistic endeavors. He abandoned his goal of the reform of Japanese literature because he doubted the possibility of ever realizing it. He was well aware that the normative values that determined what was considered modern narrative were those of the West and that Japan would be on the margins as long as that remained the case. In a sense his personal difficulties were confirmations of the intellectual position he had already adopted. He was simply being true to his convictions and his experience when he turned his back on fiction.

Futabatei was not the only writer of his generation to abandon the writing of fiction for a significant period in his life. Mori Ōgai, Yanagita Kunio, and Kōda Rohan all underwent similar experiences to greater or lesser degrees. Since the personal circumstances of these men varied, it is probably fruitless to look for a single reason to explain this behavior. However, all of them started with the notion that new fiction, unlike the works of the *gesaku* tradition with which they were all very familiar (and seemed to have enjoyed), should serve a serious purpose, and they were all disillusioned by their recognition of the essential rhetoricity of fictional narrative: a recognition that no narrative, however serious its intent, could escape its inherent falseness. Although their seriousness of intent, and the self-consciousness that it implies, did make them different from Tokugawa writers, their perception that formally their work was not that different from *gesaku* was enough to create doubts about the usefulness of the undertaking.

The depth of Futabatei's disenchantment with fiction can hardly be doubted, since his self-imposed silence lasted nearly twenty years. Why, then, did he start writing again? He was not newly certain about the value of literature; he kept his doubts to the very end of his life. The tendency to question, however, stirred him to explore other outlets for his critical and literary views. In 1908, less than a year before his death, he summed up his feelings on the matter.

> For me, literature is somehow trivial and of scant value. When I take up the brush and look down upon the paper, for some reason I cannot concentrate. I cannot help being distracted by things. I cannot get worked up by literature, nor give my life to it, nor lose myself in it. I have been troubled about this for a long time. . . . However, in the case of international problems—and by "international problems" I mean, according to my personal interpretation, something different from so-called diplomatic relations and the like—I can get worked up about them, I can give my life to them, I can devote myself to them. I should die quite contentedly for the sake of such problems. I cannot feel that way about literature. I feel as though literature is not my place of death. I do not consider it my mission.[5] (*FSZ*-C 4:301–2)

On one level, Futabatei is admitting that the *gesakusha* were right all along and that literary pursuits are frivolous. He does not explain why that should bother him so, except that perhaps he felt he was wasting his considerable talents. What he called "international problems," on the other hand, did interest him keenly, and this interest affected his notions about the function of literature. As a result of his years of reading and translating the works of Russian authors, he came to share their concern for social problems, which he viewed within an international context—that is, he looked at problems confronting Japan, problems involving social inequities or economic exploitation, not as parochial concerns but as issues confronting all nations. Perhaps such a view allowed him to adopt the pretense of dealing with universal problems, which made his own efforts seem less marginal. In that limited context, literature could still perform a role, by helping to alleviate these problems, and though he was not doctrinaire (unless one considers his skepticism dogmatic), it may be said that he wrote with ethical concerns in mind. In the notebooks dated from 1905 to 1906, he explores such issues as the problem of individuality in a tradition-bound society, the question of generational differences and the exploitation of youth, and the nature of economic inequality. He came to believe that literature could at least serve as a medium to express his views on such matters, and his social criticism served as the basis for his return to fiction.[6]

A number of changes in his personal circumstances also facilitated his return to the literary world. For almost six years after taking the job at the Government Printing Office, Futabatei produced very little writing of any kind. In 1893 he married Fukui Tsune, but their life together was not happy, and he divorced her in 1896. He quit his position the following year and began teaching. During this period, he began to translate more actively, and at the urging of Shōyō and Roan, he became involved in a modest way with the activities of the *bundan* (the literary establishment). He married again in 1902 and then spent much of the next two years working in China and Korea. When he returned to Japan in March 1904, he took a job in the Tokyo office of a daily newspaper, the *Asahi shinbun*. He did not particularly like journalistic work, but his editor, Ikebe Yoshitarō, was a strong-willed individual who managed to keep him on the staff. This job marked his reemergence on the literary scene.

The Russo-Japanese War provided the stimulus he needed to try his hand at another novel. The war held special significance for Futabatei. Twenty-five years earlier, he had begun his study of the Russian language under the influence of what he himself termed a kind of imperialism that made him consider language study essential for the security of the nation. He never entirely ceased viewing Russia as a potential threat, but his long association with that country created severe doubts about the course of his own nation's modernization. He shared the nationwide sense of revulsion over the terrible costs of victory, for which no compensation could be adequate, and this feeling was amplified in his case by his personal ambivalence about the war. His moral values had been shaped to a large extent by Russian authors, and so his perspective on events was broader than that of most observers at the time.

He was approached by the editors at the *Asahi shinbun* to write a story depicting the domestic troubles created by the war. The end product, *Sono omokage,* has little to do with the events of the conflict, but its subject grew out of the original topic he chose to explore—the difficulties faced by women widowed by the fighting. He first looked at this question, and outlined his ideas for a story based on it, in an essay titled "Mibōjin to jindō mondai" (Widows and problems of humanity). He began a novel, *Chasengami* (Tea-whisk hair, named after a hairstyle worn by widows, in which the hair is drawn up in a short ponytail that resembles a tea whisk), based directly on the outline in this essay but abandoned the project when the original conception of the book began to change. His investigation into the problems of women cut off from family and economic support because of widowhood gave way to a wider examination of the family system and of the rights of the individual, especially women, within that system—which came under fire in a number of works of the period for maintaining what were perceived to be vestiges of feudal society. *Sono omokage,* the novel that grew out of this change in conception, was serialized in the *Asahi shinbun* between October 10 and December 31, 1906.

Sono omokage shares many of the elements found in *Ukigumo*. At a basic level, it may be said that both works are attempts to portray realistically the consequences of the failure of an individual to cope with the pressures of personal and social obligations. In *Sono omokage,* however, the author's ideas have evolved and deepened, and a much more mature artistry is at work. The protagonist of *Ukigumo,* Bunzō, is a man so hamstrung by his scruples that he is incapable of rising to heroic action to achieve success in the world and thereby win Osei, the woman he loves. Ono Tetsuya, the protagonist of *Sono omokage,* is also a stubborn, ineffectual antihero. Yet his characterization is far more complex, both because he rouses himself to have a self-destructive love affair with his sister-in-law, Sayoko (whose character is based on that of the young widow Yukie in *Chasengami*) and because we see him constantly questioning the nature of his actions and thus get a clearer idea of the defeats and disappointments that have created him. Tetsuya is not a self-portrait of the artist, any more than is Bunzō, but certainly an older author was able to draw on the experience of defeat and disappointment to create a different and darker fictional world. Moreover, *Sono omokage* shows a greater formal consistency that is perhaps the result of the author having finally settled into a skeptical frame of mind.

Kindly received on the whole, the work was generally taken to be a modest success for its author. A few people, including Natsume Sōseki, were greatly impressed by it, indicating if nothing else the respect in which Futabatei was held by his peers.[7] Still, if it is possible to damn with faint praise, that is the fate the work suffered, and ironically it was the criticism of his lifelong supporter Shōyō that other critics tended to follow. Shōyō felt that the new novel was a fine effort and much more polished than *Ukigumo*, but he also felt that the books were very much alike, especially in their characterizations, and that there was little if anything new or of major interest in *Sono omokage*. Hakuchō makes similar observations, claiming that *Sono omokage* merely repeats the themes of *Ukigumo* and wondering if this repetition did not reveal a weakness in its author's creative powers.[8] In the end, *Sono omokage* was relegated to a secondary place in Futabatei's oeuvre.

Other circumstances also contributed to the lukewarm reception. The years immediately following the Russo-Japanese War were extremely lively ones in the literary world, and the emergence of Sōseki and the rise of the naturalists were events that overshadowed Futabatei's effort. The novel was published in the same year that Tōson brought out *Hakai* (The broken commandment). It was also in 1906 that Sōseki finished his serialization of *Wagahai wa neko de aru*, and the following year Katai's *Futon* appeared. Because *Sono omokage* does bear some superficial similarity to *Ukigumo*, it must have seemed out-of-date given the new trends of the time. Moreover, the historical importance of *Ukigumo* was just being recognized, and it and Futabatei's early career were being idealized in some respects. His second novel, coming as it did after a twenty-year lapse, was bound to suffer by comparison. The naturalists were especially eager to claim his first novel as one of their own, in spite of Futabatei's reservations about the movement, and tended to misread the realism of *Ukigumo* and the portrait of Bunzō as representing an early confessional mode. To them, *Sono omokage* failed to extend the earlier achievement, and they saw their own efforts carrying on the true line of development.

Futabatei's narrative breakthrough was a product of his ambivalence about literature. According to his Confucian heritage, all fiction, but especially *gesaku*, was lacking in the quality of seriousness essential to great literature. This heritage, though supporting the Western notion of seriousness as an important literary value, clashed with Western assumptions concerning the applicability of seriousness to prose fiction. The value of seriousness is also at odds with Futabatei's own fondness for *gesaku* and his use of *gesaku* techniques to create a realistic colloquial narrative. It was perhaps to reconcile these conflicting thoughts that he argues in "Shōsetsu sōron" that the novel serves to reveal ideas, suggesting that fiction grows out of the process of looking for truth. This concept helped determine his development of the realistic style that the naturalists later misread, seeing in the self-questioning of the text a narrative method to get at the truth. But to Futabatei, the narrow factuality created by a writer like Tōson did not resolve the larger problem of the purpose of fiction. On the contrary, the shifting narrative perspective he employed, fundamentally different from the introspective "I" used by many of the naturalists, was a means of representing his belief that the truth could never be known absolutely.

The techniques Futabatei developed in the course of composing *Ukigumo* were brought to bear on his second novel, and even though Shōyō and others were disappointed that he seemed to be returning to his original experiments instead of striking out in new directions, they at least acknowledged that *Sono omokage* was a more polished work. Futabatei perfected his narrative in a number of ways. The novel deals with the family of Ono Tetsuya. As a young man, Tetsuya had been a poor but promising student. In order to complete his education, he had married Tokiko, the daughter of a moderately successful merchant named Ono Reizō, and was adopted into his wife's family in order to provide a male heir. The Ono family in turn paid off his debts. This arrangement remained viable until Reizō died. Reizō had lived beyond his means, and though he had supported his family in an atmosphere of comfort and luxury, he left them with no means to continue that lifestyle. The considerable financial burdens of the household thus fell on Tetsuya's shoulders. Tetsuya, who is reluctant to accept his responsibilities as head of a household, is not capable of fulfilling his obligations. Complicating his situation is the fact that he has been adopted. Though he is nominally its head, he never gains control over his family, and his wishes are almost always ignored.

The novel traces how this fundamental problem goes beyond the point of resolution. Having grown accustomed to luxurious living, Tokiko and her mother, Takiko, are completely dissatisfied with Tetsuya's approach to his new responsibilities. Because they measure success in material terms, they force him to take several teaching jobs in order to support household expenses. Once his energies have been spread so thin, Tetsuya finds himself in a situation in which it is impossible for him to advance. His continued failure adds to the unhappiness of his wife and mother-in-law, and a terrible cycle of distrust and recrimination begins. As life becomes unbearable for Tetsuya, his marriage begins to disintegrate, and because both husband and wife feel justified in their complaints, what they say about each other being ostensibly true, a reconciliation becomes impossible. Divorce is no solution because Tetsuya cannot get the money he needs to settle his educational debt, and even if he could get the money, his departure would leave the Ono family destitute.

One other element complicates this story: Reizō's illegitimate daughter, Sayoko. Although he had tried to care for this daughter, her presence in the house was a painful affront to Takiko. Sayoko was moved out, and she spent much of her childhood in Christian boarding schools. When her father died, she had been forced to leave school and get married. Unfortunately, she was widowed shortly afterward and had had to return to Tetsuya's house. Her return is perceived by the other women as not just a burden but a threat. Because of Tetsuya's strained relationship with Tokiko, Sayoko begins to look after him, performing many of Tokiko's wifely duties.[9] Tetsuya already feels sorry for Sayoko and wants to help her in some way; when she begins to look after him, he sees her as his only source of comfort and then as his ideal love.

Tokiko is alarmed by her husband's attitude and searches for ways to get Sayoko out of the house. At this point, a family friend, Hamura Kōsaburō, approaches Tetsuya with a job offer for Sayoko, thinking that recommending her as a governess to his boss, Shibuya, may further his career. Tetsuya wavers; Shibuya has an unsavory reputation, and there have been rumors that the man has raped some of his female servants. But Tetsuya is too weak-willed to make a firm decision, and he cannot bring himself either to refuse or to accept his friend's proposal. Hamura then goes over his head to Tokiko and her mother. The two of them jump at the opportunity to be rid of the potential threat to their security, and once again they ignore Tetsuya's desires. Sayoko is sent off to the Shibuya house, only to return soon after when, as feared, her master tries to rape her. This precipitates a violent argument during which Tokiko strikes Sayoko. Sayoko decides to leave the family for good, intending to join a Christian group in a rural province. Feeling a sense of obligation to Tetsuya, however, she contacts him at his school just before her departure.

He convinces her to stay, and they become lovers, living together in a hideaway.

Their life quickly deteriorates. Tokiko vows that whatever happens between her and Tetsuya, she will do all she can to keep Sayoko away from him. In spite of this attitude, Tetsuya feels pity for her, and he becomes desperate to find a way to leave with Sayoko without placing Tokiko in a hopeless position. A solution seems to present itself when he is unexpectedly offered a job teaching in China. He accepts the position, but before he can flee, his hideaway is discovered. The leaders of the Christian group that Sayoko had originally planned to join take her away, and Tetsuya is unable to find her. Psychologically broken, he becomes an alcoholic and eventually disappears in China. The Ono house is ruined, and Tokiko and her mother are forced to return to their ancestral home in the countryside. Sayoko reportedly becomes a nurse on a hospital ship. The only figure in the book who ends up successful in material terms is Hamura.

The main characters in this story are unable to achieve reconciliation because they each believe utterly in their own versions of the truth. Even though Tetsuya tries to understand events from the viewpoint of Tokiko or Hamura on a number of occasions, he never doubts that he is justified in his attempt to get away from his family burdens and achieve personal happiness. Throughout the novel, there is an implied criticism of the inflexibility and narrow absolutism not only of the family system but also of the actions of the characters, and this criticism is the product of an intellectual position that refused to acknowledge the possibility of a single narrative version of the truth. This skepticism affects the structure of the novel in two ways. First, the perspective of the story is constantly shifting. Second, Futabatei refuses to utilize heroic action as a way to achieve some sort of resolution to the problem.

In *Sono omokage,* Futabatei makes more complete use of the technique he developed as he grappled with the difficulty of writing *Ukigumo.* For much of the novel, the authorial voice is greatly diminished. Apart from the opening description of Tetsuya and Hamura and the closing *ubi sunt* passage, both of which show vestigial traces of *gesaku,* a separate narrative voice rarely intrudes directly. Of course a narrator relates information throughout to provide context for characters' remarks or thoughts, and these often determine the interpretation of events, as in the following scene, which takes place after the argument between Tokiko and Sayoko:

Takiko came in quickly. As soon as she sat down she said, "What do you think you're doing? You've made a terrible mess of things." No matter what excuses Sayoko made, Takiko would not listen to her. She scolded and complained over and over, and asked her, "Now that you've done this, what do you plan to do about it?" Sayoko thought enviously, "Of course, mother, you believe what Tokiko says, but you never listen to me." But then she felt as if she did not care anymore. "I'll go to Chiba," she said. "Mrs. Katsumi said that she'd look after me, so I'll become a Bible Woman. That's like a nun who reads sutras." She explained herself in simple terms so the old woman would comprehend. (*FSZ*-C 1:309)

The narrator's presence is apparent here at those points where the reader is let in on Sayoko's thoughts and the reason for Sayoko's explanation of "Bible Woman" is given. But the perspective is a privileged one that makes Sayoko a sympathetic figure. The narrator is given a smaller role than in *Ukigumo* and rarely confronts the reader directly.

Unlike the experiments of the naturalists, Futabatei does not try to create the pretense of an unmediated narrative. The characters view themselves and each other in very different ways, and because there is no single objective account of the events, the credibility of the text shifts according to whose perspective is being presented. The relative nature of narrative truth is illustrated by the use of a number of techniques. One method is to undercut established expectations in the reader. A series of scenes involving Tetsuya and his wife provides an example of this. The first scene takes place shortly after Sayoko has been sent to the Shibuya household. Tokiko comes to Tetsuya and asks him to increase her household allowance so that she may hire a maid to take over the duties that Sayoko had been performing. Since it is clear that Sayoko was doing duties that for the most part should have been Tokiko's responsibility and since it is also clear that Tokiko squanders some of the household budget on frivolities like the theater, the sympathy of the novel here moves toward Tetsuya and Sayoko. After they become lovers, however, there occurs another scene between Tetsuya and Tokiko that produces a different interpretation of Tokiko's motives. Although Tokiko has many faults, the narrative presents a number of reasons for her behavior. She is an attractive woman who cannot win the affection of a man who is described as slightly seedy and dirty. At one point, she recalls a night years before when Hamura and Tetsuya came home drunk, and Hamura made advances to her. Although she feigns embarrassment over the memory, it is obvious that it is a fond one for her because it proves she was once attractive to men. Now, after eight years of marriage, she remains childless, sleeping away from her husband most nights. Tetsuya's personality has darkened the atmosphere of a household that was once bright and lively. His failure to live up to his early promise has stifled the family. Thus, even though she may have driven her husband and sister together, Tokiko's characterization, and her role in the plot, is determined by more than just her own flaws as a wife. Her jealous fears prove justified, and though she is aware of her faults, she cannot help what she is. Her complaints gain credibility, and she becomes a figure to be pitied.

Soon after Sayoko leaves the house, Tokiko suspects that she and Tetsuya are living together. One night, when Tetsuya returns late, she breaks down in front of him and begs him to leave Sayoko. She admits that her jealousy drove her to hate her sister but tries to make Tetsuya see that their unhappiness is not all her doing. Her words strike home:

> Even though he hated the woman who was speaking, tonight, unlike all those other times, he was touched. After all, they had lived together for eight years, and she had not always been repulsive to him. Especially when he thought back to the days when they were first married, he could not believe that they were the same couple. Tokiko had always been self-centered, but now she did not look that way, and it was probably not an idle statement when she claimed that he was her sole means of support. When he thought of how pathetic she would be if he deserted her, he was very moved. The figure of Tokiko, who had forgotten her pride and thrown herself down before him, would have touched even the most determined heart. He thought that maybe she was right, and that he was cruel for thinking of walking out on her. He was prepared to forget all his grievances and accept the blame. He felt like telling her so. (*FSZ-C* 1:352)

But Tetsuya hesitates, and his chance to speak up is lost. In fact, he has no precedent—no emotional language, in effect—to guide him in properly responding to his wife. Tokiko interprets his silence as proof of his cruelty. She makes her threat to keep him from Sayoko, and any hope for reconciliation is gone. Yet from Tetsuya's perspective, the narrative has provided a view of Tokiko that undercuts what had previously been established about her and shifts the blame back toward her husband.

A third scene that further undercuts what had been established previously takes place near the end of the novel, after Sayoko has been taken away from Tetsuya. Tetsuya, who cannot back out of his job commitment, must go to China by himself. Tokiko wants to talk with him and try to work out their problems, but in the rush of preparations she never has the chance. To make matters worse, Tetsuya has begun to drink heavily, usually coming home late to fall asleep in a drunken stupor. The day before he is scheduled to leave, Tokiko asks him to come home early from a farewell party he will attend with his university colleagues. Again he returns late and very drunk. She pleads with him to stay awake and listen to her. She knows he cannot forget Sayoko and so tells him that he should divorce her and take Sayoko with him to China. He cannot respond to her sacrifice, however, because he has fallen asleep. Her weeping wakes him, and in a fit of remorse he too breaks down and cries. He blames himself for not having the courage to kill himself with Sayoko and promises Tokiko that he will come back from China a different man. His honesty consoles her, even though it does nothing to resolve their problems. In portraying the sorrow of this unfortunate couple, the narrative has suddenly suspended judgment on them. It has moved beyond the causes of events to their emotional consequences; it has moved from the singular truths of the multileveled accounts of events to create the illusion of a more complex, affective notion of truth.

The text not only undercuts the expectations it creates but also calls into question at certain points the reliability of the perspectives through which the story is related. At moments of stress, the characters mistake the appearances of things around them, revealing their own selfish desires or fears. When Sayoko leaves the Ono house for the last time, she is in a state of emotional turmoil. She wonders if she should tell her brother-in-law what has happened, and on the way to the station she mistakes a total stranger for Tetsuya. This mistake shows the extent of her preoccupation. Up to that point, it is not clear if she feels anything akin to love for Tetsuya, and her mistake does not by itself prove that she does. Nonetheless, it creates a doubt, and when she then decides to call Tetsuya and tell him she is leaving, she creates the opportunity for their affair to begin. That she should make the mistake in a moment of crisis throws a very different light on the protestations of innocence that she had made to her sister a few hours earlier.

A similar kind of confusion occurs near the end of the novel when Tetsuya is leaving with the other teachers for China. His family and friends come to see him off, but his behavior is cold and tense. He confides in Hamura that he thinks he saw Sayoko at the station, but his friend tells him that it could not have been she, implying that he knows her whereabouts. Recognizing his blunder, Hamura tries to cover up, but his actions only heighten Tetsuya's suspicion. After the train has left, Tokiko tells Hamura that she too thinks she saw Sayoko, who is supposed to be in Nagoya, and when she learns that Tetsuya also claimed to have seen her, she is convinced that it was indeed her sister. Hamura remarks that it sounds like a parting scene in a love story and insists that Tokiko's jealousy made her imagine she saw her rival. Tokiko retorts that she is no longer jealous, but neither her remarks nor Hamura's rationalization determine for us whether Sayoko was actually at the station. The narrative remains inconclusive, illustrating how dependent its descriptions are on the subjective and not wholly reliable viewpoints of the characters.

The unreliability of the voices that relate the story is vital to the design of *Sono omokage*. Because the text never gives a clear-cut reason for believing one character's story over another, the fundamental contradictions are beyond resolution in narrative terms. The story of Sayoko illustrates this dilemma. For the most part, she is depicted favorably, and there is little doubt that she does not deserve the treatment she receives. Yet the pathetic quality of her life story and her apparent devotion and innocence make her attractive to Tetsuya, and there are a number of instances when she tries to use that attraction to her advantage: for example, to persuade Tetsuya not to send her to the Shibuya household and to enlist his help when she leaves the family. It cannot be said that she has no ulterior motives. Once she becomes Tetsuya's lover, however, she suffers from a terrible sense of guilt. She is not being hypocritical when she expresses concern for her sister. No matter how badly she was treated by Tokiko, Sayoko's Christian principles cause her to feel a strong sense of remorse, and her pity for Tokiko is one way she can express her beliefs. She cannot relinquish her moral values, for they have been her means of survival. Tetsuya does not understand her beliefs, but he has been attracted to her in part because of them. Her moral values, her Christian ideals, which from Sayoko's standpoint should be above reproach, are responsible in part for her adulterous affair. This literary representation of the contradictions in human relationships that give rise to suffering is yet another indication of a profound skepticism about the absolute nature of any values.

Futabatei's skepticism is also evident in his refusal to use heroic action to resolve his plot. The realistic mode he developed in *Ukigumo* involved more than moving away from the reliance on stock figures and improbable action. If fiction was to reflect or record the realities of modern society, then the means by which the characters try to overcome their difficulties had to involve commonplace actions. For example, in Tokugawa drama and fiction, the device of double suicide was frequently used to resolve the otherwise irreconcilable conflict between the desires of the individual and the dictates of social behavior. In choosing to die, the lovers in Tokugawa literature opt for a difficult, heroic course of action. The literary convention of double suicide reflected a real contradiction in society, where individual rights were subordinated to social obligations; it also tacitly acknowledged the primacy of those obligations. If in a modernizing society a critique of older social customs was to have any force, then the actions taken in the past to overcome the conflicts caused by those customs had to be rejected. To the extent that literary conventions reflect the nature of social conflicts, heroic action had to be redefined. It was his failure to do so in his first novel that left Futabatei dissatisfied with the work.

The conflicts in *Ukigumo* have the potential for either a comic or a tragic resolution, but in his effort to stress the realism of the work, Futabatei realizes neither of these potential resolutions fully. In particular, the decision not to be tragic, not to make use of heroic action, suggests that he could not find a notion of heroism acceptable for a new literature. In fact, the concern with the impossibility of heroism becomes one of the major themes in *Sono omokage,* and it naturally centers around the alienation of Tetsuya. He is described through the reported comments of his students as a dry and boring lecturer who is nonetheless straightforward and dutiful. He is later described by the narrator as a man without any psychological support. Hamura teases him for his rigid principles, especially his squeamishness about sending Sayoko to work for Shibuya, and says that his ideals have the purity of old books. The cumulative effect of these comments is to create a portrait of a mediocrity: a man for whom the promise of youth has not been fulfilled. He has learned to tolerate this state of affairs, but he is just as frustrated as his wife. When Sayoko treats him kindly, he is at once attracted to her, but he tries to hide his love behind a facade of reasonable concern over the treatment she has received and justifies his actions as the natural result of his outrage. The vestiges of his promising past, the rationalizations of his feelings toward his wife, his idolization of Sayoko, the ideals he holds up for himself, and finally the alcoholic, haunted shadow of a man that he becomes together point to the lack of credibility of Tetsuya and indeed of the narrative as well, suggested by the word *omokage,* the insubstantial, shadowy figure of the title.

Unlike Bunzō, however, Tetsuya is not totally passive. He takes a tentative step toward heroic action by consummating his love for Sayoko. Perhaps because of her principles, Sayoko is more direct in her calculations. When she realizes that her love for Tetsuya has put her in an impossible position and that she must either destroy Tokiko by staying with Tetsuya or destroy Tetsuya by leaving him, she truly displays the purity of old books—the purity of Ukifune's renunciation or of the choice of suicide made by the courtesan Koharu in Chikamatsu's *Amijima shinjū*—by suggesting that the only way out is death. In a scene that is the turning point in the novel, Tetsuya at once shrinks from the prospect. He understands her reasons for wanting to die, and he feels great pity for her.

> Even so, he could not bring himself to die with her. There are people in the world who dismiss all love suicides as foolish. Many of these people are simply superficial types who could never kill themselves. They are the clever crowd who think that love is a foolish infatuation and that anyone who died for it must also be foolish. Thus they mock love suicide, and are unable to do it. But because Tetsuya was not one of this clever crowd, he neither completely approved nor disapproved. There is no person who does not cherish life, and so when someone takes the drastic step of suicide for love, there must have been unbearable circumstances beyond the comprehension of a casual observer. Whenever he heard about a double suicide, he thought how sad it was. Thus, because he viewed things from an intellectual standpoint, he felt no disdain for Sayoko. If you looked at their present situation according to moral ideas, or if you thought about its advantages and disadvantages, then it was best that they should separate. But if they could not bring themselves to separate, then Sayoko's attitude, which ignored morality and the calculation of profit and loss, was admirably heroic. When he thought about it this way, he had to conclude that he was insincere and had neither her honesty nor her passion. He felt somehow ashamed and could not help being stirred by the words of Sayoko, who had thought so deeply about it. Yet, for all that, he could not bring himself to die. He thought that perhaps the clever crowd was right after all and that it was foolish to die. (*FSZ-C* 1:372)

Tetsuya admires the ideal of death as a solution, but he cannot bring himself to perform the actual deed. His "intellectual" position only further alienates him by destroying the possibility of resolving his crisis. It also denies the narrative a traditional resolution of the plot, for tragedy is not possible in a work that is so self-conscious about that possibility. However, unlike *Ukigumo,* the story of Tetsuya finds an original variation on the love-suicide narrative. Although he turns his back on the tragic, heroic action of death, Tetsuya's life, and the lives of those around him, are destroyed. His fate is determined by his own weaknesses, and his mediocrity prevents him, and the novel, from attaining traditional heroic proportions. This modern tragedy, in which the characters are not simply defeated but also alienated, denied the possibility of heroic defeat because of the self-awareness of their situations, is reflected in the structure of the narrative. Nothing is resolved in an absolute way, and the characters are left adrift. There is no tragic apotheosis, but a final, ironic account of how each of the characters fared.

Sono omokage is more than a polished effort. It is perhaps the first work of its era to explore fully the ambivalent nature of tragedy in an age preoccupied with the modern, and it is also the first truly sophisticated treatment of the central dilemma that confronted Meiji writers: how to reconcile the formal necessities of literature with contemporary ideals and principles. Futabatei's skepticism led him to develop a narrative mode through which he created antiheroic elaborations on traditional characters and situations. It was one thing to try to achieve realism, but quite another if in the attempt the rhetorical qualities that gave value to the novel as an art form were lost. The striking originality of *Sono omokage* is the result of the way in which the dilemma of its main characters reflects the formal dilemma of the narrative. If you cannot know the truth of any narrative, then is serious narrative really a possibility? *Sono omokage* does not resolve that dilemma. Futabatei was well aware that the question of the possibility of a new literature had not been laid to rest, and his next novel, *Heibon,* further explores that problem.

◆

chapter seven
Like the Slobber of
a Cow: A Mediocre
Literary Life

Heibon, Futabatei's final novel, was published serially in the *Asahi shinbun* from October to December 1907. It added to his critical reputation[1] and helped him return to a position of some prominence within the *bundan*. But for a number of reasons he viewed the attention he was receiving as a mixed blessing. He had garnered acclaim early in his career, but he had not handled it well. More importantly, he had reemerged at a time of important developments in Meiji literature. The rise of the naturalist movement in particular had created a lively atmosphere in which the purpose and nature of literature were being reconsidered. The terms and assumptions of literary discourse diverged from those that had guided Futabatei in his youth, and the issues he had addressed in *Sono omokage* brought him to a reconsideration of the value of literature. It was a cautious man who faced the reading public in 1907.

The uncertainty that Futabatei felt toward his profession had been present at an early age, and the sometimes-unhappy course his life had taken after *Ukigumo* contributed to that feeling. This ambivalence was more than a matter of personal disappointment; it reflected a critical view that placed him at odds with the notion that literature could arrive at factual knowledge through careful, so-called scientific observations of life. He had struggled with the problem of realism and had concluded that the effort to use fiction to achieve serious aims, especially those set out by the naturalists, was misguided. The structure of *Sono omokage* reflects that conclusion, which owes a great deal to the views of *gesakusha* whose bantering statements of contempt for the frivolousness of their own writing arose from an awareness of the fictionality of narrative.[2] By the time Futabatei returned to fiction writing after his years of silence, he was no longer able to believe in any universal manifesto for literature. Less than a year before his death, he summed up his beliefs as follows:

> People talk about "life," but what in the world is that? Is it not just a mere notion? I really want to question our modern group of writers about this "life" that they so often say they must touch on. When we read works we distinguish between those that somehow move us and those that miss the mark. Yet would we not be a little hasty to make our standard whether they touch on life or not? Is there not a large gap between the questions of whether they arouse a strong reaction and whether they touch on life? I feel strongly that there is. (*FSZ-C* 4:255)

Other writers, particularly the naturalists, were keenly aware of Futabatei's ambivalent attitude because it challenged their own work. Both Tōson and Tayama Katai felt the need to answer this challenge. In their memorial essays of 1909, they make prominent mention of his skepticism. Although Futabatei was only slightly older than these men, they saw him as belonging to another literary generation, and Katai even asserted that the works of Futabatei were the true foundation of modern literature in Japan. However, neither he nor Tōson believed that Futabatei was being serious when he questioned the truthfulness of literature. Katai acknowledges Futabatei's statement that his dislike of fiction stemmed from its inability to portray true feeling but then points to the rhetorical skill of Futabatei's writing as a refutation of that dislike.[3] Tōson concurs, writing that "while ridiculing the absurdity of participating in literature, Futabatei wrote works over which he exerted the utmost care and effort. *Heibon* is the sad memento of a spirit that continued to be destroyed."[4]

These comments reveal the narrow theoretical approach taken by these men, two of the most influential of the naturalists. Because of their emphasis on sincerity in literature, through which they believed they could transcend the rhetorical restraints of fiction and reveal their true thoughts and feelings, accepting any doubts about the matter would have completely undermined their own critical values. Therefore they sought to question the sincerity of Futabatei. They also reveal a sensitivity to the ambivalent attitude Futabatei brought to his work. He could not overcome his doubts about the fundamental nature of literature, and yet he understood the artistic potential of fictional narrative as well as any writer of his generation.

The circumstances leading to the composition of *Heibon* suggest that the novel was an attempt to clarify the reasons for this ambivalent attitude. After *Sono omokage* was finished, Futabatei agreed to take on a translation as his next project. He was not especially eager to do another translation, and this decision was made primarily for financial reasons. He may also have been professionally envious of the success that his fellow writer-in-residence at the newspaper, Natsume Sōseki, was enjoying with *Gubijinsō* (Red poppy, 1907). In any case, he began work on a new novel.

Once he had started, further incentive was provided by two novellas that he read during the period of composition: *Futon*, by Katai, and *The Kreutzer Sonata*, by Tolstoy. *Futon* was both a popular sensation and the center of critical discussion. Though written as a third-person narrative, the novella was considered daring and courageous for purportedly representing the real-life experiences and feelings of the author. For Futabatei, the book presented a challenge, because it used an implied confessional mode as a means of achieving credibility; that is, the power of *Futon* rested not on the merits of its rhetoric but on the extrinsic knowledge that the story supposedly revealed secrets of the author's life. The rhetorical power of a confession lies at least in part in the assumption that the narrator must be telling the truth because he is exposing things he would not want others to know under normal circumstances.

The most compelling evidence of *Futon*'s influence is found in the extensive changes Futabatei made to the early draft of *Heibon*. The first part written was the section dealing with the boyhood of the narrator, centering on the boy's attachment to his pet dog, a story based on Futabatei's remembrance of a favorite dog of his own (his working titles for the early version of the novel were *Pochi*, the name of the dog, and *Hatsukoi*—First love). Futabatei changed his original third-person narrative voice to the first person after reading *Futon*, suggesting that he was attempting to emphasize the confessional aspects of his story.[5] Of course *Heibon* is not intended to be taken for a confessional novel in the sense that Katai had in mind, and certainly the narrative voices of the two works are strikingly different. But Futabatei was willing to experiment in that mode because of the claim that its immediacy lessened the distance between fiction and reality and thus provided a way to create a truthful narrative. In *Heibon,* he sought to expose the rhetorical, formal nature of the confession.

The title *Heibon* is one indication of the confessional approach taken in the novel. It suggests a kind of self-parody that calls attention to the inherent artificiality of the first-person narrative. It also recalls the mediocrity of the characters in his earlier works, as if to point out that modern literature can no longer deal in absolutes such as heroic action. The self-conscious nature of the title undermines the immediacy of the confessional form, for it indicates that there is nothing of interest to confess and the work is an empty, formal exercise. As Oketani Hideaki has put it, "What Futabatei attempted in *Heibon* was a confession that focused on a fundamental misgiving about and a denial of literature, as if to throw cold water on Katai's faith in art, a faith that, whatever else it doubted, could not doubt literature."[6]

The parodic use of first-person narrative is a feature that sharply distinguishes *Heibon* from naturalist literature, and as the comments of Katai and Tōson make clear, the importance of this technique to Futabatei was not overlooked by his contemporaries. He was not above taking advantage of the narrative possibilities of the confessional mode, and he was able to achieve an intimacy in the tone of the narrative that draws the reader at once to the narrator. He convincingly adapted a naturalist mode without being able to believe that he was conveying any truth in his narrative. The opening lines are typical:

> This year I turned thirty-nine. Since the average life span is fifty, I don't think I'll be crawling into a hole any time soon. But however far away the future may seem, it arrives very quickly. As it passes by, in fact, it seems to come too quickly. While we are still saying "not yet, not yet," before we know it our time in this world is up, and the moment of farewell arrives. When that moment comes, no matter how much we may struggle and squirm, it is to no avail. If we are to resign ourselves to our fate, the time to do so is now.
>
> Even though I am not ready to die, I feel I have grown old. There are those who will say that thirty-nine is a bit early to consider oneself old, but it is best that my attitude be older than my years. It is safe that way.
>
> I do not know why it is that I have come to feel aged like this. It is not necessarily the fault of hardship. Everyone has experienced as much suffering as I. And yet there are some people who are always happy and not at all defeated by their troubles. There are also some who have the temperament

of a monk. They never lose their youthful spirits, as if all their difficulties were superficial and did not penetrate to their hearts. Still, generally speaking, all of us succumb to hardship; we grow older than our years; we grow cowardly and fully domesticated; and on our way home from the office we like to come back dangling some salmon wrapped in a couple of pieces of bamboo bark. That's normal. At least I comfort myself thinking that it is. (*FSZ*-C 1:417–18)

The credibility of this opening depends to a great extent on the familiarity of the narrating voice, and that familiarity is established in several ways: (1) the language, while not radically different from the language in the later sections of *Ukigumo,* is in an accessible colloquial style that echoes what had become the stylistic norm (an irony not lost on Futabatei); (2) the subject, the ephemerality of human life, is a traditional theme in Japanese literature; and (3) by the self-questioning tone of the passage, the narrator tries both to draw the reader into an acceptance of his concerns and experience and to cover the artifice of his narrative.

The narrator does not try to disguise his fictionality for too long, however, and he soon admits the formal quality of his utterance. The self-consciousness reflected in the title appears over and over in the novel. In chapter 2, even as the narrator begins to tell us about his personal background, he decides right in front of us the subject and mode of his narrative:

> The truth is, although it is an extremely private story, my present circumstances are such that I must count myself among that number of people known as low-salaried clerks. But in the old days I was a man of letters known a little in certain circles by such and such a pseudonym. Indeed, even now I have old acquaintances in the literary world, and if I were to swallow my pride and go sniveling to them, there are a few who would really put themselves out for me, sending off manuscripts to some publisher or other and making something out of them. If I were to do that, then the end of this year would probably be better than last. And it would all be for the sake of my dear wife and children. In any case, let me try to write.
>
> Well now, a title . . . "What should I do for a title? These matters have always been damned hard for me to decide" . . . And so, thinking aloud like this for a moment, I suddenly slap my knee. *Mediocrity!* That's the title. When a mediocre person writes about his mediocre half-life with his mediocre pen, that title's a natural.
>
> Now for the style of writing, although that is not something you can really plan out. I hear that of late it has become the rage to write out all manner of trivial things experienced by the author, just as they are without adding

Like the Slobber of a Cow

any artifice, like a cow dribbling slobber. That style is called naturalism, or something of the sort. In any case good things are always popular, so that's for me.

So let's see. My title is *Mediocrity*, and my style of writing will be as natural as the slobber of a cow. (*FSZ-C* 1:420)

Futabatei is poking fun at the sort of automatic writing he associated with his own efforts at realism. His attack is less on a particular school of writing than on an approach he has concluded is fundamentally wrong. As I noted in chapter 5, Shimizu Shigeru has suggested that Futabatei seems never to have been able to get beyond the *gesakusha*'s view of their own fiction, which he extended to literature generally. This skeptical attitude is apparent at those points in the novel (including the passage just cited) where the narrator intrudes on the story in a way that undermines the sincerity of the confessional style. At the end of the book, in fact, there is a sudden and unexpected intrusion when the text is abruptly broken off, and we get a new narrator, pretending to speak in the voice of the real author, who supposedly discovered the manuscript of the novel:

> Futabatei will speak now. I obtained this manuscript while shopping for some books one evening, but the ending was torn out and lost. I know it is a bit like having the telephone cut off while you are in the middle of a conversation, but I am afraid it cannot be helped. (*FSZ-C* 1:533)

The ending of *Heibon* has been criticized for taking the easy way out and for being emotionally unsatisfying. But it is comprehensible within the context of Futabatei's skeptical view of literary art, and it may be said that, at least in intellectual terms, it is the most appropriate conclusion. The text has been made fragmentary and open-ended, pointing to a central aspect of both a literary life and literary form. In any case, the effect of this type of intrusion is to introduce a strong sense of ambivalence into the narrative. Nakamura Mitsuo has observed this ambivalence, though he describes the narrative voice in different terms, and notes that it may prove troublesome for some readers. "*Heibon*, of his three novels, is the one in which we feel closest to the author's psyche, and to that extent we best understand the propensities of his heart. The reader who becomes intimate with his personality gets the impression that he is listening to a conversation in which the author is letting his hair down. Yet there are perhaps people who, seeing a frivolous pose in the clumsy gestures of diffidence, are repelled by that."[7]

Whereas the impact of *Futon* on *Heibon* is seen mainly in its narrative voice, the influence of Tolstoy's work shows most in the ideological underpinnings of the novel. *The Kreutzer Sonata* forced Futabatei to take up again the question of the possibility of literature as a vehicle for expressing moral ideals. His reaction to *The Kreutzer Sonata* suggests that he gained not so much a new direction for his ideas as a confirmation of previously held beliefs. Even so, the conviction that buttressed Tolstoy's idealism was a serious challenge to his skepticism, and to confront that challenge honestly, it was vital that he reconsider the notion of idealism. In chapter 40, the narrator discusses Tolstoy's philosophy.

> Tolstoy is said to be the philosopher of the North. And what kind of things does this philosopher say? In the epilogue to *The Kreutzer Sonata* he writes that ideals that can be completely realized are not true ideals. If they cannot be realized then truly they are ideals. To be free of sin is the ideal of Christianity. Thus it is inevitable that it cannot be realized. Saying that Christians must pursue this ideal to the end of their lives, he exhorts the husbands and wives of the world to live as much as possible like brothers and sisters.
>   What was that? I don't get it at all. If pursuing perfection is impossible, then must we not die an agonizing death? (*FSZ*-C 1:492–93)

The narrator challenges the notion that an ideal must be unattainable on the grounds that the denial of self implicit in Tolstoy's vision would undermine the very formulation of an ideal, let alone its realization.

Heibon is not a polemical attack on Tolstoy's notion of idealism, although Futabatei did not abandon his skeptical outlook. The novel is an examination of the possibility of maintaining ideals in the face of the disappointments of life. The confessional mode is used as a means of examining idealism while maintaining a skeptical frame of mind. That Futabatei was uncomfortable with the contrivance of the confessional pose does not, I think, alter the seriousness of his purpose in undertaking to write. Addressing the broad theme of the ideal of human love, the novel consists of three main stories, each dealing with a love relationship of importance to the narrator, whose emotional relationships are shaped by his youthful commitment to literature. These stories involve his grandmother, his dog, and his father, respectively, and each exemplifies a different kind of love. The novel takes the form of a personal memoir that shows the growth in the consciousness of the narrator, Furuya Sekkō, as he comes to grips with the loss of these three figures and comes to understand the nature of love.

Like the Slobber of a Cow

The story of his relationship with his grandmother takes place when the narrator is very young. She is depicted as something of a tyrant who uses her position in the household to bully the narrator's mother. One way in which she exercises power is to pamper her grandson and protect him from the discipline of his parents. Furuya tells us that, although so young, he soon learned how to manipulate the situation to his advantage, and though he caused his mother many problems, he also secretly thought that his grandmother was foolish to be taken in by his childish calculations. When his grandmother died, Furuya says that he made a show of grief but did not really feel any loss until after the public mourning was completed. Only after he returned to the normal routine of the household did he feel the absence of the grandmother, and he speculates that what was taken to be a love relationship was instead nothing more than the selfish gratification he and his grandmother gained by using one another.

Love has no real meaning for Furuya the child except in its most narrow and grasping sense until he comes to a different understanding of it through caring for a pet dog. Of all his relationships, he tells us, it is his love for this animal that he regards as the highest type of love in his experience: a love valued because it was selfless and natural. And of all the incidents in the narrator's life, it is the death of the dog at the hands of a dogcatcher that prompts his deepest speculations on the ideal of love. After telling us how the dog was killed and how the episode affected him, Furuya abruptly interrupts his narrative.

> Today for some reason my head is heavy and I cannot write at all. So let me just jot down a few things.
>
> Love unifies all existence.
> Love must be experienced, not intellectualized.
> With love, life has meaning; without love, it has none.
> When you consider life from an objective view, you see that in the end it is an impossibility.
> Seeing a purpose in life or seeing none, both are mere intellectual exercises.
> When you gouge out the eye of the intellect and see no purpose, then you have the best experience.
> Ideals are fantasies.
> The mediocre man lives in experience; his whole life is an ideal.
> The poet-philosopher lives outside experience; an ideal is his whole life.
> The mediocre man is a miniature saint.
> The true meaning of life is not found in ideas; fortunate people can transcend ideas.

> For civilization in the twentieth century, people must strive to transcend thought.
>
> I could go on scribbling such things, but having just written them I'm bored. They are all lies. I would like to write just one thing that isn't a lie. For a long time after Pochi was killed, the faces of people all looked like dogcatchers. That alone is the truth. (FSZ-C 1:452–53)

The aphorisms here show a deep distrust of the intellect and a reliance on intuited experience as the basis of the narrator's skepticism. The inadequacy of rationalism thus appears to be a crucial argument at this point. However, the intuitive faculty is not being idealized either. These aphorisms carry more rhetorical than intellectual weight, and Futabatei uses them to good effect to make us feel the grief and resentment of the young man. The emptiness of intellect, which is the faculty that idealizes, is revealed in its contrast with innocent emotion. The effect of the passage is to confirm the importance of emotional attachments while showing that such attachments are never permanent and cannot become an ideal. This recalls what takes place in *Sono omokage* when that novel shifts near the end from the question of credibility to that of emotional consequences. The truth that each of the aphorisms tries to express gives way before the formal literary effect of the passage, which creates the illusion that the final statement about human brutality is an absolute truth.

We soon learn that this skeptical view of ideals extends to literature. Almost half of the novel deals with the education of the narrator. The turning point in his education comes when, as a middle-school student, Furuya obtains his parents' consent to go to Tokyo to study. It is arranged that he will stay and work in the home of his uncle while attending school. There his cousin, Yukie, arouses his first pangs of adolescent love, but she turns out to be a shallow young woman, and he is disappointed. He also grows indignant at the treatment he receives from his uncle, who uses him like a servant. As a result, he strikes out on his own, moving to a boardinghouse where he becomes friendly with some young men who are interested in literary pursuits. He affects a literary name, Sekkō, which is the Sinitic reading of the characters for Yukie, and he portrays his early literary endeavors as a youthful, pretentious kind of romanticism. Soon, however, Furuya comes to look on his involvement with literature as a corrupting influence. Looking back on that time of his life, he feels that he was seduced by the notion that literature provided a way to get at the truth, to describe reality. "The reality of literature embellishes human corruption with rhetorical flourishes and only makes spiritless people all the more spiritless. Is my view prejudiced? Am I looking only at the evil and not the good? And yet is not the reality of literature that evil wins over good? Isn't the reality of literature already more prejudiced in favor of evil than my view of it?" (*FSZ-C* 1:497).

Furuya tells us that he enjoyed some early critical successes with his writing but was hard-pressed to continue because he really did not have the imagination to create fiction. To compensate for his weakness, he decided to try writing according to the formula of some artistic doctrine, and the one he eventually settled on resembles naturalism. At this point, the narrative folds over on itself, with the narrator telling in a mock-naturalist style about himself as a young author, who writes as an insincere naturalist. Once he had adopted this literary creed, he concluded that reality depends on the subjectivity of the author and that he must therefore broaden his experience as much as possible. This leads him to a meaningless relationship with a woman named Oito, and it is in this section of the novel that Futabatei makes his sharpest attack against the methods of the naturalists. In his exposé of the pretense that underlies the honesty of the confessional mode, he foreshadows the critiques by Shiga Naoya and Akutagawa Ryūnosuke of Tōson's novels *Ie* (The family) and *Shinsei* (A new life), which deplored the hypocrisy of an author who absolved himself of ethical responsibility in real life by literally using the novel as a confessional.

When Furuya first embarks on his literary career, he is estranged from his parents, and the lifestyle he leads with Oito causes him to neglect them further. This becomes a serious matter when his father falls gravely ill. When his father dies, Furuya is shocked into the realization that he has been chasing after false values and ideals, and he comes to feel that this new understanding is somehow inextricably bound up with his views about literature.

> What literature is I haven't the faintest idea. If you listen to idle talk, then you may think of it as something that turns fantasy into life. Because the nature and humanity that appear in works of literature are reproduced through fantasy, even when the author directly touches humanity or nature and seems to achieve true feelings, they are not real. Even when you are able to picture them and draw near the truth, they are not real. They are shadows of reality and contain the elements of fantasy. Even in the sense that

you have touched them there is a diversion somewhere; that is, in works of literature there is always an element of playfulness. It is natural that you cannot achieve the sincerity that comes when you touch on the humanity and nature of real life. I have always been steeped in literary emotions only, and because I did not brace myself with sincere emotions, it was inevitable that a man like me should become lazy and sodden, that a good-for-nothing should become even worse. (*FSZ-C* 1:532)

These remarks, which come right before the abrupt ending of the novel, are a recapitulation of the doubts about literature that Futabatei struggled with for most of his life. He sees a strong link between idealism and literature in the formal, intellectual, and thus fictional qualities they share. He is skeptical of both because they lack reality, and it is on this point that he sees moral and literary questions overlapping.

But if that were all there was to his position, then surely he would not have bothered to write *Heibon* at all. Skepticism was central to his thought and to his writing, and it was predicated on a fundamental paradox. He defined that paradox as the irresolvable conflict between the ideal and the practical, which in turn he thought reflected a larger crisis within Meiji culture. He was ambivalent about the novel, recognizing its emotional power and artistic potential yet unable finally to find in it the kind of seriousness he thought was needed to create a new literature. He remained uncomfortable striking a literary pose, even if it allowed him to deal with serious issues. "*Heibon?* A complete failure, I'm afraid. It was not originally intended to be a satire, and yet, I suppose because I was the theme, it turned into a satire in the end. At first I grandly intended to set forth a theory from a straightforward viewpoint, but when I tried to write I fell into a bantering tone. Again and again I tried to become serious, but it did no good. In the end it turned out totally playful. In that sense it was an utter failure" (*FSZ-C* 4:246).

This self-critique cannot be taken at face value, for it is an extension of the attitude he reveals in his fictional confession. He suggests that *Heibon* is a failure because it is literary, because it depends on formal conventions that are neither truthful nor serious and prevent us from ever getting at the facts about ourselves, let alone the world around us. The title suggests a self-conscious stance that considers all modern literature vulgar and mediocre. If one can make literature out of the commonplace, then literature has the potential to level everything and make it mediocre. Futabatei's constant struggle with the literary conventions of the past in his effort to create a new literature becomes a near-obsession with the formal qualities of literature and their implications for the ability to comprehend or describe the world—that is, for the possibility of ever knowing truth. He never advocated a return to the playfulness of the *gesaku* tradition, but to the extent that that tradition was true to its conventions and accepted them for what they were, he preferred it to the position of the naturalists, which mistook the formal truth of literature for an absolute.

In June 1908 Futabatei left for St. Petersburg to work as a special correspondent for the *Asahi shinbun*. Shortly after he arrived, he suffered a nervous collapse and spent most of the rest of the year recuperating. The following February he was diagnosed as having either pneumonia or tuberculosis (probably the latter). He entered a hospital in March, but a high fever persisted. In April 1909 he was sent home. He went to London first, where he boarded a Japanese ship. The following month, while the ship was docked in Singapore, Futabatei died. The circumstances of this last year make it difficult to determine if *Heibon* was meant to have been his valedictory novel. Had he lived longer, it seems possible that he might have written more fiction. His own comparison of his late novels suggests that he was aware of his development as an artist and that he was still interested in experimenting with literary forms.

> At the time I wrote *Sono omokage*, the order I gave to myself was to create a living doll, and since I was trying to bring to life a realistic human being, I put a great deal of emphasis on nature and character. However, when I came to *Heibon* I was not concerned with things such as the character of a person. Not that it is not there, but character dropped to secondary importance for me, and I kept my eye on something else. That "something else" is the attitude people have toward life. Although I dislike trifling with words, I am referring to the attitude of a certain type of person, not of people in general, nor of a specific individual. That type of person is a writer. I mean by this the various senses of writer throughout human history and not necessarily a writer in the modern sense only. Therefore, in *Heibon* I look only at the attitude a writer holds toward life. Since I was not trying to create a realistic person, I have not done so. This is the difference in my views between the times I created *Sono omokage* and *Heibon*. (FSZ-C 4:251)

Sono omokage is one of the most formally complete works of realistic fiction produced in Meiji Japan. *Heibon* is one of the earliest narratives of the period to make the problem of literary truth a central concern.[8] In spite of their differences, however, these novels share the single, constant element in Futabatei's career: his profound skepticism about the possibility of creating a new literature or of expressing the literary self. This skepticism defines both the modern in his work and the nature of his influence on other writers. The issues he dealt with serve as a guide to the main preoccupations of Meiji literature.

part three

◆

Inner Horizons:
The Modern Narrative
Voice

As authors realized the ambiguity inherent in the project of creating a new cultural identity, a crisis arose in Meiji literary culture. Narrative experiments in perspective and voice during the period are consistently torn between the need to make a radical break with the past to establish a sense of a modern Japanese self and the desire to invoke the tradition, to make use of an already established and intelligible literary language, as a way of recovering continuity in the face of change. Cut off from their cultural past and marginalized by the Western norms used to define the modern, Meiji writers increasingly relied on subjective experience, the inner horizons of their private lives, as the constitutive element of their fiction. They viewed the objective, external horizons established by the tradition as no longer relevant, and their turn inward is reflected by the general tendency to try to blur the distinctions between the narrator, who was often a central figure in the story, and the implied and real-life author. This tendency, most obvious in certain works by the Japanese naturalists and in the development of what came to be termed the "I-novel" (*shishōsetsu*), created its own difficulties, for the emphasis placed on the authorial voice often brought with it feelings of isolation and alienation.

The emphasis on individual experience quite literally left Meiji authors to their own devices—a situation that created a dizzying sense of liberation, of unbounded possibilities. Writers were forced to look for objective validation of their particular experiences either by claiming to represent the only legitimate continuation of the tradition, as, for example, Masaoka Shiki tried to do with his efforts in *shaseibun* and the reform of poetic practice, or by looking elsewhere to discover larger truths, as in the depictions of nature in the works of men like Kunikida Doppo or Tokutomi Roka. Looking at the experiments of the 1890s, especially the romantic movement, it is tempting to conclude that Meiji literature followed, in a compressed fashion, a trajectory similar to that of literary developments in the West. And in certain respects, such a conclusion is justified. The heightened subjectivity of Meiji narratives exploded not only the language of the tradition but also the romantic notion of nature as the source of art and inspiration. As in the West, the turn inward was a reaction to the romantic conception of the process of artistic creation. The individual artist came to be viewed not as a conduit or medium with a special sensitivity to the beauty and significance of nature but as the source or locus of the aesthetic values that define modern art. But Meiji writers were more completely alienated, more self-conscious about their inability to be the source of modern values than were their Western counterparts, who were cultural heroes to their compatriots. They were much more acutely troubled by the impossibility of being modern, and thus their search for an objective grounding for the experience of the individual artist led to a recurring and generally inconclusive tendency toward narrative experimentation and the fragmentation of the tradition.

Futabatei located the source of the dilemma of the modern in the contradictory impulses of a narrative voice that self-consciously exposed its own fictionality and thereby threatened to undermine the pretense of sincerity and seriousness that, it was believed, would distinguish modern literature from the tradition. Like many of his generation, he believed the Meiji period was the age of *bunmei kaika,* of civilization and enlightenment that triumphed over the stifling past, freeing individuals to redefine their relationship to their culture. At the same time, Futabatei was attracted to his native tradition and felt disinherited from it as a result of the search for a new, realistic narrative form. European and American cultural assumptions had radically altered the literary landscape. The old formal conventions by which the artist expressed his identity no longer served as adequate guides, yet the wholesale adoption of Western conventions was not simply impractical but impossible: it would have meant the annihilation of the Japanese cultural self. As many elements of Futabatei's work indicate, he needed the past in order to write because it counterbalanced the fact that the standards defining the modern were alien to him and to his culture. He instinctively backed away from the extreme discontinuity created by cultural modernization, but in doing so he had to face the fact that the language he relied on was as rhetorical and artificial as that of the late Tokugawa tradition. Futabatei's inability to resolve the irreconcilable conflict between the ideal and the practical led him as an artist to strike the pose of a skeptic.

Futabatei confronted the major problems that, in one form or another, plagued all Meiji writers. I have argued in the preceding chapters that he was a representative writer of his time; in this section, I shall broaden my examination by looking at the different responses to the dilemma of the modern taken by a number of important contemporaries of Futabatei. My selection of authors, which includes Shimazaki Tōson, Iwano Hōmei, Natsume Sōseki, Mori Ōgai, and Nagai Kafū, is not exhaustive, but it is representative. All these writers worked in forms in which the narrative voice either overtly controlled the narrative or was the protagonist. Although they achieved markedly different results, their efforts exemplify the radical literary experimentation of their age. More importantly, though each of these writers defined the dilemma of the modern according to different sets of critical terminology, they all did so in a way that resonates with the struggle Futabatei experienced in his efforts to reinterpret his tradition and create a new cultural identity through literature.

◆

chapter eight
The Dilemma of the
Modern and the
Autobiographical Confession

I argued that Futabatei's importance to his contemporaries was not only his influence in matters of narrative technique but also his presence as a symbol of the struggle to produce a modern literature. Futabatei's literary response to the dilemma was to embrace the fact that there was no resolution. His early efforts at realism ran into the problem that the formal necessities of fiction distorted the view of reality he wanted to present. This is reflected in the theme of alienation, which he first explores in *Ukigumo,* and to which he gives full expression in the story of Tetsuya in *Sono omokage.* Tetsuya, who is trapped in an unbearable present, is unable to recover the promise of his past and resolve the competing claims on his life. He ends up both physically cut off from his homeland and spiritually destroyed. Futabatei further explores the theme of alienation in his last novel, *Heibon,* but there he ties the issue directly to the question of the literary artist's life and suggests that creating a new literature will always end in alienation for the narrator. He remains skeptical of the power of art to provide form, or closure, to open-ended modern experience, and his skepticism is a direct response to the efforts of writers like Katai who saw in the arts a means of self-definition and redemption.

The Dilemma of the Modern

Futabatei cast his final work in the autobiographical, confessional mode of *Futon* in order to show that the form shared the fundamental problem of all narrative, which is that the conventionality of form undermines the truth, or reality, of the artistic vision. Although Futabatei doubted the efficacy of the form, his work is no less typical of the period for that conclusion. The autobiographical confession became increasingly important in late Meiji literature, indeed perhaps its central form, because it best expresses the impulse for self-assertion and liberation while at the same time conveying the alienation of the authorial voice. Whether or not they agreed with Futabatei about the limits of the form, all the authors discussed in this section used it.

The autobiographical confession allows the author to create the illusion of a narrator who speaks directly and truthfully about himself to the reader, even in cases where the intent may be satirical or humorous. To the extent that the confessional narrative is an act of telling about a literary self, it is also an act of self-creation. Moreover, the confession is closely connected with the idea of sin, or crime. Confessing is an assertion of the self against ethical or social conventions. It is an act of individuation, of opening up, that, like the Fall, is a sin insofar as it disrupts authority, stasis, and repetition. In literary terms, it is a sin in which the fictionalizing self breaks with tradition to define his individuality and make narrative possible. The incidents narrated may be of the past, but the act of revelation is ongoing and always directly in front of the reader. The confession is a narrative of the present moment, and as such it is the ideal mode to represent the problems posed by modernization because it both defines and alienates the individual.

Hōjōki vividly presents this dilemma: while the necessities of the age and the desire to find salvation force the narrator to separate himself from the world, the act of separation/individuation is a hindrance to his redemption. Saikaku's *Kōshoku ichidai onna* is a fictitious autobiography that parodies the sentiments of the confessional mode, asserting instead the "religious" value of individual love and pleasure. Because that value is transitory, however, it too is beyond attainment; and by showing that the individual is left alienated by the very act that defines the self, the narrative, for all its subversive humor, ends by affirming conventional ideals.

Although the confessional mode was widely popular during the Meiji period, Ōgai's *Maihime* (The dancing girl, 1890) being perhaps the first important example, the naturalists made especially heavy use of this narrative technique. They were aware of the difficulties inherent in this choice, and the connection between the assertion of the self and the notion of sin is explicit in most major works of the school. *Hakai* (The broken commandment, 1906), by Shimazaki Tōson, although not an autobiographical piece, provides an early example of this awareness. The protagonist, Segawa Ushimatsu, is alienated by the knowledge of his true identity. He is a member of the outcast society, the *eta,* or *burakumin,* but he has promised his father that he will keep his identity secret. This promise not to tell of himself, not to narrate the truth about his identity, robs him of the language he needs to project a sense of himself, much as Bunzō was denied self-expression in *Ukigumo*. To make matters worse, Ushimatsu is constantly confronted with a model of such a language in the confessional writings of the character Inoko Rentarō, an *eta* who has disclosed his identity and who is devoted to the fight for equal rights for outcasts. Yet Inoko's language, his solution to the problem of self, is not available to Ushimatsu. At one point, on reading Inoko's work, he thinks,

> The circumstances surrounding the time Inoko confessed his background were recorded in detail in *Zange roku* (A confessional record). Ushimatsu was greatly moved. Soon, reading became too painful, and closing the book, he shut his eyes. Sympathy is a strange thing, and there are times when you cannot reconcile it with your ulterior motives. Further, Rentarō's work was the kind that made you think rather than the kind that made you read for interest. In the end, Ushimatsu read on, completely detached from what was written, concentrating only on his own life. (*STZ* 4:12)

Tōson's handling of the relationship between Inoko and Ushimatsu suggests that his purpose is less to plead for civil rights than to present an image of alienation. In this respect, the way in which Ushimatsu reads his mentor, especially his observation that Inoko's work was "the kind that made you think rather than the kind that made you read for interest," exemplifies the tension between the artistic spirit that seeks for self-expression and the reforming spirit that seeks to right a social wrong.[1]

When he at last confesses the truth about himself, Ushimatsu gains his individuality, although it is at the price of a more complete alienation. A wealthy outcast named Ōhinata, who has suffered a number of humiliations because of his background, has devised a plan to begin farming in Texas, and he invites Ushimatsu to join him and start his life over. This sudden intervention following the damaging confession is a rather clumsy deus ex machina, but, clumsy or not, the decision to leave is as much an exile as a chance for liberation, for the act of confession has totally separated Ushimatsu from the culture that had heretofore defined him. The novel ends with the image of Ushimatsu's sledges moving over the snow. This image is double-edged, for earlier in the story, immediately following his decision to confess, Ushimatsu felt that he had at last taken possession of the world of snow (*STZ* 4:291, 297). The sense of hope inspired by his new life is qualified by its association with a barren, wintry symbol of isolation and death.

The fundamental question posed by *Hakai*, its plot mechanism, is whether to tell, and the resolution of Ushimatsu's torment comes with his confession. The creation of a sense of individual identity is a purely narrative act that points to a key element of Tōson's conception of the self, a conception that, as a number of commentators have noted, contains elements of both the native tradition and Western ideas about the individual. For example, Janet Walker locates the source of self-expression in the contact of certain writers with Western notions, especially the "myth of individual freedom associated with the rise of the middle class." She goes on to locate a similar myth in the Tokugawa defense of the natural self, the instinctual man, which thinkers like Norinaga posed against neo-Confucian orthodoxy, and cites the influence of that ideology first in the *ninjōbon* of the late Tokugawa period and then in the confessional mode of Meiji literature, which, she argues, "was surely a continuation of the . . . *ninjōbon*'s interest in the aesthetic-emotional aspect of the individual."[2]

Edward Fowler takes issue with the notion that Tokugawa ideology somehow paved the way for the importation of Western ideas about the individual, noting that "modernity and selfhood are more properly characterized as historical processes emerging from a particular intellectual tradition than as commodities readily available for consumption, like so much technological hardware." He goes on to write that "modernity in the Japanese intellectual context takes on this paradoxical meaning: it is no more—and no less—than the institutionalized process by which Japanese continue to apply traditional (and specifically non-western) modes of thinking to contemporary social, economic, and political issues; selfhood, again paradoxically, is the state of separation from society ('premodern' or 'modern') that Japanese can attain, although not without certain material and psychological risks."[3] Similarities between Western and native ideologies may have made alien assumptions more readily comprehensible, but they neither constituted nor ensured a continuation of the Tokugawa view of the individual. However, Fowler's statement that modernity in Japan is nothing more than the application of traditional modes to contemporary issues is an overcorrection that in its own way implies a strong ideological continuity. Seeing how Meiji writers reread their native tradition requires an understanding of that tradition on its own terms, but those terms were unquestionably determined in the Meiji period by the process of reading the West.

While it is certainly misleading to see in Meiji ideas of the individual a mirror of Western concepts, to view the separation of the literary self through confession as something "peculiarly Japanese" is an exaggeration. Fowler defines this selfhood as "a nonparticipatory and nonconfrontational existence by which a Japanese, normally the most social of social animals, turns his back on society and loses himself in the aesthetic life and in nature."[4] Apart from the doubtful generalization about Japanese sociability, this rather pastoral characterization of Japanese selfhood minimizes the conflicts, sacrifice, and even self-extinction that are alternative expressions of self-identity. The sense of discontinuity and displacement that defines Meiji culture resulted from a shift from one dominant ideology to another, not from a specific ideology of the individual, either native or Western. These competing ideologies of course set the boundaries within which cultural identity developed in Meiji Japan, but the tension created by the contact of competing notions of selfhood, more than the particular notions themselves, was the crucial factor in determining the narrative strategies adopted by Tōson and his contemporaries.

With *Hakai*, Tōson broke important ground in the use of the narrative problem inherent in the confession: the tension between the need to expose the true identity of the self and the recognition of the danger of isolation. Still, it was a fictional account, and it did not bring the problem of confession to bear directly on the literary artist. Tōson's efforts with autobiographical material go back to his association with the literary journal *Bungakkai* and its founder Kitamura Tōkoku (1868–1894), the acknowledged leader of the romantic movement of the 1890s.[5] Tōson first made his reputation late in that decade as a lyrical poet who took himself as the primary subject of his work. A few years later, under the influence of *shaseibun*, he shifted his romantic inclinations toward prose sketches of nature, which he eventually published as *Chikumagawa no suketchi* (Sketches of the Chikuma river, 1912). Following his decision to write prose fiction and with the publication of *Hakai*, he turned to an even fuller examination of himself and his association with romanticism in the novelistic account of his youth, *Haru* (Spring, 1908). He then attempted to explore the conflicting ideas of the self fully through the autobiographical confession in *Ie* (The family, 1910). The novel was initially serialized in the *Yomiuri shinbun* with the concluding chapters appearing in the journal *Chūō kōron* the following year under the title *Gisei* (Sacrifices). Looking back at this period of his career in an essay titled "Mitsu no chōhen o kaita tōji no koto" (Circumstances at the time I wrote three novels), Tōson informs us that, "while I was writing *Hakai*, *Haru* had already sprouted within me. Then, while I was writing *Haru*, I conceived of writing *Ie*. However, by the time I finished *Ie* a fourth long work had yet to float up in my heart. That period was a lonely one for me" (*STZ* 22: 117). The sources of Tōson's loneliness appear to have been both the deaths in his family that occurred during this period of his life and the writer's block he suffered on completing *Ie*.

The paradoxical nature of the struggle of the individual to separate himself from society is suggested by the two titles of the novel, *Ie* and *Gisei*. All the characters are defined not in terms of their personal relationships but as members of a larger, impersonal social institution that blocks their individual aspirations. The sacrifices indicated by the alternative title are the human losses incurred either by subordinating oneself to that institution or by trying to break free from it. The design of the novel reflects this primary conflict. It is loosely organized; there are breaks in the narrative chronology, and the story is told for the most part in an anecdotal fashion through groupings of short scenes that do not always progress in a linear fashion. However, the account is given a center by the character of Sankichi, Tōson's alter ego, who relates three main stories: the decline of the Koizumi family, especially as related to the business failures of Minoru, Sankichi's oldest brother; the decline of the Hashimoto family, Sankichi's in-laws through his sister, Otane; and the establishment of Sankichi's own family.

Within each family, the individuals attempt to accommodate themselves to the institution or try to break free of it, and almost everyone is crushed as a result. Minoru, for example, is driven by an idealistic desire to restore the prestige and fortune of the Koizumi family, which had been lost as a direct result of the economic changes brought about by the Meiji Restoration. He is portrayed as trapped by social circumstances into pursuing business ventures doomed to failure by his personal limitations. Similarly, Koizumi Morihiko, Sankichi's second-oldest brother, has been compelled to set aside his aspirations in order to support his family by taking unfavorable positions that eventually leave him poverty-stricken

(*STZ* 9:159–162). Sankichi's oldest sister, Otane, is destroyed by a marriage system that has no concept of the rights of women. Her husband, Hashimoto Tatsuo, deserts her and physically destroys her by passing on the venereal disease he contracted from one of his many lovers. Another example of how the institution crushes the individual is provided by the pathetic figure of Sōzō, Sankichi's younger half-brother, born of an adulterous affair between their mother and a Buddhist priest. Throughout his life, Sōzō feels victimized by his birth; he fails at every school and job he attempts, and in asserting himself against his family he leads a life of dissipation that eventually destroys him. Indeed, for all of these characters, the destructive effects of the family institution on the happiness of the individual, either through social pressures or through hereditary factors, is a recurring theme.

Sankichi's determination to establish his own family is partly a reaction to the decline of his family fortunes and partly a romantic expression of independence. This struggle between the demands created by a socially displaced family and an idealistic vision of that family is carried on in the relationship of Sankichi and his wife, Oyuki. Because Sankichi has idealized the marriage institution, he is disappointed with the realities of married life, and his attitude creates instead an unloving and stiflingly conventional marriage. He sees himself and his wife as slaves to one another, and he resolves at one point to redefine their relationship not as husband and wife, but as older brother and younger sister (*STZ* 9:147–149, 176–177). Although it is a speculative point, the influence of Tolstoy's *The Kreutzer Sonata* seems apparent in Sankichi's attempt to save his marriage by redefining it in this idealistic manner. By the end of the novel, the couple nears some form of reconciliation, but the outcome of their efforts is left unstated.

Just as his relationship with Oyuki defines his attitude toward the Koizumi family, Sankichi's other important relationship, with his nephew, Shōta, ties the Hashimoto story to the larger narrative. Shōta and Sankichi are actually close in years, and this bond is made stronger by mutually shared aspirations. Their closeness is such that at one point Shōta refers to Sankichi and himself as lovers, indicating a spiritual affinity that from Sankichi's point of view is the ideal transcending the relationships created by social institutions (*STZ* 9:175). When Shōta dies without realizing a restoration of his house or achieving any degree of personal satisfaction or accomplishment, it is a major blow to Sankichi, who then vows to write the truth, both the good and the bad, about Shōta's life in order to achieve his ideal through his narrative.

The social struggle of the individual against an institution such as the family becomes the image for the narrative struggle, that is, the struggle to find a voice for self-expression. Because the similar problem of finding a voice drives the plot in *Hakai,* it is important to consider possible reasons for the shift from the fictionalized confession of the earlier novel to the more clearly autobiographical mode in *Ie.* First, Tōson shared with others of his generation an ambivalent attitude toward fiction, rooted in the general devaluation of Tokugawa fiction on the grounds of its uncritical embrace of rhetorical techniques for their own sake. Second, his ambivalence also grew from the concern with presenting the pose of a truthful narrative and thereby creating a serious literature. Such a concern is related closely to his ideas about projecting sincerity in his work. From the viewpoint of Tōson's aims, the move toward an autobiographical confessional mode was the natural culmination of a process that both addressed traditional literary practices and gave scope to romantic notions of the centrality of the literary self.

The impulse to focalize the narrative through an alter ego, which is marked in the works of Tōson and other naturalists by their almost exclusive reliance on the events of their own lives for the substance of their fiction, is not merely due to the influence of Western romanticism; it is in part a legacy of narrative conventions in the classical tradition. This fusion is most readily apparent in the idea of sincerity—the notion that personal utterance was closer to emotional reality—that permeates Tōson's novels.[6] This concept was not at all foreign to the Japanese tradition, in part because the confessional mode inherently assumes a pose of sincerity and in part because sincerity was seen, paradoxically, as a means of realizing the objectivity and lack of self-consciousness of nature (as evidenced, for example, in the studied casualness of Genji's aesthetic or in the attempt of Chōmei's narrator to achieve the indifference of nature). I do not mean to suggest that this native romanticism paved the way for Western ideology, any more than native concepts of the self made the importation of Western individualism possible. However, the existence of a native concept of sincerity, together with the influence of Western romanticism, provided the kinds of narrative resources that enabled the experiments with autobiographical confession. By using sincerity as his justification, Tōson was able to emphasize personal utterance and a strong emotional commitment to make his writing original.[7] His concern with sincerity was shared by other Meiji writers. Tayama Katai, in outlining the rise of naturalism, writes, "What was our expectation [aim] in mingling together? It was novelty and sincerity. In addition we desired to emulate modern foreign literature, especially continental literature. Further, we disliked the factionalism of the literary establishment, and we felt that we wanted to distance ourselves from it. So quite naturally we quietly came together. First, Kunikida wrote *Unmei,* then next Shimazaki wrote *Hakai,* and I, being the tardiest, wrote *Futon.*[8]

Placing Tōson within a romantic tradition requires some clarification of his ties with naturalism in Japan. It has become a commonplace of literary history to see Japanese naturalism as diverging sharply from its European counterpart, the implication sometimes being that this was a sign of how little writers in Japan understood what was going on in the West.[9] But though modern Japanese literature is characterized by the dramatic shift to autobiographical confession, the use of one's life as a literary source seems to be more an extension of European naturalist theory than an abandonment of it. The question of literary influence becomes extremely complex at this point, for the translation or importation of Western literature meant that there was a chronological compression of differing schools, with naturalism, realism, romanticism, and the art nouveau movement of the late nineteenth century all emerging in Japan at roughly the same time.

Such a compression revealed the affinities between these movements as much as their differences. Jay Rubin argues that

> Naturalism's single greatest contribution to the development of modern Japanese literature—and society—lay in its messiness. The very fact that it never was—and never has been—successfully defined; that no two of its writers (when they could be identified) ever fit neatly into any of its theories; that it represented no ideology; that "it" was actually many writers who took a variety of positions with regard to change and the status quo; all this is ample demonstration that "naturalism" was merely a convenient and misleading label for the beginning of the representation of "variousness, possibility, complexity, and difficulty" in Japanese literature.[10]

While I agree in the main with Rubin's description of naturalism as a school, I disagree with his characterization of the term itself as "a convenient and misleading label." Even if no two writers agreed on the meaning of the term, many individual authors had a clear and programmatic notion of what it represented. More importantly, Rubin's own description contradicts the implied notion that naturalism as a critical term is meaningless, for clearly he has identified it in terms that correspond to such basic assumptions of liberal democratic ideology as pluralism and individualism. However, it is not really necessary to give an all-encompassing definition of the term, for in its various manifestations it provided a point of reference for writers whose sense of displacement otherwise threatened to silence them. Its method was the pretense of a greater objectivity through detached, scientific observation, and though it held that the fate of the individual was determined by social and environmental factors, naturalist fiction nonetheless attempted to foster a fundamental respect for the individual's right to achieve autonomy and self-realization. According to this view, literature was an instrument for social change to achieve an essentially romantic vision of the individual.

Tōson's approach is best revealed in his insistence on close observation and personal experience to get at the truth.

> Though I speak of the struggles involved in writing, each work has its own difficult points. However, as an example, let me talk of the time when I wrote *Ie*. In that novel I wrote only of things that took place within the house, and writing from the vantage of the kitchen, of various rooms, and of the garden, I felt that I was building my work in that manner. As far as possible I did not write of things that took place outside, and even when I did write of outside things I used only those incidents that entered into the house. Although the work is very long, I hardly wrote at all of outside events. I wrote of the family activities that occurred in the old house in Kiso, but I gave no explanations concerning the Kiso district. I tried to write by limiting the scope of my expression to the conditions inside the house that could only be seen in that rural area, to the people who came there, and to the sound of the Kiso River, which could be heard inside the house. (*STZ* 22: 287)[11]

Tōson's rereading of his own novel, and the architectural metaphor he uses, in the manner of a latter-day Genji or Chōmei, suggests growth, development, and thus an open-ended view of the artistic self. The narrative voice he uses in *Ie* developed out of this view. The social displacement Tōson experienced led him to create a narrative edifice that emanated from his literary alter ego. By emphasizing the importance of the fictional self in this manner, Tōson appears to be unconcerned about the extreme subjectivity of his perspective, but the matter-of-factness with which he chronicles his life suggests that he also wanted to achieve an objective style.

In focusing the narrative on himself, Tōson greatly limits the range of his observations, but the major difference, as he saw it, between his approach and that of the European naturalists stemmed not so much from dissimilar ideas of the goals of narrative as from different concepts of knowledge. He even remarked that European naturalism was not possible in a country like Japan, where there was no background of science. In the essay "Kinō, ototoi" (Yesterday, the day before yesterday), he writes,

> Will our country finally never produce a writer like Balzac? There are people who ask why Japanese naturalism has not given birth to stronger works, but that which gave birth to the works of Balzac, which are like looking at a stone building of many layers, is not the power of literature alone. We must keep in mind that lurking in the background is the power of French science created by the bacterial research of Pasteur, or by the mathematics and astronomy of Poincaré. Perhaps we can say that many authors in Japan are impressionists by nature. That is both the strength and the weakness of us Japanese. (STZ 18:92)

This opinion is very similar to that expressed by Sōseki in his essay "Bungei to dōtoku" (The literary arts and ethics). I shall return to this essay in the next chapter, but it should be noted here that although Sōseki believed a scientific outlook was not native to Japan, unlike Tōson he did believe it was a part of the outlook of Meiji Japan. For Tōson, the subjective, emotional knowledge he gained by self-examination was valid because he could at least be certain of it himself. Reliance on intuited knowledge, taken together with the underlying rationalism of Tōson's method of observation, creates an ambivalence in his work that allowed him to justify its novelty as a Japanese variant on a European model.

Relying on autobiographical material provided a means for Tōson to achieve the illusion of sincerity, because the difficulties involved in the decision to confess are laid out for all to see. The authorial voice is depicted as choosing to alienate itself in order to express a subjective vision of the truth. The problem is that reducing that vision to narrative requires calculations and formal choices that undermine the illusion of sincerity and call into question the honesty with which the self is depicted. In Tōson's case, the inability to sustain an honest subjectivity eventually led to severe criticisms about his hypocrisy, especially in connection with *Shinsei* (A new life, 1918), a highly personal confession that exploded his scandalous affair with his niece as the affair was going on. Akutagawa Ryūnosuke wrote about *Shinsei* that "he had never encountered such a crafty hypocrite as the hero of *Shinsei*" (4:64). Tōson felt that Akutagawa had misinterpreted his purpose, and he wondered if others also saw *Shinsei* as an unnecessary work. He responded, "At the time I wrote with a troubled heart, but my intention was to drive a pickax into the extreme decadence of our age. If I could unearth our debauched hearts, my aim was to resurrect them from that living hell. It makes me feel forlorn that there will never come a day when I can get Akutagawa to reread my work" (*STZ* 22:62).

Because the autobiographical confession is based on real-life experience, the reader is forced by the pretense of the narrative to decide whether to judge the sincerity of the account according to its adherence to fact. Doing this, however, leads to a very narrow conception of truth. Knowing, for example, that the hypocritical way Sankichi treats his wife's aspirations for happiness while pursuing the poet Chiyo as his ideal love and that the sacrifice of his three daughters' lives for the sake of his art are incidents based on Tōson's own life may make the reader perceive the author to be sincere, but that perception is quickly undermined by the realization that the confession is an act of expiation and is therefore self-serving.

Perhaps the most irritating thing about an autobiographical confession is the way in which it flouts the distinction between ethical and artistic considerations. An author can literally get away with murder in a confession, for the form not only re-creates the crime but so separates the narrator from conventional standards of judgment that it serves as both punishment (the narrator's alienation) and absolution (the reward for his sincerity). The autobiographical confession attempts to forestall judgments about the narrator on either aesthetic or moral grounds. That Tōson exploited this aspect of the confession so thoroughly is damning evidence not only of his insensitivity but of his lack of imagination. Yoshida Sei'ichi takes a rather tactful approach to the question of Tōson's creativity, arguing that "when people discuss naturalism, they at once assume that it values the truthfulness of reality and furthermore that it depicts reality just as it is. However, that is not necessarily the case. Nor is it necessarily accurate to think of the claims of naturalism as standing on a primitive materialistic footing. Fundamentally, it has always stood atop the opposition between the objective that views and the subjective that is viewed, and it makes observation its main tool. What the naturalists were searching for was not 'creativity' but 'discovery.'"[12] Uno Kōji is more critical of Tōson's methods. In an essay on Tōson's later novel *Yoakemae* (Before the dawn, 1935), Uno concludes that Tōson's subjective view of the narrative is always dissatisfying and that even when Tōson touches directly on peasant life or townsman life, his lack of a sympathetic imagination prevents him from doing so with real understanding.[13]

If Tōson were an isolated figure in Meiji literature, it might be easy to dismiss his use of the confessional form as an aberration. Yet, despite his weaknesses as a writer, his work is representative of the experimental trend in the literature of the time. A fair judgment on the importance and failings of his work thus requires a comparison of it with other efforts in this form. One writer whose literary theories and practice provide a good point of comparison is Iwano Hōmei, a man whose work is not widely read now but who gained a degree of notoriety during his lifetime.

Hōmei, whose given name was Yoshie, was born on January 20, 1873, on the island of Awaji in the Inland Sea.[14] His family, originally from Edo, were low-ranking samurai who served as retainers in the residence of the Hachisuka family of Awa. At the time of the restoration, the fortunes of the Iwano family, like many of the same class, declined, and Hōmei's father brought the family to Awaji, where he worked as a provincial police officer.

When Hōmei was fifteen, he was sent to study at a Christian academy in Osaka. He converted to Christianity and even planned to serve as a missionary.[15] In 1888 his family moved back to Tokyo, where his father worked first as a policeman and then as owner of a boarding house. Hōmei finished the school year in Osaka and then rejoined his family in Tokyo, where he entered Meiji Gakuin, a Western-style Christian academy established in 1886, one class behind Tōson.

The two young men received very different educations at the school. For Tōson, the years at Meiji Gakuin were generally happy ones that he recalled with excessive nostalgia and sentimentality in *Haru*. It was a period of exciting liberation, marked by the strong adolescent romanticism that sometimes mars the work of his maturity. Yoshida Sei'ichi, commenting on Tōson's Christianity at the school, describes him as being a member of the "soft" faction among the students. Hōmei, on the other hand, belonged to the "hard" faction, and he grew xenophobic while at the school, hating his foreign teachers and frequently skipping classes.[16] His earlier idealistic faith in Christianity waned, and he eventually renounced his belief.

In 1889 Hōmei left Meiji Gakuin to study law and economics. He considered a career as a politician but later wrote that his youthful interest in politics was something of a sham and that he considered the movements for freedom, people's rights, and democracy to be symbolic ideals that held no substance (*HZ* 11:12). Instead, he was attracted to political notions of individual autonomy and to figures of strong personal authority. He became fascinated with Emerson at this time and published a translation and study of him in 1891. He was also interested by the novel *Keikoku bidan* (Laudable stories of statescraft, 1883), by Yano Ryūkei, and wrote his own historical novel, never published, about the Persian king Cyrus.[17] The political ideas Hōmei developed during this period of his life distinguished him from other writers who came to be associated with naturalism. He saw in the works of his contemporaries a reaffirmation of an essentially bourgeois ideology, and his skepticism toward that ideology led him to adopt a more radical stance in his own work, which he consistently referred to as *Shin-shizenshugi* (New Naturalism).[18] The admiration for strong men and the elements of hero worship in Hōmei's ideology reflect an awareness of the irresolvable struggle between the practical world of human actions and the ideal world of literature and art. He shared this awareness with men like Futabatei, and indeed saw himself as much closer in ideology and literary practice to writers like Doppo and Sōseki than to more mainstream naturalists like Tōson or Tayama Katai.[19]

In 1891 Hōmei moved to Sendai, where he studied at Tōhoku Gakuin until 1893. It was during this period that he settled on a literary career. Like Tōson, he started out as a poet, and he wrote plays and criticism as well. During the 1890s he brought out several volumes of poetry, much of it autobiographical. The choice of himself as material may have been suggested to him by the romantic movement of the time, but the impulse to write such poetry was more deeply rooted in his dislike of convention, an attitude previously revealed by his revolt against authority at Meiji Gakuin, and in his desire to create a literature free from the past and from Western assumptions.

His dissatisfaction with the literature of the day was compounded by personal disappointments and a very unhappy marriage. Hōmei married his first wife, Kō, in 1895. The couple had several children, most of whom died. In view of Hōmei's clearly expressed desire to escape the relationship, the couple remained together a remarkably long time. In 1908, however, he began an affair with a prostitute named Masuda Shimoe, and the following year he fled to Sakhalin, where he tried to start a crab-canning business. After the failure of this project, he spent a year wandering around Hokkaido before returning to Tokyo. In 1912 he finally divorced his wife and married Endō Kiyoko, a writer and activist for women's rights whom he had met in 1909 and subsequently had lived with in Osaka in 1911. They remained together until 1915, when they separated after Hōmei met Urahara Fusae. Kiyoko retaliated by publishing a story about their situation, but Hōmei stubbornly rode out the scandal and divorced her in 1917. He married Fusae, and his personal life was less colorful for the remainder of his life. He died of bleeding ulcers in 1920.

It is interesting to note one point of similarity in the backgrounds of Hōmei and Tōson—a factor that may help to explain their affinity for autobiographical confession. Both came from families that had not adjusted well to the social changes following the Meiji Restoration, and they perceived themselves to be on the margins of society compared to other literary figures. This contrasted sharply, for example, with the experience of the major writers of the Shirakaba-ha, men such as Arishima Takeo, Mushanokōji, and Shiga, who were members of a social and cultural elite. Their educational backgrounds also set them apart. Many of the most influential writers of the day either were educated at Tokyo University—as were Ōgai and Sōseki—or at least attended mainstream educational or journalistic institutions—as did Shōyō and Futabatei.

Even more important than institutional affiliation may have been the general difference between the nature of their educations and those of writers only a few years older. This generational difference must not be given undue importance but it does permit some differentiation among the responses to the modern that shaped the development of Meiji literature. It is a rough generalization, but it may be said that Ōgai, Sōseki, the older members of the Ken'yūsha, and even Futabatei, for all his skepticism, were more sure of themselves intellectually in the sense that they were better grounded not only in Western languages but also in their native tradition and in Chinese literature than were Hōmei and Tōson. They faced the challenge of Western culture on a more equal footing, as suggested by Ōgai's successful personal experience in Germany or Sōseki's confidence in his critical understanding of the British tradition. To be sure, these men were also aware of Japan's marginal status in the face of Western imperialism, and the fact that on occasion they felt the need to assert their equality signals misgiving as much as confidence. Nonetheless, within their own society, they were certainly more central figures than were Hōmei and Tōson, who, along with several other naturalists, were trained at Western-style Christian academies. This difference does not negate the similarity in outlook that resulted from the sense of crisis shared by Meiji writers generally, but being less sure of the native tradition and being on the margins of society (at least at the beginning of their careers) produced a more profound alienation that helps explain the important role autobiography played in their novels.

Hōmei, who began to receive a measure of critical praise in the years just before his death, took as one of his central tenets the idea that his life and his art were inseparable. Throughout his life, he challenged social conventions and responsibilities. He not only felt but was compelled to embrace the cultural discontinuities of his age. He did not try to compromise his vision to make it palatable to conventional tastes, and in this respect it may be said that for all the hurt he caused others, he was more forthright in his dealings with people and in his literary accounts of them than was Tōson. His sense of discontinuity was different not so much in kind as in degree, and having no other resources for his literature, he gave voice to his predicament through the narrative convention of the confession, creating a literary testament to his sense of displacement.

Hōmei's most representative work is a group of five novels that chronicle his life from about 1908 to 1914. These are *Hōrō* (Wandering, 1910), *Dankyō* (Broken bridges, 1911), *Hatten* (Debauchery, 1912), *Dokuyaku o nomu onna* (A woman who drinks poison, 1914), and *Tsukimono* (The possessed, 1918). He was especially proud of *Dokuyaku o nomu onna* and compared it to the best works of Shakespeare and Goethe. The novel covers the period when his first marriage was at rock bottom and he began his affair with Masuda Shimoe before leaving for Sakhalin in 1908 and 1909. Masuda, who was the inspiration for the character Otori who appears throughout the series of five novels, is the woman of the title. An understanding of the precise relationship among real-life figures and their fictional counterparts has no bearing on the formal effects of the novel itself, but in Hōmei's case the closeness of this relationship does point to the attitude that governed the narrative form: his belief that literature is life and that art is action. The intensity of his confessional technique is crucial to his conceptions of the individual and the narrative voice.

Hōmei took the honesty of the autobiographical confession to an extreme by publicizing events in his life not to justify or expiate them but to shock. Where Tōson sought redemption and even justification for his actions after the scandal with his niece broke, as if he wanted to assert his individuality while not being wholly cut off from the social norms against which he sought to define himself, Hōmei was brutal in his depiction of his literary alter ego and made no secret of his desire to be free of social obligations, no matter the consequences. The most notorious example of this desire is depicted in *Dokuyaku o nomu onna,* when he gives an almost verbatim account of a real-life argument he had with his first wife, Kō, at the hospital where one of his children had just died of diphtheria. Hōmei evidently made it clear in a loud voice that he did not care about the child. The fictional treatment of this incident is remarkably direct, lacking the circumspection of Tōson's account in *Ie* of his children's deaths. The narrator simply states his reasons for his actions:

> Thinking back, his first child had also suffered from diphtheria and had died while trying to grasp the little lamp at the head of her pillow. His third child also caught the disease and died in his mother's arms with a look that seemed to ask why was he suffering. He had been bothered by the death of the little girl, not only because she was his first child, but also because he had certain memories of her from her two years and two months of life. Yet he felt no remorse for the boy because it was the second to die, and because it was only nine months old. As for the new baby, he didn't care at all. He had hardly ever seen it, and he was sure it would die as well. (*HZ* 3:458–459)

This treatment of the event forces the reader to confront directly the motives of the narrator. Although the sentiments expressed are harsh, it is not impossible to sympathize with the narrator's position, since the cost of emotional attachment could be so destructively high. Nevertheless, the voice here is harshly pragmatic. It sets out the terms of selfhood in such strong opposition to conventional values that we are both emotionally engaged and repelled. Hōmei achieves the separation of the self, that is, the creation of the narrative alter ego, through the rhetorical pretense of a severe, honest voice.

Hōmei's conceptions of narrative voice and perspective are expressed in his critical ideas concerning the attitude the author brings to his fictional characters. In the essay "Gendai shōrai no shōsetsuteki hassō o isshin subeki boku no byōsha ron" (My theory of description, which should lead to the reform of present and future conceptions of the novel), he presents four possible types of relationship between the author and the characters in a novel (*HZ* 10:545–548).

The first type of relationship, equated with the flat or surface description (*heimen byōsha*) advocated by Tayama Katai, occurs when the author tries to present objectively each separate character in order to give a truthful account of events. Such a scheme maintains a distance between author and character and can apply even to autobiographical novels where the author presents his fictionalized self but does not tell the story solely through that character. The second type of relationship arises through a closer identification between the author and his fictionalized self. The pretense of objectivity is abandoned as a formal convention, and the characters are portrayed from a single perspective. The difference in the degree of identification, Hōmei writes, is the same as the difference between a simile and a metaphor. Comparing himself with other naturalists, he states,

> If we were to try to contrast Tayama with Hōmei, the first thing we would readily understand is that their difference is the difference in attitudes represented by types 1 and 2. He stated once, concerning my *Dokuyaku o nomu onna,* that although there should have been more observation of the woman, I stopped halfway. As I replied in my defense at the time, I created a woman only within the limits seen by the man who is the hero, and even though there may be other points of view by which to observe her, I omitted those, or intentionally did not show them, in order to make concrete the personality and life of the hero instead. Tayama, being attached to the misconception of flat description, does not understand this point. (*HZ* 10:557–558)

The third and fourth types of relationship are elaborations on the first two. The third scheme relates to the structure in which a story is told by an author who gives separate narrative voices to his characters. The fourth deals with the variety of narrative in which the author is identified with one of the characters but is not the only voice relating the narrative.

In all cases, Hōmei rejects the possibility of truly objective description and instead looks for literary truth through the extreme of intense, subjective honesty. His position leads him to confuse the author with narrative voice, but that mistake is crucial, for it allows us to observe better the ideas fundamental to his understanding of narrative voice. His conclusion is that there can be no absolute reference point outside the individual narrative perspective, a view that leads him to adopt a kind of formal relativism. The truth of his portrait of Otori in *Dokuyaku o nomu onna,* for example, has nothing to do with objective notions of accuracy; rather, it is achieved by the degree of consistency he maintains in the narrative perspective of the character. The truth of the text depends on the observations of that voice. It is not truth in an external, objective sense but truth that derives from a radical shift to the interior of the literary self.

It is difficult to judge the conduct of Yoshio, Hōmei's fictional alter ego in *Dokuyaku o nomu onna,* toward Otori and Chiyoko, Yoshio's wife, in part because the narrative perspective so blatantly challenges conventional ethical standards. This desire to break from convention and to find a new aesthetic expression for the self is apparent in the imagery the narrator employs to describe Yoshio's relationship with the two women.

> He was silent and did not answer. The smell of the woman assaulted him. Only the right side of his nose worked, and this odor, which he could sense on one side alone, was now his sole comfort. Of late he had come to ignore the stench of the gutter outside. Once he climbed up into this room, even unpleasant things could not upset his nerves. This smell of Otori, however, had become like the smell of an *eta* to him, no matter how he tried to think of it another way. At the same time, it was not a wholly disagreeable sensation, more like the smell of an armpit.
>
> In any case, this room, with its warm smell, was better than the thin, cold place of Chiyoko, which in the evening seemed to be surrounded by the scent of plum trees.
>
> If this smell of Otori were not here, he would have instead a very lonely feeling. (*HZ* 3:444)

The squalor of Otori's life becomes an image of her attractiveness to Yoshio, while a well-worn image of feminine beauty, the scent of plums, holds only negative connotations. This reversal is not unlike that created by the shocking image of the opening lines of Eliot's "The Love Song of J. Alfred Prufrock." The essential condition of Yoshio's life is his loneliness, which he willfully fosters by rebelling against the social conventions represented by his marriage. His preference for Otori has less to do with her personal qualities than with the fact that she is somehow more alive and physically real to him and with the way in which Yoshio uses those qualities to create an alternative set of values for his life and art.

Nevertheless, Yoshio feels trapped in both relationships and seeks to escape by ridding himself of Otori as well. To this end, he seeks the help of a man named Kashū, a writer who pretends to be helping Yoshio but in fact has no intention other than to make Otori his plaything. Yoshio finally forces Otori to choose between him and the other man, and when he discovers how deep her relationship with Kashū has become, he abandons her. He justifies his actions by blaming Kashū, but the argument that ensues between the two men in front of Otori turns the blame in her direction, and their cruelty leads her to attempt suicide for a second time in her life. Having left her after this scene, Yoshio, aware of her emotional instability, returns to her room to find that she has swallowed poison. She survives, and he nurses her back to health before leaving for Sakhalin.

Yoshio feels justified in the cruelty of his relationship with Otori not only because it suits his own selfish desires but also because the words and

The Dilemma of the Modern

actions of the other characters at times support his perspective on the story. Even Otori seems to accept his view of things, and she supposedly attempts suicide not in response to his callousness but because of the guilt she feels for having betrayed him by her affair with Kashū. The fact that she is almost always portrayed through Yoshio's perspective makes her admission of guilt seem coerced. But this coercion is justified on the grounds that in a world where objective standards of truth are no longer possible, truthfulness derives solely from an intensely subjective consciousness through which the individual is able to confront alienation.

The close identification between the author and the narrating self is necessarily reflected in the style of writing. The novel has a narrative drive and a sense of immediacy that convey the urge to break from convention and the subsequent loss of objective standards. The intensity of his style is apparent from the opening scene.

> "The old woman must have some sort of divine inspiration."
> "Divine inspiration? What's that?"
> "It's a god-given power to read other people's minds."
> "Don't be silly, there's no such power."
> "You can never be sure. People like you wouldn't understand it. In any case I don't mean divine inspiration in the Christian sense. There's no such god to give it. I just mean that some people have a special power deep inside."
> "There's no such thing."
> "It's not impossible. By the way, did you say anything to the Haradas about us being here?"
> "Me? I didn't say anything. At first I thought it'd be OK to mention it, but then I thought if they told my family about this place it'd cause trouble."
> "But they do know. At least they know we are staying in a place near a wood."
> "A wood? That could be anywhere."
> "I suppose you're right." Yoshio said nothing more to Otori of his worries. He certainly did not tell her that Chiyo was apparently trying to kill her with some form of curse. Otori was already neurotic, and to upset her further would have meant nothing but trouble. (*HZ* 3:436-437)

Even if the reader is unfamiliar with the situation as outlined in Hōmei's earlier novels, the opening provides a complete, if oblique, explanation and establishes the tone for the entire narrative. The desperation of life and the depravity of the human relationships are conveyed by images of filth and darkness, of gutters and foul smells. When more conventionally beautiful images appear in the narrative, as in citations from Poe and

Rosetti in the second chapter, they are used as a counterpoint to emphasize just how far the world has moved away from those ideal images and how that separation denies the possibility of achieving love in a conventional sense.

The intensity of the narrative voice arises from the pretense of the implied author's virtual identification with his literary self. The perspective Hōmei uses makes no concessions to the reader. The ideological justification for this formal experiment is laid out in his essay "Shinpiteki hanjūshugi" (Mystical semibestialism, 1906), which summarizes and critiques the work of Swedenborg, Maeterlinck, and Emerson (*HZ* 15:107–14).[20] He did not agree with the mystical philosophies of Swedenborg and Emerson and instead located the reality of life solely in the corporeal, animalistic struggles of humanity. Hōmei felt that this marked an advance in his thinking, and he ties his materialistic philosophy directly to the rise of naturalism in Japan, asserting in a remarkable piece of revisionist literary history that he had written the essay to help bring naturalism into being. The title points to the dual, contradictory nature of man, a being half-god, half-animal, with one foot in eternity and the other in the material present (*HZ* 15:69–70, 73–78). Hōmei outlines three extremes of human existence that arise within the boundaries defined by these aspects of human nature: a state of extreme desire and emotion; a life of genius, or essential self-awareness; and a state of fatigue, which is like paralysis in life. These extremes occur in a universe that is essentially chance and aimless, and he accordingly adopts a fatalistic stance in which alienation is relieved only through a complete awareness of the self (*HZ* 15:59–60, 68). Hōmei's philosophical terminology restates the fundamental dilemma of the modern, the impossibility of narrative duration, which his literary experiments then sought to resolve. The concern with narrative voice indicates an attempt to reach what he understood to be the state of artistic genius.

Perceiving themselves to be cut off from the past—indeed, desiring to be cut off—and yet living in a present without objective standards, Hōmei, Tōson, and other writers who made use of the autobiographical confession set out to redefine literature through an increasingly personal and inward vision of the self. For these artists, the literary form of the confession was virtually synonymous with the creation of a new cultural identity. The autobiographical confession quickly became a mainstream form for the Japanese novel, in spite of the radically experimental ways in which the mode was initially employed by Meiji writers. It is difficult to

The Dilemma of the Modern

give a single reason for this rapid acceptance, but the fact that there were traditional precedents for this type of narrative helped reduce the marginality of the Japanese literary self with respect to Western models. The widespread use of the confession may thus be due at least in part to the perception that it offered a possibility to resolve the dilemma of the modern. However, the extreme relativism of the approach taken by the naturalists created its own difficulties. The fragmentation of the tradition destroyed the possibility of ideal or universal values, although Tōson, Katai, and even Hōmei seem not to have been quite so preoccupied by the question of the impossibility of a modern literature as were other writers. The faith these men held in their literary projects—a faith that appears to be common to the various manifestations of naturalism—suggests that they believed they had found a way to overcome the dilemma of the modern.

I do not in any way suggest that the personal crises faced by the naturalists in their writings were any less consequential than those Futabatei confronted. But the lower degree of skepticism they exhibited toward the limits of narrative conventions may have been due to a stronger personal need to recover a sense of continuity, which in turn led them to adopt very nearly unquestioningly the autobiographical confession as their primary mode of self-expression. Considering the narrow aims of the project most naturalists set for themselves, the autobiographical confession was not, in fact, a major formal innovation, in spite of its influence on the subsequent development of twentieth-century literature in Japan. The problem of perspective was a central preoccupation of Meiji writers, but doubts about the ability of any narrative form to create a self not limited by the particularities of place and time is, according to my use of the term, a crucial component of the modern. In that respect, Futabatei is a more truly innovative writer, as are those authors who expressed serious reservations about the aims and practices of naturalism.

◆

chapter nine
The Sense of an
Ending: The Apocalyptic
Individualism of
Natsume Sōseki

In his memorial to Futabatei Shimei, Natsume Sōseki dwelt on the fact that although they both worked for the *Asahi shinbun* they never really had the chance to get to know each other. He writes of his surprise at Futabatei's appearance when they were introduced, and he talks of his admiration for Futabatei's novels, especially *Sono omokage,* regretting that the nature of the memorial did not allow him to go into the reasons for his admiration.[1] There is throughout the tribute a warm sense of humor about their relationship tinged with regret that they never had the opportunity to draw closer. He ends with an account of their final meeting, which

> took place a few days before his departure [for Russia]. When he set foot inside my house it was for the first and last time. Looking about as he walked through the rooms, he remarked that the place reminded him somehow of a Buddhist monastery. He had come merely to take his leave, so we talked about nothing particularly important, except that he requested over and over that I look after the Mozume sisters, Kazuko and Yoshiko, and one other person from a northern province who were his pupils.
>
> A day passed, and I went to make a return visit. Unfortunately, he was not in, so I was unable to meet him. I did not see him off in the end. As it

has turned out, I cannot meet Hasegawa any more. I received a single postcard from him while he was in Russia. It sounds rather feeble, he wrote, but I'm not at all suited to the cold here. I remember thinking as I read that card that although I felt sorry for him the situation also had its humorous side. That was because I never imagined it was so cold he would die. Nonetheless, it appears it was that cold. Hasegawa died after all. He died without ever understanding me and without my understanding him. Even had he lived, we perhaps would not have associated with one another any more than we had. Then again, perhaps the chance would have arisen for us to have drawn closer. I will never know. I am a distant friend who has no other recourse but to remember the Hasegawa I described above as Hasegawa. The Mozume sisters entrusted to me drop by from time to time. I have had no word from the person from the north.[2]

Like most of the authors in the memorial volume, Sōseki, in describing his relationship with Futabatei, tells us more about himself than about his subject. This is no doubt due to the fact that he did not know Futabatei well. His reflections on the death of his literary compatriot are a meditation on his own career to that point, and they reveal an attitude that became increasingly important and characteristic of his late fiction. The memorial essay was written at roughly the same time that *Sore kara* (And then) was being prepared for serialization in the *Asahi shinbun,* and it expresses the sense of isolation that he explores more thoroughly in his treatment of Daisuke, *Sore kara*'s protagonist. Sōseki saw a kindred artistic spirit in Futabatei, and his regrets at never being able to connect with his contemporary in any deep sense seem to be genuine. At the same time, his tribute is among the most contrived, with the strongest narrative line, of all the essays in the volume. The story of his failure to get to know Futabatei somehow confirms the larger theme of the isolation of the individual central to so much of his fiction. It is as if the only way he can make sense of his experience of knowing Futabatei, and thus overcome his feelings of isolation, is to treat it as a narrative. He ends the essay with a reference to Futabatei's disciples, to whom he tries to do his duty. Yet the sense of something being lost, of never quite connecting, is brought home by his inability to carry out his obligations to the unnamed disciple.

It is easy to attribute Sōseki's brooding sense of isolation to his difficult childhood. He was given up for adoption by his elderly parents as an infant, only to be returned to them when he was nine years old. Certainly, the subsequent feelings of rejection, which he carried with him his entire life, were profound; however, I do not want to place too much stress on the role of his personal circumstances in the creation of his literature. With the exception of his last complete novel, *Michikusa* (Grass on the wayside, 1915), his writings do not take his personal life as their immediate focus. And even in *Michikusa,* the structure of the novel, which takes advantage of the serialized format to create dramatic breaks and suspense at moments of importance in the story, shows a greater concern with the formal requirements of narrative and a greater degree of overt fictionalization than is found in most autobiographical novels of the period. This tendency suggests that Sōseki instead made his writing the focus of his life.

Sōseki's expression of the discontinuities in his own life was not limited by the naturalist concern with sincerity as a purely narrative attitude, and he sought wider validation for his acute sense of personal isolation in the larger discontinuities of his historical moment. Etō Jun argues that the source of Sōseki's art is to be found at the juncture between his desire to create a more certain identity for himself and his awareness of the larger historical dislocation that Meiji Japan was undergoing. This dislocation provided Sōseki with the image he needed to create his literature. Etō writes,

> Sōseki wrote *Michikusa* when he was forty-nine years old, a year before his death. It is a work of the very last year of his authorial life. The fact that he sincerely and repeatedly set down in the autobiographical novel written in his last year the question he himself was probably asked, "Whose child are you really?" indicates that this was a question he had to answer his entire life.
>
> In short, to use a word that has finally become widespread recently in Japan, it is a question of the problem of identity, of where do I belong, of what is my true character. This question was the problem of Sōseki's life.
>
> Now, expanding our frame of inquiry, if we ask what sort of an age was the Meiji Period, and what was the fundamental problem of that age, again it is the problem of identity. . . .
>
> Therefore, these questions—just what kind of a person am I? where have I come from and where am I going?—that Sōseki as an individual continually asked within his unique circumstances were precisely the questions of his age. Sōseki had to ask that question out of his own personal sense of individual inevitability. Yet the age that surrounded him and that changed so rapidly reached the point where it also posed the same question. That is the deepest meaning of the encounter of Sōseki with his age.[3]

Etō's reading of Sōseki's work as a convergence of an individual voice with the spirit of the times runs the risk of creating a circular reading of the significance Sōseki attached to literature. James Fujii argues against what he sees as a tendency in Etō Jun's historical approach "to reduce the complex, interanimating relationship of a text and its historical moment to a static, self-validating binarism." This critique is important to note here, for my own use of the term *modern* stresses that what determines the creation of narrative is not only historical context but also the constantly evolving process of rereading the past. Even so, it strikes me as difficult to define the limits of historicism precisely, since any discussion of a work within its historical or cultural context establishes self-validating relationships. Indeed, when Fujii writes that "Sōseki's odd fusion of narrating subject with language reminded his reader that what was fast becoming the standard form of narration was merely a convention recently naturalized, and one among many possible forms of literary expression," he reaches essentially the same conclusion as Etō, who connects Sōseki's self-consciousness about the rhetorical nature of narrative form to the linguistic crisis of Meiji Japan.[4] This self-consciousness concerning the literary project is apparent in certain elements of Sōseki's fiction. First, there is an overtly stated desire to narrate as a means to overcome the sense of dislocation. Second, his work presents an apocalyptic vision of the individual that stems from the identification of the literary self with a particular and significant present. Since these elements express his concept of the individual, it will be useful to look more closely at that concept to examine how it shaped the contours of his fiction.

In his essay "Bungei to dōtoku" (The literary arts and ethics, 1911) Sōseki explicitly argues against both a separation of art and ethics and the narrow notion of art for art's sake and looks for a synthesis of the two as a way to define the social function of modern literature. His analysis reveals a tendency to reread the past according to present-day standards, and his classification of ethical thought reflects the same dilemma confronted by Futabatei. Sōseki asserts that in the past, by which he means specifically the Tokugawa period, morals were absolute, and the individual was subordinated. The reason for this was that "people in the past lacked a critical psychology. This was the result of the combination of a strong conviction that ideas like filial piety or chastity, which had been transmitted from earlier ages, could be reproduced in their ideal forms and of the lack of a sensibility that looked critically on those ideal models. In short, it is correct to say that [the lack of a critical psychology] was due to the fact that science was not very advanced" (11:369–370). Unlike Tōson, Sōseki did not see this lack of a critical psychology as precluding modern literature from assuming a social function. Instead, he felt that what distinguished the Meiji period was the greater freedom of the individual that grew out of a scientific outlook. The collapse of moral absolutes lowered ethical standards and made them more realistic, and as a result, the world became easier for the individual to live in.

Yet with the willingness to admit limitations there comes a considerable diminution. In another short essay, titled "Bungei to hiroikku" (The literary arts and the heroic, 1910), Sōseki describes one aspect of this diminution by noting that naturalism, the movement that gave literary expression to the modern scientific sensibility, is never equated with the heroic. *Heroic*, in fact, is never a term that applies to the modern, and it can only be used to describe earlier people and ages (11:240). Sōseki makes a similar point in his essay "Bungei no tetsugakuteki kiso" (The philosophical foundation of the literary arts, 1907).

> There has never been a generation so lacking in heroism as the present, nor a literature that promotes heroism so little as present-day literature does. It is also clear that in the present age not a single tragedy has appeared that arouses the feeling of sublimity [or solemnity—*sōgon*]. So the ideals of modern literature are not beauty, goodness, or sublimity, but simply truth [or sincerity—*makoto*].[5] If I were to provide examples to prove this, this essay would run on too long, and if I try to provide evidence, then it will be very difficult. Since I cannot do anything about that, I shall simply leave it as my assertion that truth/sincerity is the ideal of modern literature, especially fiction. (11:66)

In "Bungei to dōtoku," Sōseki connects literary practice with ethics by noting that over the previous forty years two literary modes, romanticism and naturalism, had dominated. He does not limit his use of these terms to the literary sphere; in his mind, the movements correspond to the two different ethical systems operating in Tokugawa and Meiji societies. Romanticism expresses absolute or ideal ethics because it avoids depiction of imperfection. Naturalism must show imperfections in order to achieve an honest depiction, honesty being the basis of morality (11: 379). This analysis finally suggests that the two approaches are, from the standpoint of creating a narrative voice, necessary and yet mutually incompatible, and the awareness of the futility of trying to reduce these competing ethical claims to narrative indicates the degree to which the dilemma of the modern guided Sōseki's literary practice.

Sōseki discusses similar concerns in "Watakushi no kojinshugi" (My individualism, 1914), a later and better-known essay that provides some insight into his ideas about the literary self, although its generalizations are not entirely pertinent to the novels that predate it. But keeping in mind that each work represents a separate stage in the development of his ideas about the individual, it can be observed that Sōseki's fundamental definition of individualism is indebted to a social contract theory reworded in terms of Confucian notions of individual duty to the primary social relationships. He reduces his definition of individualism to three main points: (1) developing individuality requires that the individuality of others be respected; (2) the assertion of the self and the power of the individual must be accompanied by an awareness of duty to others; and (3) showing individual financial power requires a respect for the responsibilities of that power (11:454). He cites England as the model of an individualistic society in which the expression of the self is unhindered so long as it does not impinge on the development of others' individuality.

Although Sōseki is apparently naturalizing Western notions of individualism, that is not his main purpose in the essay. Most important is the significance he attaches to literature in his own search for individuality. The self-reflective title suggests that the essay's aim is not just to define the concept of individualism but to define himself through that concept. At certain points, he explicitly relates that search to his struggle to define what literature is. He tells of his years studying English literature under James Main Dixon at Tokyo University but confesses that after three years of labor he still had no idea what it was. This, he claims, "was the root cause of my anguish" (11:441). Not knowing what his calling should be, he felt lost and trapped and had no idea what would become of him. Finally, he came to the conclusion that there was no other way to save himself "except to create by my own powers a fundamental concept of what literature is" (11:442).

> Next, in order to strengthen—or perhaps in order to build anew—my viewpoint toward literature, I began to read books that had no connection with literature. In a word, I finally conceived of the term *self-centered,* and in order to substantiate that self-centeredness I became absorbed in scientific studies and philosophical speculation. Now, because the times are different, I expect that the need for self-centeredness should be clear to anyone with a head on his shoulders, but back then not only was I immature, but also, because the world was not all that advanced, the way I proceeded was unavoidable.
>
> After grasping the term *self-centered* in my own hands, I became very strong. I had the backbone to question others. For me, who up to now had been in a daze and lost, the term *self-centeredness* truly was what instructed me where to stand and which way I must take on this road.

If I may confess, I started out anew from this idea of self-centeredness. I thought that if I could properly put forth the unshakable reasoning that it is unreliable to follow others blindly, to make a fuss about nothing as they do now, and that it is all right not to imitate Westerners, then it would make me happy and give people pleasure. And I thought I could make my life's work the accomplishment of that goal through literature. (11:444–45)

Sōseki restates here the central dilemma that gave rise to the crisis of Meiji literature, and he explicitly connects his sense of the modern with the creation of a new self. The past was no longer relevant, but the complete adoption of Western ideas, especially Western ideas about literature, was a hindrance to the development of the self and to the realization of individuality in Japan. He asserts a relativist position toward the critical interpretation of literature, claiming that his own readings of Western literature are valid, even if they differ from the readings of Westerners, precisely because his individuality gives autonomy and thereby authority to his opinions. Sōseki's denial of Western influence on his notion of individuality is more than a literary pose, since he could point to precedents within his native tradition. The strange thing about his argument is that he never explains why his search for identity is so closely related to his search for an explanation of what literature is. Moreover, he is extremely vague about what it is about his cultural background that supports his relativistic view of the value of his own critical opinions. It is significant that a fundamental element in his definition of individualism, excluding concepts borrowed from social contract theory, rests not so much on a philosophical foundation as on an emotional need to assert the self. His notion of the individual suggests a process of separation/individuation rather than any specific set of cultural or social values; it is the naturalist process of narrating a new identity. The specific notions of the self and of duty are less important to his work than the basic impulse to define himself, which he sees as essentially a narrative process.

The impulse to establish a sense of selfhood through narrative was for Sōseki a temporary resolution of the basic question of how to define his individuality. However, he was also acutely aware that creating a new identity led to different sorts of problems. In asserting individuality, the past and its conventions are lost to the present-day writer, and all that remains is for the individual to be brave enough to look into the void, into the discontinuities of the present, and set about re-creating a different order and a new sense of continuity.

To speak more simply, individualism is an ideology possessing the relative merit of avoiding cliquishness. The individualist does not form factions or create groups to run blindly after political or financial power. For that reason, a loneliness unknown to people is concealed beneath the surface of this ideology. Because once there are no more cliques, insofar as I must selfishly follow my own path and at the same time not obstruct the paths others must take, then at certain times and in certain circumstances people will separate. That separation is what is lonely. (11:457)

Sōseki presents an ambivalent view of individualism. He seeks to recover a rationale for traditional notions of ethical behavior by claiming that respect for personal freedom leads to an acceptance of responsibility and thus to moral behavior, but the price of individualism is alienation.

Etō Jun argues that there is an important connection between Sōseki's work and the decadent (art nouveau) movement in British art of the end of the nineteenth century. Seeing a similarity between the Meiji and Victorian periods in that both witnessed a rise in nationalism at the expense of culture, he argues that the modern begins with those writers who understood the collapse of culture and made it the source of their literature. "In his 'Theory of Literature' Sōseki gives an extremely sympathetic account of the Pre-Raphaelites and of the French impressionists who were led by Manet. Was this not perhaps because he possessed an extremely sensitive ear that could make out the sound of the footsteps of 'delicate death' that was moving about the fin de siècle, that is, the world [at the turn of century]?"[6] The influence of English literature on Sōseki may not be so much a matter of technique as of mood. The isolation of the literary self, which is the paradoxical result of the act of narrating the self into being, is linked closely to an apocalyptic view of the present. The act of reducing the self to a narrative, of defining one's individuality in the present moment, is also a symbolic death: living in a significant present gives meaning to the self but creates the dilemma of isolation, a figurative death.

The novel that most clearly illustrates this apocalyptic sense of the self is *Kokoro* (1914). The title of the work, which may be translated "spirit" or "heart," suggests that the author identifies the spirit of the individual with the spirit of the age, an interpretation supported by the fact that Sōseki began work on the novel partly in response to the suicide of General Nogi after the death of Emperor Meiji in 1912. Nogi's death, the implications of which are discussed in the narrative, was a ritual form of suicide called *junshi* (following one's lord in death) that recalled all the older values of a feudal era. The death of the emperor was by itself enough to suggest the passing of an age, but the double suicide of Nogi and his wife was a sensational event that riveted the nation's attention and called to mind all the basic questions the Japanese were confronting concerning their traditional values and their national identity during an age of unparalleled social and cultural transformation. Sōseki was not the only author profoundly affected by this event, but, given his intellectual and emotional sensitivity to questions of cultural identity, he was especially moved by the implications of Nogi's action.

In terms of narrative voice, *Kokoro* may be considered part of the trio of books that also includes *Higansugi made* (To the vernal equinox and beyond, 1912) and *Kōjin* (The traveler, 1913). It has also been grouped with *Michikusa* (1915) and *Meian* (Light and dark, 1916) to form a trilogy that is the culmination of his life work, but the structure of the novel makes the earlier grouping more appropriate. Certainly, it shares one major point of similarity with *Higansugi made:* both novels break roughly into two different narratives, the first half being a type of detective story, and the second revealing the details of that story. Although the detective element is not overt in *Kokoro*, the first half of the book, comprising parts 1 and 2, deals with the efforts of the narrator, a young man referred to as "I" throughout, to discover the identity of his mentor, a man who is referred to simply by the honorific title of *Sensei*, teacher or master. The second half of the narrative is a long suicide letter written by *Sensei* that helps to unravel some of the mystery surrounding the older man.

The young narrator meets *Sensei* while vacationing in Kamakura. He wonders about the older man and then is seized by a desire to find out more about him. The reasons for this initial interest are never fully explained, except that the young man does say that he thinks that he has seen *Sensei* somewhere before. After introducing himself, the young man gradually becomes more familiar with *Sensei*, though their relationship is not especially close because of the older man's aloofness. Much of the first half of the work is then taken up with the young narrator learning about the present situation of *Sensei* and his wife, but he never gains an understanding of the reasons for the older man's gloomy disposition.

The next section of the book relates the ties between the narrator and his family. The key event he tells about is the illness of his father, who is suffering a slow decline because of kidney failure. His father wants to secure his son's future before he dies, but the narrator is so reluctant to follow his family's wishes that he asks *Sensei* to find a position for him in

Tokyo, even though he knows that *Sensei* claims that he cannot really do anything for his young friend. The final events of the story are played out against the deaths of the emperor and of Nogi and his wife during the late summer and autumn of 1912. The narrator's father is near death when at last the letter the narrator has been expecting from *Sensei* arrives. It is very long and deals not at all with the question of the young man's future occupation. It is instead an explanation of why *Sensei* has chosen to die. The young man is shocked and in his confusion takes the drastic step of leaving his father's deathbed to hurry to Tokyo. It is already too late to do anything, and the narrator's rash, unfilial act will no doubt estrange him from his family. As he rides the train to Tokyo, he reads the letter through, and the voice of *Sensei* narrates the final part of the novel.

The letter is a confession that puts together many of the pieces of the puzzle of *Sensei* that the young narrator had tried to solve by himself. The confessional mode suits *Sensei*'s purpose because it allows him to present the truth about himself and to confront the discontinuity that results from his loneliness and isolation. He does not write to his young friend merely out of a sense of obligation. In fact, he has chosen to live a lonely life, seeking either willfully or by circumstances "to live a lifestyle that as much as possible cuts down on my obligations" (6:153). He claims that he is weak and cannot stand the pain his kind of life inflicts, and so to avoid the discomfort of guilt, he undertakes the letter. However, that is not his only rationale for writing.

> Beyond that, I wanted to write. Apart from my duty the fact is that I wanted to write about my past. Because my past is my experience and mine alone, then I may be permitted to call it my property and mine alone. It would be regrettable, would it not, if I should die without passing it on to someone. In any case, that is how I feel about it. Nonetheless, I think it would be better to bury these experiences along with my life than to give them to someone who cannot accept them. In truth, if there had not been someone like you, my past would have ended as my past, never known even indirectly by anyone else. Of all the millions of Japanese people, it is to you alone that I wish to tell of my past. For you are sincere. Because once you said sincerely that you wanted to learn from life itself.
>
> Without hesitation I am about to cast the shadow of the dark world of humanity upon your head. However, do not be afraid. Stare deeply into the darkness, and pluck out of it whatever will be instructive to you. When I speak of darkness, of course I mean moral darkness. I am a man who was born ethical. I am a man who was raised ethical. It may be that my conception of ethics differs greatly from that of young people today, but however

wrong my ethics may be, they are my own. They are not some rented tuxedo I borrowed as a temporary expedient. Thus I think my experiences will provide a lesson to someone like you, who wants to grow from this. (6:153–154)

Sensei's justification for writing about his past, which is ostensibly didactic in nature, resembles Georges Gusdorf's observation (cited above in chapter 1 in connection with Prince Genji's impulse to fix his own image as the heroic ideal) that a person who writes autobiography is more aware of discontinuities than continuities and thus seeks to leave behind an image of himself as a means to arrest the flux and change of human experience.

The act of writing the letter, of reducing his past to narrative, is equated with *Sensei*'s death. The connection between confession and death suggests that it is the ultimate act of separation. *Sensei* quite literally creates himself by narrating the facts of his life for his reader. For that reason, the sincerity of the reader is an important element in the motivation to confess, a fact that *Sensei* takes into consideration in choosing the young man as his audience. Like the autobiographical confessions of the naturalists, the sincerity of the narrative is seen to be a crucial component of the truth of the story, but at the same time there seems to be a greater knowingness of the formal, conventional nature of this undertaking. The implied reader is a fictional party of one, but Sōseki's narrative strategy is to draw the real-life reader as well into the "crime" of the confession (in narrative time, after all, we are reading through the letter at the same time as the young man). Sōseki takes the question of sincerity a step further by placing on the reader some of the burden for the sincerity of the text, and thus the truth it conveys. This strategy of implication and isolation relies on the pretense that the reader alone is being let in on the secret of *Sensei*'s isolation and consequently must share in the man's loneliness.

Sensei warns his reader that he is about to cast the shadow of moral darkness over him, and the narrative voice is that of one isolated individual reaching out to another. This relationship between narrator and reader determines the moral dimensions of *Sensei*'s story. David Pollack argues that Confucian notions of duty to human relationships play an important role in understanding the expression of individualism in *Kokoro*.

> *Kokoro* is, in fact, a teacher's lesson about the human "heart," and we are left in no doubt as to exactly what sort of human heart it really is. In the end, then, I think we must disagree with Jay Rubin's assertion that in his later novels "Sōseki's increasingly dark view of man and world never lacks

for despair, but it stops short of condemning human nature as inherently evil." The novel is a practical demonstration of Hsün Tzu's vision of man's inherently evil nature in the face of the opposing Mencian ideal supported by Meiji ideology.[7]

Sōseki no doubt attempted to recover the language of an adversarial strain of neo-Confucianism to highlight the predicament of *Sensei* as a man out of his time, but in pressing this argument Pollack reads the ideological parameters of *Kokoro* as set by a thoroughgoing Confucianism. Such a reading is not convincing. First, it fails to account for *Sensei*'s assertion that he was "born ethical," a statement that at the very least suggests a vision of man's moral nature that does not correspond to Hsün Tzu's. Second, and more importantly, it fails to examine how Hsün Tzu's vision of human nature is refracted through the modernist structure of the narrative. The life of *Sensei* and his view of the human heart revealed in the suicide letter are ironic both because we know that the letter is a justification for *Sensei*'s death and because it is not the sole perspective of the novel. Accordingly, neither claim by Rubin or Pollack that *Sensei*'s outlook is the final word on the subject (in that it corresponds to Sōseki's own view of human nature) is supportable.

The purpose of the letter is to explain and perhaps to instruct, but above all it is to force the reader to confront the isolation of the narrative voice. *Sensei* has looked into the shadows created not only by his alienation and loneliness but also by his realization that there are no moral absolutes in human life. The notion of being forced to gaze into the dark void of discontinuity evokes—intentionally, I believe—the image of Conrad's "Heart of Darkness" and recalls the apocalyptic sense of the self that Sōseki shared with British writers at the end of the last century. *Sensei* declares that the darkness of life is a moral darkness, but that does not mean the sole purpose of his confession is an ethical one. We are presented with a statement of the relative nature of moral values that Sōseki would expand on in his lecture on individualism, which was written a few months after the completion of *Kokoro*. In a world where there are no longer any moral absolutes, the individual must seek a way to give meaning to his life and to find an identity for himself. The lesson of *Sensei*'s experience is not expressed directly through the language of a specific moral ideology but obliquely through his choice of lifestyle, his acceptance of the relativism of values, and his assertion of his individuality.

The bulk of the letter deals with the incidents that led to *Sensei*'s isolation and loneliness. He lost both his parents while he was young, an obvious echo of Sōseki's own experience, and his inheritance was administered by an uncle. This uncle proves to be dishonest and swindles the young man of a large portion of his fortune. *Sensei's* character, he tells us, was forever shaped by this event.

> My frame of mind was already pessimistic when I left my home province for the last time. The conviction that people could not be relied on appears to have penetrated to the very marrow of my bones by that time. I began to think of my uncle, my aunt, and all the other relatives I had come to hate as representative of the entire human race. Even boarding the train I began indirectly to scrutinize those next to me. When on occasion someone spoke to me, I became even more vigilant. My heart was melancholy. From time to time I felt painfully oppressed, as though I had swallowed lead. Yet my nerves, as I said, were razor sharp. (6:177)

He distrusts people in matters of money, but he says that he has not yet learned to doubt love. For this reason, he feels conflicting emotions when he falls in love with the daughter of the woman from whom he rents a room in Tokyo. He is also capable of feelings of true friendship toward another young man who is called K. K is an extremely high-minded man of principle who cuts himself off from the support of his family in order to pursue his own goals. *Sensei* is attracted to his idealism, although naturally wary of the consequences of K's actions, and he tries to do his duty by his friend in whatever way he can. When K finally loses all financial support, *Sensei* invites him to stay in his boardinghouse. This act of friendship leads to the crime that is the motivation for the confession.

Sensei soon perceives K as a threat to his own romantic pursuit of his landlady's daughter. His fears are realized when K confesses his love for the young woman. To fight back, *Sensei* betrays his friendship for K, first acting as his confidant, then torturing him by pointing out the contradiction between K's ideals and his passions. The predicament of K is in turn linked to the general dilemma of his age.

> That age was a time in which words like "the age of awakening" and "the new life" did not yet exist. However, it was not because the conception of the modern person was lacking in him that K did not wholeheartedly discard his old self and run off in new directions. For him, the past was so valuable he could not discard it. It might even be said his past was the reason he had lived until today. Thus the fact that K did not rush straight toward the object of his love does not necessarily mean that his love was lukewarm. Though his emotions burned passionately, he could not be moved impulsively. Not

only was there never an opportunity for the impulse to forget the past and the future to arise, but also K always had to stop short a little and look back on his own past. By doing so he had to continue following along the road his past had laid out for him to that point. (6:253–254)

K's crisis of identity causes him to delay openly confessing his feelings to the mother and daughter, and *Sensei* takes advantage of this interval to destroy K by proposing marriage to the young woman. In taking this action, *Sensei* dooms himself to precisely the same sort of crisis that immobilized his friend. "In short, it had been my intention to follow the path of honesty, but finally I was a fool who lost my footing on the way. Or else I was a cunning man. The only ones who noticed that were Heaven and my own heart. However, I had fallen into the dilemma that, in order to regain my footing and start out again on the path of honesty, the people around me had to learn of my dishonesty. I wanted desperately to hide my wrong. At the same time, I had to start back on my former path. Caught in this dilemma, I was paralyzed" (6:264).

K commits suicide, and that act sets the course for the isolation and inactivity of *Sensei*'s life. The contradiction between his ideals and his actions is a heavy burden, but it is not that conflict alone that troubles him. The inevitability of loneliness that comes with any assertion of the self against the ideal is the dark truth that *Sensei* is finally forced to acknowledge.

> All the while I pondered over and over the causes of K's death. Perhaps because at that time my mind was under the sway of love, my observations were simplistic and straightforward. I quickly decided that without a doubt K died for the sake of lost love. However, as I gradually regained a calmer state of mind, when I looked at the same event again, it appeared to me that such a simple explanation would not do. Was it the clash between reality and his ideals? —Yet that explanation was also insufficient. In the end, I wondered if he had not suddenly resigned himself to death as a consequence of feeling helpless over experiencing, as I had, an absolute loneliness. I shuddered as soon as I thought of that, because the premonition that I was following the same path K had trod blew from time to time across my breast like a chill wind. (6:280)

K killed himself to escape the burden of isolation that resulted from the assertion of his desire and his individuality. His death was the only possible resolution of the contradictory impulses between the ideal and the self. K, in trying to create a new identity, wants to maintain the emotional and intellectual ideals of the past, but he is of course doomed to failure.

Inner Horizons

When *Sensei* finally decides to confess his own crime and then to die, his realization that he is treading the same path is also a recognition that in spite of all his efforts to withdraw from the world, he now has no other recourse but the absolute withdrawal of death.

The decision to die is not made until the death of Emperor Meiji, and Sensei's letter ends by joining the predicament of the individual to the predicament of the age. When he suggests to his wife that with the passing of an age he is now an anachronism, she jokingly suggests *junshi* as a solution to his problem. He replies that if he does commit *junshi*, it will be out of loyalty to the age, not to the emperor, but her remark makes a strong impression. Listening to the sound of the cannon on the evening of the funeral, it sounds to him like "the herald of the passing of Meiji" (6:286). Soon after, he learns of Nogi's death, which is explained as an act of atonement for having dishonorably lost his banner to the enemy in the Seinan War thirty-five years before. *Sensei* sees a parallel to his own life and wonders if Nogi suffered more pain from the suicide or from having waited so long to complete his atonement. He does not share the same motivation as Nogi, whose death is a reaffirmation of older feudal values, but from the viewpoint of his relativistic individualism, Nogi's act still makes sense even in the present age. This apocalyptic vision of the self is finally what drives *Sensei* to the narration of his life and then to his suicide. The two are in essence the same thing.

> More than ten days have gone by since I decided to die, and I want you to know that I used most of the time to leave behind this long autobiography for you. At first I felt that I wanted to meet with you to talk about my life, but having written this I feel instead that I was better able to give you a clearer picture of myself this way, and I am happy. I am not someone who writes on a whim. The past that gave birth to me is part of human experience, and because there is no one else besides me who can tell of it, my efforts to set it down truthfully will not be useless to you or to others in learning about humanity. Just recently I heard the story that Watanabe Kazan postponed his death for a week in order to complete his painting "Kantan" (Vanity).⁸ Looked at from another person's point of view, this can be interpreted as a needless act, but then again perhaps such a thing is inevitable, since the needs appropriate to the person concerned are in that person's heart. My efforts are not intended just to keep my promise to you. They are more the result of having been stirred by my own needs. (6:287–288)

The various aspects of Sōseki's preoccupation with the present and his apocalyptic views of the age and of the individual come together in *Sensei's* justification for his confession and death. The predicament caused by the conflict between the ideal and the practical, by the need to assert individuality in the face of isolation and alienation, and by the loss of absolute values and the emergence of a relativistic worldview is the fundamental issue Sōseki addresses again and again in his fiction. He recognizes that the turn inward toward subjectivity requires constant redefinition of the past, which makes the renewing of life and values possible, but it also means that nothing is permanent or settled. In 1915, a year after he completed *Kokoro,* he turned to the autobiographical confession to present yet another statement of this vision in *Michikusa.* The main plot of the story concerns the strained relationship between Kenzō, Sōseki's literary self, and his former foster father, who uses his connection to extort money from his former charge. When, near the end of the story, the foster father is paid off and agrees in writing never to bother Kenzō again, Kenzō's wife is certain that will be the end of their troubles. The novel, however, ends on an ominous tone of uncertainty. "'Hardly anything is settled in this world. Once things happen they go on forever. It's just that because things take different forms no one understands them.' The tone of Kenzō's voice was bitter, as if he were spitting out his words. His wife silently held their baby. 'Oh, good baby, good baby. We don't understand what father's talking about, do we?' she repeated over and over, kissing its red cheeks many times" (6:592).

Kenzō's sentiments are a Nietzschean expression of the terrible costs of understanding the reality of human nature, of asserting the autonomy of the self, and of looking into the dark chasm created by cultural discontinuity. However, it is misleading to describe this apocalyptic vision in terms of Western concepts such as eternal recurrence. Setting aside the personal dislocations that affected him, Sōseki had native models to provide him with an image for his literary self. There is a strong connection between the dilemma posed by the act of narration in *Kokoro* and that presented in *Hōjōki,* a work that Sōseki, as a young man, translated into English at the urging of James Main Dixon. Chōmei's presentation of the dilemma of modern must surely have struck a chord. Recognizing that Japanese culture was marginal with regard to Western imperialism and faced with the discontinuity this situation created, Sōseki sought to center the narrative voice in his works in order to decenter all culture, Western and Japanese. His vision of the lonely individual facing the world without the aid of any absolute references is a powerful expression of the dilemma of the modern.

◆

chapter ten
The Individual in History:
The Narrative Voice of
Mori Ōgai

Sōseki's concept of individualism allowed him to justify his pursuit of art and literature as an extension of the self and as a response to the personal dilemma he faced concerning his cultural identity. His message to the students at Gakushūin (Peers' school) was that what worked for him was a willingness to seek out a personal means to narrate himself in the modern age. Like Futabatei, Sōseki never thought his experiments with the novel could provide an ultimate resolution to the dilemma of the modern, for any personal resolution is temporary and must pass away with the individual who has found it. This approach is representative of the literary experiments of the age generally, and it is central to the specific literary problems that preoccupied Mori Ōgai, who is frequently cited along with Sōseki as one of the towering figures of the time.

Ōgai was temperamentally very different from Futabatei and Sōseki, but his literary career and his conception of the novel bear some overall similarities to those of his contemporaries. In particular, Ōgai seems to have shared the distrust of fictionality or rhetoric so crucial to those writers who were concerned with creating a realistic mode early in the Meiji period. He was a key figure in the burst of experimentation in the 1880s and early 1890s, making his name as a poet, translator, critic, theoretician, and novelist. From about 1894 to 1909, however, he found himself on the margin of literary developments.

A number of factors explain this situation. First, his early efforts did not lead to the sweeping changes in literary practice that he was seeking, and, like Futabatei, he interpreted the lack of change as a sign of his own failure. Looking back on his early career through the mid-1890s, Ōgai writes,

> At that time, Rohan said to me, "You like debating with people, and so far you've won every time, but people who swim a lot sometimes drown, and those who ride a lot are sometimes thrown. Sooner or later a great debater will appear, and you will be muddied in defeat." In one sense, Rohan was proven correct. In fact, he was more than correct. The age has produced not just one great debater, but an endless number of them. They are the teachers of the new B.A.'s. If you look first, say, at the early volumes of *Teikoku Bungaku*, at the various magazines that followed Hakubunkan's *Taiyō*,[1] which appeared at the same time, and at the different newspapers in Tokyo, you will see that many bullets riddled the name Ōgai. The name Ōgai could not be heard amid the clamor. Ōgai Gyoshi died at that time. (23:138–39)

Second, although he seems to have been more confident of the importance of literature than Futabatei, who was genuinely torn over the direction his career took, Ōgai experienced pressures of a different sort that pulled him away from his artistic activities. As an officer in the Army Medical Corps, Ōgai eventually rose to the post of surgeon general, and the irreconcilable conflict between his public and private pursuits is reflected in the years of what he termed his "exile" from the literary world—an exile that was made real when he was transferred to a provincial post in Kokura to serve as chief medical officer from 1899 to 1902. This exile was the result of Ōgai's struggles with his rivals and superiors, particularly with the surgeon general, Koike Masanao, who often criticized his writing as an activity inappropriate for a military officer.

Although the transfer was in fact only superficially related to his writing career, the alienation and frustration it caused affected his opinion about his work. For all his outward worldliness and aura of confidence, Ōgai shared deeply one of the common experiences of his generation: he came face to face with the conflict between his ideals and the practical limitations imposed by his public life. In an article he wrote in 1900, he looked back on his early literary career.

I have not called myself by the name Ōgai Gyoshi for a long time. Whenever I hear it, it sounds like the name of another person—another person not of my generation, but of a different age altogether. For a short time during the Meiji period, if you spoke of literature, it was said that there were Rohan, Kōyō, Shimei, Kōson, Ryokū, and Bimyō for fiction, and Shōyō and Ōgai for criticism. This idea was bandied about by these writers, and the public, responding to that, came without reason to count me among these men of genius. In speaking about the men who were included in this group, all of them made their living by writing. The only exceptions were Shimei, who became a government official, and Shōyō, who became a college teacher. I alone am a doctor, and an army doctor at that. Then, together with the spread of my false reputation, people outside the field of literature blurred the distinction between fiction and criticism, and they began to say of me, "he's a novelist." (23:134–35)

After his return to Tokyo, Ōgai was soon promoted to the post of director of the war ministry's bureau of medical affairs, and his public career was back on track. The pressure of his new duties, coupled with the outbreak of the Russo-Japanese War in 1904, was enough to keep him from concentrating on literature and, more than his disillusionment, may explain why he was not such an active figure in the literary world in the early years of the century. Nevertheless, his personal frustrations had a lasting effect on his work and would lead him to the experiments that evolved into the narrative modes most often associated with him, the *rekishi shōsetsu* (historical novel) and the *shiden* (historical biography).

The initial step in Ōgai's development was the attitude he adopted during his period of isolation. He came to see himself as an onlooker, *bōkansha,* a person on the margins of society who can observe but has no practical effect on his age. This attitude was shared by many of his peers, who saw a state of isolation and alienation from society as a necessary element in creation and wanted to find in that isolation a kind of objectivity. This attitude easily translated into a narrative perspective identical to the classical outlook embodied by the convention of the hermit or of the narrator of a diary. Ōgai located in his own experience the essential nature of his individuality as well as the paradox of asserting his selfhood as a writer. In an essay titled "'Resignation' no setsu" (An explanation of "Resignation," 1909) he tries to extend his attitude to an aesthetic position. "If I were to say how best to describe my feelings in words, 'resignation' would seem to be appropriate. This does not apply to the arts alone. This feeling is with me wherever I go and whatever I do in the world. Thus, while others are thinking that perhaps I am troubled by personal matters, the fact is that I am indifferent. Of course, it may be that the state of 'resignation' is cowardly. I will make no special effort to defend myself on that count" (19:527).

Ōgai's response to his circumstances, his act of stepping aside, of stoically withdrawing to the margins of society, was both a personal and an artistic necessity, but it was not an act that he saw as particularly heroic. It may be that in adopting the attitude of resignation he precluded the possibility of heroism. Mishima, looking at Ōgai's statement and trying to understand what kind of a man would take that stance, writes,

> Even though pessimism is cowardice, the endurance of suffering is courageous. The malaise [byōhei] of the age in which Ōgai lived has of course not continued in that form to the present, but in any age there hides within what appears to be the courageously heroic, positive spirit of action the heart of a coward [hikyōsha] opposed to the age. Ōgai, at the very least, was not that kind of coward. His resignation may be thought of as narrating with a single word the serene courage and the spiritual pain of a man who would not abandon his position even at the very end.[2]

Mishima's remarks point to the main conflict in Ōgai's sense of himself, and it is this conflict that fuels the developments in his writing over the last decade of his life. If the only appropriate action for the artist was to step back from the world, then how could he record his vision of himself and his age?

The approach taken by the naturalists, and to a certain extent by Sōseki, was to rely on the subjective vision of the artist as the arbiter of truth. For Ōgai, this was not satisfactory. He believed that subjectivity was not a reliable means by which to ascertain truth. In *Vita sexualis,* his parody of Japanese naturalism published (and, in a farcical turn of events, banned by the government) in 1909, he argues through the voice of his narrator, Kanai, that often such a point of view is itself abnormal.

> Whenever he read a naturalist novel, he observed that the characters in those works, in the short span of their daily routines, are accompanied by sexual images for everything, and he observed that criticism recognized such writing as a true portrait of human life. He wondered if human life was really like that, and at the same time he also wondered if he did not deviate from the psychological state of most people and was indifferent toward sexual desire. More specifically, had he been born with an abnormal propensity that could be called frigidity? Such speculations occurred when he read Zola's novels. For instance, Kanai thought about his own personality when he observed the passage in *Germinal* where a laborer from the peasant village reached an

extreme of misfortune and then went to peep at a couple making love. It was not that he thought such things impossible. Such things did happen. He only wondered why the author had written about them. In short, he wondered if the author's own sexual imagery was not abnormal. People like novelists or poets did have abnormal sexual appetites. This was related to the problem of genius on which Lombroso and others had expounded. Möbius and his disciples seized on famous poets and philosophers and made the argument that they were all mentally ill the foundation of their theories. However, the naturalists who had arisen recently in Japan were different. Many writers appeared at the same time writing about the same things. Critics recognized their work as human life. Because, according to psychiatrists, this thing called life gives a sexual coloring to every image, Kanai's doubts became even deeper than before. (3:245–46)

Ōgai focuses his criticism on what he sees to be the single-minded propensity of the naturalists, but his basic concern is very similar to the problem of presenting life in art that Futabatei had expressed the previous year.[3] Even if one accepts that the modern artist's only recourse is to use a subjective view of reality as the basis of literature, a faithful adherence to that vision does not guarantee the truthfulness of narrative. After all, reducing the experience of subjective truth to a narrative form destroys its subjectivity—its presentness—and thus distances both author and reader from the vision of truth that prompted the literary work in the first place. The relativistic sense of knowledge implied by the reliance on the validity of each individual's understanding of life means that absolute knowledge is impossible and that the individual artist must always be alienated from all sense of certainty and continuity.

These issues not only brought Ōgai back to an active literary career but also stimulated his most important literary experiments. He explored the problems of narrative in *Vita sexualis* and *Seinen* (Youth, 1910), both novels perhaps marred by the heavy-handed insertion of their author's intellectual positions on art and philosophy; however, the work that most clearly reveals in formal terms his struggle with these questions is *Gan* (The wild goose), a novel serialized in the journal *Subaru* from September 1911 to May 1913. This novel was his last major fictional piece before he became preoccupied with narratives based on historical events. Ironically, the process of working against his own distrust of fiction produced what is perhaps his finest fictional narrative at just the point when he decided to abandon the form altogether.

Gan is often described as a romance, and it is on that basis that most criticisms of the novel are made. Richard Bowring, for example, feels that there is an "uncertainty of touch in the narration," a carelessness on the author's part that damages the structure of the work and gives an inconsistent portrait of the characters. "One looks for realism and instead one finds idealized characters. . . . In this sense it represents for Ōgai a step back into a precarious lyricism."[4] Bowring concludes that the faults of the work are due to how little time Ōgai had to write and to the fact that literature was still a part-time occupation for him. This critical reading, which is representative of views of the novel,[5] fundamentally misrepresents the structural effects of the work and the conception of the novel that guided those effects. The assumption that one should read *Gan* with the expectation of finding realism is particularly misplaced, for it ignores the fact that Ōgai was concerned with exploring the limits of just that type of narrative. *Gan* is not a romance, and it is not a step back to lyricism. It is an experimental work perhaps best described as an antiromance, a parodic narrative that turns the convention of the romance on its head in order to deal with the issue of the credibility, or reliability, of fiction as a means of conveying truth.

The concern with credibility is apparent in the narrator's efforts to show how he has covered the gaps in his knowledge and thus presented a truthful account. The work opens with the narrator setting the scene of the action within a historical context in order to give himself the surface appearance of plausibility. He is primarily concerned with explaining how he came by the details of the story, many of which involve privileged information. He briefly expresses a worry over that problem at the beginning of chapter 4 but waits until the end of the novel to explain himself and the method of his narration.

> Having completed writing this, I tried counting on my fingers and found that thirty-five years have passed since that time. I observed half the story during my close association with Okada, and the other half I heard when I unexpectedly became acquainted with Otama after Okada had left. This story was created by illuminating together what I observed before with what I heard after, like viewing as one image two pictures, left and right, that have been set under a stereoscope. I may be asked how I came to know Otama, and under what circumstances I heard her story. However, my answer to this, as I said before, is outside the scope of my tale. Because it is beyond question that I do not possess the requisite qualities to become Otama's lover, it is best that the reader not make any idle speculations. (5:419)

The elements of romance are in the details of the lives of Otama and Okada, yet the assertion of authorial control through a concern with demonstrating the reliability of those details takes us out of the realm of the romance. The effect of this blatant intrusion by the narrator resembles the *gesaku*-like effect at the end of *Heibon* and makes it abundantly clear that without that intrusive narrative voice there could be no story.

The intrusion of the narrator is not just a matter of his concern with credibility. We also learn that it was the accidental intervention of the narrator that prevents the potential affair between Otama and Okada from developing. The climax of *Gan* is actually an anticlimax, because the potential lovers fail to meet at a time when they could begin their affair. The responsibility for that anticlimax is borne by the narrator. On the very evening Otama has arranged to express her true feelings to Okada, the narrator invites Okada to come with him on a walk. The reason the narrator wants to go out is that his landlady has served a meal of boiled mackerel in bean paste, a dish he loathes. Since Okada is accustomed to taking walks, they follow one of his normal routes, which takes him by Otama's house. Okada and Otama don't really know one another, but she has watched him on these excursions and has fallen in love with him. Okada is attracted to her but does not understand her feelings. On the night the narrator suggests that he and Okada go out together, Otama is waiting to meet Okada and confess her love, but she is deterred by the presence of the narrator, who later concludes, "Just as great events happen because of a single nail, Otama and Okada were never able to meet on account of a dish of boiled mackerel that was on my dinner tray at the Kamijō" (5:419).

Gan is an antiromance because the very structure of the story is built on the lack of action. In spite of the promise of the ambivalent opening sentence, "*Furui hanashi de aru*" ("It is an old story," or "It happened long ago"), which not only sets the time of the novel but also assures us that we are in store for an old form of narrative, there is no illicit affair, no heroic action, nothing of interest at all from the standpoint of a traditional romance. If the narrator makes it clear that without him the story could not be told, then he makes it equally clear that his very presence in the story renders the traditional narrative impossible. This is also suggested by the presentation of the two would-be lovers. Okada is an antihero. He has the potential to be a traditional hero, in that he is strikingly handsome, well mannered, thoughtful, and intelligent, but the narrator blocks his potential, not only during the crucial scene, but through the very nature of his friendship with Okada. He idealizes his friend much in the way traditional romances idealize the hero, and it is important to note that the friendship begins through their mutual interest in the classic Ming novel, *Kinpeibai* (in Chinese, *Chin P'ing Mei*). Apart from its moralizing aspects, this particular novel is famous for its graphic descriptions of sexual love, and the innocent-seeming choice of it—which glosses over the nature of the text—further suggests an idealization on the part of the narrator. As it turns out, the effects of traditional romances on Okada have little to do with either morality or sex.

> Okada liked *Yü Ch'u hsin-chih,* and among the stories he could practically recite all of "Ta t'ieh ch'ui chuan" by heart. Long before that time, he had wanted to try his hand at the martial arts, but because he had never had the opportunity, he had made no effort. In recent years, after having taken up rowing, he became more enthusiastic, and the fact that he progressed to the point where he was urged by his colleagues to become a competitor was due to the overall development of his will.
>
> In *Yü Ch'u hsin-chih* there is one story Okada liked in particular. That was "Hsiao Ch'ing chuan." The woman in that story, if I were to describe her in modern terms, was a woman who made beauty her life, to the extent that she could keep the angel of death waiting outside the door as she quietly applied her cosmetics. Such a woman aroused Okada's sympathy. For Okada, a woman was something merely beautiful, something that must be adored, that must be content no matter the circumstances, and he felt that her beauty and lovableness had to be protected. His view of women was probably the result of the influence he had unknowingly received by reading run-of-the-mill poems in the *kōrentai* style and by reading the sentimental and fatalistique works of the so-called geniuses of Ming and Ch'ing.[6] (5:279–80)

Part of the idealization of Okada in the narrative is to make him an idealizer of women. His is an aesthetic sensibility not at all suited to the realities a love affair would require him to confront. Indeed, he appears to be a fictional embodiment of the literary and ethical romanticism that Sōseki, in his essay "Bungei to dōtoku," argued was the epitome of Tokugawa sensibility. Throughout the novel, Otama remains for Okada (when he thinks of her at all) a storybook beauty, an ideal that he cannot touch. Okada's heroism is idealized to the point that he is not capable of true heroic action. Indeed, the only action he does take is mock heroic when, like a miniature St. George, he kills a garden snake that is threatening Otama's caged birds. It is worth noting as an aside here Uno Kōji's observation that a characteristic element of Ōgai's work is his preference for passive characters. He writes that, when the topic is love, "at the very least in *Gan* and *Seinen,* and even in *Vita Sexualis,* Ōgai wrote more cleverly about passive characters than about active characters. On the other hand, he became all too easily mediocre when he wrote about active characters in love."[7]

Otama is treated in considerably more detail, and her motivations are given some psychological depth. Her self-awareness grows throughout the story, and she changes according to her circumstances. The way in which she and Okada are treated in the narrative gives further support to reading the novel as an antiromance, for their characterizations reverse the normal type of roles they would represent. In *Gan,* the male hero is rendered passive, while the heroine not only develops a sense of herself but becomes an active plotter.

> Because Otama had no other aim than to give happiness to her father, she became a mistress, forcibly convincing her stubborn father to let her do so. Seeing that she had fallen as far as she could fall, she found a kind of solace in her altruistic act. However, when she learned that the man she relied on for her support was a usurer, this excess of trouble left her at a loss. She was unable to expel the torment in her breast on her own, and she thought that she would open her heart to her father and share her troubles with him. So she thought, but when she visited her father in the house by the pond and saw the blissful life he was leading, she couldn't stand pouring a drop of poison into the sake cup the old man held in his hand. However painful her thoughts might be, she decided to keep them folded up in her heart. The moment she made this decision, Otama, who had up to now known only dependence on others, for the first time felt as though she were independent. (5:355–56)

The assertion of her individuality, the claim she makes for the importance of her own desires, makes it possible for Otama to try to influence the course of the narrative. She carefully arranges an opportunity to meet Okada and consummate her love.

Gan is not a failed attempt at a romance. It deliberately undercuts both realistic and romantic conventions by overtly discussing the nature of fictional narrative and the possibility of conveying truth through that medium. The emphasis on historical accuracy that frames the story suggests that Ōgai was seeking to renew the narrative form by adapting the techniques of the popular histories that he had read in his youth. The fact that he never returned to this kind of overtly fictional narrative does not necessarily mean that he was frustrated by the form or that he thought this particular work was a failure. His experimental approach moves ambivalently between the ideals represented by the factuality of traditional historical narrative and the model of the Western novel that had such an enormous impact on his generation. The ambivalent quality of the narrative voice in *Gan* represents a crucial step in the development of Ōgai's concept of fiction: it makes central the difficulties created by the influence the narrative voice—even a detached, supposedly objective voice—asserts on the story.

Given the inherent subjectivity of the author, narrative is never really able to achieve universality. This is a concern in which the interests of the literary artist and the historian intersect. As is well known, Ōgai was prompted to start writing his historical narratives by the suicide of General Nogi, who was his mentor and friend. The first work he published, "Okitsu Yagoemon no isho" (The testament of Okitsu Yagoemon), which appeared soon after Nogi's death in the October 1912 issue of *Chūō kōron,* was based on materials Ōgai had long had in his possession, so it would be misleading to claim that Nogi's death by itself moved Ōgai toward an interest in historical subjects. Clearly, however, the sensational death of an officer he knew personally prodded him finally to begin to make use of that type of material for literary purposes. The fact that in his last decade he concentrated solely on historical narrative is often interpreted as a major change in the direction of his literary interests, but it is perhaps more appropriate to view it as an extension of the general concerns about narrative form he struggled with during his entire career.

"Okitsu Yagoemon no isho" and the next story he wrote, "Abe ichizoku" (The Abe family) both deal with the subject of *junshi,* but there is a difference in the emphasis he places on historical accuracy in the two stories. "Abe ichizoku" is a considerably less personal story that tries to present an objective, critical account of the injustices that may arise as a result of the custom of *junshi*. The first version of "Okitsu Yagoemon no isho," by contrast, is told in the voice of the man who commits ritual suicide and as such deals directly with the reasons and, by implication, the self-justification for the act. Since the story itself had long interested Ōgai, it is unlikely that he ever meant it to be taken as a defense of Nogi. Rather, the work seems like the response of a man trying to come to grips with why someone he admired would choose to end his life in such an anachronistic manner. More relevant than his reasons for undertaking the story is the fact that he was dissatisfied with it and within the coming year rewrote it to conform more to the approach taken in "Abe ichizoku." In particular, Ōgai added more background material to provide an objective context by which to judge better the suicide of his protagonist, and he radically altered Okitsu's motives after he realized that he had made a serious factual error in the first version by writing that Okitsu knew he was disobeying the ban against *junshi,* when in fact the practice was not banned until after Okitsu's death.

The preoccupation with historical accuracy is a different manifestation of the problem of narrative reliability. The writer who chooses historical subject matter must balance the claims of accuracy with the requirements of narrative form. Ōgai's awareness of these competing claims appears to have been with him from the outset. Not only did he rewrite the story of Okitsu to bring the emotional impact of the story back into balance with historical fact, but in "Ōshio Heihachirō," which was written in late 1913 and published in the January 1914 issue of *Chūō kōron,* he was willing to exploit the dramatic possibilities of the civil insurrection in Osaka led by Ōshio on February 19, 1837. He was extremely careful about selecting his sources for this story, relying primarily on a biography of Ōshio written by Sachida Seiyu. He was also even-handed in his judgment of the causes of the rebellion, citing the natural disasters that led to food shortages, the personal failings of the main players, and the shortcomings of the bureaucratic system. At the same time, the structure of the story is brilliantly conceived, and even though the prose makes no concessions to the reader, the work achieves dramatic impact. The story begins in medias res, and there is an atmosphere of imminent crisis. Ōgai never plays loose with his facts, right down to the accuracy of his geographical descriptions, yet within his rigid accuracy the narrative moves about effortlessly, shifting locales, going back in time to set the context of the events, and showing the personal motivations of the main actors.

In spite of his desire to create an objective, fact-based literature, Ōgai's response to the problem of balancing the need to assert the literary self with the desire for reliability led in the end to a very subjective conception of narrative. Ōgai has had virtually no imitators; his achievement is unique in formal terms. The reason for this is perhaps to be found in his notions of historical method, which share certain affinities with neo-Confucian historiography. More importantly, Ōgai not only adapted the traditional methods of the historian but also appropriated a kind of historical writing called *gaishi,* the informal or unofficial histories of lower-ranking warrior families that were popular in the Tokugawa period, in order to create a narrative form compatible with his concept of the role of the authorial voice.[8]

Official Tokugawa historiography was based on the assumption that history served two purposes: to show the way to correct current evils through a study of the past and to legitimize the present regime. According to the second purpose, the historian ideally should not criticize the present regime but remonstrate with it through historical example (the best examples are Hayashi Razan and his descendants). There was thus a split in the private and public roles of the Tokugawa historian, on the one hand needing to be true to the private, methodological demands of his profession, while on the other providing support for the status quo. These conflicting demands indicate that the Tokugawa view of history assumed that it would reflect both objective reality and the normative ideals of Confucian orthodoxy that supported the state. Kate Nakai writes,

> The traditional evaluation of Confucius' achievement in writing the *Ch'un ch'iu* epitomized this assumption. Confucius was held to have simply described things as they were: his successors also believed that through his selection of what to record and what to leave out, and by his choice of terms to refer to those involved in the events recorded, Confucius had clarified the ways in which the figures appearing in the *Ch'un ch'iu* had succeeded or failed in fulfilling the moral norms specific to their status and situation. "Confucius simply described things as they were," claimed Chu Hsi, "and right and wrong became apparent of themselves."[9]

The ideal historian, as epitomized by Confucius, bridges the gap between subjective vision and objective fact. The selection, ordering, and linguistic categorization of facts is a literary activity that succeeds as history only if it presents things as they are—that is, if it shows us the inherent order and meaning in history.

This notion of historiography is at the heart of Ōgai's discussion of historical narrative, "Rekishi sono mama to rekishibanare" (History as it is and history divergent), which he wrote in December 1914 and published the following month. The reason for writing the essay, he says, is that some of his friends were debating whether his historical narratives were novels. Ōgai states that such a judgment is difficult in an age where few people hold to a normative criticism that prescribes the exact formal requirements a work must fulfill in order to be called a novel. In a sweeping contrast, he echoes the distinction between "naturalistic" Meiji and "idealistic" Tokugawa Japan that Sōseki espoused. He then points out that in the historical narratives he has written to date, there are great disparities in the extent to which he observed the material in an "objective" manner (23:505).[10] To illustrate, he cites two of his works, a story titled "Kuriyama Daizen" and a play, *Nichiren shōnin tsujizeppō* (Wayside sermons of the priest Nichiren, 1904). The first he describes as a bare outline, a historical text. The play, in contrast, uses historical fact rather loosely. That freedom of choice, he claims, is the essence of fiction.

In the end, however, Ōgai rejects the methodology represented by those two examples, a rejection seen as well in the shift in method between the first version of "Okitsu Yagoemon no isho" and "Abe ichizoku." He gives us two reasons for his rejection:

> "I wanted to try investigating historical materials and I was careful to respect the 'nature' I discovered in them. It was distasteful to me to change it arbitrarily. This is one reason. I noticed also that people living now write about their private affairs just as they are, and if it is all right for the present to write just as things are, then it is appropriate for the past. This is the second reason. (23:506)

Ōgai touches here on a fundamental distinction between types of narrative. He shares the historian's concern for preserving what he terms history's "nature," its factuality or narrative inevitability—a choice of words that calls to mind the traditional ideal of the objectivity and lack of self-consciousness in nature. At the same time, he turns to his own use the propensity of the naturalists to emphasize the importance of subjective truth, the contingency of narrative, in their literary projects. He also seems to be aware that the rhetorical demands of narrative create some strange reversals. Although constrained by the demand that they record events as they are or were, historical narratives must always suggest the contingency of events, the possibility of different outcomes, not merely to create aesthetic interest but to create space for the interpretation of events. Fictional narratives, on the other hand, are always limited by what is perceived to be the arbitrary choice of the author, and thus they must always suggest the inevitability of events, the impossibility of other outcomes, in order to make a claim for truth or, at the very least, for verisimilitude.

Ōgai tries to have a laugh at the expense of his contemporaries, but his justification for historical narrative runs into the problem of the rhetorical overlap between narrative types. His appropriation of naturalist theory for his own cause brings him back to the nagging problem of the reliability of the narrative voice even in works where the aim is an objective narrative form determined by unchanging, and thus universal, historical facts. He moves on to remark that many of his friends characterize his work as essentially intellectual, in comparison to other, more emotional writers. Ōgai concurs in this judgment, calling his own work Apollonian and claiming that he has yet even to try to write a Dionysian work (23:506). This reference to Nietzsche is not merely an attempt to place his work within the mainstream of Western aesthetics; it also implies that Ōgai was seeking some philosophical image to describe the imbalance he perceived in his writing. The reference also connects him once again with the critical vocabulary of Futabatei and Sōseki in that it suggests that Ōgai saw his work as moving between, and limited by, the two aesthetic poles of the ideal and the particular. He disliked changing the nature in history, but he felt constrained by a history he could not experience and thus could not know.

Ōgai felt that he had to resolve the inherent ambiguity in narrative, and to achieve the kind of perspective that would help him do this, he returns to his philosophy of resignation and says that his aim is to write dispassionately, to arrive at an intuited objectivity through a subjective, but aloof, observation of historical nature. Instead of altering history, he seeks to participate in it and thus allow the reader to participate as well. He is not bothered by inserting editorial judgments of his own, for the absence of such remarks could also be interpreted as a form of subjective bias. His approach is to enter the subjective, particular world of his characters, presenting the facts, incidents, and traits by which they would evaluate and understand themselves. In a sense, this approach does not differ significantly from the method of the Confucian historian, whose method might involve case-by-case studies. However, Ōgai is no Confucianist. Where the Confucian historian would say that ultimately right and wrong are reducible to principle, Ōgai's training in Western scientific methods and his self-consciousness about the philosophical problems of perspective did not allow him to go that far. He could assert his own individuality against history for the sake of creating a narrative voice, but he could never claim his method provided an absolute viewpoint that resolved the question of narrative reliability.

The formal qualities of Ōgai's historical narratives represent a unique development in Meiji literature. Historical narrative was finally the only appropriate mode for him because it involved not the creation of wholly new forms, which required an authorial intrusion that was too subjective, but the transformation of one narrative, the narrative of historical fact (or "nature"), into a more inward, personal account. Sensing the discontinuity of the age, an age in which he was a major spokesman for scientific rationalism and skeptical change and in which he had to come to terms with the emotional pull of the past as represented by Nogi's *junshi,* he sought to create a new literature by fusing a subjective narrative voice with an ideal form of historical narrative. Ōgai's struggle to achieve that fusion grew out of the same modernist outlook apparent in the struggle of Futabatei with the *gesaku* tradition or the struggle of Sōseki with the problem of identity.

◆

chapter eleven
Nostalgic Narratives:
The Primitivistic Voice
of Nagai Kafū

Nagai Kafū certainly agreed with Sōseki that the heroic was not a characteristic of the modern, but for him distress over what had been lost in the present, which in his view was dwarfed by an idealized past, was not balanced by an equal sense of gain. Many of his fictional characters are depicted as deeply discontented and longing to return to Japan's past. For example, in "Mihatenu yume" (Unattainable dreams, 1910), a loosely autobiographical story, the protagonist is a man drawn to the vestiges of Edo culture who tries to lose himself in the arts of that time and in his affairs with geisha. He is a man who chooses to be out of his time and to turn his back on the present. "The primary reason for this was his inability to maintain interest in any aspect whatsoever of the newly risen Meiji period. In a word, the external appearances of his own times were crude, and its tastes were uncultured. On the basis of that view, he was a man who violently cursed twentieth-century civilization, and he dreamed of the frivolous eighteenth century, trampled across by the muddy boots of the lower classes, and of the Edo period, which had suffered the attacks of Mizuno Jūrōzaemon, lord of Echizen" (*KZ* 5:239).[1] Similarly, Chōkichi, the young protagonist of *Sumidagawa* (The Sumida River, 1909), longs to escape the modern world, with its mindless schooling, rigorous examination system, and colorless bureaucratic careers, in order to become a Kabuki actor and marry the love of his youth, Oito, who has become a geisha.

The frequent appearance of figures like these in Kafū's work has prompted many readers to stress his antimodernity and his one-man revolt against the loss of the urban culture of Edo as the salient feature of his fiction. As Etō Jun has put it, "All through his life, Nagai Kafū continually fled from the realities of modern Japan. Among modern Japanese writers, no one maintained his isolation as carefully as he, nor has anyone so fastidiously rejected things that threatened that isolation. On the surface, at least, his was the life of an isolationist."[2] In this view, Kafū is a fugitive from modernity, a writer with no social vision who simply deplored what he saw around him.

The overtly antimodern stance of many of Kafū's narratives, and the nostalgic, elegiac moods he so often evokes to convey that stance, is central to his work, but that characteristic is often emphasized to the point that he is described as a complete anomaly, a throwback to the age of the scribbler of *gesaku* fiction.[3] This judgment is exemplified by Seidensticker's translation of Kafū's personal choice of epitaph, *sanjin,* as "scribbler." Yet Seidensticker's choice strikes me as misleading, emphasizing the triviality and frivolity of the act of writing fiction and ignoring the nonliterary aspects of the lifestyle the word *sanjin* implies. No doubt the epitaph has a humorous quality, since the word also refers to a person of no talent or to a man of leisure, but the knowingness behind Kafū's selection suggests a seriousness of purpose that the word *scribbler* does not convey. This is not a mere quibble; Seidensticker's term is a critical categorization he uses to support the notion that Kafū's work is a throwback to *gesaku* traditions. In my opinion, the ambivalence of the meaning of *sanjin* not only precludes that interpretation but also points to a more important characteristic of Kafū's work: its effort to situate itself in the ambiguous space marked out by the changing meanings of *modern*.

There is little doubt that Kafū presented himself as a lonely eccentric lamenting the trends of his age, but that pose cannot disguise the fact that his antimodern attitude, his primitivism, reflected a literary sensibility shaped by an overpowering sense of cultural discontinuity. His nostalgia enabled him to conjure up an imagined past in which he saw the realization of all the ideals for which he longed in the present. Kafū's antiquarian interest in Edo—an idealized literary cityscape comparable to

Yeats's Byzantium—reflects a modernist aesthetic central to the structure of his fiction. Like Futabatei, he admired and emulated the playful fiction of Edo scribblers, and like Ōgai, he was fascinated with the possible uses of historical detail. However, he was also uncomfortably aware that he was trapped in an age that blocked the realization of his ideals.

A number of critics have located the origins of his isolationism and pursuit of artistic individualism in his rebellious temperament. Nakamura Mitsuo claims that Kafū's interest in both French literature and Edo culture stemmed from his desire to assert himself against his family, his father in particular, and against the larger society, often in the form of the literary establishment.

> If I were to give a reason [for his interest in French literature], then perhaps his antipathy toward his father, who governed his household like an oriental despot but who outwardly took the guise of the English gentleman, and his revulsion against the strictness of the German missionaries who surrounded his mother are the foundation. . . .
>
> His youthful intoxication with the arts of Edo was the product of his resistance to the atmosphere of his home life, which was that of a respectable Yamanote family, together with the influence of his mother, who had had an Edo upbringing, and of his rebellion against his father, who hoped to make him follow a respectable profession.[4]

As Kafū's career developed, his impulse toward isolation was transformed into aestheticism, a sensitivity to beauty and art that held no other purpose. He strove to apply the ideals of freedom and selfhood to his own life, and when it came to creating a formal, literary statement of his notions of selfhood, Kafū initially turned to the French naturalists, especially Zola, for the concepts he needed.

Early in his career he stressed the overpowering constraints of heredity and environment on the individual. The artist could attempt to deal with the environment either by becoming socially active and changing it or by withdrawing from society altogether through physical or imagined retreat. The constraint of heredity, however, could not be directly changed or avoided, and Kafū tried to resolve the problem through the liberation of personal experience: that is, through the act of re-creating himself. This self-centered aestheticism produced an idiosyncratic view of the artist and a highly personal conception of the novel. This conception owed a great deal to his experiences in America and France between 1903 and 1908; indeed, shortly after he returned to Japan in 1908 he published *Amerika monogatari* (Tales of America), whose impressionistic style and lyricism gained him a critical following.[5] The reputation he secured following his years abroad, however, should not lead one to attribute his decision to define his literary identity through isolation solely to his years abroad; that decision, in fact, is closely tied to the formal experiments he undertook before his travels. *Yume no onna,* for example, is often cited as Kafū's first successful novel, and yet its importance to his development has been overlooked because of the tendency to view the years overseas as the formative period in his art.

The twin constraints of environment and heredity are crucial elements in the story of Onami, the heroine of *Yume no onna.* Onami's life is almost a parable of the kinds of problems the individual faced as a result of the social dislocations of the Meiji period. She cannot escape from the circumstances created by the failure of her father, a retainer to the feudal lord in Okazaki (in present-day Aichi prefecture), to adjust to the modern world after the Restoration. His personal and financial setbacks force Onami to be sent off as a mistress when she is sixteen. Although she gives birth to a child, the precariousness of her social position is made clear at the beginning of the novel when she learns of the death of her benefactor. Because she is the sole means of support for her parents and her younger sister, Okinu, she agrees to become a mistress again, this time to a merchant named Otabe, who sets her up in a brothel. There is at the heart of her actions a fundamental contradiction between the filial piety that motivates her and the reality of the life she is forced to lead. In the end, her efforts come to naught, and despite her attempts to protect Okinu, the atmosphere in which her younger sister is brought up is so negative that she eventually runs away from home. When Otabe dies, Onami's hopes of escaping her circumstances are also extinguished.

Onami's life is driven inexorably by forces beyond the control of an individual, and thus the novel appears at first sight to be a youthful, mechanical imitation of a Zolaesque narrative.[6] However, Kafū, in representing the difficulties confronting the individual, produces a distinctive narrative voice that reemerges in his later writings. *Yume no onna* is the first of his novels fully to explore the primitivist response to the problem of the modern, with the past becoming both an image to describe the dislocation felt by the individual and an imaginary escape from the alienation of the present. Two passages from the novel illustrate Kafū's method. The first takes place when Onami visits her family home in Okazaki. Just before she returns to Tokyo, she goes with her mother to buy some gifts, and on the way back they pass the outer moat of the old castle. As the autumn evening settles over the houses, Onami gets the strong impression that the past is still alive. As they pass a black gate, her mother suddenly stops and asks her if she recognizes the place. It turns out to be the house where both Onami and her father were born.

> Her mother spoke in a tearful voice, but Onami was amazed. "Mother? This was father's house?" She stood open-mouthed, but could say nothing more.
> "Ah, people say you can never tell about human fortune . . . but when I think about it, it would have been best to have died." Her mother was blinking back her tears. "Let's go home now, Onami. We walked here accidentally, but if I had known we would come by this place I would have turned on to the street over there. No matter how much you cry, you can't change fate."
> "Mother? Whose house is this now? Oh, listen . . . you can hear a koto on the second floor." Onami pulled at her mother's sleeve as though she couldn't bear passing by.
> "I wonder who lives here. Everything about this area makes one think of the past. Mother, you haven't come here for many years."
> Her mother once again looked sorrowfully up at the second floor. As she did, an indescribably gentle voice sang out a verse, "The flower named Fuki . . ."
> "Mother, that's the young lady of the house. She has a lovely voice. She must be an elegant woman."
> "In the old days, you would have learned the koto." Her mother could not control herself and her tears fell.
> Onami, listening to the haunting sound of the koto at the place where she was born, was struck by a deep, inexpressible feeling that somehow her own shining birthright had been stolen by a young woman she did not know. (*KZ* 2:290–91)

The nostalgic mood of the novel is created by this and other scenes in which the sense of loss represented by the present is focused through Onami's perspective. However, that mood is not a recovery of the past, but a longing for recovery. As such, the images of the old castle and its grounds, the retainers' houses, and the sound of the koto are appropriate to the naturalist notions that shaped the narrative in that they point to the heroine's profound sense of alienation.

The images of a nostalgic past represent the only hope of social reintegration for Onami, yet realizing that hope is as impossible as solving the moral quandary in which she finds herself. As the title suggests, the dilemma of the individual in the present is irresolvable in real terms. The longing for a return to the past is balanced by a strong awareness of the ephemerality of life and of the inexorable flow of time. By the end of the novel, we are in the type of cityscape, the demimonde, that is the preferred imaginative setting for conveying the dislocations of modern life in much of Kafū's fiction. While the demimonde is less affected by the changes at the center of society and thus contains some vestiges of the past by which the individual can redefine identity, it is on the margins of society and cannot provide a lasting refuge. Again, the title of the novel suggests this reading by indicating the insubstantiality of Onami herself. Time imagery abounds in the story, but the most important image is perhaps that of flowing: the flowing of time, of the river, and of the course of life. This image is also linked to Onami's final recognition of her position in the world. Near the end of the novel, she takes a boat ride with two acquaintances, customers she has known, down the Fukagawa River through the licensed quarter of Susaki to Tokyo Bay. The strange and beautiful images of nature and of the old city fill her with a confusing range of emotions, from wonder and awe to loneliness and apprehension.

> Until that evening, Onami had never really had the opportunity to gaze up at the night sky spread out so magnificently clear and so endlessly sweeping. Except for the indistinct Milky Way, the moon, shining like a flawless gem, and all the heavenly bodies gave off a blazing, mysterious light as they drifted above the blue sky.
>
> For no apparent reason, the sky was frightening to Onami's feminine heart, and for a time she unconsciously closed her eyes, but sad, unbearable thoughts came welling up one after another in her breast. Her suffering arose from the very depths of her body. Onami had never before been so totally gripped by such a strange fear concerning the life she had come to lead. Just now, however, while looking up at the infinite sky, she confronted the long past life stirring in her heart, and while she felt thoroughly the forlornness of being alone in the wide world, at the same time she also felt as though she had completely awakened from the dream of the life she had until today been living as though it were reality. As a single woman with the power of discretion to go out into the world, she had been able up to now to shoulder the heavy responsibilities of her parents and her younger sister. She had thought that if she somehow did everything she ought to do with the fervor of her dream, then she would automatically arrive at the final great goal of human happiness. But perhaps there was no such thing in this world. Onami concluded that it would have been better to have died in her previous sleeplike state before this awakening took place. (KZ 2:377–78)

The awakening of Onami to the inevitability of her situation does not help her, but it does give rise to a critical and interpretative perspective that permits her to give new meaning to traditional images. It is this developing self-awareness that sets off the meaning of the final image of the novel. On the way back to her brothel from her father's burial, the light of the streetlamps "flowed like blood through the patches of pure white snow here and there" (*KZ* 2:389). This image conflates traditional images of sexuality and the flux of time with the naturalist concept of the flow of heredity and circumstance that traps Onami.

Yume no onna is important because its narrative strategies mark out the path Kafū's later career took. Moreover, the work's nostalgic aspects suggest that its author was part of the mainstream of Meiji developments. This is not simply a matter of the elegiac tone or the mood of nostalgia that permeates the story. Like so many of his peers, Kafū was stimulated by European models of narrative technique to explore the fundamental questions of identity and displacement specific to his time and culture and thus looked to the margins of society for the images needed to express his vision of the modern dilemma. Ironically, as a result of his narrative choices, he is often accused of lacking any social vision. Of course, many writers of the period, not just Kafū, have been criticized for turning their backs on society or lacking social consciences. Still, even though there may be some justice in these criticisms, it is more accurate to read the move toward the margins of society as a legitimate response for an author in an age where social and moral absolutes are no longer viable. *Yume no onna* is an example of a subversive tendency to make the margins of life central to narrative, a tendency manifest in the central place a primitivistic voice assumed in his later work.

Kafū's primitivism reaches its most complete statement in his late masterpiece, *Bokutō kidan* (A strange tale east of the river), which took the literary establishment by surprise when it appeared in serialized form in *Asahi shinbun* from April to June 1937. Kafū had been relatively inactive for almost two decades and had published little since 1931–1932, when *Tsuyu no atosaki* (During the rainy season) appeared. That a work of *Bokutō kidan*'s quality should have been produced by a writer who had first made his reputation in the Meiji period seemed almost miraculous, as if a previously unknown manuscript by an old master had suddenly been unearthed. That the manuscript should have appeared in a newspaper was all the more surprising, for this broke Kafū's personal rule against such publication, which he had adopted because of his intense fear and loathing of reporters. He even speaks of that fear in *Bokutō kidan* when the narrator, a writer named Ōe Tadasu, explains the precautions he takes to keep his liaison with a woman named Oyuki a secret.

> The only concern for me here was that I had to take steps to avoid running into other writers or reporters in the vicinity of Oyuki's street or on the Tōbu train. I didn't mind if I ran into people somewhere else, or if it looked as though I was being followed. I am in the position of having been given up on by austere people since my youth. And because even the children of my relatives no longer dropped by my house, now, finally, there was nothing to hold me back. The only thing I had to fear were writers and reporters. Some ten years earlier, at about the time cafés were beginning to appear on the main streets all over the Ginza, I was denounced by all those rags that considered themselves newspapers because I took to getting drunk there. The April 1929 *Bungei shunjū* attacked me as a person who "should not live on" in the world. When I saw passages that used such phrases as "seducer of maidens" I wondered if perhaps they had entrapped me and made me out to be a criminal. If they ever found out that I was crossing the Sumida River stealthily at night to play around on the eastern bank, it is hard to imagine what they might write about me now. This was something truly to be feared. (*KZ* 9:134)

Bokutō kidan shares certain elements of Kafū's work in general, including the demimonde setting and the tendency to evoke and elegize the past and its fading customs. However, the novel is different in certain ways from the work that immediately precedes it, especially *Tsuyu no atosaki*. The heroine of that work, a woman named Kimie, represents the modern demimonde, the world of the Ginza café. She is also at the center of the novel in the same way that Onami is at the center of *Yume no onna*. The central figure in *Bokutō kidan*, in contrast, is the narrator, Ōe Tadasu, and the novel is a highly personal account, a fictional memoir, that combines the overall unity provided by first-person narrative with stylistic elements gleaned from the descriptive techniques of *zuihitsu*.

The novel is based on the author's experiences in and around a newer section of Tokyo called Tamanoi, which he first visited in 1932. The district was situated east of the Sumida River, north and east of Asakusa. The area had been primarily swampland until the Kantō earthquake of 1923, which led to a replanning of the city. The brothels that had been located around Asakusa, the last vestige of the old licensed quarters, were forced to move into Tamanoi. Kafū spent a great deal of time there in 1936, using a map to find his way around the labyrinth of narrow streets. He recorded his wanderings in a diary and then in an essay titled "Terajima no ki" (A record of Terajima, 1936). *Bokutō kidan* owes its miscellaneous quality to the descriptive passages in the diary and essay.

Edward Seidensticker provides a full analysis of the connection between the diary and the novel. However, in demonstrating the importance of the diary as source material for the novel he misrepresents the impact of the personal memoir on the structure of the novel. He writes that *Bokutō kidan* "must be taken on its own terms, as a lyric and not as a novel of conflict and resolution."[7] By calling the novel a lyric and thus emphasizing the elements of mood he claims are derived from the diary, he all but sidesteps any discussion of the fictionalizing techniques that actually constitute the unique terms of conflict and resolution in the work.

Tamanoi figures as a representative locale for the imaginary cityscape that plays a recurring role in Kafū's narratives. It is an evocation of the past, of the culture of the licensed quarters of Edo, and yet it is not only a rather poor substitute but also an extremely transitory one. Dirty, haphazard, and prone to flooding, Tamanoi was a makeshift district from its inception, and it disappeared altogether after the war. Like the café scene that sprang up in the 1920s and also disappeared rather quickly, Tamanoi embodies the impermanence of a past world that is continually being lost. Kafū seeks to arrest that process of mutability by finding a timeless quality in the images of that cityscape. It is in the bringing together of those images that Kafū's narrative emerges.

The novel begins with the narrator feeling the need to escape the noise and oppressive atmosphere of the modern city, with its blaring radios and crass newspapers. His desire is to retreat from the world in order to reclaim some sense of wholeness and identity. The images that allow him to give expression to that sense are found in Tamanoi. The district is dirty, and its canals are swollen and infested with mosquitoes, but this squalor is precisely the antidote to civilization, the primitivist ideal, that the narrator longs for. All of the sights, sounds, and smells of the city are brought together in the single image of Oyuki, the prostitute with whom the narrator spends many of his summer evenings. Her rooms stand close to an open canal in a nondescript back alley, and the heat of summer and the ubiquitous insects become closely associated with her. This connection is made explicitly at one point in an exchange between Oyuki and some male passersby who heckle her while she is sitting at her window. One of them refers to her as "gutter-mosquito whore" (*dobukkajorō*), and she retorts by calling him "garbage-dump asshole" (*gomitameyarō; KZ* 9: 167).

Yet for all the vulgarity associated with her, Oyuki arouses in the narrator an ability to recover the past.

> The house by the gutter, where I had unexpectedly found peace . . . the house where the woman called Oyuki lived, was in a corner of the district that reminded me of the prosperity of the area when it was first opened in the Taishō period. This fact struck me somehow as having a deep relationship with my own circumstances, having been left behind by the tide of fortune. To get to that house you enter a certain alley from Taishō Avenue, pass the Fushimi Inari Shrine, with its stained banners unfurled, and follow along the gutter. Because it is in such an out-of-the-way place, the radios and phonographs of the main street disappear in the sounds of the passersby and can hardly be heard. On a summer's night there was probably not another spot as suitable for escaping from the noise of the radio.
>
> Throughout the pleasure quarters, according to the rules of the association, phonographs and radios were banned from four in the afternoon, when the women came out to sit at their windows, and playing the samisen was also forbidden after that hour. On evenings when the rain was falling softly, as the night grew late and the voices that called out were heard less frequently, the droning of the mosquitoes in and out of the house could be heard. Truly the loneliness of this place, which was like a back alley in some town on the outskirts, was palpable. This was not just some ordinary slum. It possessed the lonely charm of the world of the past that can be felt in the plays of Tsuruya Nanboku.
>
> The figure of Oyuki, who always did her hair up in the old Shimada or Marumage styles, the filth of the gutter, and the droning of the mosquitoes were strong stimuli to my senses and brought back phantoms of a past that had disappeared thirty or forty years ago. I want to express my gratitude, without reservation if I can, to the go-between who brought me those fleeting, strange visions. More than the actors who star in the plays of Nanboku, more than Tsuruga What's-his-name who chants *Ranchō*, Oyuki was the skilled, silent artist who had the power to call forth the past. (*KZ* 9:136–37)[8]

The narrator credits Oyuki with creating his artistic vision, but his likening of her to an artist is, at least in terms of the narrative, somewhat misleading. The portrait of Oyuki is very sympathetic. With her old-fashioned appearance, she is described at one point as being more honest, simple, and forthright than the new prostitutes of the Ginza and Ueno districts (*KZ* 9:158), and near the end of the novel the narrator says that she "possessed a personal charm and an intelligence inappropriate to a woman of such a place" (*KZ* 9:180). The narrator believes the woman's beauty and elegance is genuine within its context, and this beauty stimulates his desire to write. For all the credit he gives Oyuki, however, her beauty is his own creation, and the ideal of beauty he finds in her and in Tamanoi is embodied by the narrative structure of *Bokutō kidan*. There is an explicit connection between the nostalgic mood, arising from the narrator's disinheritance from the past, and his need to tell his story.

> Oyuki is the muse who had unexpectedly called back these nostalgic phantoms of the past to my weary heart. If Oyuki had not been drawn to me—or at the very least if I had not felt that she was—then most certainly the manuscript that had been lying on my desk for so long would have been destroyed and discarded finally. Oyuki was the mysterious encouragement who forced an aging author, one forgotten by the world, to finish a manuscript that would probably be his final work. Whenever I looked on her face, I wanted to thank her. If you look only at the results of my behavior, then perhaps I deceived a woman inexperienced in the ways of the world, and I dallied not only with her body but also with her sincere emotions. Though in my heart I want to apologize for a wrong that is hard to forgive, I regret that circumstances were such that I was unable to do so. (*KZ* 9:170)

For all the vividness with which Oyuki is described, she is, like Onami, an insubstantial figure: the inspiration and the creation of the artist. Her portrait may be realistically detailed, but to focus on that aspect of her characterization would be somewhat sentimental, as the narrator himself becomes about her, and would also miss the deeper emotional and aesthetic basis of the novel. In a sense, the idealization of Oyuki's beauty is a denial of reality, because it seeks to make permanent something whose very nature is tied up with ephemerality. On the surface, the novel is an elegy for the loss of an ideal, but there is much more to the work than the evocation of a mood. The act of narrating is a conferral of form, or an idealization, that seeks to arrest the discontinuity created by a strong awareness of the present. More than the description of Tamanoi, the self-consciously literary context in which those descriptions are presented is important to understanding the work's complexity.

The preoccupation with narrative form and with the authorial voice in *Bokutō kidan* reflects the work's sense of discontinuity. The narrator creates a fictional context for the story of Oyuki throughout the novel. He not only quotes from his own stories but includes a chapter of the novel he is working on when he first meets Oyuki. This novel, called *Shissō* (Disappearance), tells of a man named Taneda Junpei, a teacher who grows sick of his conventional family and runs off with a barmaid named Sumiko. The need for material for *Shissō* sends the narrator to Tamanoi, where he accidentally runs into Oyuki, sharing his umbrella with her during a sudden rainshower in a coincidental meeting evocative of the fiction of the late Tokugawa period. He then reflects upon his story.

> People who have read the stories of Tamenaga Shunsui perhaps know that the author would insert here and there in the narrative a few lines defending himself. When he wrote a scene in which a young girl in love for the first time forgets all reserve and throws herself at the man she loves, he then immediately urged the reader to consider this girl, her appearance and choice of words, according to the situation, and not to judge her as lascivious. There are instances in his work where, when a woman brought up in a good family reveals her true feelings, she can appear more charming and fascinating than a geisha. Or again, when he depicts instances where an experienced prostitute meets up with a male friend from her youth and fidgets like a young lady, even though she is a professional. Because these are points that all people rich in experience with these matters will recognize, it is clear that the author's observations are not inappropriate and that he wrote to be read with that in mind.
>
> In imitation of Shunsui, I shall add a superfluous word or two here. The reader may suspect that the woman I first met there on the roadside was too familiar in her attitude toward me. However, I have done no more than set down the incident as it happened, without adding any rhetorical flourishes to our actual encounter. Nor is there any artifice on my part. There are perhaps those who, seeing that our encounter took place because of a sudden thunderstorm, will laugh at the conventional narrative technique of the author, but because I was conscious of this, I did not want to deliberately set up events elsewhere. The events of that evening, which were brought about by an evening shower, seemed made to order for some traditional story, and that fact struck me as rather interesting. Because I really wanted to try writing that, I began to set things down in this volume. (*KZ* 9:119)

At first glance, the connection between life and art and the narrator's concern with credibility reflect the preoccupation with sincerity exhibited by the naturalists. The structure of the novel, however, places us very much within a literary world, such that the novel turns the naturalist premise upside down in the way that Ōgai jokingly proposed for historical fiction. Art is no longer the extension of real life. Instead, real life shares in the fictionality, the insubstantiality, of art. The interweaving of other literary works—a quotation from the drama critic and scholar of Chinese literature, Yoda Gakkai (1837–1909), various *haiku*, a poem from *The Dream of the Red Chamber*, and the valedictory poem at the end (*KZ* 9: 131, 138–39, 177, 180–82)—points to the literary self-consciousness that shapes the narrative. At one point, this becomes a major concern for the narrator, who wants to avoid the dilemma that is at the heart of Ōgai's *Gan*. He is afraid that if he imposes himself on the world of Tamanoi, it will be cut off from him. He quotes from "Mihatenu yume" to explain his aesthetic notions and states that the reason he likes such a place is that "he rejoiced more in discovering the remains of some beautiful embroidery on a scrap of discarded cloth than in finding the stains on a wall proclaimed pure white" (*KZ* 9:151). This is an implied contrast between the aesthetic notions governing Kafū's work and the approach of the naturalists. His aim is to be unflinchingly true not so much to life as to his own primitivist impulses and to find an outlet, a narrative voice, appropriate to his frame of mind. It is for this reason that he justifies his interest in Oyuki to the reader: "In order to become intimate with these women—at least in order to have them respect me and not distance themselves from me—I thought it best to hide my personal circumstances. It would have been very hard for me to take had these women thought of me as someone who shouldn't come to this kind of place. I wanted to avoid as far as was possible being mistaken for one who enjoyed looking down on them from above, as though I observed their unfortunate lives in the same way I would watch a play. Accordingly, I had to keep my identity secret" (*KZ* 9:151). The narrator denies his self-identity, becoming a kind of voyeur in order to share in the life of Oyuki and of Tamanoi. But to tell of his experience he must eventually reassert his identity as the author who, in giving his experience fictional form, idealizes it.

The paradox of fiction is that it denies reality at all levels. Ideals are nothing more than abstract, transitory fictions; and to reduce an ideal to formal expression is to deny its essence. This paradox is brought home in the treatment of the narrator's break with Oyuki. He simply stops coming to see her when the autumn arrives. He does not explain it to her, because, he believes, she would not be able to understand why he was not coming back. He gives as one reason for his decision the fear that she would become as lazy or unruly as a wife because of his own weaknesses—but this is mere rationalization. By asserting this kind of control over the narrative, the author establishes his literary identity and at the same time brings the narrative to a close. In the end, the decision to break is essentially a formal one. In a fictional world where beauty and the past are idealized, attachments are not possible, for they would destroy the idealized forms that make the narrative possible.

Bokutō kidan is more than a beautifully written elegy. It is a complex statement on the nature and reality of the act of narrating. The novel, in denying its links to reality, makes it clear that the only attachment possible in literary art is the attachment to words. The two characters whose interactions create the work never really learn anything about each other; they remain at the level of idealization, of literary type. Again, for all the vividness of her portrait, Oyuki is nothing more than a mask, the goodhearted whore who serves as the inspiration for art. The narrator is a fugitive, a poser, a voyeur, but he is also very much at the center of the text. Like a fictional Heian lover who catches a stolen glimpse—a *kaimami*—of a woman through an opening in a fence or screen, the narrator of *Bokutō kidan* does not need a detailed view of a woman to create an ideal of beauty.

The creation of narrative through the tension between an observer and an idealized character is a technique deeply embedded in works of Japanese literature that exhibit a strong sense of the modern. The primary source of Kafū's art and of his identity as an artist is the tension between the ideals of the narrator and the impossibility of reconciling those ideals with reality. There is both a triumph in the literary metamorphosis and self-expression involved in the creation of art and a sense of irrevocable loss, a symbolic death, in the reduction of ideals to narrative. This ambivalence is given full expression in the poem that closes the novel:

> A single stem of cockscomb stands
> in the corner of the garden
> where you discarded a tissue
> stained with the blood you wiped from my brow
> bitten by a mosquito lingering past its season.
> Because the frost that drops each night is cold,
> its deepening colors move me
> as its brocade leaves wither,
> not waiting for the evening wind,
> not knowing the term of its life.
> A dying butterfly flits unsteadily on wretched wings
> and must fall and die in the shade of the leaves
> of a cockscomb blooming uncertainly out of season.
> A late autumn evening
> leaves no time for fleeting dreams to form.
> I am alone, having parted from you,
> and what will become of my heart,
> which I liken to a single stem of cockscomb
> that must fall and die? (*KZ* 9:181–82)

Those who prefer to see in Kafū's work an unapologetic lyricism that affirms the validity of the artistic endeavor and the isolation of individual existence may object that my analysis emphasizes too much his narrative calculations. Yet the closing poem suggests that Kafū found the ultimate image for his views of life and art not in specific objects of nature, nor in his remembrance of things past, nor even in literary and cultural artifacts, but rather in the self-conscious, nostalgic process of writing: a process that reconstitutes those objects, memories, and artifacts and reveals their fragile, fleeting impermanence.

part four

◆

Narrative Relativism and
Cultural Amnesia

For many authors whose careers began or peaked in late Meiji Japan, cultural discontinuity was expressed as a problem of identity. The sincerity thought to be a necessary component in the creation of a new literature was directly related to the potential ability of literature to define the modern individual. Beginning with Futabatei, the authors I have examined in the two preceding sections of this book experimented with narrative voice in an attempt to situate themselves as modern Japanese by breaking free from the authority of two traditions—the native tradition, which seemed inadequate to express their sense of the modern, and the Western tradition, which threatened their cultural autonomy. Although their experiments produced different results, each of these writers stressed the validity of personal experience and observation over universal values and thus, wittingly or not, embraced a relativism that set the course for the development of narrative form throughout this century.

The convention of a personal, subjective voice was a technique to create narrative order and meaning in a changing society, but it could never serve as an absolute point of reference to define modern identity. While the fragmentation of cultural values liberated the artist, making literary renewal possible, it also isolated the artist by making normative values impossible. In general, the modern artist tries to compensate for this relativism, this loss of absolutes, either by self-consciously championing a universalist ideology or by championing the self and art as original and unique and thus worthy of elevation to the status of a cultural standard. David Harvey observes that this process of "creative destruction" at the heart of the modern was reinforced through the "commodification and commercialization of a market for cultural products during the nineteenth century." The result "was often a highly individualistic, aristocratic, disdainful (especially of popular culture), and even arrogant perspective on the part of cultural producers, but it also indicated how our reality might be constructed and re-constructed through aesthetically informed activity."[1] Though Harvey is pointing to developments in Western societies, his comments are relevant to the situation in Japan, for Japanese writers were no less concerned with producing the essential Japanese narrative than, say, American writers have been with creating the Great American Novel. Examining Western modernism in the period between the world wars, Harvey also notes that "this particular surge of modernism . . . had to recognize the impossibility of representing the world in a single language. Understanding had to be constructed through the exploration of multiple perspectives. Modernism, in short, took on multiple perspectivism and relativism as its epistemology for revealing what it took to be the true nature of a unified, though complex, underlying reality."[2]

The dilemma posed by a relativistic outlook is the dilemma of the modern itself; that is, those aspects that define the modern self, such as an open-ended sense of development or a multileveled sense of identity, make it impossible to discover or express universal values and thus lead to fragmented perspectives. The only way to avoid the debilitating effects of relativism is to make the individual perspective a type of narrative absolute—to interject a new conception of the heroic back into narrative form. This approach, which is best represented by the narrative perspective employed in certain works by Shiga Naoya, is problematic. For one thing, it implies a kind of uncritical hero worship that establishes cultural values solely through the viewpoint of a strong protagonist. Here again developments in Japanese narrative experiments may be compared with those in the West. Protofascist tendencies in a number of modernist or avant-garde movements in Europe are an example, since on one level fascism is an attempt to insert the heroic back into a skeptical, self-conscious present.³ In addition, the heroic employs the most primal of images, such as the struggle between father and son, to create a mythology of the transcendent and absolute artist. To adopt such an approach requires that the author have confidence in the essential judgment of his literary self; he must eschew an ironic view of life. Given that a literature of discontinuity tends toward relativism, in order to give primacy to the perspective of the individual, the author needs a leap of faith—an irrational acceptance of the self as absolute that transcends the fragmentation and disorder of modern culture. It is perhaps for this reason that the narrative strategies of Shiga have seemed at once so attractive and yet so troublesome to his contemporaries. For certainly the awareness of the present involves an awareness of the relativism of cultural values, and to give a true account of the self, and of the present, an author must come to terms with the reality of the loss of absolutes that attends cultural discontinuity.

In the final part of my survey, I shall examine how a number of authors attempted to deal with the limitations imposed by narrative relativism. As I just suggested, the limited perspective typical of the I-novel, and especially characteristic of the work of Shiga Naoya, is one response, and the centrality of that form in post-Meiji literature suggests that the question of selfhood that dominated Meiji writing gradually gave way to a growing concern with the effects of relativism. This concern was later heightened by the aftermath of World War II, which once again forced Japan urgently to redefine its culture in the face of defeat and American occupation. To illustrate this development, I shall first discuss very briefly how the formal experiments of Meiji were extended in the narrative perspective of certain works by Shiga Naoya. I shall then examine alternatives to Shiga's work in the writings of two young Taishō period (1912–1926) writers, Akutagawa Ryūnosuke and Kajii Motojirō. Finally, I shall examine the almost total collapse of cultural absolutes and the shattering of perspective and cultural memory depicted in *Yukiguni* (Snow country) and *Yama no oto* (The sound of the mountain) by Kawabata Yasunari.

chapter twelve
The Apotheosis of the Artist: The Transcendent Perspective of Shiga Naoya

From the standpoint of the modern artist, the challenge to create a new literature is not the responsibility of the author alone. To paraphrase Ezra Pound, if as a result of cultural discontinuity the artist must learn to write all over again, then the reader must also learn how to read all over again. There can be no compromising of the author's vision; otherwise there will be no possibility of literary creation. The group of writers that best exemplified this rigid artistic stance in Japan was the Shirakaba-ha (White Birch school), and though the individual members of that school—Shiga Naoya, Mushanokōji Saneatsu, Arishima Takeo, and Satomi Ton—possessed different temperaments and embraced different ideologies, they nonetheless shared a patrician background that gave them confidence in the correctness of their own sense of taste. In his study of the Shirakaba-ha, Honda Shūgo is careful to delineate the differences among the various members of the school, but he nonetheless stresses the common class background that shaped the group's basic tenets. Pointing to their early education in particular, he notes, "Many members of the Shirakaba-ha were heretics [*itansha*] at Gakushūin. Their heresy was due to their dual pride: the pride that liberated them from the feelings of inferiority of the nobility, and the pride that distinguished between 'the common people' and the self. In the Shirakaba-ha's assertion of the ego, the deeply rooted consciousness of a privileged class was fortified by the opposite reaction 'I too am a human being.'"[1] Honda attributes the common characteristics of the group not only to a shared class background but also to the notion that they constituted an artistic elite. Of these writers, it was Shiga who best succeeded in finding a narrative voice that expressed that elitism and certainty and who uncompromisingly challenged the reader to read his narratives on his terms.

Perhaps the most striking aspect of Shiga's writing is its extraordinarily narrow perspective. Not all of his writing exhibits this characteristic,[2] but many of his major works, including *Wakai* (Reconciliation), *Ōtsu Junkichi*, and *Aru otoko, sono ane no shi* (A certain man and the death of his sister), three loosely autobiographical novels published between 1912 and 1920, are narrated almost exclusively from the protagonist's viewpoint. Shiga also employed this perspective in his masterwork *An'ya kōro* (A dark night's passing, completed in 1937), a novel that for the most part relates the point of view of the hero, Tokitō Kensaku. In all these works, other fictional perspectives, whether other characters' or a narrator's, do not impinge in any significant way on the perspective of the protagonist. The reader shares the intimate observations and judgments of the hero but is also virtually dependent on a single perspective to understand the work as a whole.

Because of his narrowly focalized perspective and because Shiga based much of his work on his own life, he is seen as a major figure in the development of the *shishōsetsu*, "I-novel."[3] This characterization raises some questions, however: much *shishōsetsu* fiction is essentially autobiographical, an extension of the tendencies manifested early in the naturalist movement, yet Shiga's narratives are in no way autobiographical in the same sense as works by Tōson or Hōmei. Naturalism assumed that it was possible to reveal an absolute reality so long as sincerity and credibility were achieved through the subjectivity of the narrative perspective. The effect is that the narrative becomes inextricably bound up with the consciousness of the narrator, the fictionalizing mind that brings the story into being. This effect is heightened in *shishōsetsu* because the narrator is an extension of the author, his literary alter ego, and so readings of the narrative are in part determined by the assumption of some objective reality beneath the subjective perspective of the novel. *Shishōsetsu* thus rely for their formal effects on an assumption very similar to that at work in the confession, even when the story is not directly based on the author's life. For example, in certain works by Shiga, the "I" of his novels represents not so much the facts of his life as the image of himself as an artist. He does not compromise his artistic vision by falling back on the notion of some reality underlying the story. Instead, he uses his narratives to create the effect that beneath the surface is another fiction, an artistic consciousness he has created for himself.

Shiga's perspective is striking because of its unyielding single-mindedness. Nakano Shigeharu writes that it "is based on the clarity of his understanding. It is not that everything is clear. His understanding does not connote everything broadly or deeply. It is narrow. It is in truth a clarity that lies solely within the limits of himself. Prior to depiction there is selection, and only the things selected have absolutely no ambiguity."[4] What is knowable in Shiga's fictional world is limited to the direct experience of the protagonist, and that lends a certainty of tone to the narrative, a self-confidence that, while it does not pretend to objectivity, is nonetheless unambiguous. There is throughout Shiga's work an absence of irony because the protagonist depends on his intuitive judgment, not his intellect, to shape the narrative and thus does not feel any deep difference between what is experienced and what is knowable.

This feature of Shiga's perspective is apparent in the famous autobiographical short story, "Kinosaki nite" (At Kinosaki, 1917), a meditation on death in which the narrator describes his experiences at a spa he visited to recover from a near-fatal accident. He witnesses three deaths, of a bee, a rat, and a lizard, the last of which he himself causes. His observations are made from a perspective he commonly employed.

> My own room was on the second floor. There were no adjacent rooms, and it was a comparatively quiet accommodation. When I tired of reading and writing, I often went out to the chair on the balcony. To the side was the roof of the entrance hall, and the place where they joined had been wainscoted. Inside the paneling there appeared to be a hive of bees. The fat insects, with their broad tiger stripes, worked busily every day from morning until almost nightfall when the weather permitted. As the bees squeezed out from a crack in the wainscoting, they would drop down onto the roof of the entrance hall. Then, once they had neatly rearranged their wings and antennae with their front and back legs, some would walk about a little. But they all soon stretched out their long narrow wings and flew off with a buzz. As they took off, they quickly gained speed and flew away. The flowering shrubs in the thicket were just then starting to bloom, and they gathered there.

The Apotheosis of the Artist

When I was bored, I would often gaze at their comings and goings from the balustrade.

One morning I discovered a single bee had died on the roof of the entrance hall. Its legs were tucked up tightly under its belly, and its antennae were drooping haphazardly over its face. The other bees were totally indifferent to it. Though they crawled around it as they busily entered or left the hive, they did not seem particularly to mind one way or another. The bees who worked so busily gave the impression of being very much alive. Each time I looked at the dead bee beside them, whether at morning, noon, or evening, lying there facedown, never moving, I had the impression of something very much dead. It stayed there like that for about three days. I would look at it, and a very quiet feeling would come over me. It was lonely watching the little corpse left there alone atop the cool tiles at dusk, once the other bees had all entered the hive. Yet it was a very quiet feeling.

During one night a heavy rain fell. The morning was clear, and the leaves, ground, and roof were all washed clean. The corpse of the bee was gone. The other bees continued to work spiritedly, but the dead bee had been carried along the downspout and washed out onto the ground. Legs shriveled, antennae clinging to its face, it was perhaps covered with mud and lying quietly somewhere. It would probably stay there until the next change brought it back to the external world. Or would it be carried off by ants? In any case, it was very still. Still because the bee, which had lived only to work so busily, had lost all movement. I felt an intimacy with that stillness. (2: 176–77)

The focus of this descriptive passage is very narrow. The scene is finely detailed, but Shiga is careful about what he reports as fact. What is not experienced directly, including the existence of the hive itself, is qualified by the use of such words as *rashii* (seems, appears as) or *koto de arō* (is perhaps . . .), but these qualifiers appear infrequently, and Shiga mostly employs a fairly simple declarative style. He is, moreover, careful to avoid the pathetic fallacy. The feelings of solitude and quiet that the sight of the dead bee inspire in him, as well as the impression of the deadness of the bee, are not attributes of the insect. The scene is described in such a way that the external objects become an extension of the narrator's mind and moods—objective correlatives, to borrow Eliot's phrase, that create for him an epiphanic moment that is highly subjective and yet ineffable. The repetition of the words describing his mood and the repetition of certain elements of the scene, such as the busy motion of the living bees and the stillness of the dead bee, are formal arrangements that confine the observing perspective even more tightly.

The quiet and solitude of the scene arise not from the intrinsic quality of the realities perceived but from the interaction between that reality and the observer. The perspective is so focused that, although the narrator muses about what becomes of the bee, he apparently feels no need to generalize about or interpret that small death. He merely asserts his intuited understanding of the scene and the emotions he feels. Because he does not appear to be overtly contriving to shape the narrative in order to achieve a more credible account, the reader is left to accept or reject his description as it stands. The lack of self-doubt—of any questioning of the authority of the observing voice—strips the narrative of irony.

This quality of Shiga's writing can be more fully appreciated through a comparison of the passage above with a scene from Kawabata's *Yukiguni* (Snow country). The scene occurs halfway through the novel, at the beginning of what is the third visit of the protagonist, Shimamura, to the mountain hot springs.

> Since it was the season when moths lay their eggs, his wife had told him as he left his house in Tokyo to take care not to leave his clothes hanging out on a rack or on a wall for any length of time. And sure enough, when he arrived, six or seven large, maize-colored moths had been drawn into the lantern hung from the edge of the eave overhanging his room in the hotel. A small, fat-bodied moth had alighted on the clothes rack in the three-mat room next to his.
>
> The windows still had screens stretched across them to keep the summer insects out. There was a moth there as well, perfectly still as if glued to the screen. It had thrust out its antennae, like small brown feathers. Its wings were a light, transparent green. They were nearly the length of a woman's finger. The mountains on the border were bathed in evening light, and because they were already stained in autumn colors the thin green on that one spot of his vista seemed like death in contrast. The green was dark only where the back and front wings overlapped. When the autumn wind blew they fluttered like thin paper.
>
> Wondering if it were alive, Shimamura stood up and went over to it; even though he snapped his fingers at it from inside the screen it did not move. He tapped at it with his fist, and it fluttered down like a leaf, floating up lightly halfway through its fall. (*KYZ* 10:72)

My reason for choosing this particular passage, apart from the similarity of its content to that of the passage from Shiga, is to illustrate that even in a narrative narrowly focalized through the perspective of a single character, it is difficult to sustain a tone of certainty. Indeed, the credibility of such a perspective depends in part on the narrator's ironic awareness that there is sometimes a disparity between what the characters observe and

The Apotheosis of the Artist

what is real. Shimamura does not trust the feelings that arise from his observation of the moth, which he is forced to confirm somehow. In *Yukiguni,* the narrative constantly highlights the limits of Shimamura's perspective, reducing his credibility and control over how events are read. In Shiga's narratives, by contrast, the limits of the perspective are defined in such a way that the gap between what the protagonist knows and what the reader knows is greatly narrowed. Shiga's protagonists certainly have moments of hesitation, but their doubts are almost always attributed to the inability to observe or experience directly.

Shiga's style developed, at least in part, because of his family background and his literary associations. He was born in 1883 into a family of samurai origins that had achieved financial success after the Meiji Restoration. He was never forced to pursue any lifestyle other than that of a gentleman of leisure. The tone of certainty that marks his protagonists' aesthetic and moral judgments must be viewed in light of the economic security and social privileges he enjoyed. Nonetheless, his personal life was not without conflict, and his relationship with his father was tumultuous. When he was two, he was taken by his grandparents and raised by them, a situation that later caused him to question the identity of his true father. His fears were unfounded, but his revolt against his father and his questions about his origins became central elements in his fiction. In the afterword to *An'ya kōro,* for example, he tells a story about the reactions of his father and his grandfather to the death of his mother. His grandfather was visibly more shaken by her death than his father was, and that greater show of emotion caused Shiga to wonder whether his grandfather was in fact his real father. Shiga makes it clear that he knew his speculations were foolish and groundless, but the inner conflict produced by such a thought was in its way liberating. It was a fiction that provided him with the image of his own struggles as an artist needed to make the writing of *An'ya kōro* possible.

The self-centeredness and certainty of outlook evident in Shiga's narrative perspective was nurtured by his literary associations, which centered around the Shirakaba-ha. He carried on a lifelong friendship with Mushanokōji, for example, and he shared the general personal and literary goals of the group, which focused on self-realization rather than social activism. Honda has noted that for members of the group, "being an artist was the best way 'to bring the self to life,' and because they believed that to be the most appropriate way for the growth of the self, they became artists. They made themselves important, they never lost sight of themselves, and they did not misunderstand themselves. To be absolutely faithful to the self was the first condition for a person not only to become an artist, but also to mature as a human being. Being faithful to the self appeared to be the ultimate human virtue."[5] As a central figure of the school Shiga was the target of criticisms leveled at this apparently egotistical position. Attacks generally contrasted the Shirakaba-ha with the naturalists and found it wanting on the question of social awareness. For critics like Ikuta Chōkō, for example, the self-absorption and single-mindedness of many of the school's works indicated not only immaturity in both style and outlook but a dangerous retreat to a premodern irrationalism.[6]

Ikuta's critique applies to Shiga where the limitations imposed by his choice of narrative perspective block the expression of a deeper intellectual and emotional development. Rather than struggling to find a language to describe epiphanic moments that define the artistic self, Shiga often noted those moments in general or oblique ways. *Wakai* provides an example of this tendency. The story concerns the estrangement between a father and son that becomes destructive when it indirectly results in the death of the son's child. Because the novel does not give a full account of all sides in the matter, the ironies of the tragic situation are never realized, and the causes of the problem are never fully explored. This is not a question of whether Shiga is obligated to deal with the larger social conflicts created by the pressures of familial relationships—clearly he is not—however, the narrative implies that a reconciliation of just such an important conflict takes place through the intuited bond the father and son create during the climactic scene.

> The door to the study was open. I looked at the calm face of my father who was seated facing me in a chair in front of the desk. Turning his face toward a chair lined up against the window and pointing to the floor in front of me, my father said "Bring that chair here."
>
> I brought the chair over, and, facing him, I sat down. Then we were silent.
>
> "Let's hear from you first," my father said, and then, "Is Masa there?" His manner of speaking gave me a good impression. I answered, "Yes."
>
> My father stood and rang the bell on the wall. When he returned to his seat, he said, "Well?" as though urging me to break my silence. The maid came in and asked what he wanted. My father said, "Ask Masa to come here right away."
>
> "I think it's meaningless for you and me to continue quarreling like this."

The Apotheosis of the Artist

"I see."

"What's done is done, but I feel sorry for you, father. I think I was wrong in some of my actions."

"I see," my father nodded. Perhaps because I was so excited, I had spoken in a tone of voice as if I were angry. It was completely different from the calm, quiet tone I had repeatedly promised my mother I would use. Even so, it was also the most natural tone to use at that time, and I felt that for now there was no more fitting way to express the state of my relationship with my father.

"However, as I said, what's done is done. I think it would be foolish to go on acting as we have been."

My uncle came in. He sat in a chair behind me.

"Fine. And then? Do you intend a permanent reconciliation, or is this just for the sake of your grandmother while she's alive?" my father said.

"Until just a moment ago, father, I didn't want a permanent reconciliation. I thought it would be best simply to receive permission from you to come and go freely in your house while grandmother was alive. Now, however, I sincerely hope for more than that," I said, fighting back a little the tears in my voice.

"I see," my father said. He tightly pursed his lips, and tears welled up in his eyes. "To tell the truth, I'm getting older, and our falling out was painful for me. I even thought in my heart that I hated you. Years ago you said you would leave this house, and though I spoke to you over and over you wouldn't listen. I was at a complete loss. Even though I had no choice but to agree, I never wanted to force you to leave. After that, until today . . ."

As he was speaking, my father started to cry. I began to cry as well. The two of us said nothing more. (2:402–4)

This passage possesses many of the characteristic traits of Shiga's prose style. The diction is relatively simple and straightforward, and there is a single perspective, that of the narrator Junkichi, who refers to himself throughout as *jibun* (I, myself). If the style lacks irony or critical self-awareness, it nevertheless conveys settings and moods directly and without sentimentality. However, the passage cited above does not reveal the inner processes that make the reconciliation possible; in fact, the decision to attempt a permanent reconciliation is reached spontaneously with no apparent prior consideration. The scene ends when language becomes inadequate to express the mutual understanding that has been achieved, thus there is no way to share in the unspoken bond reestablished between father and son. It is as though Shiga believes the transformations that make the reconciliation possible to be beyond representation. The outcome may have been implicit for him, but the danger of such an exceedingly narrow perspective is that it makes an antirational appeal to the heroic sensitivity of the artistic genius.

It is in *An'ya kōro* that Shiga's narrow perspective most completely transforms the inward turn of Meiji narrative into a mythic statement of the artist as hero. Briefly stated, the novel presents the development of an individual, Tokitō Kensaku, within the new terms laid down by a modernizing society. To develop and achieve self-realization, the individual must actively seek a break with the past. For Shiga, this break is represented by the conflict between father and son. William Sibley has provided a thorough analysis of the typical hero in a Shiga narrative in terms of a Freudian analysis of that specific conflict, and it is unnecessary to examine further the psychological dimensions of the work here.[7] The kind of conflict Shiga narrates over and over would seem to support the notion of a literary anxiety of influence in which Shiga must struggle with and destroy his forebears in order to assert his own literary self. The Freudian terms Sibley uses to describe this struggle, however, are a little restricting, for they suggest that Shiga's narrow perspective is the result of an impulse to work out his own psychological quandaries (a reading that has wide support). Yet the psychological aspect of his stories does not simply represent autotherapy that relieved Shiga of inner turmoil; it is also a fundamental element in the development of his narrative voice. The conflict between father and son is an image that describes the literary process of asserting selfhood by creating a discontinuity that is then bridged by the narration of a new literary self. The process of self-discovery and reintegration establishes pattern and form. Sibley writes that

> among the alternatives open to the modern artist is that of a narcissistic retreat into the self; or, as the case may be, a retreat behind a somewhat confused array of identity fragments. This relation to what is known as the real world may not hold much promise for whole-some and vigorous creations, and perhaps lends itself more readily to expression through poetry, drama, and the visual arts. (Shiga once confessed that if he had another life to live he would prefer to be a painter.) Although it may not be conducive to the writing of good novels in the traditional sense, "narcissistic withdrawal," accompanied by a simple, childlike acceptance of one's natural surroundings and one's neighbors, is nevertheless a good way for a sensitive man to survive in the modern world.[8]

The process described by Sibley as a "narcissistic retreat" is embodied in the narrative perspective of *An'ya kōro*. In the prologue, Shiga begins by telling the story in a first-person voice but then mediates between the protagonist and the reader by employing thereafter a third-person narrative voice that refers to Kensaku throughout by the third-person pronominal *kare*. Even with this distance, however, the perspective is extremely limited, for events unfold almost exclusively from the protagonist's point of view. Kensaku faces two main crises in his life. The first is the conflict with his father, which reaches its climax when Kensaku's wish to marry Oei, the maid (and former mistress of his grandfather) who raised him, is opposed and thwarted. This conflict is resolved only when Kensaku finally learns that his real father was the man he thought was his grandfather—a resolution that represents a figurative death of the father and thus a release from the constraints of the relationship.

The second crisis is precipitated by what Kensaku believes to be the infidelity of his wife, Naoko. When his behavior toward her grows violent, he seeks to renew himself by retreating for a while to a mountain village. There he falls ill, but in spite of his poor health he decides to go mountain climbing. In what is the climactic scene of the novel, he succumbs to his illness and is forced to stay on the mountain overnight. He undergoes a transforming experience in which his subjective consciousness merges with objective nature, and he gains a transcendent awareness and acceptance of the world.

> Though he was exhausted, he could feel his exhaustion change into a strange rapture. He felt his mind and body now dissolving into this vast nature. Although that nature was something he could not sense with his eyes, like a vapor enveloping him, who was as small as a poppy seed, within its boundless immensity, he was dissolving into it—and that feeling was a pleasure beyond expression in words. It was a little like the sensation of falling asleep when one is drowsy and without cares. All the time he was in a state as if he were really half asleep. The feeling of being absorbed into immense nature was certainly not a first-time experience for him, but this rapture was. On other occasions up to now he had had the feeling of being sucked into it, and even though there had been a certain joy, at the same time the feeling had had a quality as though a willfulness, which tried to resist nature, had arisen of its own accord. Moreover, the feeling of resistance usually brought on a feeling of unease, but his feeling now was completely different from that. There was no feeling of resistance. He felt only the joy of melting into it without anxiety.
>
> It was a quiet evening, and he could not hear even the voices of the night birds. A thin mist was hanging below, and he could not see the lights of the villages. All he could see were the stars and, below them, the shape of the mountain, which gave the impression of the back of some huge animal

looming faintly above him. Now he was thinking that he himself had taken one step on the road that passed to eternity. He felt no fear of death. He thought that should he die now there would be nothing to regret, not even dying like this. Yet he did not think of crossing over to eternity as death. (5:578–79)

Particularly at epiphanic moments such as this, the perspective of the narrator seems almost to merge with that of the protagonist. The use of the pronoun *kare* represents not so much a narrative intrusion as simply a second voice for Kensaku, a way to present his inner thoughts and moods. The formal perspective remains self-centered and narrow, but in merging the narrator and Kensaku, the narrative attempts to objectify individual experience in order to move toward the universal and transcendent. In all other respects, however—in the sureness of tone, in the fullness of the description, and in the apparently intuited understanding of nature—this passage bears the characteristic marks of Shiga's perspective and style. The specifics of what Kensaku has discovered are not explicitly stated, for again his epiphany is beyond representation. All we are allowed to witness is the process of the integration of the individual consciousness into an absolute, allowing Kensaku to achieve a transcendent sense of identity and to overcome his feelings of isolation.

The strongest prose styles paradoxically achieve their impersonal quality through such compelling representations of experience that the reader is forced to interpret the story on the terms established by the narrative voice. In just this way, Shiga's narrative perspective asserts the validity and priority of subjective experience while striving to achieve an impersonal, transcendent quality that will make the narrative universally comprehensible. His achievement is the strength of his style, which sustains the illusion that the narrative has transcended the relativism implicit in a limited perspective. Even so, this transcendent perspective remains an illusion, because it is limited by (or, more accurately, reduced to) the formal necessities of art. Like all modernist heroes, Kensaku is threatened by the lack of duration, a problem for which the only narrative solution is to achieve, or at least to suggest, a permanent transcendence, to fix the epiphanic moment, which then brings the narrative to an end. One expedient is to suspend the hero near death, as Shiga does, achieving an apotheosis that kills the subjective hero into an objective ideal.

Shiga's effort to bring the heroic back into a self-conscious narrative form—to establish a myth of the primacy of the artistic self for the modern world—has aroused contradictory feelings of admiration and loathing among other writers. Akutagawa, for example, looked past the self-centeredness of the typical perspective that Shiga created, and in "Bungeiteki na, amari ni bungeiteki na" (Literary, all too literary, 1927) he praised what he felt was the moral purity that gave Shiga's writing an impersonal, godlike transcendence (5:134). Dazai Osamu, on the other hand, denounced Shiga in the essay "Nyoze gamon" (Thus I have heard, 1948) for what he thought was latent militarism, willfulness and patrician airs, and cunning that made an aesthetic virtue of a style and perspective that were cruel, violent, and stubborn.[9] As different as these interpretations are—one seeing Shiga's work as a solution to the modernist dilemma and the other seeing it as embodying a dangerous protofascist aesthetics—they suggest that Shiga's attempt to define a modern heroism was an effort to create the illusion of a transcendent, unassailable narrative perspective.

◆

chapter thirteen
The Narrative Subversions
of Akutagawa and
Kajii Motojirō

I argued in the previous chapter that the relativism of the typical narrative voice in Meiji literature forced writers toward increasingly radical solutions to attempt to provide objective grounding for subjective experience. Shiga Naoya, for example, tried to elevate the artist to the status of hero, resulting in an extreme form of perspectivism that had a profound effect on other writers. In this chapter, I shall look briefly at the work of two younger writers, Akutagawa Ryūnosuke and Kajii Motojirō, who were especially influenced by the problem of narrative relativism and by Shiga's example. While some of Akutagawa's narrative experiments represent an opposing extreme to Shiga's work, the narrative voice developed by Kajii strives for a middle way.

Throughout his brief career, Akutagawa was explicitly preoccupied with the implications of relativism on narrative form, and it may have been that preoccupation that made Shiga's work seem so important to him. Instead of seeking a perspective to transcend relativism's limitations, he was more interested in the formal possibilities offered by the creation of multiple perspectives that created irony and thus undercut the individual perspectives of his characters. In spite of his professed admiration for

Shiga, his most famous stories revel in the lack of an absolute point of reference. They are often based on classic tales that Akutagawa made new simply by fragmenting the perspective. The characters' viewpoints are purposely decentered to reveal the fact that viewpoint is not absolute; the irony resulting from the gap between what the characters know and what the reader knows reduces the credibility of the account and renders the truth of the story relative, dependent on individual interpretation. The compensation for this ironic denial of absolute truth is that the narrative as a whole seeks credibility by asserting that the contingency of life and art is an inevitable condition of human experience. The literary self is moved to the margins in an effort to regain narrative credibility.

The most famous example of this fragmenting of perspective is of course "Yabu no naka" (Within a grove, 1922), in which the story of the rape of a woman and the murder of her husband by a thief is told from several differing viewpoints, including those of the three main characters. Because each version of the story is self-serving and, in narrative terms, self-centered, no absolute truth is possible. Akutagawa borrows not simply the story material from the *setsuwa* tradition but also the notion that truth in human terms is relative and that reality is contingent. However, by shifting the focus of the story away from the event itself to the various interpretations of it, Akutagawa creates a new narrative reflecting a modernist preoccupation with perspective.

Akutagawa continued throughout his career to explore the gap between what his protagonists think to be the truth and other possible realities. In "Hana" (The nose, 1916), for example, the narrative is less obviously structured to show competing versions of the truth, but the tale turns on the irony that results from the gap between what the protagonist thinks will happen to him once his extraordinarily long nose is fixed and what actually happens to him. The tension created by the recognition that what the individual perceives to be the truth may have to give way to some other view of reality is one of the central effects of Akutagawa's work.

The story in which Akutagawa achieves his most complete expression of the way in which a relativistic outlook affects both narrative form and the depiction of character is "Jigokuhen" (Hell screen, 1918). Like many of his stories, it is based on material from the *Uji shūi monogatari* and from the *Kokon chomonjū*.[1] It also raises questions that are characteristic of Akutagawa's work. How can the reader trust the narrative, given the competing claims of the narrating voices (a question explored by Futabatei and Ōgai on slightly different grounds)? And if the narrating voices are not entirely trustworthy, then how does one interpret the artistic consciousness that gives form to the narrative?

The strategy employed by Akutagawa for this story resembles the ploy Ōgai adopted in *Gan,* in which the narrator makes himself the center of the story by acting as the mechanism that shapes the plot. The narrator of "Jigokuhen" pieces together the puzzle of events and motivations for us, but his account is not at all certain, and he uses the admission of his ignorance to try to make credible what he is able to present to us. The crucial example of this pose comes when he discovers Yūzuki, the daughter of the painter Yoshihide, moments after she has been raped. The perpetrator of the crime is almost certainly Lord Horikawa, Yoshihide's patron, who has exhibited a sexual fascination with Yūzuki. The narrator reports his attraction to the girl obliquely, as nothing more than rumors. However, the anonymity of the gossiping voices gives them a kind of objectivity, making the reports of Horikawa's behavior seem believable even as the narrator dismisses them as false (1:268, 271). When confronted with the evidence of Horikawa's rape of the girl, the narrator asks the crucial question "Who did it?" but then immediately excuses himself from his narrative responsibility to provide a complete account: "I was born foolish, and apart from things that I understand all too clearly, unfortunately I don't understand much. Thus I did not know what to say, and for a while I simply stood there transfixed, feeling as though I were listening keenly to the palpitations of the girl's heart. This was because I felt the sting of conscience, as if it would not be right to question her further about what had happened and why" (1:281).

The narrator, by reporting events in a way that refuses to confirm his own observations about the relationship between Horikawa and Yoshihide's daughter and by reporting rumors and opinions that undermine his own position in the story, admits his fallibility and opts instead for the credibility suggested by honestly showing us the limits of his perspective. The irony of the story is especially complex because the narrator's self-confessed limitations and his misreadings of the motivations of the main characters provide alternative narratives that make an absolute judgment of events impossible, regardless of what we think of the narrator's interpretations.

In contrast to the position of the narrator, the two main figures of the story, Horikawa and Yoshihide, struggle to make themselves the center of the plot, to shape and control the unfolding of events. This struggle is based on an elitist view of the artist. Yoshihide is depicted throughout as someone who is not quite human. His obsession with art, which makes him appear inhuman to those around him, and his repulsive features, which resemble those of a monkey, combine to create an animalistic image. Yoshihide is obsessed with his art, and he breaks all conventional rules in his dealings with his superiors, to whom he does not always show proper deference, and in his notions of himself as an artist.

> To describe his characteristics, he was stingy, he was hard-hearted, he was shameless, he was lazy, he was avaricious—but perhaps his greatest excess was that he was arrogant and haughty, and he flaunted his own work, boasting that he was the greatest painter in Japan. It would have been all right if his attitudes applied only to painting, but since he refused to give way on his opinions, he had to make light of everything else, even the customs and conventions of society. I heard the following story from one of Yoshihide's disciples of many years. One day a spirit took possession of a famous medium in his studio, and when she began to speak her awesome oracle, Yoshihide pretended not to hear, and taking up the brushes and ink there he drew an exact likeness of the terrible face of the medium. He treated the horrible curses of the spirit as though they were nothing at all. Because he was that kind of man, he used a prostitute as the model for his portrait of Kichijōten, the goddess of virtue, and he used a petty criminal as his model for Fudō [Acalanātha, one of the five Buddhist kings of wisdom and light]. When he was rebuked for his irreverence, he put up a bold front, saying "It would be a strange thing if the gods and buddhas Yoshihide painted punished Yoshihide." (1:268–69)

Yoshihide's arrogance is exhibited in his lack of concern for anything that distracts from the artistic creativity by which he defines himself. He treats his apprentices with sadistic disregard in order to obtain models for the torment he wishes to portray in what he plans to be his masterpiece, a screen depicting the tortures of hell. Applying a method very close to that of the naturalists, he is compelled to base his art on his real-life experiences. As he nears completion, he finds that he cannot continue unless he has a model for the centerpiece of the screen, which is the image of a woman in a burning carriage falling through space. He requests that Horikawa burn such a carriage for him, explaining to his lord, "As a rule I cannot paint things I have not seen. Even if I try to paint them, they lack conviction. And isn't painting without conviction the same as being unable to paint?" (1:282).

Horikawa not only agrees to this bizarre request but goes one step further by promising Yoshihide that he will burn a carriage with a woman inside it. This horrific promise turns out to be an escalation of the struggle between the two men to control one another, to control the commissioned work of art, and thus to control the narrative. It is through this contest of wills that we come to understand that Horikawa's will to control is what makes him resemble the artist. Horikawa is described at the beginning of the story as an extraordinary man whose birth was marked by a supernatural visitation and who, in an echo of Prince Genji's portrait, brought to life his own grand vision of himself through the realization of the design of the palace at Horikawa (1:265). His granting of Yoshihide's request turns out to be an act of revenge for the painter's having thwarted his designs on Yūzuki. When the night comes for firing the carriage, it is Yoshihide's daughter who is the model. At first Yoshihide is horrified, but then his anguish turns to ecstasy, and in the climax of the story the portraits of the two protagonists come together.

> Moreover, the mysterious thing was not simply that he was joyfully observing the death agonies of his daughter. In the Yoshihide of that moment there was an uncanny solemnity that somehow could not be considered human, that resembled the fierceness of a lion seen in a dream. Consequently, even the numberless birds of the night that had been startled by the unexpected fire, and that flew around in a screeching clamor, seemed—or did I just imagine it?—to avoid the area around Yoshihide's cap. Perhaps in the eyes of those artless birds there was an unfathomable dignity hanging like a halo above the man's head.
>
> If the birds acted that way, then how much more were we and even the servants transfixed, hardly breathing and never taking our eyes off Yoshihide. It was exactly like watching the spiritual awakening of a buddha, and our bodies were shaking and our hearts were filled with a wondrous joy. The fire of the carriage, which roared up to the sky, and Yoshihide, who stood there unable to move, as if his soul had been snatched from his body—together they were somehow majestic, somehow ecstatic. Only one person, our lord, was panting like some thirsty beast. His face pale, his lips foaming, clutching at the knees of his purple trousers, he seemed to be a different person altogether. (1:287)

Yoshihide achieves the transcendence that makes his work of art possible, yet that transcendence is only possible because of the vision of Horikawa, who is as sadistic and animalistic as Yoshihide. If Yoshihide created the work of art, then Horikawa created the artist. At the same time the "Hell screen" that the reader experiences is a literary work of art brought into being by neither of these artists but instead through the report of a narrator who observes the struggle by which art is created and whose reliability is doubtful. The story's structure is built of a series of regressions that goes beyond the surface irony characteristic of so many of Akutagawa's stories. "Jigokuhen" questions the very possibility of artistic control and of the creation of self through literature in the face of a loss of absolute perspectives.

The experiments Akutagawa undertook with his early stories initially yielded interesting results, but they also made it difficult for him to write longer, sustained pieces of fiction. Even when he seeks actively to center himself in his writing, as he does in his late autobiographical pieces, *Aru ahō no isshō* (The life of a certain fool, 1927) and *Haguruma* (Cogwheel, 1927), his unwillingness to abandon a detached, relativistic perspective in order to create the fiction of a transcendent self results in a hyperrational, schizophrenic narrative voice. The urgency with which he expresses his literary dilemma in these works is heightened by his personal circumstances, especially his physical and mental deterioration.

The late autobiographical stories reveal a desperate desire to break through the endless regressions of a relativistic outlook. The narrative structure of *Haguruma*, in which the narrator's life is shattered into separate levels of existence—the waking world that shifts between moments of lucidity and paranoid fear, the world of books to which the narrator seeks to escape, and the world of drug-induced dreams—indicates the impossibility of attaining that desire. The narrator's dilemma is stated most explicitly when he depicts himself reading Shiga. At one point, the narrator writes, "I tumbled onto my bed and began reading *An'ya kōro*. The psychological struggles of the hero were all poignant to me. How foolish I felt I was compared to the hero, and at some point I started to cry. At the same time my tears brought peace to my feelings. That, however, did not last long. Once again in my right eye I sensed a translucent cogwheel" (4:26–27). At a later point in the work, the narrator says that he is reading the works of Prosper Mérimée (1803–1870) and that those works "gave me again the capacity for living. However, when I learned that Mérimée had become a new convert in the last year of his life, suddenly I felt I had glimpsed his real face, which had been in the shadow of a mask. Like me, he had been alone, walking in the midst of darkness. Midst of darkness?— *An'ya kōro* had begun to change into a terrifying book for me" (4:33). Shiga's work is presented here as a possible resolution of the relativist's dilemma, but it is a resolution that, for Akutagawa, must always remain tantalizingly beyond his reach.

Though his historical position in the development of Taishō literature has been somewhat obscured by the reaction to his suicide in 1927—a reaction that ultimately devalued his work by casting him as a literary martyr whose work failed to resolve the modernist dilemma—Akutagawa's experiments in narrative perspective demonstrate a strong awareness of the limitations of the Meiji response to cultural discontinuity. The mechanistic image of the cogwheel, which he used just prior to his death to symbolize his personal dissociation, points up the potential loss of humanity that occurs when the emphasis on discontinuity as a means of defining the self leads instead to a disintegration or fragmentation of identity. As different in style, form, and substance as the writings of Shiga and Akutagawa are, the search for identity at the heart of narrative form in Meiji Japan developed for them into a common aesthetic ideology, a view of the artist as elite and transcendent, that perpetuated itself by embracing the ambiguities of the current age as the only proper subject for art. Narrative form was increasingly marked by a preoccupation with perspectivism, and even though the strategies chosen to express this preoccupation did not provide a great deal of psychological comfort, a range of authors employed them. In this regard, the experiments of Kajii Motojirō are typical of larger developments and provide a good point of comparison with those of Shiga and Akutagawa.

Kajii's literary career, which spanned a mere seven years between 1925 and 1932, was shaped largely by his struggle with tuberculosis. By limiting his activities, the disease also narrowed the range of experience he brought to his writing. It isolated him both physically and emotionally and determined the tone and perspective of many of his stories. The very act of writing took an enormous physical toll on him, and his total output comes to no more than twenty short pieces that can be called complete. In spite of these limitations, Kajii's prose style has its fervent admirers in Japan, who praise it for its polish and imaginative expansiveness. The sad paradox of his work is that his personal difficulties were the wellspring of his genius. He subverted the constraints on his life and, through his fiction, achieved a kind of liberation.

If the subversive tendency in Kajii's stories, the desire to undermine ideological certainties, was a reaction to his private circumstances, it was the product of a mind fully aware of the artistic trends of the day. Kajii was an admirer of Shiga, he was attracted to the social ideas of Mushanokōji, and he later became sympathetic to the ideals of Marxism. Finally, apart from his own literary circle, he was acquainted with the poet Hagiwara Sakutarō and with Kawabata, who had cofounded the Shinkan-kaku-ha (Neosensualist school) partly in opposition to the artistic aims of proletarian literature. While it is not possible to place Kajii's work comfortably within any of these literary approaches, their collective influence helped to shape the development of his fiction.

A strongly subversive impulse is apparent in his earliest important piece, "Remon" (Lemon), which was published in 1925 in *Aozora*, a magazine he helped to establish. The story is not explicitly autobiographical, but the portrait of the protagonist is drawn closely from the author's own experience. Poverty-stricken and ill, the young narrator is chronically depressed and suffers from the constant feeling that an "unpleasant lump" is pressing upon his heart. He wanders the streets of Tokyo seeking solace. For a brief period he was attracted to places like Maruzen, a bookstore known for its exotic and beautiful wares and its books on art. Now, however, everything about the store—its books, the students, the checkout counters—has come to seem like the "deceased spirits of bill collectors," and he is more and more drawn to the beauty of simple or even shabby things. He especially likes a particular greengrocer that he often passes on his walks. One day it becomes the starting point for the central experience of the story.

> That day I actually did some shopping for a change. Some lemons, an unusual commodity, had appeared on the stand. Now of course lemons are a commonplace fruit, but I had never seen them there like that. Even though the place was not run-down, it was, after all, a pretty ordinary greengrocery. In any case, for some reason I took a fancy to those lemons—with their pure color looking as though someone had squeezed lemon yellow paint from a tube and let it harden and with their pointed tubular shapes crammed together lengthwise—and so I finally decided to buy one. After that I lost track of where or how I walked. I walked the streets for a long time. As soon as I had grasped that lemon the unpleasant lump that was always pressing on my heart seemed to have relaxed, and I felt very fortunate there on the street. That my persistent melancholy could be relieved by a single lemon—perhaps such a dubious thing was paradoxically true. For all that, my heart is a rather mysterious thing.
>
> The coolness of the lemon was unbelievably pleasant. Around that time I had aggravated my catarrh, and my body was always feverish. In fact, just to show off my fever to my friends, I would try clasping our hands together, and my palms were always the hottest. Perhaps it was because I was so hot that the coolness of the lemon, which seemed to seep into my body through my hands, felt so refreshing.

Over and over I brought the fruit up to my nose and sniffed it. Its place of origin, California, rose up in my imagination. The words, "It strikes the nose," written in *The Words of the Orange Merchant* that I had learned in Chinese, came drifting up in fragments. Then, when I inhaled deeply the fragrant air, the remaining heat of my warm blood rose to my body and face, and never having breathed so deeply before, somehow my spirits were awakened within me. (*KMZ* 10–11)

The dense, economic style of this passage is typical of much of Kajii's writing. The strength and grace of his style are no doubt the result of the extensive rewriting and polishing to which Kajii subjected his prose. An example of the felicity of his style is provided by the vivid synesthesia achieved by the description of the lemons. The literary image is the starting point of the narrative, for through his physical experience of that single lemon we are able to share in the various sensations and thoughts of the narrator. The perspective is thus dynamic as well as economical, fusing the image of the object with the subjective appreciation of it by the narrator.

The perspective reveals a larger tension in the narrative. The narrator attempts to make his description of the lemon objective, to give it a reality apart from his subjective view of it, so the reader can experience its shape, smell, and coolness. At the same time he uses this image as a way of describing his own emotional state. It is a source of relief for his physical distress, it sends him into a series of reveries, and it revives his spirits. The narrator stresses the ordinary quality of the lemon, but it is through his experience of this everyday object that he is able to rid himself of the constraints on his world. His physical limitations provoke a desire to break free, and they force him to seek liberation within a narrow range of experience that focuses the narrative on the freshness of a lemon.

The physical feeling of liberation stirred in him by the lemon brings him to an even greater act of subversion, the figurative breaking down of the artistic barriers in his life. He goes to Maruzen and begins looking at the art books. The atmosphere seems stifling and oppressive to him, but he stays and builds a castle out of the books, literally imposing his identity on other works of art and asserting his own creativity. Finishing his castle, he takes out the lemon and, pretending it is a bomb, leaves it on a shelf.

> I felt strangely ticklish. "Should I leave, I wonder. Yes, let's get out of here," and I hurried out.
> The strangely ticklish feeling made me smile out on the street. How intriguing it would be if the mysterious villain who had come and planted the

fearful bomb that was shining yellow on a shelf in Maruzen were I, and if, ten minutes later, there were an explosion with its epicenter at the Fine Arts Section.

I intently pursued my daydream. "If that happened, then stuffy old Maruzen would be blown to bits."

I went down to Kyōgoku, where the pictures on the movie billboards colored the streets with their strange appearance. (*KMZ* 13)

The narrator wants to destroy not only Maruzen, with its luxurious goods and books that arouse in him desires that can never be fulfilled, but also the constraints that the conventions of the artistic tradition represent to him. The lemon becomes his source of self-liberation; it soothes him physically, and it becomes a symbol for the destructive impulse of his own art. He echoes Chōmei's impulse to build a literary edifice out of canonical works of art but then leaves his imaginary lemon-bomb to blast apart the canons of conventional taste.

This destructive re-creation of the tradition is an intensely private, literary act. Nothing happens outside the mind of the narrator. Although the young narrator could have been presented as a member of the proletariat, Kajii does not inject social themes into the story. The world appears transformed at the end—the streets have taken on the bizarre hues of the billboards, which are reflections from a different realm of art—but that transformation appears only through the eyes of the narrator and implies a limit on the power of the imagination to effect real change. There is no sense that the narrator has truly transcended his circumstances. An act of the imagination turns a lemon into a bomb that can destroy Maruzen, just as an act of the imagination can produce a new work of literature. Yet does the imagination really change anything? How does the artist break through the limits of his personal vision, when that vision is the source of his art? The narrator in "Remon" asserts his creative self, and there are changes in his perception of the world, but there remains the problem of how to reconstruct a vision of the world in which art is possible. Kajii seems attracted to and yet skeptical of the type of perspective Shiga developed, and he appears to have recognized this tension in his work even as he wrote "Remon," for he began to dwell more on the isolation of the individual writer's perspective and on the need for the artist to find some way to engage the reader.

Perhaps more than for any other author examined in this study, the sense of isolation Kajii felt as an artist may be traced to his physical condition. He was an invalid for so much of his life that he grew accustomed to looking at the world from the inside out. The image that best conveys his narrative perspective is the window frame. Windows are the only openings onto the world in stories such as "Kōbi" (Mating, 1931) and "Aru kokoro no fūkei" (A certain landscape of the heart, 1926), and the image of the window as a frame of perspective is used in many other stories as well. The window narrows the scope of the narrative and accentuates the separation between the observer and the observed. As literary images, windows open up confining spaces but create their own limitations. This paradox becomes a recurring theme.

An example is provided by the story "Shiro no aru machi nite" (At a castle town, 1925). The story is a collection of observations of minor events made by the narrator, Takashi, while staying at the house of his older sister in a small provincial town. The following anecdote concerns Katsuko, the niece of Takashi.

> Takashi stood next to a window that faced onto an open field and gazed out.
> Gray clouds filled the sky. They appeared to be very thick, and he thought they were hanging low to the earth.
> Everything in the vicinity had lost its brightness and was quiet. Only the lightning rod on the hospital in the distance appeared to be shining white.
> In the field some children were playing. Looking closer, he saw that Katsuko was among them. There was a boy, and it looked like he was playing some roughhouse game.
> Katsuko had been knocked down by the boy. As soon as she got up she was knocked down again. This time he had pushed her hard.
> "What in the world is he doing? He'll hurt her," Takashi thought, watching them carefully.
> Next, when that game was finished, the group of girls, three in all, stood in front of the boy as if lining up at a ticket gate at a station. Then a strange ticket taking began. The boy would pull violently on the outstretched hands of the girls. One girl fell to the ground. The next girl put out her hand. That hand would also be pulled. The child who had fallen would get up and once more go to the back of the line.
> As he watched, the boy began to change the strength with which he pulled. The girls seemed to be having fun as they waited fearfully anticipating, not knowing if he would pull hard or gently.
> When they thought he would pull hard, he would tense up his body only to pull gently. Then he would fiercely throw down the next girl. Again, he let the next girl through only lightly touching her hand.
> Although the boy was small, he looked like an adult—a sawyer or a ma-

son—and seemed to be humming while he worked. He was proud of himself.

It seemed to Takashi that Katsuko alone was being treated with excessive strength. He took that badly. It seemed that in a roundabout way Katsuko was being treated unkindly.

Perhaps the reason Katsuko was treated badly was that she was selfish, and when she played with other children she was never a good child.

Be that as it may, didn't she understand the unfairness of what was happening? It was natural that she should understand, and yet she put up with it out of pride.

As he was thinking about this, she was thrown hard to the ground again. If she were putting up with it out of pride, what must her face have looked like as she glared at the ground? When she got up her face was the same as the other children.

She was very good at holding back her tears.

Thinking that the boy might happen to look at the window, he did not move away from it. (*KMZ* 37–39)

The perspective in this scene gradually narrows until the focus is the movement between the children playing and Takashi's observations of them. He interprets their play as being unjust to Katsuko but cannot be sure that his niece is aware of that, and his inability to be certain about her reaction is troubling to him. Moreover, he is incapable of doing anything about it. He stays near the window hoping the boy will see him watching. He records the scene, but even in narrating the story he remains passive and apart.

The loneliness of Kajii's life guided the development of the perspective he brings to his stories, and he saw the predicament of the artist as analogous to his real-life situation. From both an emotional and an artistic standpoint, this predicament is the central theme in his work. He sought ways to liberate himself, as in "Remon," but he grew increasingly preoccupied with the desperate feeling that there was no way to resolve the paradox of his life and art. The assertion of his individuality as a way to create art meant that he had to accept a fragmented view of the world in which the truth of his narrative was relative. If a self-centered narrative form was a means of liberation, it also created its own limitations by making all perceptions of truth personal and interior.

In "Rojō" (On a road, 1925) Kajii presents this problem in an unusual, almost absurd manner. The narrator of the story tells about a shortcut he has discovered to get to his home. The path leads from a train station that he has not used previously, and it winds through a rural, wooded area. He prefers taking this path, and he is eager to show it to his friends, but one day he discovers that, after a rain, the path is muddy and difficult to negotiate. He slips and falls, covering himself in mud. What makes the situation worse, in a strange way, is that there is no one to witness his mishap and thus to share in it and give it some sense of reality. "Looking at the dwellings below, I thought, 'Isn't someone, somewhere watching me?' If they were watching from those houses, then I must have looked like some comic performing with all my might on this lofty stage. —No one was watching. It was a strange feeling" (*KMZ* 68–69).

This feeling of isolation is more pronounced in a later story, "Aru gakuue no kanjō" (Certain emotions atop a cliff, 1928), that takes a rather perverse twist. The story concerns two young men, Kijima and Ishida, who are talking in a café bar. The two are not close friends, and Kijima, who is drunk, does most of the talking. During the evening he confesses to being a voyeur, and the image he associates with his habit is the same as the one Kajii generally associates with the perspective of the narrator: namely, the window. Kijima says to Ishida, "To tell the truth, windows are hard for me to resist. I always think it is pleasant if other people's windows are visible from where I am. It's also very pleasant when I leave my own windows open and constantly expose myself to someone else's eyes" (*KMZ* 196–97). He tells Ishida of a road on a cliff above the town where he goes to spy on the lives of other people. Although this is really nothing more than perversity, he tries to make it sound as though he is simply leading an open life, the life of an artist who seeks to connect with his fellow man. Ishida then tells him of a travel book by a Japanese author. In the book the writer describes a night he spent in Vienna when he happened to look through a window in a neighboring hotel and saw a couple making love. Kijima laughs at this and expresses his desire to go to Vienna. The two then part company.

When Kijima returns home, we learn that he lives in a shabby room with a woman he does not especially like. His existence is dreary and pathetic. Thinking back on his earlier conversation, he debates whether he should leave his window open. His room is visible from the cliff, and he is ashamed to think that by telling this to Ishida he has tempted him to go there, where he can see the truth about Kijima's life. Kijima thinks,

> At first I was filled with goodwill toward the man. Then I felt like telling him my story of the windows. Why could I not help feeling that I wanted

to make him a puppet of my own desires? Full of goodwill, I thought I spoke with the idea that the things I love would surely be loved by others. Now I feel that there was something coercive in my manner, an unconscious urge to rub my desires onto someone else and to make a person like myself. Now I'm waiting for him. He has climbed the cliff road, spurred on by those desires, and what I had fantasized is opening the window onto our squalid reality, exposing it to that road. (*KMZ* 205)

In the end, in spite of all of his talk, Kijima cannot bring himself to open the window. He cannot confess the truth of his life and so effectively cuts himself off from any possibility of liberation.

Meanwhile, Ishida has indeed climbed the road, having given in to the temptation. He searches for Kijima's room but because Kijima has left his window closed cannot find it. Ishida is confronted instead with scenes of trivial lives of squalor and, through the windows of a hospital, of death. In desperation he searches for someone making love, but he finds no one. In their earlier conversation, both Kijima and Ishida spoke of opening up the windows of their lives in an effort to connect with others and overcome their isolation. Those windows, like the window in "Shiro no aru machi nite," are simply a different form of barrier that shows them the limitations of their own perspectives on the world and makes them more acutely aware of their inability to engage their fellow beings.

The mood that dominates most of Kajii's stories is one of despair. Following "Remon," where the narrator seeks to subvert the external constraints on his life, Kajii begins a further turn inward to confront the isolation of the artist. In "Deinei" (Muddy road, 1925) that isolation is brought home in a number of ways. The narrator is dependent on his family for support and is hurt by a delay in receiving money from them. Since he lives in Tokyo, this problem brings him to the realization that there is no one he can turn to immediately in a time of need. He has friends, but lately they have avoided him out of fear of his lung disease. His loneliness finally makes him think of himself as strange.

Although Kajii used his health problems as source material, he rarely allows his narrators to present the subject of illness in a self-pitying or maudlin manner. The pain he portrays is disquieting, but he avoids bitterness. There is a gentle satiric streak in the narrative voice of "Deinei," as when he questions a friend about why he has not come by to visit more often. The answer is obvious, and though the friend is slightly embarrassed, the object of the satire is really the narrator himself. A gentle self-prodding is apparent in other stories as well, including the passages cited above from "Rojō," "Remon," and "Shiro no aru machi nite." One way of dealing with despair is to deflate any notion of the importance of self, and it is in this impulse that we see the beginnings of a tendency to decenter the narrating voice in his work.

In "Deinei," however, Kajii does more than merely deflate the narrator's ego. After receiving the long-awaited cash from home, the narrator goes out with a friend to look at books. In the evening, after going to a bar, he returns home. On the way, he undergoes an epiphanic experience in which he momentarily escapes his situation by completely losing his sense of self and achieving an apotheosis similar to that of Shiga's character, Tokitō Kensaku.

> Leaving the main road, I came out onto a street with few lamps. For the first time the moonlight brightened the snow-covered scenery. The snow was piled up mysteriously. It was lovely. I knew that I had made up my mind and that I would continue to feel even more decisive. My shadow, having moved from left to right, was in front of me. Now that it was not being disturbed, it was distinct. I was walking, marveling at why such intimate feelings should have occurred to me a short time ago, and feeling nostalgic. My shadow was wearing a soft hat that had lost its shape, and from the delicate neck there were slightly square shoulders. As I watched I gradually began to forget myself.
>
> From within the shadow there emerged a sign of something that was alive. Whatever that living thing was thinking, it was definitely thinking something—what I had taken to be a shadow was my own vivid self!
>
> "I will continue to walk! Then, from a vantage point like that of the moon I will gaze down on myself." The ground was transparent, like some kind of glass that had been stretched out, and I felt a little dizzy.
>
> "Perhaps my shadow will walk off somewhere," I thought, a vague uneasiness beginning to take hold. . . .
>
> In a small gutter in front of a bamboo grove beside the road the hot water that had run off from the public bath was flowing. The steam stood up like a folding screen and struck my nostrils—I returned to myself. The owners of the tempura shop next to the bath were still up. I entered the dark street in the direction of my lodgings. (*KMZ* 62) [2]

The narrator finds release through a moment of transcendent experience. But instead of the self merging with nature, as was the case with Tokitō Kensaku, there is the uneasiness that comes with the sense of losing control. The narrator feels as though he is looking down on himself, a self that he equates with his shadow, as if his spirit has left his body and become one with the moonlight. The world is permanently divided into two spheres: one of the light of his imagination and the other of the darkness of his earthly existence. The anxiety he feels at the possibility that his shadow will leave him is the fear of the death of that self. These same images appear in another story, "K no shōten, aruiwa K no dekishi" (The apotheosis of K, or K's death by drowning, 1926), where a third-person narrator describes the transcendental experience of his friend, K. The narrator has observed K on a moonlit beach, where he stands as if in a trance, staring at his shadow. Later, after K has died by drowning, the narrator speculates that the spirit of K had left his body during the moments he was staring at his shadow and had ascended to the moon. Thus, the narrator reasons, only the earthly body, the shadow of the self, actually drowned (*KMZ* 134).

Among Kajii's stories, "K no shōten" is unusual for its fantastic quality, but it provides a further view of the transcendental experience that offers hope of release. In "K no shōten," this liberation is equated with both death and transcendence, as it is in *An'ya kōro,* while in "Deinei," the experience is momentary, but in both stories it is clear that the realization of the imaginative world is incompatible with human life and that such realization is fleeting at best. In "Kakehi no hanashi" (The story of a conduit, 1928), the narrator describes an epiphanic experience he has while walking among the mountain forests near the convalescent home in Izu where he is staying. One day he comes across an abandoned water conduit. The sounds of the forest and the sound of the water running in the conduit send him into a reverie. The moment is unique, however, and on later walks he cannot recapture the epiphany. "When the rain didn't fall, the conduit would run dry. In addition, there were days on which my ears had no sensation. Then, just as flowers pass their prime, from about that time the conduit lost its mystery, and I no longer stopped and stood by it. However, when I walk the mountain path and pass that spot, I think about my fate as follows: 'That which has been inflicted on me is the tedium of eternity. The illusions of life accumulate with despair'" (*KMZ* 169). "The tedium of eternity" suggests the impossibility of renewal. The nature of the narrator's personal predicament so fragments his vision of the world that he cannot accept the absolute promise of an epiphany. To do so would deny the reality and meaning of his own suffering in this world. Liberating flights of the imagination coexist with despair over the isolation and impotence confronted in life and art.

The tension between the desire to break free and the sense of hopelessness reaches a critical point in the story "Fuyu no hae" (Winter flies), written in 1928. The narrator compares his life to the struggle to survive of the winter flies in his room at a convalescent home. He notes that they have lost all the liveliness of summer flies but they stubbornly cling to life. The sight of these flies oppresses him, and he feels that he must escape in order to prove that he too has the will to live. He runs away from the home for a few days, but the exertion is detrimental to his health. When he returns, he must spend several days recovering.

> One day, all of a sudden, I noticed that not one fly was left in my room. I was completely surprised. I thought about it. Was it perhaps that while I was away no one opened the window and let the sun in or lit a fire and warmed the room, so that they died from the cold? That seemed likely. The conditions under which they existed depended on my quiet lifestyle. And while I was fleeing from my depressing room, tormenting myself and my body, they actually died from cold and hunger. For some time I was depressed by that. Not because I was hurt by their death, but because I felt as though there were capricious conditions that somehow kept me alive and that at some point would kill me. I thought it was like looking at the broad backs of those flies. That was a new vision that destroyed my self-respect. I felt that my life would contribute more and more to the melancholy that arose from that vision. (*KMZ* 192)

The despair of this passage is deepened by the recognition of the randomness of life. Realizing that his desires and views of the world are not absolute but marginal, the narrator knows that he exercises little control over his life.

Paradoxically, this blow to selfhood revealed in this story is also the beginning of a new attempt by Kajii to resolve the conundrum of his art, if not of his life. He arrives at a kind of acceptance of his destiny: an attitude that permits him to explore different perspectives in his literature. Turning away from the self-absorbed, isolated narrating voice that dominates most of his work, he begins to explore the narrative possibilities of multiple perspective as a way to achieve a literary apotheosis.

The acceptance of his destiny is fully dealt with only in the final story of his career, "Nonki na kanja" (A carefree patient). This piece was published in *Chūō kōron* in January 1932, two months before Kajii's death, and it illustrates the new direction his art had begun to take. The protagonist is a man named Yoshida, and "Nonki na kanja" is the record of his stay in a hospital. The dispassionate account of the horrors of tuberculosis is truly harrowing. Still, unsentimental descriptions abound in Kajii's work, and what gives this story its special power is the penetrating perspective of the narrative, which, although told in the third person, is tightly focused through the protagonist. The reactions of Yoshida's mother to his illness are presented with such understanding that the mediating presence of the protagonist seems to disappear at points. The same effect is achieved in the portraits of the many people who advise Yoshida, out of superstitious belief or false hope, to take some peculiar form of medication or in that of the woman who tries to convert him to religion in order to cure his illness. There is no malice in the descriptions, which are never judgmental about these characters. Instead, the story reveals a different aspect of his isolation. The people who try to help him are not being insincere, but they are unable to see what it really means to be in his position.

Understanding that all viewpoints are relative leads Yoshida to observe that his position, his isolation, is a condition ultimately shared by everyone. This conclusion, that the basic condition of humanity is loneliness and unpredictability, is not attractive. Nonetheless, it forces Yoshida to confront the reality of his own life, and this new-found understanding gives him the ability to break through his self-centeredness to comprehend the motivations of those around him and to understand how incapable they are of connecting with him.

This is perhaps the greatest act of subversion in all of Kajii's stories, and it is typical of a modernist sensibility. Charles Taylor has argued that as art in this century has shifted inward, "It has explored new recesses of feeling, entered the stream of consciousness, spawned schools of art rightly called 'expressionist.' But at the same time, at its greatest it has often involved a decentring of the subject: an art emphatically not conceived as self-expression, an art displacing the centre of interest onto language, or onto poetic transmutation itself, or even dissolving the self as usually conceived in favour of some new constellation."[3] The perspective in "Nonki na kanja" is comparable to the image of the "invisible eyeball" that Emerson used to describe the transcendent observer. Like the formal successes in the best stories of Akutagawa, "Nonki na kanja" succeeds because it takes advantage of the narrative possibilities of a highly personal viewpoint to transform the narrative into a transpersonal meditation on the ephemerality of human life. Revealing that truth is small comfort, however, and the final lines of the story sum up Yoshida's hard-won wisdom.

There were certain figures that Yoshida daily kept in mind. Of the percentage of people who died of tuberculosis, according to statistics, over ninety percent were poor, and fewer than one percent were from the upper class. Of course, these were only the statistics of people who had died of tuberculosis, and they did not include the mortality rates of the rich or the poor vis-à-vis the disease. Further, he did not understand to what extent those who had tuberculosis were poor or were rich. It was, however, enough to cause Yoshida to speculate as follows:

In short, the vast majority of tuberculosis patients now continue to die. Only about one percent receives the best possible treatment, so how many of the ninety percent or so of the patients who are poor go to their deaths without taking any sort of medication?

Yoshida merely abstracted these thoughts from the statistics, and though he thought they corresponded with his own experience, when he thought about the death of the daughter of the kitchenware merchant and further about the suffering he himself had endured for several weeks, he had no choice but to think about these things ambiguously. When he considered the ninety-odd percent of poor people in the statistics, certainly they included men as well as women, old people as well as children. If there were people who could go on strongly enduring their poverty and the pain of illness, then surely there were also very many who could not endure it at all. Still, sick people are never granted exemptions like those given for a school march to people who are weak and cannot do it. Until they reach the final goal of death, both the courageous and the cowardly follow the same line, shuffling along whether willing or not. (*KMZ* 269–70)

The statistics imply some hope of survival, but their impersonal objectivity is challenged by Yoshida, who denies such hope. All patients are headed for the same end. The statistics also imply a criticism of social inequalities, but Yoshida does not dwell on that point. His thoughts turn to the far deeper paradox of human life: that we are bound by mortality yet can imagine eternity; that we can construct the ideal even within the randomness of reality; that we can recognize our common bonds yet remain isolated. In Kajii's vision, we are all patients. Yoshida, however, is a "carefree patient" because he confronts the truth of human existence and tries to subvert the limitations on his life by accepting that truth. At the same time, Kajii's vision ultimately denies the possibility of such subversion, calling into question the efficacy of the formal achievements of his literary art.

Kajii's death was not widely noted at the time. It was unspectacular and unpleasant and did not bring about the kind of soul-searching—often a self-serving reevaluation—that followed the deaths of Futabatei or of Akutagawa. Yet Kajii's literature shared a number of tendencies with that of his more famous contemporary. The circumstances of his disease isolated him and made him acutely aware of his loneliness and of the differences between individual perspectives. His illness also forced him to confront and somehow try to reconcile as an artist the fact that the only thing he shared absolutely in common with others was his mortality, a common bond that he knew would eventually silence his voice. Like Akutagawa, Kajii tried to take formal advantage of the relativism implied by the assertion of individual perspective and to overcome the threat of artistic death by moving the self out of the center of the narrative, giving priority to a formal presentation of competing perspectives. The aim was to surmount the limitations of the self, but the impossibility of that goal brought Kajii back again and again to the primary dilemma of the artist with an acute awareness of his predicament. As with the work of Shiga and Akutagawa, Kajii's experiments with perspective and his concern with the problems of narrative relativism reflect a persistent struggle between the liberating and debilitating effects of discontinuity.

◆

chapter fourteen
A Dizzying Descent into
Self: Kawabata and the Problem
of Cultural Amnesia

The search for identity that typifies much of Meiji literature was a reaction to the cultural discontinuity created by Japan's modernization. The limits of that search are revealed in the increasingly personal and fragmented perspectives that dominate the literature of the Taishō and early Shōwa periods. The self-absorption of so much of the literature of twentieth-century Japan, while it represents a serious search for a resolution of the dilemma of the modern, nonetheless results in an endless regression in which the act of narrating the self came to be viewed paradoxically as both a source of discontinuity and a means to overcome it. The tendency toward fragmentation and relativism in Meiji fiction was given greater impetus by the events leading up to and following the Second World War. The physical destruction of the Japan created in the Meiji period swept away even the tentative certainties that had been created to deal with cultural discontinuity. The war severed Japan from its past just as thoroughly as had the government policies that followed the Meiji Restoration. The defeat and occupation were wounds to the national psyche that, by violently separating the present from the past, threatened what might be termed *cultural amnesia.*

A Dizzying Descent into Self

The term *cultural amnesia* carries with it a negative sense, as though what was lost was inherently good, or necessary, and essential to recover. This is potentially misleading because it suggests the existence of a cultural memory—a set of shared images and myths that establish a common sense of self. But cultural memory is a construct that always represents the economic, political, or aesthetic interests of those in power; consequently, cultural amnesia implies a sentimental longing or nostalgia on the part of social elites whose order is threatened by cultural change. Since it suggests a validation of particular values and interests, therefore, *cultural amnesia* must be used with considerable caution as a descriptive term.

In spite of its descriptive limitations, however, cultural amnesia provides a useful image by which to look at narrative developments after Meiji. For one thing, the relationship of memory to the act of narrating became a central theme in a large number of works in the immediate postwar period. In addition, the concept of amnesia provides, as I argued at the outset of this book, an analogy to the dilemma of the modern. Narrative relativism, the fragmentation of perspective, and the decentering of the literary self are, as I have shown, particular extensions of that dilemma, and the heightened sense of discontinuity brought on by the war led a number of writers to extend their efforts to explore the problem of cultural memory. An example of the effects of extreme discontinuity on narrative form is provided by comparing two famous works by Kawabata: *Yukiguni* (Snow country), which was written mostly before and during the war, and *Yama no oto* (Sound of the mountain), his most important postwar novel.

To think of Kawabata as a novelist of discontinuity is a reading at odds with general critical perceptions of his work. He is often looked at as representing the traditions of Japan and as owing a larger-than-normal debt to the classical tradition—a judgment at the heart of his Nobel Prize citation.[1] In a narrow sense, he resembles Kafū in that his conscious invocation of the classical is a sign of his modernism. His first popular success came in the mid-1920s with *Izu no odoriko* (The Izu dancer), so he began reaching a wider audience not through his earliest experimental pieces but with a somewhat more conventional novella. Following that work, he became involved with Yokomitsu Riichi in the activities of the Shinkankaku-ha (Neosensualist school). One of the goals of that movement was to provide a corrective to the tendencies of the proletarian writers, who, in seeking a socially active literature, were taking the theories of Western Marxist critics as the basis for their aesthetic concepts, at the expense of the continuity of the native tradition. Kawabata's position toward the proletarian writers grew out of a legitimate artistic concern, although it must be said that in the politically charged atmosphere of the time, his position was also relatively safe.[2] Through the support of men like Kikuchi Kan, the powerful publisher of *Bungei shunjū*, he rapidly became an influential figure in the literary establishment, and he seemed to cultivate the image of the master writer who was a defender of older cultural values. I do not mean to discount the fact that he was extremely well versed in the classics of the Heian period, but the image of Kawabata as somehow maintaining cultural traditions should not be allowed to obscure the fact that his use of the tradition was self-conscious and thus an indication of his awareness of the gulf between the past and the present.

Certainly on the surface the classical aspects of *Yukiguni* are readily apparent. The famous opening lines—"*Kokkyō no nagai tonneru o nukeru to yukiguni de atta. Yoru no soko ga shiroku natta*" (Emerging through the long tunnel at the provincial border, it was the snow country. The very depths of the night had turned white)—are a distillation of Kawabata's art. The very first word, *kokkyō* (provincial border), hearkens back to pre-Meiji Japan. The cultural differences and isolation suggested by the snow country, a province figuratively frozen in time, provide the images (like Kafū's Tamanoi) for the poetic landscape into which the protagonist, Shimamura, can escape from the modern world. Train travel itself fuses a modernist image of progress with older religious and literary associations. It is a metaphor for the unsettled nature of human existence and suggests that in Kawabata's story we are moving not just spatially but culturally and psychologically into a realm created by art.

Yukiguni is an imaginary landscape created out of images that are archetypal and resonate strongly in the cultural memory of Japan. At the heart of the novel is the image of the geisha, Komako, a symbol of the transitory beauty of the floating world. She is, like her Heian literary forebears, a static figure: the waiting woman who depends on a male to create her story. That story is in turn archetypal in that it follows a pattern of decline and abandonment. The man that brings Komako's story to life is Shimamura, who also possesses certain stock characteristics. He is a traveler—an interloper, really—whose presence in Komako's life is temporary. He is weak and vacillating, and his relationship with Komako is played out against an elaboration of the seasonal progression found in love stories in classical poetry anthologies. Although the narrative chronology is different from the seasonal chronology, the affair begins in spring, when

Komako is not yet a geisha. The death of Yukio, the son of Komako's music instructor, brings to an end his unexplained relationship with Komako, and it occurs during Shimamura's second visit in the winter. The end of Shimamura and Komako's affair also takes place in late autumn/early winter, completing the poetic seasonal cycle of their love story.

Within the larger archetypal patterns of the narrative are a host of recurring images that echo the literary tradition. Images of insects abound, many reinforcing the seasonal progression of the story, and Komako is connected with those images in Shimamura's mind by the association of her rooms with silkworms and cocoons. The dominating colors of the novel are red and white, traditionally auspicious colors connoting a range of ideas that include purity, sexual desire, and death, all of which are associated by Shimamura with Komako. The image of the mirror is a symbol of the art of the geisha, and thus of the transitory beauty of women. The mirror also provides an oblique way for Shimamura to observe the beauty of Komako and of Yōko, the bright-eyed young woman he sees on the train at the opening of the novel who has important but unexplained ties to Komako.

The characterization, seasonal progression, and imagery are tied together by a minimalist plot that nonetheless reflects the contrivances of traditional plotting. The story depends on two coincidences: the arrival of Shimamura on a day when all the geisha are occupied at a large banquet, leaving available only Komako, who performs music part-time; and his chance sighting of Yōko on the way to his second meeting with Komako. The second coincidence in particular is reminiscent of a *kaimami*, the stolen glimpse of a woman that set any number of Heian literary love affairs in motion, and it reinforces the passive characterization of Shimamura, who is an onlooker, or voyeur, through whom the story of Komako is focused.

This brief catalogue of narrative elements illustrates how Kawabata attempted to invoke his literary tradition, and the clear presence of these elements is the basis for readings that stress the novel's classicism. However, there is also a general critical tendency to stress the realism of the work and of the portrait of Komako in particular. This reading appears to stem from Kawabata's sympathetic treatment of her and from the emotional impact of her affair with Shimamura. Itō Sei, for example, links the lyricism of the novel to the power of Komako's portrait.[3] His reading is echoed by other critics, such as Masao Miyoshi, who sees Komako as "one of the few life-sized and full-bodied female characters in Kawabata's novels," and Donald Keene, who thinks of her as a successfully drawn female character who "would have earned him [Kawabata] the reputation of a master of feminine psychology" even if he had written nothing else.⁴ The problem with such readings is that they view the narrative mode of *Yukiguni* as essentially realistic, in the sense of trying to establish psychological verisimilitude. This misreading leads in turn to several literal-minded interpretations of one of the crucial scenes of the novel, when Shimamura switches from calling Komako "a good girl" to calling her "a good woman." Edward Seidensticker's view of this exchange, and of Komako's hysterical reaction, is that Shimamura has betrayed her; Miyoshi's is that no moral reading can be made of the scene because of the narrative's neutrality concerning Shimamura's behavior.⁵ The problem with these two readings is that they see Shimamura as nothing more than a cipher or foil for Komako, who is taken as the only fully embodied, tangible figure in the story, an emphasis that distorts crucial aspects of the narrative perspective. More importantly, the notion that Komako is betrayed does not take into account the fact that Shimamura's verbal slip does not actually reveal anything that she does not already know. However his behavior is judged in moral terms, it is not unexpected to her nor, given the archetypal pattern of the story, to the reader. Reading *Yukiguni* as a realistic account of Komako may reflect the vividness and sympathy with which she is drawn, but it fails to explain the narrative strategies by which Kawabata utilizes the elements of his tradition to create a new literary form.

A stronger reading of *Yukiguni* must connect the psychological tensions depicted in the story with the modernist variations of formal convention that create the narrative context. It has long been noted that *Yukiguni* is an extended elaboration on the No, especially on plays about women, and that elaboration must be the starting point for understanding both the structure of the narrative and the relationship between the lovers.⁶ Shimamura's role in the story, as has been often noted, is similar to the role of the *waki,* usually a traveler or itinerate priest, who introduces the locale of a No play and the poetic associations or legendary stories connected with it. Komako is the main figure, the *shite,* and her affair with Shimamura provides the interaction through which we begin to learn who she is and through which her character is transformed. This reading is useful in two ways. First, it points to the archetypal quality of the story and of Komako's characterization. She is throughout the novel reduced by Shimamura's perspective to an ideal image of purity and cleanliness that resembles a Nō mask.

> The thin, high nose was a little lonely, but the small, budding lips beneath it were smooth and glistening, like a beautiful circle of leeches. Because you felt as though they were somehow moving even when she was silent, if they had been wrinkled or if their color had not been good, then they would have looked unclean. However, that was not the case, and they were moist and shining. The corners of her eyes neither rose nor fell, and they seemed funny in a way, as though they had been drawn straight across intentionally. The downward sloping brows, with their thick, short hairs, arched over the eyes in just the right way. Her round, convex face had rather ordinary contours, but her skin was like white porcelain tinged with a light crimson, and because the base of her throat was still slender, she was clean and pure rather than beautiful. (*KYZ* 10:29–30)

We never view Komako directly but see her refracted through Shimamura, who in turns observes her in the reflections of mirrors or breaks her into descriptive fragments, figuratively dismembering her.

Reading the novel as an elaboration on the Nō points up the problems of interpreting *Yukiguni* as a realistic work, and it helps to explain the somewhat troublesome and enigmatic ending. Applying the *jo-ha-kyū* musical structure (preface, exposition, rapid finale) loosely to *Yukiguni* helps to make the ending somewhat more coherent without imposing speculative resolutions to the relationship between Komako and Yōko (which is never fully explained). Having learned about Komako through Shimamura, who decides, finally, that he must withdraw from her world, there is nothing more to be revealed. The novel ends at the scene of a fire at a cocoon warehouse. Just when it looks as though everyone has escaped safely, a body is seen falling from the upper floor. Yōko has been trapped, and she is described by Shimamura as transformed, as a being from an unreal world caught between life and death. Her piercing eyes are closed as the fire illuminates her face.

> With a start Shimamura recalled the appearance of that moment some time ago when the lamplight on the mountain had hovered in the middle of the reflection of Yōko's face on the train he was taking to meet Komako at this hot spring. Again his breast shuddered. His time with Komako seemed to blaze up in an instant. For some reason a heartrending pain and sadness was here.
>
> Komako rushed away from Shimamura's side. She screamed and covered her eyes at the same time, just as the throng of people gasped.

> Amid the water-soaked and charred fragments of wood scattered here and there, Komako staggered, pulling the long skirts of the geisha. She struggled to return, clasping Yōko to her breast. Beneath her desperately straining face, Yōko's face, with its vacant stare of the dead, was hanging down. Komako looked as though she were embracing either her sacrifice or her punishment.
> The throng of people, which had been holding back, raised their separate voices and broke forward in a rush to surround the two.
> "Get out of the way, please get out of the way!" Shimamura heard Komako cry. "This girl. She's insane! Insane!"
> Shimamura tried to draw near to Komako, whose voice sounded as though she were insane herself. But he was pushed aside by some men who tried to take Yōko from Komako and stumbled backward. As soon as he regained his ground and looked up, it seemed that the Milky Way was rushing down inside Shimamura with a roar. (*KYZ* 10:140)

This closure, for all its ambiguity, makes formal sense if read as an elaboration on the Nō. The scene is like the frantic final dance of the *shite*, whose story is already known to the audience. The ending is not so much a resolution of the story as a ritual re-creation of the literary convention of the abandoned woman.

Nevertheless, such a reading still does not fully explain certain elements of the narrative, in particular the role that Shimamura plays. It helps to clarify the structural relationship among the other traditional elements of the story, but it does not explain what is new about Kawabata's treatment. He was, after all, very much aware of the work of modernist writers in Europe and was involved in introducing the theoretical works of the surrealists in particular.[7] Indeed, I suggest that Kawabata owes the final image of the story, the Milky Way flowing down into Shimamura, to Breton's claim in 1930 that surrealism is directed "to the complete recovery of our psychic force through a means none other than the dizzying descent into ourselves, systematically illuminating hidden places and progressively darkening others, a perpetual walk in the heart of the forbidden zone."[8] Once the archetypal story of Komako has been played out, Shimamura's narrative function is exhausted, and the internalized, abstract world he has created to constitute himself through his relationship with Komako collapses in on him in a dizzying descent.

The modernist elements in *Yukiguni* are apparent in certain qualities of Kawabata's style, in the treatment of various aspects of the structure of the plot, and in the narrative perspective provided through Shimamura. One of the features of Kawabata's prose style, though certainly not unique to him, is its tendency toward fragmentation and minimalism. It may be argued that this tendency also reflects his attempts to recapture traditional

A Dizzying Descent into Self

elements of style, and undoubtedly the associative quality of his writing suggests a solid basis for locating Kawabata's models squarely within the tradition. Even so, this associative quality seems quite modern, lending a kind of psychological verisimilitude, a stream-of-consciousness realism, to descriptive passages; and whatever the influence from Western forms of modernism might have been, Kawabata's style unquestionably belies the associative quality of classical poetic style and reflects a far greater sense of discontinuity, abstraction, and detachment. For all the classical familiarity of his imagery, the strange and jarring juxtapositions he creates at times lend a surreal quality to his writing. This is apparent, for example, in both the description of Komako's face, with the image of her lips as leeches, and in the image of the Milky Way that closes the text.

The important effect of this style is the way in which it conveys the dissociation of Shimamura, through whom we obtain these fragmented images. Kawabata's style perfectly reflects the state of mind of his protagonist and is one of the master strokes of the novel. The following passage is representative:

> Shimamura was translating Valéry and Alain and treatises on the dance by French literati from about the time that Russian ballet was in its full flower. He intended to publish it as a luxury volume in limited edition through a vanity press. The fact that the book would be useless to the present dance world in Japan could be said to have actually brought him some comfort. Sneering at his own work was an indulgent pleasure. Perhaps it was from this tendency that his pathetic fantasy world was born. Off on a trip, there was absolutely no need to hurry.
>
> He observed in great detail the death agonies of insects.
>
> As the autumn grew colder, there were insects dying on the tatami mats of his room every day. When the stiff-winged insects turned over on their backs, they couldn't get up. A bee walked a little, rolled over, walked again, and then collapsed. It was a quiet death that accompanied the dying of nature according to the change of the seasons. However, when he came closer to look, it was struggling, shaking its legs and antennae. The eight-mat room looked enormously wide to serve as the scene for such a small death.
>
> While Shimamura picked up the corpse with his fingers to throw it out, he suddenly remembered the children he had left behind at home. (*KYZ* 10:105)

Shimamura embodies a modernist sensibility—an extreme self-consciousness and an abstract comfort in forms and surfaces. Because he is given to abstraction, he cannot provide us with a connected view of reality. This is reflected in the surreal image of the dead insect on the empty, geometrical grid of the tatami mats. Reality is heightened not because of the detail of the description, which is actually rather vague, but because the description is so fragmented, reduced to its essential elements. This reduction or fragmentation is reinforced by the jarring association of the insect with Shimamura's children in Tokyo.

The fragmented, associative quality of Kawabata's style is what is most often cited as poetic about his work. The effect is similar to that achieved by the miscellaneous structure of *Hōjōki* or by the anecdotal style of Saikaku, and it is perhaps not inappropriate to liken its effect to that of linked verse, in that it tries to emulate the ephemeral flow of experience. It is this quality that led Kawabata to claim that his novels lack formal structure in the ordinary sense of the term, but it is also a clear indication of his debt to modernism as an aesthetic ideology. Feeling incapable of writing a sustained novel, a concern he seems to have shared with Akutagawa, he was reduced to writing opening chapters that he then proceeded to vary by stringing together image and experience in an open-ended, episodic pattern. Although the resemblance to No cannot be ignored, *Yukiguni's* structure is obviously much looser, and the method of composition and publication—the work took shape over a series of short installments that appeared between 1934 and 1947—would seem to bear out Kawabata's observation about his own work.[9] What emerges is a narrative in which the succession of images and experience cannot be reduced to separate meanings. They depend on their formal relationships for significance, and that form is provided through the perspective of Shimamura. Just as the style of the work is used to convey his sensibility, so the structure of the novel reflects the abstracting, fictionalizing mind of the main character.

As I noted above, there is a tendency to see Shimamura as somewhat peripheral to the story, but he performs a much more important function as the focus of the narration and thus goes beyond the role that, for example, the *waki* plays in the No. The relationship between Shimamura and Kômako is best described as that of the observer and the observed. It is through Shimamura that we are told Komako's story, and the act of narrating in that sense places him at the very center of the novel. Komako needs Shimamura to tell her story, and yet in his narration she is reduced to an ideal, a type. If this is the source of Shimamura's artistic control, however, it is also the source of his own dilemma in the novel. He observes Komako and creates her story, but in reducing her to art he is finally unable to become involved on any real emotional level. Were he to get involved, the ideal would be destroyed, and the narrative rendered impossible.

A Dizzying Descent into Self

The dilemma faced by Shimamura is an expression of the dilemma the modern artist faces in his relationship with the tradition. For Shimamura, the world becomes an abstraction, and he cannot connect with it. The result is that he not only cuts himself off from the past but is cut off from the present as well. His spirit is, in Komako's words, broken and scattered (*KYZ* 10:95), and the sense that all the action in the novel is "futile action," a term that Shimamura uses to describe Komako's life but that could very well apply to his own, reflects the alienation and repetitiveness of modern life. Played out against the immensity of nature—the white blankness of the snow country and the blazing emptiness of the winter sky—all human activity becomes trivial and futile.

Komako's story has been enacted again and again in the tradition, and it cannot exist unless she is abandoned. To think that she is betrayed by Shimamura is to read a great deal of sentimentality into the story. Her anger and tears do not spring from a sense of betrayal; they are prompted by the realization that her story is complete—that she is being written out of the narrative. This reading of Shimamura's narrative function moves the focus of the novel away from the plight of Komako. The achievement of *Yukiguni*, its power to move us emotionally, lies not in the hackneyed story of an abandoned geisha but in the way Kawabata has managed, through the narrative perspective of Shimamura, to express the larger human costs of the fragmentation of experience.

In *Yukiguni*, elements of narrative form and style are brought together in such a way that they furnish a penetrating portrait of the emotional and aesthetic dilemmas confronting a modernist sensibility. Kawabata would further develop those elements following the war in his finest novel, *Yama no oto*, where he not only presents a deeper analysis of the impact of discontinuity on the individual but also indicates its larger social and moral implications. The techniques Kawabata brings to this novel, which was serialized between 1950 and 1954, are generally very similar to those he used in *Yukiguni*, but he extends them. For example, the characteristics of the prose style he employs in *Yukiguni* are in some ways more exaggerated in *Yama no oto*. The style is even more fragmented and minimalist, virtually reducing the narrative to its most fundamental units of experience. The flow of experience is created by an associative technique that links the observations, thoughts, and images presented in the narrative, but the juxtapositions are at times even more jarring than in *Yukiguni*, and the surrealistic nature of the descriptions seems more striking.

The key function of the prose style is to convey the observing consciousness of the protagonist, an older man named Shingo. Although a third-person narrating voice is present, as in *Yukiguni,* so much of the story is focused through Shingo's perspective that it is essentially a record of his consciousness. The fragmented, minimalist style of the prose dictates for the most part how we read Shingo's fictional experience, and to that extent it largely determines the structure of the novel. Since that style is so fragmented, the associative quality of the prose determines the coherence of the narrative. The succession of images and thoughts, and the brief moments of experience, cannot be reduced to any separate or precise meaning. The tendency on the part of both Shingo and the reader to want each episode to make sense is inappropriate to the narrative. The problem is not how much information is given to us (privileged perspective is not a problem here), but how to give order and form to that information. Clearly, the units of experience presented through Shingo only gain meaning collectively, through the relationships they create in the flow of an individual's life. By "collectively," I refer to two things: the process of memory, the personal associations that the characters, mainly Shingo, bring to each moment of experience, and the process of cultural or social memory, the larger associations and points of reference that give meaning to experience independent of personal associations. *Yama no oto* is a chronicle of the narrating process, the process of memory, that is used to represent the essential nature of human experience and of the flow of life.

Viewing the book as a chronicle of Shingo's memory helps to explain the novel's loose structure and provides some justification for the open-ended conclusion. The flow of Shingo's consciousness is not, however, rational and linear. It is random and unpredictable at points. The degree of his involvement in the plot, specifically in the affairs of his children, varies a great deal—to the point that he even surprises his wife, Yasuko, on one occasion by the forcefulness with which he injects himself into the story. At the same time, we are always watching Shingo placing patterns on his own experience, interpreting them almost like a detective piecing together the facts in a case. It is the constant interaction between Shingo and his experiences that shapes the story for us.

The parallel relationships set up in the novel—grouping Shingo's daughter, Fusako, his wife, Yasuko, and his granddaughter, Satoko, on one side, and his daughter-in-law, Kikuko, and his deceased sister-in-law on the other—provide examples of how Shingo's observations control the way we read the story. Similarly, the parallel plots that involve the marital problems of Fusako and of Shūichi, Shingo's son, and especially

A Dizzying Descent into Self

the pregnancies of Kikuko and Kinuko, Shūichi's lover, are associated for us only through Shingo's consciousness of them. Framing the plots of the stories of his children is a series of recurring personal and cultural associations. These include anecdotal stories about the deaths of a number of Shingo's acquaintances, including a friend dying of cancer, a man named Kitamoto who goes mad trying to pull out all his gray hair, and an acquaintance named Mizuta who dies at a hot springs while making love to a young woman. There are also a number of images of the past—a Nō mask Shingo buys from Mizuta's widow, the memory of a dwarf maple tree he associates with Yasuko's dead sister, a regenerated two-thousand-year-old lotus he reads about in the paper, and ink paintings and utensils associated with the tea ceremony—that link his personal experiences and contemplations with a larger store of cultural associations of death and rebirth.

The flow of images and associations is given additional depth and form by the various levels at which they appear in the narrative. Many of these associations occur in the interaction of Shingo with his family and with his associates. In many scenes in the novel, the associations arise in the interaction between Shingo and the natural world. These coexist with the associations created by his memories and his dreams, and this interaction at various levels creates a more complex narrative structure. As we move about through these levels, we are constantly forced, together with Shingo himself, to reevaluate both the meaning of his experiences and his understanding of them. The novel's fragmented structure may be understood as reflecting Shingo's consciousness, but the very form of the novel gives rise to a different problem: how far we can trust the reliability of the narrative perspective?

Kawabata explicitly relates the effect of discontinuity and the question of narrative reliability to the problem of memory. The difficulty is not the disjointed associations or jarring juxtapositions created by the narrative perspective of Shingo; rather, it is a question of how far we can trust the reality of the individual experiences and images that make up the story. If we cannot trust those individual moments of experience, then how can we trust a narrative created by the collective associations of discrete images and experience? The primary perspective in the story is that of a man who is slowly losing his memory. The novel opens with Shingo trying unsuccessfully to remember the name of his former maid. He is constantly in need of prompting from those around him and at one point even forgets how to tie his necktie. He is acutely aware of the problem and wistfully tells Kikuko at one point that he would like to have his head sent out to be cleaned. His problem forces him to question the very associative process by which the narrative takes shape for us. When Fusako returns home from her unhappy marriage to Aihara, she carries her belongings in a cloth bundle that had once belonged to Shingo's sister-in-law, a woman he secretly desired. The cloth leads to the following chain of associations:

> In the country town, the hobby of Yasuko's father had been dwarf trees. He was especially fascinated by dwarf maples. Yasuko's elder sister had helped him take care of the trees.
> In bed, with the storm raging outside, Shingo remembered her figure among the shelves of dwarf trees.
> Probably her father had given her a tree when she was married. Maybe she had wanted one. However, when she died, it was most likely returned, because it was such an important tree to her father, and because there was no one in the husband's family who could care for it. Maybe her father went to fetch it.
> The maple with blazing red leaves that now filled Shingo's head was the tree in Yasuko's family altar room.
> Shingo wondered if her sister had died in autumn. Autumn came early in Shinano.
> But would they have returned it right after her death? It seemed all too convenient that it should have had red leaves and been in the altar room. Wasn't this just a nostalgic reverie of his memory? Shingo had no confidence. (KYZ 12:288)

Not only the reliability of his memory is in doubt; so is the way in which Shingo gives order to his experience. The very act of putting his experience into some form forces him to question the reality of that experience. This is true of his memory, and it is true of his dreams, insubstantial visions that he is constantly trying to interpret, a number of which he relates in the novel.

The problem of reliability goes even deeper than that, however. The process of memory, the associations that create the narrative, allows him to interpret his experience, but it also has a profound effect on the reliability of his perceptions of immediate, waking reality. This is brought home to him one day on his way to work, shortly after Kikuko has had an abortion to protest Shūichi's affair with Kinuko, who is also pregnant.

> "In Heaven, a great wind. In Heaven, a great wind." For no apparent reason he repeated the inscription on his forged Ryōkan painting. Then, looking

out at the Ikegami grove, "What in the world!" He made as if to leap out of the window on his left.

"Those pines, maybe they're not in the Ikegami grove. They're closer."

The two pines, which stood out taller than the other trees, seemed to be in front of the Ikegami grove when he looked at them this morning.

Whether it was the fault of the spring or of the rain, their distance had never been clear until this moment.

Shingo continued to look out the window to make sure. Because he stared at them every morning he felt that he wanted to go at least once to the place where they were growing to find out.

However, although he claimed to look at them every day, in fact he had only just recently discovered the two pines. For many years he had passed by looking vacantly at the grove.

Yet he made the discovery that those tall pines did not appear to be in the Ikegami grove for the first time today. Perhaps because the May morning air was so clear.

Shingo had twice discovered the two pines, their upper trunks tilting toward each other and their upper branches seeming to embrace.

After dinner the night before, when Shingo was telling about how he had searched out Aihara's house and had helped out Aihara's mother a little, the enraged Fusako had fallen dead silent.

Shingo pitied Fusako. He thought he had discovered something in Fusako, but whatever he had discovered, it was by no means as clear as his discovery about the Ikegami pines.

Those were the Ikegami pines, but two or three days earlier, while Shingo was staring out at them, he had questioned Shūichi on the train and forced his confession about Kikuko's abortion.

So the pines were no longer just pines. Kikuko's abortion was entwined with them. Each time he looked at the pines on his commute to and from work, Shingo would probably be reminded of Kikuko.

So it had been this morning.

On the morning Shūichi confessed, the pines appeared dimly in the wind and rain, melting back into the grove. This morning, however, separated from the other trees, entwined with the abortion, the pines looked a dirty color. Perhaps the weather was too good. (*KYZ* 12:441–43)

The confusion that arises in Shingo's mind about the reliability of his own experiences, his admission that he may be putting things together incorrectly, is a narrative strategy that makes him both sympathetic and, insofar as his unreliability reflects the nature of human consciousness in general, psychologically credible. Nevertheless, his confusion, which extends even to uncertainty over how to count his age or tie his tie, raises the most important questions in the narrative about his relationships with those around him. The uncertainty of the process of memory creates doubt as to the reality of his experience and the forms by which he constructs his identity. If the meaning of his life story derives only from the relationship of individual moments of experience, then his real life is no more real than his dreams or his faulty memories.[10]

When individual memory is called into question, what happens to the notion of cultural memory? This problem is not really explored in any great depth in *Yukiguni,* perhaps because that novel was largely written before the defeat and occupation; however, the cataclysmic event of the war colors *Yama no oto,* giving it a deeper emotional and moral resonance. The sense of discontinuity that shaped *Yukiguni* becomes even more urgent, as though Japan's cultural memory had suffered a debilitating blow. Likening cultural discontinuity to amnesia in this manner seems appropriate in describing Kawabata's conception in *Yama no oto.* Shingo's lapses of memory are on one level symptomatic of a greater cultural loss, and his effort to recover the past, to recover a narrative sense of himself, is an attempt to stop the futility of his life and the wasting of time.

This development in Kawabata's art is apparent in the different treatment he accords two similar scenes, one from *Yukiguni* and the other from *Yama no oto.* Shimamura realizes that his own perception and interpretation of his experience is faulty, but that realization is not the central problem of the text, which deals primarily with how his propensity for narration, for creating the story of Komako, prevents him from achieving any real emotional contact with another human being. At the very end of the first part of the book, after his second visit is finished and he is returning home on the night Yukio dies, Shimamura feels that he is being "borne away in emptiness" and allows himself to imagine how the story will develop at that moment. Was Yukio dead? Would Komako see him before he died? He is greatly moved by his own fancy, and his propensity for confabulation leads him to imagine a connection between the only other people in his railcar: a middle-aged man and a young woman.

> However, when they came to a station where there were the smokestacks of a silk factory, the man hurriedly took down a wicker trunk from the baggage rack, and, while dropping it from the window onto the platform, he said to the young woman, "Maybe by chance we'll travel together again sometime," and got off the train.
>
> Shimamura suddenly became tearful and was surprised at himself. Then he thought of his solitary trip home and of his parting with the woman.

A Dizzying Descent into Self

He never dreamed that the two had simply met by coincidence on the train. The man was perhaps a traveling salesman. (*KYZ* 10:71–72)

Shimamura's misinterpretation underscores his tendency to abstract or fictionalize human relationships. His recognition of his self-created isolation, however, does not lead to any great transformation within him. The story plays itself out according to its models, with Shimamura unable to overcome his inability to connect with Komako and finally deciding that he must leave her. The treatment of Shingo, on the other hand, is different. While Shimamura's propensity for abstraction is the source of his dilemma, it becomes for Shingo the only means, albeit not a very reliable one, to give meaning to his life. Near the end of *Yama no oto*, as Shingo and Shūichi, who has finally abandoned Kinuko, are returning home on the train, Shingo observes a middle-aged man sitting next to a young woman. The two look so much alike to Shingo that he automatically assumes they are father and daughter. They never exchange a word, however, and the woman gets off first. Shingo is astounded, though his son gives the matter little thought. It seems to Shingo that he has witnessed a remarkable resemblance, and yet the connection he has created between the two is completely unreal. This is essentially the same experience Shimamura undergoes, but it takes on greater significance for Shingo. He wonders whether he has participated in some sort of miracle, and he asks himself what it could possibly mean, "creating a man and woman who resembled each other like father and daughter, and having them come together for a mere thirty minutes out of their whole lives, and showing them to Shingo?" (*KYZ* 12:527–28). Unable to get the two out of his mind, he tries to convey the significance of his experience to Shūichi.

> "But maybe they really are father and daughter. It just now occurred to me, but maybe she's a girl he fathered somewhere and left behind. They've never met, so they don't know each other."
>
> Shūichi looked away. Shingo regretted it after he had spoken. However, having made the innuendo, he continued with his thought. "Twenty years from now that may happen to you."
>
> "Is that what you wanted to say? Well, I'm not that kind of sentimental fatalist myself. The bullets whistled right by my ears, but not one touched me. Maybe I fathered a bastard in China or in the South Pacific. It's nothing at all to meet your own bastard and not know it once you've had bullets whistling by your ears. It's no danger to your life. On top of that, it's not certain that Kinuko will have a girl, and if she says it isn't mine, then I'll believe her."

"War and peace are different."

"Maybe now a new war is pursuing us, and maybe the previous war inside of us is still pursuing us, like a ghost." Shūichi spoke hatefully. "Father, you were secretly attracted because there was something a little different about her, and so you babble on with your bizarre thoughts. Men always get caught when a woman is just a little different from other women."

"You think it's all right to have a woman give birth and raise a child because she's a little different?"

"I don't want it. It's the woman who does."

Shingo fell silent.

"The woman that got off in Yokohama? She's free."

"Free?"

"She's not married, and if you called, she'd come. She may look high-class, but she doesn't make an honest living, and she's tired of the insecurity."

Shingo was taken aback by Shūichi's observation. "I'm shocked at you. When did you become so depraved?"

"Kikuko's free too. She really is free. She's not a soldier or a prisoner." He spit out his words like a challenge.

"What do you mean your own wife is free? Have you said that to her?"

"Why don't you say it to her?"

Shingo held back his anger. "Are you saying you want to divorce her?"

"Not at all." Shūichi was also controlling his voice. "I'm saying that the girl who got off in Yokohama is free. . . . Don't you suppose you thought those two looked like father and daughter because she is the same age as Kikuko?"

Shingo was caught off guard. "That's not so. If they weren't father and daughter, didn't they look enough alike to think it a miracle?"

"But it's nothing to be as impressed with as you say."

"Well I was impressed." But having been told by Shūichi that Kikuko had been on his mind, he felt his throat tightening. (*KYZ* 12:529–31)

Shūichi challenges his father's perspective on the events of their lives and on the couple on the train. Shingo is bothered by the fact that what he took to be a miracle is exposed to be the empty creation of his own fancy and, by implication, of his sexual preoccupation with Kikuko. More than that, however, he is bothered by the implications of his son's amoral view of life. Earlier Shingo was troubled by the degree of his involvement in the story of Kikuko's abortion and feels that he has somehow had a hand in the death of his grandchild. Shingo cannot stand the randomness and chaos represented by his son's point of view and by the encroaching failure of his memory, which threatens to cut him off from the things that give his life order. In contrast to the characterization of Shimamura, for whom the act of narration isolates him from humanity, Shingo is a man for whom narration represents the only way to affirm his values and his selfhood. He is forced to acknowledge what might be termed the epistemic relativism of his life, but he cannot accept that such a condition condemns him to ethical relativism. Shūichi, on the other hand, is certain in what he knows—he has faced death and seen his life reduced to its most elemental qualities. He is not bothered by the knowledge that existence is relative and contingent, for the war still rages inside him. Shūichi is too clever to be fooled, like his father, and yet his own pragmatic acceptance of the reality of the world cuts him off from all ethical bearings. Shingo is justifiably appalled that his son rejects the personal and social norms and values by which the self and the culture are created.

Shingo is a man who is losing, or has lost, his memories. His only recourse is to re-create them through new narratives. Such narratives may be relative and ultimately false, but they are signs of a fundamental need and represent the essential, ephemeral quality of human life. The open-ended structure of *Yama no oto* conveys that quality. On the surface, domestic peace has been restored in Shingo's household by the end of the novel. Shūichi has abandoned his lover, and Fusako, determined to put her unhappy marriage to Aihara behind her, asks her father to help her open a little shop. Kikuko, demonstrating the new-found independence she gained with the abortion, even offers to help Fusako—an offer greeted with surprise and scorn by Shūichi. Shingo, however, does not give Fusako a definitive answer. He suggests instead that they all go off to their ancestral home in the country to view the maples. Neither of Shingo's children wants to accompany him, which suggests that the resolution of the family problems is tenuous and that the restored balance in their relationships is precarious. This seems to be confirmed by the final lines of the novel, in which Shingo calls to Kikuko that the gourds she has planted are ripe and heavy. His voice, which cannot be heard over the sound of dishes being washed, is lost in the flow of experience.

Like the ripening plants, the process of maturation and change in human life is inescapable. In thematic terms, the image of the gourds provides an appropriate sense of closure. That the scene ends without a response, however, creates the ambivalent feeling that the narrative, like the flow of Shingo's associations, is open-ended and could potentially continue. Shingo wants to arrest the flow of experience, to make it certain and permanent, but to do so would change the very nature of experience.

Kawabata has chosen to break off the narrative at a brief moment of stasis, and his choice stresses the paradoxical quality of the process of narrative the better to show that it is emblematic of all human experience. The achievement of *Yama no oto* is that its own formal qualities so completely mesh with and convey that view of human life. It expresses the dilemma of the modern artist while at the same time providing an affirmation of art.

epilogue

◆

I have used the terms *discontinuity* and *dilemma of the modern* to suggest that there is a dual, contradictory movement in narratives that exhibit a heightened awareness of the significance of the present. On the one hand, there is a turning inward to a reliance on the subjective consciousness of the individual as the ultimate arbiter of reality. This turn inward is accompanied by a heightened skepticism toward the act of narration, by an acceptance of narrative relativism, and by an increasing fragmentation of perspective. Formally, this movement is marked by open-ended architectural constructions of the self, such as confessional narrative, autobiography, parodic narrative, and *bildungsroman*. On the other hand, there is a concurrent displacement outward, a decentering of the self reflected in concerns with language, in mythic notions of the heroic, and in appropriations of the tradition that lead to canon reformation, primitivism, and nostalgia.

By presenting a broad historical survey of Japanese fictional narratives, including several pre-Meiji works, I have also suggested that the dilemma of the modern is not an anachronistic concept. The method of my study—looking at specific understandings of the modern to find recurring patterns of expression in fictional narrative—has been to replicate as far as possible the tension inherent in the effort to achieve permanent or universal significance for the particular experience of the present moment. As Paul de Man has argued, "The appeal of modernity haunts all literature. It is revealed in numberless images and emblems that appear in all periods—in the obsession with a *tabula rasa*, with new beginnings—that finds recurrent expression in all forms of writing. No true account of literary language can bypass this persistent temptation of literature to fulfill itself in a single moment. The temptation of immediacy is constitutive of a literary consciousness and has to be included in a definition of the specificity of literature."[1] A common obsession with new beginnings does not mean that all literature necessarily achieves formal innovation. Nonetheless, each of the narratives I have examined in this book not only expresses parochial concerns and values shaped by particular historical moments, or particular discontinuities, but also employs rhetorical strategies necessitated by a recognition of the impossibility and the undesirability of completely achieving an absolute break with the past. This recognition leads to self-consciousness about the act of narration, and that self-consciousness is the defining characteristic of the modern.

I want to close by proposing once more that the dual nature of the modern is not culturally specific but rather inherent to the narrative process. This aspect of the modern has great significance for readings of the literature of the Meiji period, a historical moment marked by extreme material and ideological discontinuity. The understanding of the modern in Meiji Japan is not simply a product of either Western or native influences. Certainly the formal qualities of both Western and pre-Meiji narratives provided models for Meiji writers, who were preoccupied with what they believed to be a crisis of language. There were ample precedents in the native tradition alone for a knowing, ironic authorial voice or for concepts of heroism that gave priority to subjective consciousness. But the use of such models always constituted an appropriation or misreading that sought to validate individual experience, either by moving Japanese literature into the so-called mainstream of world literature, becoming modern in the Western understanding of the term, or by decentering those Western values that threatened the sense of a native Japanese identity.

If it is misleading to describe Japanese literature in terms of standards that reflect Western notions of modernity, then it is equally misleading to see the problem that Meiji writers faced in defining a modern Japanese

Epilogue

identity as simply one of trying to break free of the cultural hegemony of the West. Although the critique, or deconstruction, of modernization theory in the West seeks to free our readings of Japanese (or of any other non-Western) narratives from culturally bound assumptions in order to return us to a supposedly native reading of the Japanese tradition, in fact such a critique is itself a nativism that binds us ever more tightly to our own assumptions. The only means to break through these cultural boundaries, I believe, is an exhaustive survey of the ways in which individual authors construct a modern Japanese identity through narrative. This book is a step toward achieving that end.

notes

◆

Introduction

1. For a more complete discussion of the usages of these words, see Isogai, "Kindai kara gendai e," 1–10. The distinction between *kindai* and *gendai* in Japan is identical to that which came to be drawn in the West between *modern* and *contemporary*. For a discussion of that distinction, see Calinescu, *Faces of Modernity*, 86–88.
2. Chamberlain, *Things Japanese*, 1, 3.
3. Nakamura M., "Kindai e no giwaku," 328–29.
4. Ibid., 331. I have translated *seishin* as "identity" here, because Nakamura's use of the word assumes that *seishin* (spirit) is a defining national trait.
5. Taylor, *Philosophy and the Human Sciences*, 2:258.
6. Hulme, *Speculations*, 3; Barthes, *Writing Degree Zero*, 87–88.
7. Sacks, *The Man Who Mistook His Wife for a Hat*, 105. In a recent article, Sacks extends his clinical observations by examining the case of a painter with an extreme capacity for remembering that allows him to paint scenes of his boyhood home in Italy with photographic precision. The man can neither misremember nor stop remembering, and his dual gift and burden leads Sacks to speculate that "one is not born with a disposition to recollect; this comes only with changes and separations in life—separations from people, from places, from events and situations, especially if they have been of great significance,

have been deeply hated or loved. It is, thus, discontinuities, the great discontinuities in life, that we seek to bridge, or reconcile, or integrate, by recollection, and, beyond this, by myth and art" ("Neurologist's Notebook," 60).

8. Sacks points to the case of a man he calls William to illustrate this predicament, writing that

> paradoxically, then, William's great gift—for confabulation—which has been called out to leap continually over the ever-opening abyss of amnesia—William's great gift is also his damnation. If only he could be *quiet,* one feels, for an instant; if only he could stop the ceaseless chatter and jabber; if only he could relinquish the deceiving surface of illusions—then (ah then!) reality might seep in; something genuine, something deep, something true, something felt, could enter his soul.
>
> For it is not memory which is the final, "existential" casualty here (although his memory *is* wholly devastated); it is not memory only which has been so altered in him, but some ultimate capacity for feeling which is gone; and this is the sense in which he is "de-souled." (*The Man Who Mistook His Wife for a Hat,* 109)

Sacks, perhaps understandably, backs away from the truly frightening implication of his observation, which is that our normal capacity for memory is itself nothing more than a deceiving surface of illusions—that perhaps we are all "de-souled."

9. Sakai writes, "Universalism and particularism reinforce and supplement each other; they are never in real conflict; they need each other and have to seek to form a symmetrical, mutually supporting relationship by every means in order to avoid a dialogic encounter which would necessarily jeopardize their reputedly secure and harmonized monologic worlds. Universalism and particularism endorse each other's defect in order to conceal their own; they are intimately tied to each other in their accomplice" ("Modernity and Its Critique," 105).

10. Although the question of whether Japan is (or has been for some time) postmodern lies outside the scope of this study, Lyotard's definition of *postmodern* is relevant here in that it is an extension of the dilemma of the modern. If the modern is marked by the inherent impossibility of completely idealizing the present, then the postmodern "would have to be understood according to the paradox of the future (*post*) anterior (*modo*)" (*Postmodern Condition,* 81). When the impossibility of achieving an absolute break with tradition is realized, that is, when it is understood that the modern moment lacks duration, the response is to try to empower the present by "working without rules in order to formulate the rules of *what will have been done*" (ibid.). The postmodern is the modern in extremis, desperately continuing the effort to empower.

11. Harry Levin, citing the works of Freud, Lovejoy, et al., points out the paradox of the modern by arguing that in primitivism this drive toward freedom manifests itself as a sense of discontent with civilization. See *Myth of the Golden*

Age, 5. For a rather similar treatment of the subject, see Trilling, "On the Modern Element in Modern Literature," 76–77.

12. Sakai describes the bias of modernization theory in the case of Japan, writing that

    a privileged object of discourse called Japan is thus constituted in order to show *us* the supposedly concrete instance of a particularism, in contrast to which *our* universalism is ascertained. Japan is defined as a specific and unitary particularity in universal terms: Japan's uniqueness and identity are provided insofar as Japan stands out as a particular object in the universal field of the West. Only when it is integrated into Western universalism does it gain its own identity as a particularity. In other words, Japan becomes endowed with and aware of its "self" only when it is recognized by the West. It is no accident that the discourse on Japanese uniqueness (*Nihonjinron*) mentions innumerable cases of Japan's difference from the West, thereby defining Japan's identity in terms of deviations from the West. Its insistence on Japan's peculiarity and difference from the West embodies a nagging urge to see the self from the viewpoint of the Other. But this is nothing but the positing of Japan's identity in Western terms which in return establishes the centrality of the West as the universal point of reference. ("Modernity and Its Critique," 104–5)

    While Sakai persuasively points out the extraordinary difficulty Japanese writers have defining the modern on their own terms as a result of Western cultural imperialism, his critique is excessively reductive. Every interpretation is an appropriation of other narratives that allow the reader to create a new, purportedly universal narrative. Indeed, recent attempts to reread Japan as postmodern are just such a critical swerve, and Sakai's critique is applicable to virtually every article in *Postmodernism and Japan* (Miyoshi and Harootunian, eds.), including his own.

Introduction to Part 1. Mutability and the Floating World

1. Baudelaire, *Baudelaire as a Literary Critic,* 292–93. Baudelaire's definition is notable because it assumes that beauty arises only through a fusion of the temporal and the timeless, rather than being immanent in nature. This definition also sets up his later famous remarks that

    modernity is the transitory, the fugitive, the contingent, the half of art, of which the other half is the eternal and the immutable. Every painter of the past had his own modernity; most of the beautiful portraits that remain to us from bygone days depict the costumes of their period. They are perfectly harmonious because the costume, the coiffure, and even the gesture, the glance and the smile . . . form a whole that is completely alive. As for this transitory, fleeting element whose metamorphoses are so frequent, you have no right either to scorn or to ignore it. By suppressing it, you are bound to fall into the emptiness of an abstract and indefinable beauty, like that of the one woman before the first sin.... In a word, if any particular modernity is to be worthy of becoming antiquity, it is necessary to extract from it the mysterious beauty that human life involuntarily gives it. (296)

2. De Bary, *Learning for One's Self*, 4–6. The terms I use to discuss narrative voice immediately below are derived from De Bary's discussion of individualism in Confucian thought in China.
3. Kermode, *Continuities*, 21.

Chapter 1. The Makings of a Modern Hero

1. See Waley, introduction to Murasaki Shikibu, *The Bridge of Dreams*, 22–23.
2. Waley, *The Pillow Book*, 9–11.
3. Woolf, "Mr. Bennett and Mrs. Brown," 320.
4. For a discussion of the possible interpretations of the word *oya* (parent or ancestor) as it is used in the context of the picture contest, see Nakano Kōichi, "Monogatari no idekihajime no oya," 96–100.
5. Mitani, "Heian bungakushi no hōhō," 395. See also ibid., 397.
6. For a discussion of the mode of argumentation in the second round of the preliminary contest, see ibid., 395–96, 398.
7. For a discussion of this poetry contest as a source for Murasaki Shikibu, see Ishida J., "Eawase to Tentoku yonen Dairi uta-awase," 111–15.
8. It should be noted that formal realism is in this sense a product of so-called low culture because it aims for inclusiveness. Although it may seem odd to speak of works written by an elite class of court women as products of low culture, my use of the term is meant to convey a distinction in the mode of narrative representation, not a relative difference in social status between noble men and women. In *Genji monogatari tama no ogushi* (The Tale of Genji: A small jeweled comb), Motoori Norinaga (1730–1801), the great Edo period philologist and critic, defines the distinction between *deep* and *shallow* in terms of their relation to low and high culture. He sees the quality of depth as a property of *kanbun* (Chinese writings—e.g., works from foreign countries, or the *Nihon shoki* [Chronicles of Japan, 720]), which women could not easily read. Shallow works, especially *monogatari*, made use of kana and were written in more accessible language. See Motoori, *Motoori Norinaga shū*, 264.
9. See Cranston, *Izumi Shikibu Diary*, 70.
10. Walker, "Poetic Ideal and Fictional Reality," 173.
11. Ibid., 135. Walker equates the idealistic mode with the term *romance* as used by Northrop Frye to describe a narrative mode that is closely related to either a seasonal or a class ritual and shows a preference for ideal types and didacticism.
12. Cranston, *Izumi Shikibu Diary*, 116.
13. The McCulloughs observe that "in Heian usage the word *monogatari* referred most commonly to the kind of more or less factual stories told by one person to another in ordinary conversation—anecdotes, gossip, simple accounts of

everyday happenings. The derivative use to refer to written fiction was of decidedly less frequent occurrence" (*Tale of Flowering Fortunes*, 7).
14. Iwahashi, "Murasaki Shikibu," 8.
15. See Bowring, *Murasaki Shikibu*, 32–34.
16. Gusdorf, "Conditions and Limits," 29–30.
17. Motoori, *Motoori Norinaga shū*, 273.
18. Barthes, *Writing Degree Zero*, 38–39.
19. See Field, *Splendour of Longing*, 22–28.

Chapter 2. The Burden of the Future

1. For a discussion of the hermit as a literary figure, see Lafleur, *Karma of Words*, 60–69.
2. Freud, *Civilization and Its Discontents*, 28.
3. I have relied primarily on Yasuraoka, *Hōjōki*, 237–57, for the biographical sketch of Chōmei here.
4. Chōmei's poetry master was Shun'e, a monk at the Tōdaiji temple who had a number of students from the Fujiwara and Minamoto families. His music instructor was Nakahara no Ariyasu, who tutored a number of noble families and became head of the Bureau of Music in 1194.
5. Cited in Yasuraoka, *Hōjōki*, 253. *Minamoto no Ienaga nikki* is a one-volume diary covering the years 1197–1207. It is not organized chronologically, but it does provide insights into the retinue of Go-Toba.
6. See Matsunaga and Matsunaga, *Foundation of Japanese Buddhism*, 2:58–59. Hōnen, who established Pure Land Buddhism as an independent sect, retired for several years to Kurodani in 1148.
7. See Tamura, *Nihon bukkyōshi*, 248 ff.
8. Watson, *Japanese Literature in Chinese*, 64.
9. See Ozawa, *Mappō to masse no shisō*, 11, 12–13.
10. See Matsunaga and Matsunaga, *Foundation of Japanese Buddhism*, 1:219–21.
11. See Ishida M., *Nihon bukkyō shisō kenkyū*, 107–12.
12. Kermode, *The Sense of an Ending*, 94; 101–2.
13. Ozawa argues that it was in part a matter of historical timing that linked Pure Land practices with the doctrine of *mappō*. He writes:

> The second half of the sixth century, when Buddhism was introduced into Japan, corresponds to the first peak period of Pure Land teaching through the work of Tan-luan, Tao-ch'o, Shan-tao, Huai-kan, and others. Accordingly, the various Pure Land scriptures that form the foundation of the doctrine of *mappō* were likely transmitted together with later Buddhist teachings, though the formation of a Pure Land sect had to wait until Hōnen. For this reason, it is perhaps in the nature of Pure Land thought to recognize in the present-day world the degeneration of the law and to renounce it as corrupt. In Japan, after the establishment of the *ritsuryō* system of government following the Taika Reform, Buddhism was maintained and controlled within that system

as a state religion with the function of protecting and civilizing the nation. The attitude of the people toward Buddhism at that time, which was an anticipation of the secular, magical effects of promoting good fortune and warding off evil, is contrary to the fundamental character of Pure Land teachings.

Under these circumstances, although the doctrine of *mappō* took shape in Japan as a historical consciousness, there was initially little concern about the periodization outlined in the scriptures. Only when the doctrine was fused with an awareness of danger by the clergy and the laity that this was the final age, which had an individual dimension that developed with the deterioration of *ritsuryō* government, did the doctrine of *mappō* for the first time take on a magical fatalism with a social dimension. In Pure Land thought, the individual historical consciousness that views the present as the final age is fused with the view of *mappō* that religious orders explained as the destruction of the law; but in the case where that individual consciousness is sublated by a social dimension, *mappō* begins to acquire the social and psychological power to regulate people's actions and mental lives. (*Mappō to masse no shisō*, 14)

14. See Matsunaga and Matsunaga, *Foundation of Japanese Buddhism*, 2:27–28.
15. See Chappell,"Early Forebodings," 31. For the linking of Pure Land Buddhism to *mappō*, see Ishida M., *Nihon bukkyō shisō kenkyū*, 459. See also Matsunaga and Matsunaga, *Foundation of Japanese Buddhism*, 1:113–14 and 2:25–26.
16. See Matsunaga and Matsunaga, *Foundation of Japanese Buddhism*, 2:59.
17. See Hare, "Reading Kamo no Chōmei," 192–98.
18. See Matsunaga and Matsunaga, *Foundation of Japanese Buddhism*, 2:60–72. Hōnen denied that the practice of *nenbutsu* was an act of *jiriki*, and his emphasis on faith over good works created tensions with both the Enryakuji and the Kōfukuji temples, and even his disciples disagreed concerning the effectiveness and proper practice of the *nenbutsu*.
19. See Hare,"Reading Kamo no Chōmei," 200–203. Hare provides an exhaustive list of the possible readings, meanings and interpretations of *fushō*. From a grammatical standpoint, no one reading is wholly persuasive, but I have chosen to interpret the word according to its *on* reading, *fushō*, rather than its native *kun* readings, *kowazaru* or *kowazu*, for two reasons. First, its use in connection with Amida has scriptural precedents in the *Vimalikīrti nirdesa* sutra and in the *Muryōjukyō*. Second, the scriptural use overlaps with one sense of *kowazaru*, which means "without being asked or sought after."
20. LaFleur, *Karma of Words*, 114.

Chapter 3. Epiphanies of Modernism and the Floating World
1. Taylor, *Sources of the Self*, 419. See also ibid., 456.
2. Ooms, *Tokugawa Ideology*, 86. See also Nosco, introduction to Nosco, *Con-*

fucianism and Tokugawa Culture, 11, where Nosco makes essentially the same observation:

> It is remarkable how quickly, deeply, and widely interest in neo-Confucianism spread in Tokugawa Japan. The Japanese, like the Koreans some centuries earlier, appear to have taken Confucian thought seriously, almost passionately, and even if the degree of official interest in neo-Confucianism may have been exaggerated, it would appear likely that the bakufu's interest in Confucian thought, and the attendant prestige which such interest bestowed, contributed to the currency of Confucian thought in Japan.

3. Ooms, *Tokugawa Ideology,* 289.
4. Nosco, introduction, 20–21. One sign of that crisis was the attempt in 1790 to assert the neo-Confucianism represented by the Bakufu College and the Hayashi family as the sole orthodoxy through "The Kansei Prohibition of Heterodox Studies" drafted by Matsudaira Sadanobu. The crisis was felt not so much in the intolerance of heterodox views as in the restorationist aims of the edict—aims implicitly admitting that the regime was facing mounting problems that could be overcome only by returning to the true ways of the past. This particular reform nonetheless reveals the built-in mechanism for self-renewal in neo-Confucianism and thus points to the obstacles this conservative orthodoxy raised against the creation of competing ideologies. It could always reform itself by drawing on new interpretations of the past that it presented as a return to a true orthodoxy.
5. The assessment of Saikaku as a realist is for the most part a construct of Meiji criticism and as such represents a retrospective understanding of what constitutes formal realism. I shall return to this issue in the next chapter.
6. For a more complete description of the *kana-zōshi,* see Keene, *World within Walls,* 149–66.
7. Watt, *Rise of the Novel,* 32, 13.
8. For an example of this type of criticism, see Morris, introduction to Saikaku, *Life of an Amorous Woman,* 41–42. Morris writes that "we must, of course, avoid judging Saikaku's books by the standards of the modern novel" (41) and then proceeds to make just such a judgment by trying to explain away Saikaku's flaws—which exist only by contrast with Western expectations of the novel form.
9. Hibbett observes that ". . . whether burlesquing literature or life, Genroku writers were able to examine and criticize their own society at the same time that they amused it. For the incongruity thus exploited was exactly what heightened their sense of the reality of their own world. In Japan, as in the West, parody and burlesque were important techniques in the development of realism" (*Floating World,* 95–96).
10. Morris writes that "his interest in the pursuit of individual happiness, his assertion of the physical joys of life, his advocacy of the 'way of the merchant,'

his statement that only the double sword makes the *samurai* different from other men—all this may lead us to view Saikaku as a precursor of a more liberal age. In the opinion of the present writer, however, there is little justification for regarding him as a great humanist, or his *ukiyo-zōshi* as a literature of protest" (introduction, 38).

11. Ihara, *Nippon eitaigura,* 21–22. The name *Koikaze* literally means "the breeze of love."
12. For a more detailed discussion of Saikaku's debt to Kenkō, see Takahashi T., *Saikaku ronkō,* 146–55. Takahashi also discusses the connections between certain passages from *Tsurezuregusa* and *Kōshoku ichidai onna* in his *Saikaku zappitsu,* 219. See also Kawamura, *Iyō no ryōiki,* 66–67. Kawamura has located a preference for the strange in the writings of Yoshida Kenkō, who gave aesthetic priority to unusual narratives because they transcended what was normally encountered in human reality.
13. This function of linking is more fully described in Ramirez-Christensen, "Essential Parameters of Linked Poetry," 585–86.
14. Yamaguchi, *Chosakushū,* 93–94.
15. Nishida, *Mujō no bungaku,* 225. This description of the *haikai* concept of beauty is akin to Wallace Stevens's statement in "Sunday Morning" that "death is the mother of beauty." This comparison is especially apt in that "Sunday Morning" shows both the radical tendency to challenge orthodoxy (in this case religious orthodoxy) and the artist's conservative impulse to reassert a mythic order that define modernism.
16. Hattori, *Sanzōshi,* 545–46. I have translated *makoto* as "sincerity," but the word presents some difficulties. *Makoto* conveys senses of purity of emotion or intention and of truthfulness or reality. In using *sincerity,* I have emphasized the intentional aspect of the word, but I have done so because it also implies a concern with truth or reality.

    It should be noted that not only does Hattori give a second-hand report of critical ideas, but the ideas he ascribes to Bashō are cast in a vocabulary that is heavily indebted to traditional critical terms and methodology. An example of this is provided by his discussion of the origins of Japanese poetry (519–20), which is not much more than a rehashing of ideas from Ki no Tsurayuki, among others.
17. Mukai Kyorai (1651–1704) also presents a record of Bashō's precepts in which he explicitly states that *fueki ryūkō* is a fundamental teaching. Kyorai's account of *haikai* is very similar to Hattori Dohō's. At one point he writes, "Kyorai says, 'In Bashō's school there are verses that will last forever and verses that are fashionable for but a moment. Bashō taught us that *haikai* breaks down into these two types, but that there is a single basis for them both.

    " 'Without knowing immutability there is no foundation. And without knowing fashion you cannot renew *haikai.* Immutability [constancy] is that which was considered good in the past and has retained its appeal in later ages.

Fashion is that which changes according to specific periods. Yesterday's fashion is inappropriate for today. Because you cannot use today's fashion tomorrow, it is a fashion of the moment. It is something popular' " (*Kyōraishō*, 496).

18. See Nakamura Y., *Kinsei shōsetsu no kenkyū*, 285–89. The critical distinction between classical and vulgar styles of writing became widespread in the early eighteenth century primarily among scholars of Chinese fiction, especially *kogaku* (ancient learning) scholars, who used the terms to describe components of Ming vernacular style. The distinction is one part of the larger influence of Chinese vernacular fiction on Tokugawa fiction and is closely tied to the strong editorial sensibility that sought to rework older materials and showed a preference for collections of materials—both of which contributed to anecdotal formats and strong juxtapositions between classical literary modes and vulgar, contemporary subject matter and language.

19. One way that authors could create jarring juxtapositions of classical and vulgar elements was to exploit the possibilities for puns and double entendres that were inherent in the language. Hibbett observes that

> often there is an ironic contrast between the kind of language and its subject. ... Bold spending may be described in military terms, brothel-visiting in Confucian or Buddhist ones; and such a contrast may extend throughout an entire work, as in Kiseki's *Courtesans Forbidden to Lose Temper*. Indeed, parodic techniques account for much of the flavour of Genroku writing. And there are a great many kinds of parody in Tokugawa literature. Nearly every genre was parodied—in poetry as well as native forms—and all the Heian, Kamakura, and Muromachi classics received this sort of attention. (*Floating World*, 90)

In "The Playful Gloss," Chieko Ariga discusses an even more extreme form of parody, the creation of parallel texts through the use of glosses, or *rubi*. Her analysis shows clearly the extent to which vulgar and classical elements could be used to play off each other in the service of parody. However, I would add that these works, though they ran afoul of paranoid authorities, do not necessarily represent, as Ariga suggests, a coherent or strong political critique. As Ariga herself points out, the double meanings created by the use of *rubi* nullify or trivialize each other. The fusing of separate linguistic elements through such glosses prevents either an orthodox or a subversive reading from wholly gaining the upper hand. Such parody certainly deflated orthodoxy and the authorities that supported it, but conversely it did not elevate subordinated levels of society. The effects of political expression were thus diffused, placing limits on protest even as the pomposity of authority figures was exposed.

20. See Yamaguchi, *Chosakushū*, 97–137. Yamaguchi provides detailed analyses of a number of Saikaku's *haikai* versions of classical texts. He sees clear parodies of the "Uji" chapters of *Genji monogatari* in *Kōshoku nidai otoko* (A man of passion of the second generation), of *Ujishūishū* (Stories gleaned at Uji) in *Saikaku shokoku hanashi* (Saikaku's tales from the provinces), and of the Nō in *Kōshoku gonin onna*. Yamaguchi is so convinced of the importance of *haikai*

practice to Saikaku that he sees the imperfect parody of *Sagoromo monogatari* (The tale of Sagoromo) in *Kōshoku sandai otoko* (A man of passion of the third generation) as evidence that the work is not by Saikaku.

21. Moriyama, *Saikaku no kenkyū*, 124.
22. Karatani, *Nihon kindai bungaku no kigen*, 87–88.
23. In *Chosakushū*, 114, Yamaguchi argues that *Yu hsien k'u* is one of Saikaku's most important sources. Apart from the debt to the erotic elements in the Chinese novella, Yamaguchi points to the noticeable presence of certain Chinese characters in *Kōshoku ichidai onna* (such as for the words *utsukushi, hohoemi, tahafure, itosuji,* and *kahobasenayoyaka*), which do not regularly occur in other *ukiyo-zōshi*, to establish a close link between the two texts.
24. See Yamaguchi, *Chosakushū*, 113.
25. Taniwaki, *Ihara Saikaku*, 169.
26. The choice of Uji Bridge as the locale, with the play on the word *ushi,* calls to mind the dual meanings of *ukiyo*. This type of wordplay was possible because the early orthographic representations of the syllables *shi* and *ji* were indistinguishable. Although the addition of diacritical marks made it possible to represent clearly the difference between these syllables, by Saikaku's day this particular play on words had become conventional. The wordplay between *Uji* and the *uki* of *ukiyo* is based on the fact that *uki* is the modifying form of the adjectival *ushi*, which is the sentence-ending form.
27. *Onna yūhitsu* originally referred to a woman employed by a noble family to carry out the responsibility of correspondence. Here it means both a writing instructor and a substitute writer who knows the proper etiquette for composing a letter.
28. Saikaku anticipates Bashō's reaction to Matsushima, described in *Oku no hosomichi*. Bashō is incapable of composing a suitable verse, and his own failure to be inspired is attributed to the mysterious beauty of the place. He concludes, "Perhaps someone will properly take up the brush and express in words the divine ingenuity of this creation" (Matsuo, *Bashō bunshū*, 82). The apocryphal poem "Matsushima ya/Aa, Matsushima ya/Matsushima ya" (Is it Matsushima?/Yes, it is Matsushima!/Well then, if it's Matsushima . . .) is an extreme expression of this pose in which the *utamakura* (literally, "poem pillow"— words and images, especially place names, that have conventionally determined poetic meanings or associations), Matsushima, is so conventional that it becomes self-referential and stands for the function of all *utamakura*, which is to signify the ineffable.

Chapter 4. Literary Darwinism

1. See Yamamoto, *Genbun'itchi*, 26.
2. Such efforts were not limited to translations. In his preface to *Ninin bikuni: iro zange*, Kōyō says that he decided against the colloquial style of *genbun'itchi*

but then provides what amounts to a concession of the need for realism in his choice of literary styles. Forgoing the older fusion of vulgar and classical elements, he instead strives for a new style, especially in spoken passages, where he combines elements of *jōruri* speech with contemporary colloquial elements. See Ozaki, *Ozaki Kōyō shū*, 6.

3. One such example, *Berabōme, kabochabatake ni ochita tako ja aru mee shi, otsu uitsukaranda koto o iinasan na,* might be translated as "Listen, asshole, I'm not some kite that just fell into a pumpkin patch, so watch your lip!" Futabatei does not cite his source.

4. Tayama Katai, *Kindai no shōsetsu* (Modern fiction, 1923), cited in Yamamoto, *Genbun'itchi*, 8.

5. Cited in Yamamoto, *Genbun'itchi*, 8. Tōson makes essentially the same point in the essay "*Bungakkai* no umareta koro" (When *Bungakkai* was born), and in "Mitsu no chōhen o kaita tōji no koto" (Circumstances at the time I wrote three novels) and "Kinō, ototoi" (Yesterday, the day before yesterday), he explicitly cites Futabatei as the writer who opened up the world of prose fiction for him and who was the most important influence on the composition of his novel *Haru*. See STZ 18:89; 22:114, 226–28.

6. See Yamamoto, *Genbun'itchi*, 13–14.

7. The Ken'yūsha was founded in 1885 by Ozaki Kōyō, Yamada Bimyō, and others. It was very influential, and some of its younger members, including Tayama Katai and Tokuda Shūsei, later became important figures in the naturalist movement.

8. See Takeno, *Kindai bungaku to Saikaku,* 32–33, 46–47.

9. See Danly, *In the Shade of Spring Leaves,* 64–65, 148.

10. See Yamamoto, *Genbun'itchi,* 31–32.

11. See Bloom, *A Map of Misreading,* 35–36.

12. Cited in Yamamoto, *Genbun'itchi,* 23. Both men point to *Omedetaki hito* (An auspicious man, 1911) as the pivotal work in the naturalization of this style.

13. See TSS. See also Fowler, *Rhetoric of Confession,* 24–25. Fowler observes that it was largely the work of Shōyō that caused the term *shōsetsu* to come to refer to something roughly equivalent to the Western novel. Fowler is careful to point out, however, that the traditional meaning of the word was never totally superseded, and it retained certain negative connotations as frivolous literature.

14. Pyle, *New Generation in Meiji Japan,* 4.

15. Leutner, discussing the late works of the period, has summed up the situation as follows: "Ironically, the very fact that many species of fiction written in this period often approach modern novels in superficial aspects of form and content makes them hard to like: the surprise of recognition soon wears off, to be replaced by a growing sense that the object at hand is simply a strangely

defective and primitive sort of novel rather than a piece of fiction from a wholly different tradition that can be appreciated only on its own terms" (*Shikitei Sanba*, 5).

Chapter 5. The Limits of Realism and the Dilemma of Futabatei

1. Mori, "Hasegawa Tatsunosuke shi," Shimazaki, "Hasegawa Futabatei shi o itamu" (Grieving for Hasegawa Futabatei), and Masamune, "Futabatei shi," in Tsubouchi and Uchida, *Futabatei*, 2:3–4, 16–17, and 87–88.
2. Leutner, *Shikitei Sanba*, 66. See his discussion, 66–70.
3. Again, for a more complete description of this literary technique, the *rubi*, see Ariga, "The Playful Gloss."
4. Rosenberg, "Literary Form and Social Hallucination," 648.
5. See Ryan, *Japan's First Modern Novel*, 178–84.
6. Shimizu, "Shikitei Sanba to Futabatei Shimei," 185.
7. This explanation of the pseudonym, Futabatei Shimei (double-leaf pavilion, four doubts), seems revisionist to me. Another explanation for the origin of the name points to the reaction of Futabatei's father on learning that his son wanted to become an author. This sounds not only less melodramatic but more in keeping with Futabatei's own comic impulses. The use of the elegant-sounding element "pavilion" echoes the names of many Edo authors (e.g., Kyokutei Bakin, Ryūtei Tanehiko, and of course Shikitei Sanba) and of oral storytellers contemporary with Futabatei (e.g., San'yūtei Enchō). The meaning, however, is obviously inelegant, revealing a self-deprecating humor that expresses at once a debt to Tokugawa conventions and a critique of them. It should be noted that Masao Miyoshi's statement in *Accomplices of Silence* (22) that the pseudonym is derived from *futabatte shimei* appears to be a misprint.
8. Miyoshi, *Accomplices of Silence*, xv.

Chapter 6. The Skeptic as Artist

1. See M. Nakamura, *Futabatei Shimei den*, 137–38.
2. See ibid., 141–42 and 155–56. The series was titled *Shincho hyakushu*. Eighteen volumes were eventually produced. The first volume was *Ninin bikuni: iro zange* by Ozaki Kōyō. Rohan's *Fūryūbutsu* was also published in this series.
3. See Nakamura, *Futabatei Shimei den*, 146–47.
4. The italicized words and sentences are in English in the original. *Wholeman* appears as a single word.
5. Futabatei uses the English word *mission*, written in katakana, in the original.
6. For a brief discussion of how the issues he discussed in his notebooks shaped the development of his late fiction, see Nakamura, *Futabatei Shimei den*, 286–91.
7. See Natsume Sōseki, "Hasegawa kun to yo," in Tsubouchi and Uchida, *Futabatei*, 2:37.

8. Cited in Nakamura, *Futabatei Shimei den*, 278. Parallels may be drawn between most of the major characters in the two works. Apart from the ineffectual protagonists, Omasa and Takiko are almost stock figures, being scheming, mother-in-law/stepmother types; Osei and Sayoko are women who, though idolized by Bunzō and Tetsuya, respectively, find themselves in situations where they have no control over their future or their happiness. Noboru and Hamura are crass social climbers who achieve material success at the expense of ethical considerations. The opening scenes of the two books are also very similar, and judged on that basis alone it is no wonder that Hakuchō felt that Futabatei's creative powers were waning.
9. There is an implication here that their relationship is in a figurative sense incestuous, the family system having created an artificially close bond between them. Their eventual affair thus represents the breaking of social restraints and taboos in rebellion against that system.

Chapter 7. Like the Slobber of a Cow

1. See M. Nakamura, *Futabatei Shimei den*, 301.
2. See Leutner, *Shikitei Sanba*, 4.
3. See Tayama, "Futabatei Shimei kun," in Tsubouchi and Uchida, *Futabatei*, 2:49.
4. See Shimazaki, "Hasegawa Futabatei shi o itamu," in Tsubouchi and Uchida, *Futabatei*, 2:17.
5. See Nakamura, *Futabatei Shimei den*, 308.
6. Oketani, *Futabatei Shimei*, 277.
7. Nakamura, *Futabatei Shimei den*, 312. I do not agree with Nakamura's view that the author and narrator are virtually one and the same, but it is noteworthy that even though he sees the novel as more of a true confession than I do, he still feels the ambivalence created by the narrative voice.
8. The relationship between these works, if considered from a postmodernist vantage, is that of a modern novel and a postmodern novel. The formal satisfaction of *Sono omokage* provides, to use Lyotard's phrasing, a kind of "solace" in the face of irreconcilable conflicts within the narrative. *Heibon*, on the other hand, seems to subvert the notion of formal completeness, fitting Lyotard's definition of the postmodern as "that which searches for new presentations, not in order to enjoy them but in order to impart a stronger sense of the unpresentable" (Lyotard, *Postmodern Condition*, 81).

Chapter 8. The Dilemma of the Modern and the Autobiographical Confession

1. Tōson claimed to have been enormously influenced by Futabatei, and it is perhaps out of the desire to stress this connection that his memorial essay discusses the tensions in Futabatei's life in terms that could be used to describe Ushimatsu's dilemma—that is, the tension between the artist and the reformer.

See Shimazaki, "Hasegawa Futabatei shi o itamu," in Tsubouchi and Uchida, *Futabatei*, 2:16–17.
2. Walker, *The Japanese Novel*, 3, 15–16.
3. Fowler, *Rhetoric of Confession*, 75, 77.
4. Ibid., 77.
5. McClellan observes that

> Tōson was apt to talk about "the sense of discovery," "insight into reality" and the like that he thought he found in the best writers of the past, both Japanese and Western. Solemn statements of this sort can make us shy, but the fact is that he was referring to a very important aspect of the development of the modern Japanese novel. The lack of involvement on the part of writers like Shōyō, Bimyō and Kōyō was indeed a reflection of their inability to understand that realism in fiction must at least in part grow out of the desire to communicate such "insight."
>
> The relatively mature realism of *Hakai*, then, is due more to the presence of such a desire in Tōson than to some readily identifiable influence of the Western novel. And it is not at all paradoxical that the realism of his novels should be ultimately traceable to the romantic poetry of his early period when he was one of that group of passionate young writers who ran the literary journal, *Bungakkai* ("the world of literature," 1893–1898). For it was through his association with the *Bungakkai* . . . that he first learned to express his consciousness of his own identity, of the loneliness of modern youth; and it was this consciousness which led him eventually to write his so-called naturalistic novels, and which was mostly responsible for their modernity. ("Tōson and the Autobiographical Novel," 367–68)

6. For a more complete discussion of the importance of sincerity in Meiji literature, see the chapter on the subject in Fowler, *Rhetoric of Confession*, 43–70.
7. See McClellan, "Tōson and the Autobiographical Novel,", 366.
8. Cited in Yoshida, *Shizenshugi kenkyū*, 8.
9. For an example of this critical view, see Keene, *Dawn to the West*, 221. See also Seidensticker, *Kafū the Scribbler*, 13.
10. See Rubin, *Injurious to Public Morals*, 184.
11. In Keene, *Dawn to the West*, Tōson is quoted as similarly remarking, "When I wrote *Ie*, I constructed it block by block with sentences as if I were building a house. I excluded all that occurred out-of-doors, and tried to limit events to those inside the house. I described the house from the kitchen, from the entrance vestibule, and from the garden. I wrote about the river only after walking into a room where I could hear its sound. Thus I tried to build *Ie*" (262).
12. Yoshida, *Shizenshugi kenkyū*, 44.
13. Uno, *Uno Kōji zenshū*, 399.

14. For the details of Hōmei's life I have relied primarily on Funahashi Sei'ichi's biography, *Iwano Hōmei den*.
15. His zeal was such that he undertook extreme puritanical practices, such as averting his eyes whenever a young woman appeared. This sort of behavior is evidence of a volatile personality, especially in light of the fact that Hōmei was sexually initiated at a very young age: with an older woman when he was nine, and with a girl his own age when he was eleven.
16. See Yoshida, *Shizenshugi kenkyū*, 175. For Hōmei's xenophobia, see Ban, *Iwano Hōmei ron*, 34. Hōmei's dislike for his foreign teachers eventually developed into an ideology of Japan's cultural uniqueness, *Nihonshugi* (Japanism), through which he tried to rationalize the dilemma of writing a new literature based on foreign models.
17. Ibid., 45. The novel was never published. See Hōmei's reminiscence, "Boku no kaisō," in *HZ* 11:115–22.
18. There is a brief, acerbic portrait of his fellow naturalists in the opening chapter of Hōmei's *Dokuyaku o nomu onna* (A woman who drinks poison). The scene is a meeting of the Ryūdōkai, a literary club whose membership includes Tōson, Tokuda Shūsei, et al. The conventional nature of their moral beliefs is exposed in their discussion of the recent death of Kunikida Doppo.
19. See Funahashi, *Iwano Hōmei den*, 180–81.
20. I have given the original title of the essay. In 1912 Hōmei dropped the word *shinpiteki* (mystical) because he felt his ideas had been misunderstood.

Chapter 9. The Sense of an Ending

1. See Sōseki, "Hasegawa-kun to yo," in Tsubouchi and Uchida, *Futabatei*, 2: 37.
2. Ibid., 2:38–39.
3. Etō, *Etō Jun bungaku shūsei*, 1:391. See also ibid., 392, and 396–98.
4. Fujii, "Contesting the Meiji Subject," 554, 562.
5. It should be noted that Sōseki's use of *makoto* here differs somewhat from his use in "Bungei to dōtoku." There he states that *makoto* was a characteristic of the romantic morality of the past that is no longer viable, with *makoto* seeming to refer to the idealistic high-mindedness that Sōseki claims dominated Tokugawa ethics—a high-mindedness that was looked on as false in Meiji Japan. See 11:383–84.
6. Etō, *Etō Jun bungaku shūsei*, 1:210. The words "delicate death" are in English in the original and refer to a line from Whitman's "When Lilacs Last in the Dooryard Bloom'd." Etō traces the connection between Sōseki and the British decadents in a number of essays: "Sōseki to Eikoku seikimatsu geijutsu" (Sōseki and British fin de siècle art); "Sōseki to Rafaeru zenpa" (Sōseki and the Pre-Raphaelites); and "Sōseki to Aasaa-ō densetsu ni tsuite" (Sōseki and the Arthurian legend).

7. Pollack, "Framing the Self," 426.
8. The title "Kantan" refers to the ephemeral and illusory nature of human experience and alludes to a T'ang story in which an ambitious young man receives a pillow from an immortal. On using the pillow, he dreams of fifty years of adventure and glory only to awake and find that the lamp by his bed has hardly burned down at all and that he has slept but a very short time.

Chapter 10. The Individual in History

1. *Teikoku Bungaku* was published between 1895 and 1920, and *Taiyō* between 1895 and 1928. Ōgai Gyoshi was an early pen name.
2. Mishima, *Sakkaron*, 23.
3. It seems to me that Ōgai was greatly influenced by Futabatei at this point in his career. Not only does he address the same issues in language similar to Futabatei's, but *Vita Sexualis* resembles *Heibon* in its conception. In particular, the endings of the two novels resemble one another, with *Heibon* being presented as an incomplete manuscript and *Vita sexualis* concluding with the author tossing the work onto a dusty shelf to be left there unread.
4. Bowring, *Mori Ōgai*, 149–50.
5. See, for example, M. Miyoshi, *Accomplices of Silence*, 48–49. Miyoshi's reading is far more sympathetic than Bowring's, but he nonetheless remarks at one point that "the narrative structure of *The Wild Goose* is a bit awkward, a frequent problem with Japanese novels" (48).
6. *Yü Ch'u hsin-chih* (Yü Ch'u's new records) is a collection of stories compiled by Chang Ch'ao (1650–ca. 1703). The stories are mainly biographies of lesser historical figures, and they provide a model for later Tokugawa writers of *gaishi* (external history). These *gaishi*, both Chinese and Japanese, were an important influence on Ōgai that profoundly affected the narrative structure of *Gan*. "Ta t'ieh ch'ui chuan" (The tale of the great iron hammer) is by Wei Hsi (1624–1681) and appears in the first volume of *Yü Ch'u hsin-chih*. The story is a biography that tells of a hero, the dependent of a Sung general, who through his great courage defeats some rebels with his iron hammer. "Hsiao Ch'ing chuan" also appears in volume 1 of the same work. It is the story, by an unknown author, of the unfortunate life of the beautiful poetic genius, Hsiao Ch'ing. Hsiao Ch'ing is loved by a young nobleman, but she becomes the object of envy and hatred of one of the man's older concubines and dies at the age of eighteen. *Kōrentai* refers to a style of classical Chinese poetry first classified in the early T'ang period that deals with the sensuous emotions of love between men and women. I have used the Japanese reading of the characters because the term became part of classical critical vocabulary in Japan. The words *sentimental* and *fatalistique* are written in roman characters, so I have left them as they appear in the original.
7. Uno, *Uno Kōji zenshū*, 152.

8. The most important example of this genre is *Nihon gaishi*, completed around 1811 by Rai San'yō (1780–1832), an enormously popular work in the late Tokugawa and early Meiji periods.
9. Nakai, "Tokugawa Confucian Historiography, 66.
10. I have rendered the word Ōgai uses here, *kanshōteki*, as "objective," but it also carries with it the sense of being able to grasp the fundamental nature of reality through subjective observation and wisdom and is used as an aesthetic term meaning "contemplation," in the sense of an unmediated understanding of beauty. *Kanshōteki* thus carries the dual sense of objectivity as both dispassionate observation and subjective intuition, a sense that clearly echoes neo-Confucian historiographical practices.

Chapter 11. Nostalgic Narratives

1. Kafū's hero shares with Ōgai's character Okada a taste for imaginative, romantic literature, especially the *kōrentai* poetry of the Ch'ing period. Jūrōzaemon (d. 1664), a leader of the *hatamoto* (direct retainers to the shogun) in Edo, inherited his father's position in 1650. The following year saw an attempted coup by disgruntled *rōnin* (masterless samurai). During the decade after this uprising, Jūrōzaemon mustered *hatamoto* who had no political or financial support and led them in a series of violent and unlawful acts. He was ordered to commit seppuku by the shogunal authorities.
2. Etō, "Nagai Kafū ron," 352.
3. Keene, for example, describes Kafū as the last of the *gesaku* writers. See *Dawn to the West*, 431.
4. Nakamura, "Kafū no seishun," 405. Seidensticker takes essentially the same line in his *Kafū the Scribbler*.
5. See the reviews reprinted in Nihon bungaku kenkyū shiryō sōsho, *Nagai Kafū*, 229 ff.
6. Just after the turn of the century, Kafū had begun to read Zola in English translations and had started to learn French. In 1902 and 1903 he published three novels, *Yashin* (Ambition), *Jigoku no hana* (Flower of hell), and *Yume no onna*, all of which closely emulate Zola's social concerns and his narrative mode.
7. Seidensticker, *Kafū the Scribbler*, 149. For the full discussion, see ibid., 144–49.
8. Tsuruya Nanboku (1755–1829) was a Kabuki actor and a highly popular playwright. His most famous works, such as *Tōkaidō Yotsuya kaidan*, are characterized by the volatile mix of vulgar humor, expansive emotionalism, fantastic subject matter, classical allusion, and naturalistic style that also marks the fiction of the late *gesaku* tradition. *Ranchō* is a *shinnai*, a type of *jōruri* or ballad typical of Edo period *sewamono* (domestic dramas) featuring domestic triangles between a husband, the prostitute who is his lover, and his wife. *Shinnai* was a style originated by Tsuruga Wakasanojō (1712–1786).

Introduction to Part 4. Narrative Relativism and Cultural Amnesia

1. Harvey, *Condition of Postmodernity*, 22.
2. Ibid., 30.
3. For a brief discussion of the connection between the manifestos of Italian futurism and the political language of fascism, see Rawson, "Italian Futurism," 243–58. See also Harvey, *Condition of Postmodernity*, 31–35, on the phase of so-called heroic modernism between the wars.

Chapter 12. The Apotheosis of the Artist

1. Honda, *Shirakaba-ha*, 74.
2. A well-known example of a narrative that employs multiple perspectives is "Han no hanzai" (Han's crime, 1913). This story not only presents a number of differing accounts of the death of Han's wife but bases the judge's exoneration of Han on Han's honesty in admitting that he himself is uncertain whether he killed his wife intentionally or by accident. This admission removes all certainty from the so-called facts in the narrative (and establishes Han's sincerity) by making the one perspective, Han's, that could be absolute in determining what really happened relative and thus indeterminate.
3. Fowler writes that "It is no accident that Japanese literature's most highly lauded stylist (*bunshō no kamisama*) was also its most highly lauded 'realist' (*shōsetsu no kamisama*). Shiga's purpose as a *shishōsetsu* writer was never the complete, unerring depiction of lived experience, but rather the authoritative demonstration of his moral integrity" (*Rhetoric of Confession*, 188–89). Fowler concludes that Shiga's aims stem more from his interest in achieving inner peace "than in searching at all costs for the meaning of 'self.' This very limited and concrete notion of selfhood—true to the traditional epistemology and the product of a particularized narrative voice—is of course what characterizes the *shishōsetsu* in general and so much of Japanese literature. Shiga saw his task as one of resolving the contradiction within himself as observer and actor, as writer and as private man" (247).
4. Nakano S., "*An'ya kōro* zatsudan," 429.
5. Honda, *Shirakaba-ha*, 38.
6. See Ikuta Chōkō, "Shizenshugi zenpa no chōryō," 141–48.
7. Sibley writes of Shiga,

   Whatever the subject, when his "attitude" has determined that his work is to be fiction (that is, a *shōsetsu*), the focus is most often inward and backward, introspective and retrospective. As is the case with all deeply subjective fiction, much of Shiga's raw material is unmistakably rooted in his own inner experience, we may conclude; for he could scarcely know another's mind so thoroughly. But one may not find very interesting or particularly germane the dubious game of correlating closely the outward events of his life with the representation of psychological effects supposedly produced by them. (*Shiga Hero*, 4)

Notes to Pages 222-260

8. Ibid., 125. Sibley's description of "the alternatives open to the modern artist" also applies to pre-Meiji writers like Kamo no Chōmei.
9. See Dazai Osamu, "Nyoze gamon," 364–67, 369–70.

Chapter 13. The Narrative Subversions of Akutagawa and Kajii Motojirō

1. *Uji shūi monogatari* is a collection of *setsuwa* compiled for the most part between 1212 and 1221, with some stories evidently added at a later date. *Kokon chomonjū* (Old and new stories heard from authors) is another *setsuwa* collection, completed in 1254. The story from the *Uji* collection is "E-bōshi Yoshihide, ie no yakuru o mite yorokobu koto" (The painter Yoshihide, his joy at watching a house burn) from volume 3. The *Kokon chomonjū* story, "Hirotaka no jigokuhen no byōbū o kakeru jidai" (The time when Hirotaka painted a hell screen), appears in volume 11.
2. The narrator's return from his state of reverie is represented by a space in the text, which I have reproduced in the citation.
3. Taylor, *Sources of the Self,* 456.

Chapter 14. A Dizzying Descent into Self

1. The Nobel committee noted that Kawabata, like Tanizaki before him, "was clearly influenced by modern European realism but that he also clearly demonstrated a tendency to follow faithfully the path of Japan's classical literature, to maintain and support traditional Japanese forms" (Nihon bungaku kenkyū shiryō kankōkai, *Kawabata Yasunari,* 293–94).
2. For a brief summary of Kawabata's activities with the Shinkankaku-ha, especially his theoretical writings for the group, see Shindō, *Denki,* 152–65. See also Kawabata's essay "Bunshō in tuite" (On style), in *KYZ* 32:98–102.
3. See Itō, "Kawabata Yasunari no geijutsu," 42–43.
4. Miyoshi, *Accomplices of Silence,* 106; and Keene, *Dawn to the West,* 815.
5. See Seidensticker, introduction, ix; and Miyoshi, *Accomplices of Silence,* 108-9.
6. M. Nakamura, *Contemporary Japanese Fiction,* 82.
7. For a discussion of Kawabata's connection with surrealist theory, see Sasabuchi, "Kawabata bungaku to shūrurearizumu," 262–68.
8. Breton, *Les Manifestes,* 111.
9. For a discussion of the method of composition of *Yukiguni,* see Senuma, "*Yukiguni* no seiritsu ni tsuite," 199–203.
10. This relativistic view of existence is analogous to the Buddhist view of the ultimate emptiness and contingency of human experience, a view that does not deny reality but rather insists that nothing can exist except in relationship with something else. Matsunaga and Matsunaga, in their summary of the philosophy of *sūnya* (emptiness), note that "*sūnya* was initially used to denote 'emptiness' or 'devoid of reality' in the sense that it denied the existence of any form of Absolute being (or substance), unchangeable and eternal. Every

Note to Page 266

existent was viewed as a product of Interdependent Origination, subject to change and impermanence, hence in the Buddhist definition unreal" (*Foundation of Japanese Buddhism*, 1:69). For the full discussion, see ibid., 1:69–70.

Epilogue
1. De Man, *Blindness and Insight*, 152.

bibliography

♦

Abe Akio. *Genji monogatari no monogatari ron* (The discussion of tales in The tale of Genji). Tokyo: Iwanami shoten, 1985.
Akane Shōichi. *Mujō no shisō* (The ideology of mutability). Tokyo: Renga shobō, 1980.
Akiyama Mitsukazu. "*Genji monogatari* no kaiga ron" (The discussion of painting in The tale of Genji). In *Genji monogatari kōza* (The tale of Genji symposium). Vol. 5. Tokyo: Yūseidō, 1971.
Akutagawa Ryūnosuke. *Akutagawa Ryūnosuke zenshū* (The complete works of Akutagawa Ryūnosuke). 9 vols. Tokyo: Chikuma shobō, 1958.
Anderer, Paul. *Other Worlds: Arishima Takeo and the Bounds of Modern Japanese Fiction*. New York: Columbia University Press, 1984.
Ariga, Chieko. "The Playful Gloss: Rubi in Japanese Literature." *Monumenta Nipponica*, vol. 44, no. 3 (autumn 1989).
Asō Isoji. *Edo bungaku to Chūgoku bungaku* (Edo literature and Chinese literature). Tokyo: Sanseidō, 1957.
Ban Etsu. *Iwano Hōmei ron* (On Iwano Hōmei). Tokyo: Sōbunsha, 1977.
Barthes, Roland. *Writing Degree Zero and Elements of Semiology*. Trans. Annette Lavers and Colin Smith. Boston: Beacon, 1967.
Baudelaire, Charles. *Baudelaire as a Literary Critic*. Trans. Lois Boe Hyslop and Francis E. Hyslop Jr. University Park: Pennsylvania State University Press, 1964.

bibliography

Beasley, W. G., and E. G. Pulleyblank, eds. *Historians of China and Japan*. London: Oxford University Press, 1961.

Bellah, Robert. *Tokugawa Religion: The Cultural Roots of Modern Japan*. New York: Free Press, 1985.

Benamou, Michel, and Charles Caramello, eds. *Performance in Postmodern Culture*. Madison: Coda, 1977.

Berger, Peter L., Brigitte Berger, and Hansfried Kellner. *The Homeless Mind: Modernization and Consciousness*. New York: Random House, 1973.

Bloom, Harold. *The Anxiety of Influence: A Theory of Poetry*. New York: Oxford University Press, 1973.

―――. *A Map of Misreading*. New York: Oxford University Press, 1975.

Bowring, Richard. *Mori Ōgai and the Modernization of Japanese Culture*. New York: Cambridge University Press, 1979.

―――. *Murasaki Shikibu: Her Diary and Poetic Memoirs*. Princeton: Princeton University Press, 1982.

Bradbury, Malcolm. *The Modern World: Ten Great Writers*. London: Secker and Warburg, 1988.

Bradbury, Malcolm, and James MacFarlane, eds. *Modernism 1890–1930*. New York: Penguin, 1976.

Breton, André. *Les Manifestes du Surréalisme*. Paris: Sagittaire, 1946.

Buchloh, Benjamin, Serge Guilbaut, and David Solkin, eds. *Modernism and Modernity: The Vancouver Conference Papers*. Halifax: Press of the Nova Scotia College of Art and Design, 1983.

Burgin, Victor. *The End of Art Theory: Criticism and Postmodernity*. Atlantic Highlands, N.J.: Humanities Press International, 1986.

Calinescu, Matei. *Faces of Modernity: Avant-garde, Decadence, Kitsch*. Bloomington: Indiana University Press, 1977.

Chamberlain, Basil Hall. *Things Japanese*. London: Kegan Paul, Trench, Trübner, 1891.

Chang, Wen-ch'eng. *The Dwelling of Playful Goddesses*. Trans. Howard S. Levy. Tokyo: Dai Nippon, 1965.

Chappell, David W. "Early Forebodings of the Death of Buddhism." Research paper, University of Hawaii at Manoa, 1977.

Chefdor, Monique, Ricardo Quinones, and Albert Wachtel, eds. *Modernism: Challenges and Perspectives*. Urbana: University of Illinois Press, 1986.

Cogan, Thomas J., trans. *The Tale of the Soga Brothers*. Tokyo: University of Tokyo Press, 1987.

Cranston, Edwin A. *The Izumi Shikibu Diary*. Cambridge: Harvard University Press, 1969.

Danly, Robert. *In the Shade of Spring Leaves: The Life and Writings of Higuchi Ichiyō*. New Haven: Yale University Press, 1981.

Dazai Osamu. "Nyoze gamon" (Thus I have heard). In *Dazai Osamu zenshū* (The complete works of Dazai Osamu). Vol. 10. Tokyo: Chikuma shobō, 1977.

bibliography

De Bary, Wm. Theodore. *Learning for One's Self: Essays on the Individual in Neo-Confucian Thought*. New York: Columbia University Press, 1991.

———. *Neo-Confucian Orthodoxy and the Learning of the Mind-and-Heart*. New York: Columbia University Press, 1981.

De Bary, Wm. Theodore, and Irene Bloom, eds. *Principle and Practicality: Essays in Neo-Confucianism and Practical Learning*. New York: Columbia University Press, 1979.

De Man, Paul. *Blindness and Insight: Essays in the Rhetoric of Contemporary Criticism*. New York: Oxford University Press, 1971.

Doi Tadao, ed. *Nihongo no rekishi* (A history of the Japanese language). Tokyo: Shibundō, 1959.

Ebara Taizō. *Edo bungaku kenkyū* (Studies in Edo literature). Tokyo: Kadokawa shoten, 1958.

Egan, Ronald. "On the Origins of the *Yu hsien k'u* Commentary." *Harvard Journal of Asiatic Studies*, vol. 36 (1976).

Eliot, T. S. *Four Quartets*. New York: Harcourt, Brace and World, 1971.

Ellman, Richard, and Charles Feidelson Jr., eds. *The Modern Tradition: Backgrounds of Modern Literature*. New York: Oxford University Press, 1965.

Etō Jun. *Kindai izen* (Before the modern). Tokyo: Seikyōsha, 1985.

———. "Nagai Kafū ron" (On Nagai Kafū). In Nagai Kafū, *Nagai Kafū shū* (Collected works of Nagai Kafū). Vol. 24 of *Gendai Nihon bungaku taikei* (Outline of modern Japanese literature). Tokyo: Chikuma shobō, 1969.

———. *Natsume Sōseki*. Tokyo: Shinchōsha, 1974.

———. *Shinpen Etō Jun bungaku shūsei* (The collected works of Etō Jun). 5 vols. Tokyo: Kawade shobō, 1984.

Field, Norma. *The Splendour of Longing in the Tale of Genji*. Princeton: Princeton University Press, 1987.

Foucault, Michel. *The Archaeology of Knowledge and The Discourse on Language*. Trans. A. M. Sheridan Smith. New York: Pantheon, 1972.

Fowler, Edward. *The Rhetoric of Confession: Shishōsetsu in Early Twentieth-Century Japanese Fiction*. Berkeley: University of California Press, 1988.

Freud, Sigmund. *Civilization and Its Discontents*. Trans. James Strachey. New York: Norton, 1961.

Fuchie Fumiya. "Hotaru." In *Genji monogatari kōza* (The tale of Genji symposium). Vol. 3. Tokyo: Yūseidō, 1971.

Fujii, James. "Contesting the Meiji Subject: Sōseki's *Neko* Reconsidered." *Harvard Journal of Asiatic Studies*, vol. 49, no. 2 (December 1989).

Fujii Sadakazu. "Monogatari ron" (The discussion of the tale). In *Kōza: Genji monogatari no sekai* (Symposium: The world of The tale of Genji). Vol. 5. Tokyo: Yūhikaku, 1981.

Fujimura hakushi kōseki kinenkai (The Fujimura memorial lecture association), ed. *Kinsei bungaku no kenkyū* (Studies in Tokugawa literature). Tokyo: Shibundō, 1936.

bibliography

Funahashi Sei'ichi. *Iwano Hōmei den* (A biography of Iwano Hōmei). Tokyo: Kadokawa shoten, 1971.
Futabatei Shimei. *Futabatei Shimei zenshū* (The complete works of Futabatei Shimei). 9 vols. Tokyo: Iwanami shoten, 1981.
———. *Futabatei Shimei zenshū* (The complete works of Futabatei Shimei). 5 vols. Tokyo: Chikuma shobō, 1984 and 1985.
Gamache, Lawrence B., and Ian S. MacNiven, eds. *The Modernists: Studies in a Literary Phenomenon.* Cranbury, N.J.: Associated University Presses, 1987.
Garvin, Harry R., ed. *Romanticism, Modernism, Postmodernism.* Lewisburg, Pa.: Bucknell University Press, 1980.
Gerstle, C. Andrew. *Circles of Fantasy: Convention in the Plays of Chikamatsu.* Cambridge: Harvard University Press, 1986.
Gluck, Carol. *Japan's Modern Myths: Ideology in the Late Meiji Period.* Princeton: Princeton University Press, 1985.
Gotō Shōko. *Genji monogatari no shiteki kūkan* (The historical dimensions of The tale of Genji). Tokyo: Tōkyō daigaku shuppankai, 1986.
Gusdorf, Georges. "Conditions and Limits of Autobiography." In James Olney, ed., *Autobiography: Essays Theoretical and Critical.* Princeton: Princeton University Press, 1980.
Habein, Yaeko Sato. *The History of the Japanese Written Language.* Tokyo: University of Tokyo Press, 1984.
Habermas, Jürgen. *The Philosophical Discourse of Modernity: Twelve Lectures.* Trans. Frederick G. Lawrence. Cambridge: MIT Press, 1991.
Hare, Thomas Blenman. "Reading Kamo no Chōmei." *Harvard Journal of Asiatic Studies*, vol. 49, no. 1 (June 1989).
Harper, Thomas. "Motoori Norinaga's Criticism of the '*Genji monogatari.*'" Ph.D. diss., University of Michigan, 1971.
Harootunian, H. D. *Things Seen and Unseen: Discourse and Ideology in Tokugawa Nativism.* Chicago: University of Chicago Press, 1988.
Harvey, David. *The Condition of Postmodernity.* Oxford: Basil Blackwell, 1989.
Hasegawa Izumi. *Kawabata bungaku no kikō* (The structure of Kawabata's literature). Tokyo: Kyōiku shuppan sentaa, 1984.
———. *Ōgai bungaku kanki* (A personal view of Ōgai's literature). Tokyo: Meiji shoin, 1987.
Hattori Dohō. *Sanzōshi.* In Kuriyama Riichi, ed., *Haironshū* (Collection of theoretical writings on *haikai*). Vol. 51 of *Nihon koten bungaku zenshū* (The complete works of classical Japanese literature). Tokyo: Shōgakukan, 1973.
Hayashi Fusao and Izawa Kinemaru. *Rekishi e no shōgen: Mishima Yukio, senketsu no ikun* (Witness to history: Mishima Yukio, teachings left in blood). Tokyo: Kōyū shuppan, 1971.
Hayashi Fusao and Muramatsu Takeshi, eds. *Romanjin Mishima Yukio: sono risō to kōdō* (The romanticist Mishima Yukio: His ideals and actions). Tokyo: Roman, 1973.

bibliography

Hibbett, Howard. *The Floating World in Japanese Fiction*. New York: Oxford University Press, 1959.

Hino Tatsuo. *Norinaga to Akinari*. Tokyo: Chikuma shobō, 1984.

Hirakawa Sukehiro and Tsuruta Kinya, eds. *Kawabata Yasunari: Yama no oto kenkyū* (Kawabata Yasunari: Studies of The sound of the mountain). Tokyo: Meiji shoin, 1985.

Homma, Kenshiro. *The Literature of Naturalism: An East-West Comparative Study*. Kyoto: Yamaguchi, 1983.

Honda Shūgo. *Shirakaba-ha no bungaku* (Literature of the White Birch school). Tokyo: Shinchōsha, 1950.

Hulme, T. E. *Speculations: Essays on Humanism and the Philosophy of Art*. Ed. Herbert Read. London: Routledge and Kegan Paul, 1924.

Hutcheon, Linda. *A Poetics of Postmodernism: History, Theory, Fiction*. New York: Routledge, 1988.

Huyssen, Andreas. *After the Great Divide: Modernism, Mass Culture, Postmodernism*. Bloomington: Indiana University Press, 1986.

Ihara Saikaku. *Five Women Who Loved Love*. Trans. Wm. Theodore De Bary. Rutland: Tuttle, 1956.

———. *Ihara Saikaku shū (1)* (Collected works of Ihara Saikaku, part 1). Vol. 47 of *Nihon koten bungaku taikei* (Outline of classical Japanese literature). Tokyo: Iwanami shoten, 1961.

———. *Ihara Saikaku shū (1)* (Collected works of Ihara Saikaku, part 1). Vol. 38 of *Nihon koten bungaku zenshū* (The complete works of classical Japanese literature). Tokyo: Shōgakukan, 1971.

———. *Kōshoku ichidai otoko* (The life of a man of passion). Vol. 50 of *Nihon no koten* (Classics of Japan). Tokyo: Shōgakukan, 1986.

———. *The Life of an Amorous Woman and Other Writings*. Trans. Ivan Morris. Norfolk, Conn.: New Directions, 1963.

———. *Nippon eitaigura* (The eternal storehouse of Japan). Vol. 52 of *Nihon no koten*. Tokyo: Shōgakukan, 1983.

———. *Some Final Words of Advice*. Trans. Peter Nosco. Rutland: Tuttle, 1980.

Iijima, Takehisa, and James M. Vardaman Jr. *The World of Natsume Sōseki*. Tokyo: Kinseidō, 1987.

Ikuta Chōkō, "Shizenshugi zenpa no chōryō" (The domination of the prenaturalists). In Tanaka Yasutaka, ed., *Kindai hyōron shū, II* (Collection of modern critical essays, part 2). Vol. 58 of *Nihon kindai bungaku taikei*. Tokyo: Kadokawa shoten, 1972.

Inagaki Tatsurō. *Mori Ōgai no rekishi shōsetsu* (The historical fiction of Mori Ōgai). Tokyo: Iwanami shoten, 1989.

Ishida Jōji. "Eawase to Tentoku yonen Dairi uta-awase" (The "Eawase" chapter and the imperial poetry contest of 960). In *Kōza: Genji monogatari no sekai* (Symposium: The world of The tale of Genji). Vol. 4. Tokyo: Yūhikaku, 1980.

Ishida Mizumaro. *Nihon bukkyō shisō kenkyū* (A study of Buddhist thought in Japan). Vol. 3. Tokyo: Hōzōkan, 1986.

Ishihara Shōhei. "Eawase." In *Genji monogatari kōza* (The tale of Genji symposium). Vol. 3. Tokyo: Yūseidō, 1971.

Isoda Kōichi. *Bungaku: kono kamenteki na mono* (The mask that is literature). Tokyo: Keisō shobō, 1969.

———. *Shisō to shite no Tōkyō* (Tokyo as an idea). Tokyo: Kokubunsha, 1978.

Isogai Hideo. "Kindai kara gendai e" (From modern to contemporary). In Miyoshi Yukio and Takemori Ten'yū, eds., *Gendai bungaku no taidō* (The emergence of contemporary literature). Vol. 5 of *Kindai bungaku* (Modern literature). Tokyo: Yūhikaku, 1977.

Itō Kazuo, ed. *Kindai shisō: bungaku no dentō to henkaku* (Modern thought: Tradition and change in literature). Tokyo: Meiji shoin, 1986.

Itō Sei. "Kawabata Yasunari no geijutsu" (The art of Kawabata Yasunari). In Nihon bungaku kenkyū shiryō kankōkai (Japanese literary research materials publication association), ed., *Kawabata Yasunari*. Nihon bungaku kenkyū shiryō sōsho (Japanese literature research materials series). Tokyo: Yūseidō, 1973.

Iwabuchi Etsutarō. *Kokugoshi ronshū* (Collected essays on the history of the Japanese language). Tokyo: Chikuma shobō, 1977.

Iwahashi Koyata. "Murasaki Shikibu no shigaku shisō" (Muraskai Shikibu's concepts of historical studies). *Kokushigaku* (Studies in Japanese history), vols. 72–73 (March 1960).

Iwano Hōmei. *Hōmei zenshū* (The complete works of Hōmei). 18 vols. Tokyo: Kōbunko, 1971–1972.

———. *Iwano Hōmei shū* (Collected works of Iwano Hōmei). Vol. 21 of *Gendai Nihon bungaku taikei* (Outline of modern Japanese literature). Tokyo: Chikuma shobō, 1970.

Japanese National Commission for UNESCO, ed. *Essays on Natsume Sōseki's Works*. Tokyo: Japan Society for the Promotion of Science, 1972.

Kajii Motojirō. *Kajii Motojirō shū* (Collected works of Kajii Motojirō). Vol. 63 of *Gendai Nihon bungaku taikei* (Outline of modern Japanese literature). Tokyo: Chikuma shobō, 1970.

———. *Kajii Motojirō zenshū* (The complete works of Kajii Motojirō). Vol. 1. Tokyo: Chikuma shobō, 1966.

Kamei Hideo. *Futabatei Shimei: sensō to kakumei no hōrōsha* (Futabatei Shimei: A wanderer amid war and revolution). Tokyo: Shinkōsha, 1986.

Kamisaka Nobuo. "Heian-chō bungaku ni okeru *Genji monogatari*" (The tale of Genji in Heian literature). In *Genji monogatari kōza* (The tale of Genji symposium). Vol. 1. Tokyo: Yūseidō, 1971.

Kamo no Chōmei. *Hōjōki* (The record of a ten-foot-square hut). Ed. Nishio Minoru. Vol. 30 of *Nihon koten bungaku taikei* (Outline of classical Japanese literature). Tokyo: Iwanami shoten, 1957.

bibliography

Karatani Kōjin. *Nihon kindai bungaku no kigen* (The origins of modern Japanese literature). Tokyo: Kōdansha, 1980.

Katō, Hilda. "The *Mumyōshō* of Kamo no Chōmei and Its Significance in Japanese Literature." *Monumenta Nipponica,* vol. 33. nos. 3–4 (1968).

Katō, Shuichi. *A History of Japanese Literature.* Trans. Don Sanderson. London: Macmillan, 1983.

Kawabata Yasunari. *Kawabata Yasunari shū* (Collected works of Kawabata Yasunari). Vol. 52 of *Gendai Nihon bungaku taikei* (Outline of modern Japanese literature). Tokyo: Chikuma shobō, 1972.

———. *Kawabata Yasunari zenshū* (The complete works of Kawabata Yasunari). 35 vols. Tokyo: Shinchōsha, 1980–1984.

Kawabata Yasunari bungaku kenkyūkai (Kawabata literary research association), ed. *Fūin no sōkoku* (Conflicts of elegance). Kawabata Yasunari kenkyū sōsho (Kawabata research series), vol. 6. Tokyo: Kyōiku shuppan sentaa, 1979.

Kawamura Minato. *Iyō no ryōiki* (The realm of the strange). Tokyo: Kokubunsha, 1983.

Kawashima Hidekazu. *Shimazaki Tōson ronkō* (Observations on Shimazaki Tōson). Tokyo: Ōfūsha, 1987.

Keene, Donald. *Dawn to the West: Japanese Literature of the Modern Era.* Vol. 1. New York: Holt, Rinehart, and Winston, 1984.

———. *World within Walls: Japanese Literature of the Pre-Modern Era, 1600–1867.* New York: Holt, Rinehart, and Winston, 1976.

Kermode, Frank. *Continuities.* New York: Random House, 1968.

———. *The Sense of an Ending: Studies in the Theory of Fiction.* New York: Oxford University Press, 1967.

Kikuchi Yūjirō. "Heian bukkyō no tenkai" (Development of Heian Buddhism). In Ienaga Saburō, ed., *Nihon Bukkyōshi* (History of Japanese Buddhism). Vol. 1. Kyoto: Hōzōkan, 1972.

Kitagawa, Joseph M. *Religion in Japanese History.* New York: Columbia University Press, 1966.

Kitagawa Yoshio. *Mori Ōgai no kanshō to gen'ei* (The contemplations and vision of Mori Ōgai). Tokyo: Kindai bungeisha, 1984.

LaFleur, William R. *The Karma of Words: Buddhism and the Literary Arts in Medieval Japan.* Berkeley: University of California Press, 1983.

Leitch, Vincent B. *Deconstructive Criticism: An Advanced Introduction.* New York: Columbia University Press, 1983.

Leutner, Robert. *Shikitei Sanba and the Comic Tradition in Edo Fiction.* Cambridge: Harvard University Press, 1985.

Levin, Harry. *The Myth of the Golden Age in the Renaissance.* New York: Oxford University Press, 1969.

Lippit, Noriko Mizuta. *Reality and Fiction in Modern Japanese Literature.* White Plains, N.Y.: Sharpe, 1980.

Lukàcs, George. *Essays on Realism*. Ed. Rodney Livingstone. Trans. David Fernbach. Cambridge: MIT Press, 1980.

Lyotard, Jean-François. *The Postmodern Condition: A Report on Knowledge*. Trans. Geoff Bennington and Brian Massumi. Minneapolis: University of Minnesota Press, 1984.

Maruyama, Masao. *Studies in the Intellectual History of Tokugawa Japan*. Trans. Mikiso Hane. Princeton: Princeton University Press; Tokyo: Tokyo University Press, 1974.

Masubushi Shōichi. "Rekishi monogatari e no eikyō" (The influence of The tale of Genji on historical novels). In *Genji monogatari kōza* (The tale of Genji symposium). Vol. 8. Tokyo: Yūseidō, 1972.

Matsuda Takeo. "*Genji monogatari* no monogatari ron" (The discussion of tales in The tale of Genji). In *Genji monogatari kōza* (The tale of Genji symposium). Vol. 5. Tokyo: Yūseidō, 1971.

Matsumoto Hiroshi. *Natsume Sōseki: gendaijin no genzō* (Natsume Sōseki: The development of a modern). Tokyo: Shinchi shobō, 1986.

Matsumura Masaie. *Meiji bungaku to bikutoria jidai* (Meiji literature and the Victorian era). Tokyo: Yamaguchi shoten, 1981.

Matsunaga, Daigan, and Alicia Matsunaga. *Foundation of Japanese Buddhism*. 2 vols. Los Angeles: Buddhist Books International, 1974.

Matsuo Bashō. *Bashō bunshū* (Collected prose works of Bashō). Vol. 46 of *Nihon koten bungaku taikei* (Outline of classical Japanese literature). Tokyo: Iwanami shoten, 1959.

Matsuo Satoshi, ed. *Genji monogatari to joryū nikki: kenkyū to shiryō* (The tale of Genji and women's diaries: Studies and sources). Tokyo: Musashino shoin, 1981.

Matsuo Yasuaki. *Kinsei no bungaku: Bashō, Saikaku, Akinari* (Tokugawa literature: Bashō, Saikaku, Akinari). Tokyo: Bunka shobō, 1963.

McClellan, Edwin. "Tōson and the Autobiographical Novel." In Donald Shively, ed., *Tradition and Modernization in Japanese Culture*. Princeton: Princeton University Press, 1971.

McCullough, Helen Craig. *Ōkagami: The Great Mirror*. Princeton: Princeton University Press, 1980.

McCullough, Helen, and William McCullough. *A Tale of Flowering Fortunes*. Stanford: Stanford University Press, 1980.

McHale, Brian. *Postmodernist Fiction*. New York: Methuen, 1987.

Miller, Roy Andrew. *The Japanese Language*. Chicago: University of Chicago Press, 1967.

Miner, Earl, ed. *Principles of Classical Japanese Literature*. Princeton: Princeton University Press, 1985.

Mishima Yukio. *Mishima Yukio zenshū* (The complete works of Mishima Yukio). Tokyo: Shinchōsha, 1973.

―――. *Sakkaron*. Tokyo: Chūō kōronsha, 1974.

bibliography

Mitani Kuniaki. "*Genji monogatari* ni okeru kyokō no hōhō" (Fictional methods in The tale of Genji). In *Genji monogatari kōza* (The tale of Genji symposium). Vol. 1. Tokyo: Yūseidō, 1971.

———. "Heian bungakushi no hōhō" (Methods of Heian literary history). In Heianchō bungaku kenkyūkai (Heian literary research association), ed., *Heianchō bungaku no shomondai* (Issues in Heian literature). Kasama sōsho (Kasama research series), vol. 83. Tokyo: Kasama shoin, 1977.

Miyaji Hiroshi, ed. *Buntaishi, I* (The history of literary style, part 1). Vol. 7 of *Kōza Nihongogaku* (Symposium: The Japanese language). Tokyo: Meiji shoin, 1982.

Miyauchi Yutaka. *Hankindai no kanata e* (Beyond the antimodern). Tokyo: Ronsōsha, 1986.

Miyoshi, Masao. *Accomplices of Silence*. Berkeley: University of California Press, 1974.

Miyoshi, Masao, and H. D. Harootunian, eds. *Postmodernism and Japan*. Durham, N.C.: Duke University Press, 1989.

Miyoshi Yukio. *Nihon bungaku no kindai to hankindai* (The modern and antimodern in Japanese literature). Tokyo: Tōkyō daigaku shuppankai, 1972.

Mori Ōgai. *Ōgai zenshū* (The complete works of Ōgai). 53 vols. Tokyo: Iwanami shoten, 1951–1956.

Moriyama Shigeo. *Saikaku no kenkyū* (A study of Saikaku). Tokyo: Shindokushosha, 1981.

Morris, Ivan. Introduction to Ihara Saikaku, *The Life of an Amorous Woman and Other Writings*, trans. Ivan Morris. Norfolk, Conn.: New Directions, 1963.

———. *The World of the Shining Prince*. New York: Knopf, 1964.

Motoori Norinaga. *Motoori Norinaga shū* (Collected works of Motoori Norinaga). Ed. Yoshikawa Kōjirō. Vol. 15 of *Nihon no shisō* (Thought in Japan). Tokyo: Chikuma shobō, 1969.

Mukai Kyorai. *Kyōraishō*. In Kuriyama Riichi, ed., *Haironshū* (Collection of theoretical writings on *haikai).* Vol. 51 of *Nihon koten bungaku zenshū* (The complete works of classical Japanese literature). Tokyo: Shōgakukan, 1973.

Murasaki Shikibu. *Genji monogatari* (The tale of Genji). Ed. Yamagishi Tokuhei. Vols. 14–18 of *Nihon koten bungaku taikei* (Outline of classical Japanese literature). Tokyo: Iwanami shoten, 1958–1963.

Nagai Kafū. *Kafū zenshū* (The complete works of Kafū). 29 vols. Tokyo: Iwanami shoten, 1962–1974.

———. *Nagai Kafū shū* (Collected works of Nagai Kafū). Vols. 23 and 24 of *Gendai Nihon bungaku taikei* (Outline of modern Japanese literature). Tokyo: Chikuma shobō, 1969.

Nagata Ikuo. *Futabatei Shimei ron: niritsu haihan no seiritsu* (On Futabatei Shimei: The formation of his antinomy). Tokyo: Hōbunsha, 1975.

Najita, Tetsuo. *Visions of Virtue in Tokugawa Japan*. Chicago: University of Chicago Press, 1987.

bibliography

Nakada Tsuneyuki. *Genji monogatari no bungeigaku* (Literary studies in The tale of Genji). Tokyo: Fūkan shobō, 1972.

Nakai, Kate. "Tokugawa Confucian Historiography: The Hayashi, Early Mito School and Arai Hakuseki." In Peter Nosco, ed., *Confucianism and Tokugawa Culture*. Princeton: Princeton University Press, 1984.

Nakamura Akira. *Meibun*. Tokyo: Chikuma shobō, 1979.

Nakamura Gen, ed. *Ajia Bukkyōshi: Nihon-hen II, Heian Bukkyō* (History of Asian Buddhism: Japan, part 2, Heian Buddhism). Kyoto: Kōsei shuppansha, 1974.

Nakamura, Mitsuo. *Contemporary Japanese Fiction: 1926–1968*. Trans. Suetsugu Ryoko. Tokyo: Kokusai bunka shinkokai, 1969.

———. *Futabatei Shimei den* (A biography of Futabatei Shimei). Tokyo: Kōdansha, 1958.

———. *Futabatei Shimei ron* (On Futabatei Shimei). Tokyo: Shinrosha, 1947. Reprint, Kindai sakka kenkyū shiryō sōsho (Modern authors research materials series), vol. 14. Tokyo: Kōyōsha, 1983.

———. "Kafū no seishun" (Kafū's youth). In Nagai Kafū, *Nagai Kafū shū* (Collected works of Nagai Kafū). Vol. 23 of *Gendai Nihon bungaku taikei* (Outline of modern Japanese literature). Tokyo: Chikuma shobō, 1969.

———. "Kindai e no giwaku" (Doubts about the modern). In Takahashi Haruo, ed., *Kindai bungaku hyōron taikei: Shōwaki II* (Outline of modern literary criticism: Shōwa period, part 2). Vol. 7. Tokyo: Kadokawa shoten, 1972.

———. *Shiga Naoya ron* (On Shiga Naoya). Tokyo: Bungei shunjū shinsha, 1954. Reprint, Kindai sakka kenkyū sōsho (Modern authors research series), ed. Yoshida Sei'ichi, vol. 4. Tokyo: Nihon tosho sentaa, 1983.

Nakamura Shin'ichirō. *Shisetsu: Genji monogatari* (Historical fiction: The tale of Genji). Tokyo: Ushio shuppansha, 1975.

Nakamura Yukihiko. *Kinsei sakka kenkyū* (A study of Tokugawa writers). Tokyo: San'ichi shobō, 1961.

———. *Kinsei shōsetsu no kenkyū* (A study of the history of Tokugawa fiction). Tokyo: Ōfūsha, 1961.

———, ed. *Kinsei bungakuronshū* (A collection of Tokugawa literary essays). Vol. 94 of *Nihon koten bungaku taikei* (Outline of classical Japanese literature). Tokyo: Iwanami shoten, 1966.

Nakano Kōichi. "Monogatari no idekihajime no oya" (The parent of the novel). In *Kōza: Genji monogatari no sekai* (Symposium: The world of The tale of Genji). Vol. 4. Tokyo: Yūhikaku, 1980.

Nakano Kōji. *Zettai reido no bungaku: Ōoka Shōhei hyōron* (The literature of absolute zero: Critical essays on Ōoka Shōhei). Tokyo: Shūeisha, 1976.

Nakano Shigeharu. "*An'ya kōro* zatsudan" (Miscellaneous remarks on A dark night's passing). In Shiga Naoya, *Shiga Naoya shū* (Collected works of Shiga Naoya). Vol. 34 of *Gendai Nihon bungaku taikei* (Outline of modern Japanese literature). Tokyo: Chikuma shobō, 1968.

bibliography

Natsume Sōseki. *Sōseki zenshū* (The complete works of Sōseki). 19 vols. Tokyo: Iwanami shoten, 1984–1987.

Nihon bungaku kenkyū shiryō kankōkai (Japanese literary research materials publication association), ed. *Akutagawa Ryūnosuke*. Nihon bungaku kenkyū shiryō sōsho (Japanese literature research materials series). Tokyo: Yūseidō, 1975.

———. *Kajii Motojirō, Nakajima Atsushi*. Nihon bungaku kenkyū shiryō sōsho. Tokyo: Yūseidō, 1978.

———. *Kawabata Yasunari*. Nihon bungaku kenkyū shiryō sōsho. Tokyo: Yūseidō, 1973.

———. *Meiji no bungaku* (Literature of the Meiji period). Nihon bungaku kenkyū shiryō sōsho. Tokyo: Yūseidō, 1981.

———. *Mishima Yukio*. Nihon bungaku kenkyū shiryō sōsho. Tokyo: Yūseidō, 1971.

———. *Mori Ōgai*. Vol. 2. Nihon bungaku kenkyū shiryō sōsho. Tokyo: Yūseidō, 1979.

———. *Nagai Kafū* Nihon bungaku kenkyū shiryō sōsho. Tokyo: Yūseidō, 1971.

———. *Natsume Sōseki*. Nihon bungaku kenkyū shiryō sōsho. Tokyo: Yūseidō, 1970.

———. *Shiga Naoya*. 2 vols. Nihon bungaku kenkyū shiryō sōsho. Tokyo: Yūseidō, 1970.

———. *Shimazaki Tōson*. Nihon bungaku kenkyū shiryō sōsho. Tokyo: Yūseidō, 1970.

———. *Shishōsetsu* (The "I" novel). Nihon bungaku kenkyū shiryō sōsho. Tokyo: Yūseidō, 1983.

———. *Shōwa no bungaku* (The literature of the Shōwa period). Nihon bungaku kenkyū shiryō sōsho. Tokyo: Yūseidō, 1981.

———. *Taishō no bungaku* (The literature of the Taishō period). Nihon bungaku kenkyū shiryō sōsho. Tokyo: Yūseidō, 1981.

———. *Tsubouchi Shōyō, Futabatei Shimei*. Nihon bungaku kenkyū shiryō sōsho. Tokyo: Yūseidō, 1979.

Nishida Masayoshi. *Mujō no bungaku* (The literature of mutability). Tokyo: Hanawa shobō, 1975.

Noguchi Genta. "Monogatari-shi ni okeru *Genji monogatari*" (The tale of Genji in the history of the novel). In *Genji monogatari kōza* (The tale of Genji symposium). Vol. 1. Tokyo: Yūseidō, 1971.

Norris, Christopher. *Deconstruction: Theory and Practice*. New York: Methuen, 1982.

Nosco, Peter. Introduction to Peter Nosco, ed., *Confucianism and Tokugawa Culture*. Princeton: Princeton University Press, 1984.

Odaka Toshirō. *Kinsei shoki bundan no kenkyū* (A study of the early Tokugawa literary establishment). Tokyo: Meiji shoin, 1964.

Okazaki Kimiyoshi. *Kindai-gendai Nihon bungaku ron no tetsugaku* (The philosophy

of modern and contemporary literary criticism in Japan). Tokyo: Shinjusha, 1975.
Oketani Hideaki. *Futabatei Shimei to Meiji Nippon* (Futabatei Shimei and Meiji Japan). Tokyo: Bungei shunjū, 1986.
———. *Natsume Sōseki ron* (On Natsume Sōseki). Tokyo: Kawade shobō, 1983.
Onomura Yōko. "*Genji monogatari* to mono no aware" (The tale of Genji and the concept of *mono no aware*). In *Genji monogatari kōza* (The tale of Genji symposium). Vol. 5. Tokyo: Yūseidō, 1971.
Ōoka Shōhei. *Shōsetsuka Natsume Sōseki* (The novelist Natsume Sōseki). Tokyo: Chikuma shobō, 1988.
———. *Waga bungaku seikatsu* (My literary life). Tokyo: Chūō kōronsha, 1975.
Ooms Herman. *Tokugawa Ideology: Early Constructs, 1570–1680.* Princeton: Princeton University Press, 1985.
Ozaki Kōyō. *Ozaki Kōyō shū* (Collected works of Ozaki Kōyō). Vol. 5 of *Nihon gendai bungaku zenshū* (Complete works of modern Japanese literature). Tokyo: Kōdansha, 1966.
Ozaki Satoakira. *Kindai bunshō no reimei* (The dawn of modern writing). Tokyo: Ōfūsha, 1967.
Ozawa Tomio. *Mappō to masse no shisō* (The ideologies of the end of Buddhism and the corruption of the world). Tokyo: Yūsankaku, 1974.
Pekarik, Andrew, ed. *Ukifune: Love in the Tale of Genji.* New York: Columbia University Press, 1982.
Pollack, David. *The Fracture of Meaning: Japan's Synthesis of China from the Eighth through the Eighteenth Centuries.* Princeton: Princeton University Press, 1986.
———. "Framing the Self: The Philosophical Dimensions of Human Nature in *Kokoro.*" *Monumenta Nipponica,* vol. 43, no. 4 (winter 1988).
———. "Modernism Minceur, or Is Japan Postmodern?" *Monumenta Nipponica,* vol. 44, no. 1 (spring 1989).
Pyle, Kenneth B. *The New Generation in Meiji Japan: Problems of Cultural Identity, 1885–1895.* Stanford: Stanford University Press, 1969.
Ramirez-Christensen, Esperanza. "The Essential Parameters of Linked Poetry." *Harvard Journal of Asiatic Studies,* vol. 41, no. 2 (December 1981).
Rawson, Judy. "Italian Futurism." In Malcolm Bradbury and James MacFarlane, eds., *Modernism 1890–1930.* New York: Penguin, 1976.
Rimer, J. Thomas. *Modern Japanese Fiction and Its Traditions: An Introduction.* Princeton: Princeton University Press, 1978.
Rohlich, Thomas H. *A Tale of Eleventh-Century Japan: Hamamatsu Chūnagon Monogatari.* Princeton: Princeton University Press, 1983.
Rosenberg, Harold. "Literary Form and Social Hallucination." *Partisan Review,* vol. 27, no. 4 (fall 1960).
Rubin, Jay. *Injurious to Public Morals: Writers and the Meiji State.* Seattle: University of Washington Press, 1984.

bibliography

———. "Sōseki on Individualism: *'Watakushi no Kojinshugi.'*" *Monumenta Nipponica*, vol. 34, no. 1 (spring 1979).

Ryan, Marleigh. *The Development of Realism in the Fiction of Tsubouchi Shōyō*. Seattle: University of Washington Press, 1975.

———. *Japan's First Modern Novel*. New York: Columbia University Press, 1967.

Sacks, Oliver. *The Man Who Mistook His Wife for a Hat and Other Clinical Tales*. New York: Summit, 1985.

———. "A Neurologist's Notebook: The Landscape of His Dreams." *The New Yorker*, July 27, 1992.

Saitō Tsuyoshi. *Meiji no kotoba* (The language of Meiji). Tokyo: Kōdansha, 1977.

Sakai, Naoki. "Modernity and Its Critique: The Problem of Universalism and Particularism." In Masao Miyoshi and H. D. Harootunian, eds., *Postmodernism and Japan*. Durham, N.C.: Duke University Press, 1989.

Sako Jun'ichirō. *Akutagawa Ryūnosuke ni okeru geijutsu no unmei* (The destiny of art for Akutagawa Ryōnosuke). Tokyo: Ikkodō, 1956.

Sasabuchi Tomoichi. "Kawabata bungaku to shūrurearizumu" (Kawabata's literature and surrealism). In Nihon bungaku kenkyū shiryō kankōkai (Japanese literary research materials publication association), ed., *Kawabata Yasunari*. Nihon bungaku kenkyū shiryō sōsho* (Japanese literature research materials series). Tokyo: Yūseidō, 1973.

———. *Nagai Kafū: "daraku" no bigakusha* (Nagai Kafū: Aesthete of "decadence"). Tokyo: Meiji shoin, 1976.

Satō Haruo. *Kafū zakkan* (Observations on Kafū). Tokyo: Kokuritsu shoin, 1947. Reprint, Kindai sakka kenkyū sōsho (Modern authors research series), ed. Yoshida Sei'ichi, vol. 69. Tokyo: Nihon tosho sentaa, 1989.

Satō Kōko and Tomita Hitoshi, eds. *Nihon kindai bengaku to seiyō* (Modern Japanese literature and the West). Tokyo: Shungadai, 1984.

Seidensticker, Edward. *Kafū the Scribbler: The Life and Writings of Nagai Kafū, 1879–1959*. Stanford: Stanford University Press, 1965.

———. Introduction to Yasunari Kawabata, *Snow Country*, trans. Edward Seidensticker. New York: Perigree, 1957.

Senuma Shigeki. "*Yukiguni* no seiritsu ni tsuite" (Concerning the creation of *Snow Country*). In Nihon bungaku kenkyū shiryō kankōkai (Japanese literary research materials publication association), ed., *Kawabata Yasunari*. Nihon bungaku kenkyū shiryō sōsho (Japanese literature research materials series). Tokyo: Yūseidō, 1973.

Shiga Naoya. *Shiga Naoya zenshū* (The complete works of Shiga Naoya). 16 vols. Tokyo: Iwanami shoten, 1973–1984.

Shigetomo Ki. *Kinsei bungakushi no shomandai* (Issues in the literary history of Tokugawa Japan). Tokyo: Meiji shoin, 1963.

Shikitei Sanba. *Ukiyoburo*. Ed. Nakamura Michio. Vol. 63 of *Nihon koten bungaku taikei* (Outline of classical Japanese literature). Tokyo: Iwanami shoten, 1957.

bibliography

Shimazaki Tōson. *The Family*. Trans. Cecilia Segawa Seigle. Tokyo: University of Tokyo Press, 1976.

———. *Shimazaki Tōson zenshū* (The complete works of Shimazaki Tōson). 29 vols. Tokyo: Chikuma shobō, 1956–1983.

Shimizu Shigeru. "Shikitei Sanba to Futabatei Shimei: ketsuron no nai nōto" (Shikitei and Futabatei: Notes without a conclusion). In Nihon bungaku kenkyū shiryō kankōkai (Japanese literary research materials publication association), ed., *Tsubouchi Shōyō, Futabatei Shimei*. Nihon bungaku kenkyū shiryō sōsho (Japanese literature research materials series). Tokyo: Yūseidō, 1979.

Shindō Sakiko. *Meiji jidaigo no kenkyū* (A study of the language of Meiji Japan). Tokyo: Meiji shoin, 1981.

Shindō Sumitaka. *Denki: Kawabata Yasunari* (Biography: Kawabata Yasunari). Tokyo: Rokkō shuppan, 1976.

Shirane, Haruo. *The Bridge of Dreams: A Poetics of the Tale of Genji*. Stanford: Stanford University Press, 1987.

Sibley, William F. *The Shiga Hero*. Chicago: University of Chicago Press, 1979.

Spears, Monroe K. *Dionysus and the City: Modernism in Twentieth-Century Poetry*. New York: Oxford University Press, 1970.

Suzuki Shōzan. *Shōzan*. Vol. 14 of *Nihon no zen goroku* (Analects of Japanese Zen). Tokyo: Kōdansha, 1977.

Tahara, Mildred M., trans. *Tales of Yamato: A Tenth-Century Poem-Tale*. Honolulu: University Press of Hawaii, 1980.

Taishō bungaku kenkyūkai (Taishō literary research association), ed. *Shiga Naoya kenkyū* (Studies of Shiga Naoya). Tokyo: Kawade shobō, 1944. Reprint, Kindai sakka kenkyū sōsho (Modern authors research series), ed. Yoshida Sei'ichi, vol. 37. Tokyo: Nihon tosho sentaa, 1984.

Takahashi Hideo. *Shiga Naoya: Kindai to shinwa* (Shiga Naoya: The modern age and myth). Tokyo: Bungeishunjū, 1981.

Takahashi Toshio. *Saikaku ronkō* (Observations on Saikaku). Tokyo: Kasama shoin, 1971.

———. *Saikaku zappitsu* (A Saikaku miscellany). Tokyo: Kasama shoin, 1978.

Takeda Katsuhiko and Takahashi Shintarō, eds. *Mori Ōgai: rekishi to bungaku* (Mori Ōgai: History and literature). Tokyo: Meiji shoin, 1978.

Takeno Seio. *Kindai bungaku to Saikaku* (Modern literature and Saikaku). Tokyo: Shinkōsha, 1980.

Tamura Enchō. *Nihon Bukkyōshi* (History of Japanese Buddhism). Vol. 2. Kyoto: Hōzōkan, 1983.

Taniwaki Masachika. *Ihara Saikaku*. Tokyo: Shinkōsha, 1987.

Taylor, Charles. *Philosophy and the Human Sciences: Philosophical Papers 2*. Cambridge: Cambridge University Press, 1985.

———. *Sources of the Self: The Making of the Modern Identity*. Cambridge: Harvard University Press, 1989.

bibliography

Taylor, Mark C. *Deconstruction in Context: Literature and Philosophy.* Chicago: University of Chicago Press, 1986.

Togawa Shinsuke. *Futabatei Shimei ron* (On Futabatei Shimei). Tokyo: Chikuma shobō, 1971.

———. *Shimazaki Tōson.* Tokyo: Chikuma shobō, 1980.

Trachtenberg, Stanley, ed. *The Postmodern Moment: A Handbook of Contemporary Innovation in the Arts.* Westport, Conn.: Greenwood, 1985.

Trilling, Lionel. "On the Modern Element in Modern Literature." In Irving Howe, ed., *The Idea of the Modern in Literature and the Arts.* New York: Horizon, 1967.

Tsubouchi Shōyō. *Shōyō senshū* (Selected works of Shōyō). Ed. Shōyō kyōkai (Shōyō studies association). Vol. 3. Tokyo: Dai'ichi shobō, 1977.

———. *Tsubouchi Shōyō shū* (Collected works of Tsubouchi Shōyō). Vol. 16 of *Meiji bungaku zenshū* (Complete works of Meiji literature). Tokyo: Chikuma shobō, 1969.

Tsubouchi Shōyō and Uchida Roan, eds. *Futabatei Shimei.* Tokyo: Ifūsha, 1909. Reprint, Kindai bungaku kenkyū shiryō sōsho (Modern literature research materials series), vol. 5. Tokyo: Nihon kindai bungakukan, 1975.

Tsunoda, Ryūsaku, Wm. Theodore De Bary, and Donald Keene, eds. *Sources of the Japanese Tradition.* New York: Columbia University Press, 1958.

Tsuruta Kin'ya. *Nihon kindai bungaku ni okeru "mukōgawa"* (The "other" in modern Japanese literature). Tokyo: Meiji shoin, 1986.

Uno Kōji. *Uno Kōji zenshū* (The complete works of Uno Kōji). Vol. 10. Tokyo: Chūō kōronsha, 1968.

Waley, Arthur. Introduction to Murasaki Shikibu, *The Bridge of Dreams,* trans. Arthur Waley. Boston: Houghton Mifflin, 1933.

———. *The Pillow Book of Sei Shōnagon.* London: George Allen and Unwin, 1957.

Walker, Janet. *The Japanese Novel of the Meiji Period and the Ideal of Individualism.* Princeton: Princeton University Press, 1979.

———. "Poetic Ideal and Fictional Reality in the *Izumi Shikibu nikki.*" *Harvard Journal of Asiatic Studies,* vol. 37 (1977).

Watson, Burton, trans. *Japanese Literature in Chinese.* Vol. 1. New York: Columbia University Press, 1975.

Watt, Ian. *The Rise of the Novel: Studies in Defoe, Richardson and Fielding.* Berkeley: University of California Press, 1957.

Whitehouse, Wilfred, and Yanigasawa Eizo, trans. *Ochikubo monogatari, or The Tale of Lady Ochikubo: A Tenth Century Japanese Novel.* Tokyo: Hokuseido, 1965.

Willig, Rosette F., trans. *The Changelings: A Classical Japanese Court Tale.* Stanford: Stanford University Press, 1983.

Wilson, William Ritchie. "The Truth of *Haikai.*" *Monumenta Nipponica,* vol. 26, nos. 1–2 (1971).

Wolfe, Alan. *Suicidal Narrative in Modern Japan: The Case of Dazai Osamu.* Princeton: Princeton University Press, 1990.

Woolf, Virginia. "Mr. Bennett and Mrs. Brown." In *Collected Essays*. Vol. 1. London: Hogarth, 1966.
Yamada Norio. *Mishima Yukio: shi no bigaku* (Mishima Yukio: The aesthetics of death). Tokyo: Foto Nipponsha, 1971.
Yamaguchi Takeshi. *Yamaguchi Takeshi chosakushū* (The collected works of Yamaguchi Takeshi). Tokyo: Chūō kōronsha, 1972.
Yamamoto Masahide. *Genbun'itchi no rekishi ronkō* (Observations on the history of *genbun'itchi*). Tokyo: Ōfūsha, 1971.
Yasuraoka Kōsaku. *Hōjōki: zen'yakuchū* (The record of a ten-foot-square hut: Complete translation and annotation). Tokyo: Kōdansha, 1980.
Yoshida Sei'ichi. *Nagai Kafū*. Tokyo: Shinchōsha, 1971.
———. *Shizenshugi kenkyū* (Studies in naturalism). In *Yoshida Sei'ichi chosakushū* (The collected works of Yoshida Sei'ichi). Vol. 7. Tokyo: Ōfūsha, 1981.
Yoshie Hisaya. *Saikaku bungaku kenkyū* (Studies in the literature of Saikaku). Tokyo: Kasama shoin, 1974.

studies of the East Asian Institute: selected titles

◆

Japan's First Modern Novel: Ukigumo of Futabatei Shimei,
by Marleigh Ryan. New York: Columbia University Press, 1967.

The Japanese Imperial Institution in the Tokugawa Period,
by Herschel Webb. New York: Columbia University Press, 1968.

Shiba Kōkan: Artist, Innovator, and Pioneer in the Westernization of Japan,
by Calvin L. French. Tokyo: Weatherhill, 1974.

Private Academies of Tokugawa Japan,
by Richard Rubinger. Princeton: Princeton University Press, 1982.

Fragments of Rainbows: The Life and Poetry of Saito Mokichi, 1882–1953,
by Amy Vladeck Heinrich. New York: Columbia University Press, 1983.

Japanese Culture, 3rd ed., rev.,
by H. Paul Varley. Honolulu: University of Hawaii Press, 1984.

Japan's Modern Myths: Ideology in the Late Meiji Period,
by Carol Gluck. Princeton: Princeton University Press, 1985.

Studies of the East Asian Institute

Urban Japanese Housewives: At Home and in the Community,
by Anne E. Imamura. Honolulu: University of Hawaii Press, 1987.

The Japanese Way of Politics,
by Gerald L. Curtis. New York: Columbia University Press, 1988.

Aftermath of War: Americans and the Remaking of Japan, 1945–1952,
by Howard B. Schonberger. Kent, Ohio:
Kent State University Press, 1989.

Neighborhood Tokyo, by Theodore C. Bestor.
Stanford: Stanford University Press, 1989.

Education in Japan, by Richard Rubinger and Edward Beauchamp.
New York: Garland Publishing, 1989.

Financial Politics in Contemporary Japan, by Frances Rosenbluth.
Ithaca: Cornell University Press, 1989.

Suicidal Narrative in Modern Japan: The Case of Dazai Osamu,
by Alan Wolfe. Princeton: Princeton University Press, 1990.

Sowing the Seeds of Change: Chinese Students, Japanese Teachers, 1895 – 1905, by Paula S. Harrell. Stanford: Stanford University Press, 1992.

Nishiwaki Junzaburo: The Poetry and Poetics of a Modernist Master,
by Hosea Hirata. Princeton: Princeton University Press, 1993.

Social Mobility in Contemporary Japan, by Hiroshi Ishida.
Stanford: Stanford University Press, 1993.

The Writings of Kōda Aya, a Japanese Literary Daughter,
by Alan M. Tansman. New Haven: Yale University Press, 1993.

Japan's Foreign Policy after the Cold War: Coping with Change,
ed. Gerald L. Curtis. Armonk, N.Y.: M. E. Sharpe, 1993.

For a complete list of titles, write to
Studies of the East Asian Institute,
926 IAB, Columbia University,
420 West 118th Street, New York, New York 10027

index

Akutagawa Ryūnosuke: perspectivism and relativism in works of, 15, 226; critique of Tōson by, 135, 152–53; and Shiga, 225, 227, 232; classical sources used by, 227; and Futabatei, 227; and narrative credibility, 227; and Ōgai, 228; problems writing fiction, 231; posthumous reputation, 232; suicide, 232; and Kajii, 243, 244–45; and Kawabata, 254. Works: *Aru ahō no isshō*, 231; "Bungeiteki na, amari ni bungeiteki na," 225; *Haguruma*, 231; "Hana," 227; "Jigokuhen," 227–31; "Yabu no naka," 227
Amijima shinjū (Chikamatsu), 124
anecdotal narrative, 60–62, 64, 104
Arishima Takeo, 156, 214

Aristotle, 90
Asahi shinbun, 113, 114, 126, 165, 201
autobiography, 143, 149, 152–53, 265
Awashima Kangetsu, 92

Bakin (Kyokutei Bakin), 81, 89–91
Barthes, Roland, 10, 35
Bashō, 62–63
Baudelaire, Charles, 17, 271*n*1
Belinsky, Vissarion, 102–3
bikunimono, as source for Saikaku, 67
bildungsroman, 9, 265
Bloom, Harold, 84–85
Bowring, Richard, 185
Breton, André, 252
Buddhism. *See* Pure Land Buddhism
Bungakkai (journal), 6, 146

Index

Bungei shunjū (journal), 248
bunjin (literati), and self-cultivation, 19

canon reformation, 5, 85–86
Chamberlain, Basil Hall, 4
Charter Oath, 5
Chikamatsu Monzaemon, 55, 124
Chinese vernacular fiction, 60
Chiteiki (Yoshishige no Yasutane), 43, 44, 47
Chiu hsiang shih (Su Tung-p'o), 67–68
chōnin culture, 55, 103–4
Chu Hsi, 191
Ch'un ch'iu, 191
Chūō kōron (journal), 189, 190, 241
confession, 9, 143, 149, 265
Conrad, Joseph, 175

Dazai Osamu ("Nyoze gamon"), on Shiga, 225
Defoe, Daniel, 56
de Man, Paul, 266
discontinuity, 265; effect on narrative, 10–12; and mutability, 14; and relativism, 15, 213, 245; and modernity, 16; and canon reformation, 79; and language reform, 85; in Meiji culture, 146, 246; and problem of identity, 211; and perspectivism, 232
Dixon, James Main, 169, 179

Echigonoben, 37
Ejima Kiseki, 57, 84
Eliot, T. S., 1–2, 217. Works: *Four Quartets*, 1; "The Love Song of J. Alfred Prufrock," 160; "The Waste Land," 44
Emerson, Ralph Waldo, 155, 162, 243

Emperor Meiji, death of, 171, 173, 178
ephemeral, the: as aesthetic ideology, 77–78
Etō Jun, 166, 171, 196

fascism, 212–13
Fenollosa, Ernest, 90
Field, Norma, 35
Fowler, Edward, 145–46, 286n3
French naturalism: and Kafū, 197
Freud, Sigmund, 40
fueki ryūkō, 63
Fujii, James, 166–67
Fujiwara Shunzei, 44
fushō, 51–52, 274n19
Futabatei Shimei, 156, 164, 167, 211, 244; as representative Meiji author, 14, 79, 94, 142; on *genbun'itchi*, 82; and *gesaku*, 96, 137; on *shaseibun*, 97, 103; and Russian literature, 97, 107; and Shōyō, 102; and paradox of realism, 103–5; skepticism of, 106, 111, 115–16, 127, 136; disillusionment with fiction of, 107–8, 111–12, 136; personal history, 109–13; on uses of fiction, 112–13; response to marginalization, 113; on naturalism, 116, 137, 163; impossibility of heroism for, 122, 125; death, 137; and dilemma of the modern, 140–41; and Ōgai, 182, 193, 194; and Kafū, 197. Works: *Chasengami*, 114; *Heibon*, 104–5, 108, 126, 128–38, 142, 186; "Mibōjin to jindō mondai," 114; "Shōsetsu sōron," 102–3, 111, 116; *Sono omokage*, 108, 114, 115–26, 128, 134, 137–38, 142; *Ukigumo*, 94, 96, 100–107, 109, 115, 123, 126, 142, 144; "Yo ga genbun'itchi no

yurai," 82; "Yo ga hansei no zange," 106–7

ga/zoku (elegant/vulgar), 64, 78, 80, 88
gaishi (unofficial histories), 190–91
genbun'itchi. See language reform
gendai, 2–4
Genji monogatari, 63, 87, 149; aesthetics of transience in, 13; and Meiji literature, 13; idealization of Genji in, 19; and Proust, 21; politics in, 22, 26–27; and "Eawase" chapter, 22–27, 31–33, 35; narrative modes of, 28–29, 31; historical awareness in, 33; problematic hero in, 34; death of Genji, 36, 37; and "Ukifune chapters," 37–38; sense of exhaustion in, 38–39; parodies of, 61, 64–65, 71
gesaku, 55, 75, 81, 112
Gusdorf, Georges, 30, 174
Gyōgi, 44
Gyokuyō wakashū, 44

Hagiwara Sakutarō, 232–33
haikai, 62–63, 64, 73, 115
Hare, Thomas, 49, 50
Harvey, David, 212
Hasegawa Tatsunosuke. See Futabatei Shimei
Hattori Dohō, 63
Hibbett, Howard, 277n19
Higuchi Ichiyō, 84
Honda Shūgo, 214–15
Hōnen, 47
"Hsiao Ch'ing chuan," 187
Hui-ssu, and *mappō*, 47
Hulme, T. E.: *Speculations*, 9
Hsün Tzu, 175

Ihara Saikaku, 13, 19, 20, 100, 143; innovations of, 55–56, 74; and realism, 56–57, 60; idealistic mode in works of, 57; humanism of, 58–59; the rational and irrational in works of, 59; and neo-Confucianism, 59–60; and *haikai*, 62; and native realism in Meiji, 84, 92, 110; and Tokugawa fiction, 74–75. Works: *Kōshoku gonin onna*, 60–61, 65, 71; *Kōshoku ichidai onna*, 13, 14, 19, 56, 65–74, 143; *Kōshoku ichidai otoko*, 64–65; *Nippon eitaigura*, 58, 60; *Saikaku oridome*, 60
Ikebe Yoshitarō, 113
Ikuta Chōkō, 220
imamekashi, 22, 25
Ise monogatari, 25–26, 27–28, 34–35
Itō Sei, 249
Iwahashi Koyata, 29
Iwano Hōmei: and confession, 15, 157–58, 162–63; and Futabatei, 141, 155; at Meiji Gakuin, 154; personal history of, 154–56; and Tōson, 154–58; on Kunikida Doppo, 155; and New Naturalism, 155; and Sōseki, 155; and Masuda Shimoe, 155, 157; critique of Katai by, 158–59; narrative voice of, 158–59, 162; on art, 163; on materialism, 163; and Shiga, 215. Works: *Dokuyaku o nomu onna*, 157, 158, 159–62; *Dankyō*, 157; "Gendai shōrai no shōsetsuteki hassō o isshin subeki boku no byōsha ron," 158–59; *Hatten*, 157; *Hōrō*, 157; "Shinpiteki hanjūshugi," 162; *Tsukimono*, 157
Izumi Shikibu nikki, 27–29

James, Henry, 90
jidaimono, 87

Index

jiriki, 49–50
jōruri, and styles for language reform, 81
Jōsammi, 25–26, 27
junshi, 171, 178, 189

kaimami, 208
Kajii Motojirō: and perspective of, 15, 235–36, 242; and narrative relativism, 226, 245; and Akutagawa, 232, 243, 244–45; illness and death, 232–33, 244; and *Aozora,* 233; and Shiga, 235; sense of isolation and despair in works of, 235–37, 239; and Emerson, 243; and Futabatei, 244. Works: "Aru gakuue no kanjō," 238–39; "Aru kokoro no fūkei," 236; "Deinei," 239–41; "Fuyu no hae," 242; "K no shōten, aruiwa K no dekishi," 241; "Kakehi no hanashi," 241; "Kōbi," 236; "Nonki na kanja," 242–44; "Remon," 233–35, 237, 239, 240; "Rojō," 237–38, 240; "Shiro no aru machi nite," 236–37, 239, 240
Kamo no Chōmei: and *Hōjōki,* 13–14, 47–52, 149; and *mujō,* 19, 77; discontinuity in works of, 39–40, 77; personal history of, 40–43; ideal of hermit of, 44; and Hōnen, 47; and Saikaku, 59, 63, 67, 68; and confession, 143; and Sōseki, 179
kana syllabaries, 29–30
kana-zōshi, 56, 60
kanzen chōaku, 91
Karatani Kōjin, 66–67
katagimono, 57, 93
Kawabata Yasunari: and theme of memory and amnesia, 15–16, 213, 247; and Shiga, 218–19; and

Kajii, 233; and Kafū, 247; Nobel Prize and, 247; in *Shinkankaku-ha,* 247; and Yokomitsu Riichi, 247; critique of proletarian literature by, 248; and Kikuchi Kan, 248; style of, 252–54; and Akutagawa, 254; on affirmation of art, 264. Works: "Izu no odoriko," 247; *Yama no oto,* 213, 247, 255–64; *Yukiguni,* 213, 218–19, 247, 248–55, 256, 260–63
Keene, Donald, 250
Keikoku bidan (Yano Ryūkei), 155
Ken'yūsha, 83–84, 110, 156
Kermode, Frank, 45–46
Kikuchi Kan, 248
Ki no Tsurayuki, 30, 90
kindai, 2–4
Kinpeibai (*Chin P'ing Mei*), 187
Kitamura Tōkoku, 146
Kōda Rohan, 84, 112, 181, 182
kogaku, 75, 78
Koike Masanao, 181
Kokinshū, 28
kokkeibon, 97
Kokon chomonjū, 227
kokugaku, 55, 75, 78
Korsakov's syndrome (amnesia), 10–11
kōshaku, 97
kōshokubon, 64–65
Kreutzer Sonata, The, 128, 132, 148
Kunikida Doppo, 140, 150
kusa-zōshi, 89

Lafleur, William, 52, 273*n*1
language reform, 5, 14, 79, 80–85
Leutner, Robert, 97, 279–80*n*15
linked verse, 62
Lyotard, Jean-François, 12, 270*n*10

McClellan, Edwin, 282*n*5
Maeterlinck, Maurice, 162

Index

Makura no sōshi (Sei Shōnagon), 30
mappō, 39, 44–46, 49–50
Masamune Hakuchō: on Futabatei, 95–96, 102; on *Sono omokage,* 115
Masaoka Shiki: and *Hototogisu* (journal), 85; literary reforms of, 140; promotion of *shaseibun* by, 85, 92; and Buson, 92
Meiji Constitution, 5
Mérimée, Prosper, 231
Minamoto no Ienaga nikki, 42
Mishima Yukio, 183
Mitani Kuniaki, 24–25
Miyoshi, Masao, 107–8, 249–50
modern: discussion of, 1–12, 16–18, 265–66; and modernism, 15, 212; Heian sense of, 26; Tokugawa sense of, 53–54; and the West, 78; and re-reading the past, 167; self-consciousness of the, 246
monogatari, development of, 28–31
monogatari ron, 29, 35, 72
mono no aware, 34
Mori Arinori, 7–8
Mori Ōgai, 141, 143, 156; narrative modes of, 15, 182, 190; and "triple style," 84; and Futabatei, 95, 102, 184, 194; disillusionment with fiction of, 112, 180; dual career, 181–82; and philosophy of resignation, 182–83, 193; views on naturalists, 183–84, 192; on *junshi,* 189; and historiography, 190–93, 194; and Sōseki, 191, 194; and Kafū, 197, 206. Works: "Abe ichizoku," 189, 192; *Gan,* 184–89; "Kuriyama daizen," 192; "Maihime," 143; *Nichiren shōnin tsujizeppō,* 192; "Okitsu Yagoemon no isho," 189, 192; "Ōshio Heihachirō," 190; "Rekishi sono mama to rekishibanare," 191–92;

Seinen, 184, 188; *Vita sexualis,* 183–84, 188
Moriyama Shigeo, 66
Morris, Ivan, 58
Motoori Norinaga, 34, 87, 91, 145, 272n8
mujō, 19, 39. *See* mutability
Mukai Kyōrai, 276–77n17
Mumyōzōshi, 68
Murasaki Shikibu: and sense of the modern, 21–22, 63; views on history and fiction of, 27, 29; use of realistic and idealistic modes, 28; narrative innovations, 33. *See Genji monogatari*
Mushanokōji Saneatsu, 85, 156, 214, 232
mutability, 14, 17, 18, 77–78. *See mujō*

Nagai Kafū, 141; primitivism of, 15, 195–96; loss of heroic, 195; and Futabatei, 197; and Zola, 197; and Ōgai, 197, 206; early career, 197–98; on problem of identity, 201; and Kawabata, 247. Works: *Amerika monogatari,* 197–98; *Bokutō kidan,* 201–8; "Mihatenu yume," 195, 207; *Sumidagawa,* 195–96; "Terajima no ki," 202–3; *Tsuyu no atosaki,* 201, 202; *Yume no onna,* 198–202
Nakai, Kate, 191
Nakamura Mitsuo, 6–8, 131, 197
Nakano Shigeharu, 216
narrative, anecdotal, 60–62, 64, 104
Natsume Sōseki, 141, 156, 183, 187; on individualism, 15, 167–69, 178–80; and Shiki, 85; on-Futabatei, 115, 128, 164–65, 180; on scientific outlook, 152, 167–68; childhood, 165–66; and discontinuity of Meiji, 166–67; and

Natsume Sōseki (*continued*)
  English literature, 171; and neo-Confucianism, 174; translation of *Hōjōki*, 179; and Ōgai, 193, 194; and Kafū, 195. Works: "Bungei no tetsugakuteki kiso," 168; "Bungei to dōtoku," 152, 167–68, 187; "Bungei to hiroikku," 168; *Gubijinsō*, 128; *Kokoro*, 171–79; *Michikusa*, 166, 179; *Sore kara*, 165; "Theory of Literature" 171; *Wagahai wa neko de aru*, 85, 115; "Watakushi no kojinshugi," 168–71
naturalism, 84, 126, 150, 215–16
naturalists, 83, 139, 163
nenbutsu, 46, 49–50, 52
Nietzsche, Friedrich Wilhelm, 193
Ninin bikuni: iro zange (Ozaki Kōyō), 67
ninjōbon, 90, 145
niwaka, 97
Nogi Maresuke, 171–72, 173, 178, 189, 194

Ōjōyōshū (Genshin), 38, 48
Oketani Hideaki, 129
Ooms, Herman, 54–55
Ōta Nanpō, 75
Ozaki Kōyō, 67, 83, 84, 182
Ozawa Tomio, 273–74n13

perspectivism, 212, 226–32
Pollack, David, 174–75
Pound, Ezra, 214
Proust, Marcel, 21
Pure Land Buddhism, 43, 46–47, 273–74n13
Pyle, Kenneth, 92

rakugo, 97, 102
realism, 27–30, 56–58, 79, 84, 96
rekishi shōsetsu, 182
Rikkokushi, 28

Rosenberg, Harold, 104
Rubin, Jay, 150–51, 174, 175
Russo-Japanese War, 113, 182
Ryan, Marleigh, 105
Ryūtei Tanehiko, 75, 89

Sachida Seiyu, 190
Sacks, Oliver, 269–70n7, 270n8
Sakai, Naoki, 270n9, 271n12
Sanzōshi, 63
Satō Haruo, 85
Satomi Ton, 214
Seidensticker, Edward, 196, 203, 250
Seinan War, 178
senju nenbutsu, 47
setsuwa, 60, 227
sewamono, 87
sharebon, 97
shaseibun, 85, 140
shiden, 182
Shiga Naoya: on language and identity, 7–8; narrow perspective of, 15, 212, 215–16; assertion of modern heroism, 15, 224; critique of Tōson by, 135; as member of the upper class, 156; view of artist, 213; and *Shirakaba-ha*, 214; and *shishōsetsu*, 215; muted irony in works, 216; and family relations, 219; prose style, 219, 221–22; literary associations, 219–20; relations with other writers, 224–25; influence, 226; and Akutagawa, 231, 232; and Kajii, 232, 235, 240, 245. Works: *An'ya Kōro*, 215, 219, 222–24, 231; *Aru otoko, sono ane no shi*, 215; "Han no hanzai," 286n2; "Kinosaki nite," 216–19; "Kokugo moni," 7; *Ōtsu Junkichi*, 215; *Wakai*, 215, 220–22
Shikitei Sanba, 75, 82, 88, 97–100

Index

Shimazaki Tōson, 141; confessional mode of, 15, 144, 149, 153, 162–63; on *genbun'itchi*, 83; and Futabatei, 95, 102–3, 105, 127, 129; as naturalist and romantic, 115, 146; and concept of self, 145; and *shaseibun*, 146; career, 146–47; and sincerity, 149; and Katai, 150; on method of composition, 151; and Akutugawa, 153; and Hōmei, 154–58; faith in art of, 163; and Shiga, 215. Works: *Chikumagawa no suketchi*, 146; *Gisei (Ie)*, 147; *Hakai*, 144–46, 150; *Haru*, 146; *Ie*, 135, 147–49, 151; "Kinō, otototoi," 152; "Mitsu no chōhen o kaita tōji no koto" 147; *Shinsei*, 135; *Yoakemae*, 153–54

Shimizu Shigeru, 106, 131
Shinkankaku-ha, 233, 247
Shirakaba-ha, 85, 214
shishōsetsu, 139, 215–16
Shoku Nihongi, 3
Sibley, William, 222, 286n7
sincerity, 14, 127–28, 149, 174
Sino-Japanese War, 84
Social Darwinism, 91
sokkibon, 83
Suzuki Shōzan, 67
Swedenborg, Emanuel, 162

Taketori monogatari, 23–25, 27, 38
Tamenaga Shunsui, 88, 90, 92, 206
Taniwaki Masachika, 68
tariki, 49–50
"Ta t'ieh ch'ui chuan," 187
Tayama Katai: on *genbun'itchi*, 83; and *Futon*, 115, 128, 129, 143; on Futabatei, 127–29; views on power of art, 142, 163; on naturalism, 150; and surface description, 158
Taylor, Charles, 9, 53, 243

"Tiao wang shih" (P'an Yueh), 44
Tokutomi Roka, 140
Tokutomi Sohō, 82
Tolstoy, Leo, 128, 132, 148
Tosa nikki, 30
Tristram Shandy (Laurence Sterne), 104
Tsubouchi Shōyō: and canon reformation, 79, 86, 90–93; and Futabatei, 82, 89, 95, 107, 109, 113, 115; and evolution of the novel, 93; mentioned, 156, 182. Works: *Shōsetsu shinzui*, 86–90, 92–93; *Tōsei shosei katagi*, 93
Tsurezuregusa, 60

Uchida Roan, 95, 113
Ueda Akinari, 75
Ueda Mannen, 84
Uji shūi monogatari, 227
ukiyo, 54
Ukiyoburo, 97–100
ukiyo-zōshi, 19, 55–56, 62
Uno Kōji, 85, 153–54, 187–88
uta monogatari, 25
Utsuho monogatari, 23–35, 27

Vimalakīrti, 49

Waley, Arthur, 21–22, 28–29
Walker, Janet, 27–28, 145
Watt, Ian, 56–57
Wen-hsüan, 44, 68
Woolf, Virginia, 22
Wordsworth, William, 84

Yamada Bimyō, 82, 182
Yamaguchi Takeshi, 62
Yamamoto Masahide, 81
Yanagita Kunio, 112
Yang Kuei-fei, 35
Yokomitsu Riichi, 247

yomihon, 80–81, 90
Yomiuri shinbun, 81
Yosa Buson, 92
Yoshida Kenkō, 60
Yoshida Sei'ichi, 153, 154
Yoshioka Tetsutarō, 110

Yü ch'u hsin-chih, 187
Yu hsien k'u (Chang Tsu) 67

Zola, Emile, 197; and *Germinal,* 183
zuihitsu, 202

www.ingramcontent.com/pod-product-compliance
Lightning Source LLC
Chambersburg PA
CBHW031545300426
44111CB00006BA/177